AUG 31

UP FROM THE CRADLE OF JAZZ

New Orleans Music Since World War II

Jason Berry, Jonathan Foose, and Tad Jones

UP FROM
THE CRADLE OF JAZZ

New Orleans Music Since World War II

The University of Georgia Press  Athens and London

Published by the University of Georgia Press
Athens, Georgia 30602

Designed by Sandra Strother Hudson
Set in Linotron Meridien with Benquiat display

The paper in this book meets the guidelines for
permanence and durability of the Committee on
Production Guidelines for Book Longevity of the
Council on Library Resources.

Printed in the United States of America

90 89 88 87   5 4 3 2

Library of Congress Cataloging in Publication Data

Berry, Jason.
  Up from the cradle of jazz.

  Bibliography: p.
  Discography: p.
  Includes index.
  1. Rhythm and blues music—Louisiana—New Orleans—
History and criticism.   2. Musicians—Louisiana—
New Orleans.   I. Foose, Jonathan.   II. Jones, Tad.
III. Title.
  ML3521.B47   1986   784.5'3'00976335   85-29015
  ISBN 0-8203-0853-6 (alk. paper)
  ISBN 0-8203-0854-4 (pbk.: alk. paper)

CONTENTS

ACKNOWLEDGMENTS

Richard B. Allen, the dean of New Orleans jazz researchers and first curator of the William Ransom Hogan Jazz Archive at Tulane University, has long given generously of his time and knowledge, and we thank him for it. Curt Jerde, who succeeded Allen as curator, critiqued early chapters of the work. Bruce Raeburn, a musician pursuing graduate studies at Tulane, was likewise most helpful.

Journalist Bill Bentley and radio celebrity Vernon Winslow contributed to key areas of research. Writer Jeff "Almost Slim" Hannusch read the manuscript and provided an important critique. His book *I Hear You Knockin': The Sound of New Orleans Rhythm and Blues*, published in November 1985, is a valuable contribution to the literature of New Orleans music.

Among those who read the manuscript in its various stages was Andrew Kaslow, our most constructive and able critic, to whom we offer deepest thanks. Barry Jean Ancelet, Carl Brasseaux, Lawrence Goodwyn, John Joyce, Maurice Martinez,

and poet-author Tom Dent contributed instructive readings of different chapters. Marvin Williams and Mary Frances Berry read the entire manuscript for stylistic points, and to them a large thanks. Finn Wilhelmsen generously provided research papers on the Mardi Gras Indians.

For general and specific favors, our thanks go to Walter and Jerry Brock of WWOZ Radio, author John Broven, photographer Syndey Byrd, Quint Davis, William Ferris, William Griffin, Caroline Harkleroad, William Hammel, Frank Heebe, Roy Bryce-Laporte of the Smithsonian, Johnny L. Kidder, William Kirby, Joseph Logsdon, Lisa and Michelle LeBlanc, producer Stevenson Palfi, James Pierce, Shepard Samuel of WTUL, photographer Michael Smith, Nicholas Spitzer, John Stewart, James Tungate, and John Ware. We also are grateful to Malcolm Call, Douglas Armato, and their colleagues at the University of Georgia Press for their diligent efforts in bringing this book to fruition.

Tillie Rowlan typed the manuscript many times over and often under time pressure; to her, a deep and lasting thank you. At critical junctures Caroline Foose proofed and typed sections and was of profound assistance in editing the bibliography.

In the years it took to complete the book, we were assisted by several grants. For them we owe special thanks to Father David Boileau and James Pierce of the Louisiana Committee for the Humanities; James Isenogle of the Jean Lafitte National Park, National Park Service; and John Alexander Williams and Anne Woodard of State, Local and Regional Studies, programs of the National Endowment for the Humanities in Washington, D.C. Their colleagues and staff were most helpful as well.

Finally, among the scholars who provided critiques, Herbert Gutman was extremely helpful. Herb's untimely death in 1985 is a loss historians will long mourn. His distinguished study *The Black Family in Slavery and Freedom, 1750–1925* registers the heartbeat of a culture to which he gave greatly of his talent.

It would be impractical to list all of the musicians who gave generously of their time and memories, but several served as more than ordinary sources. To Harold Battiste, Earl King, David Lastie, Deacon Frank Lastie, Paul Longpre, Allison "Tuddy" Montana, and Charles Neville, we extend our heartfelt thanks.

PROLOGUE

by Jason Berry

On a freezing Sunday noon in January of 1977, there came a pounding at my door. The night before had been long; I struggled downstairs in fading bathrobe to greet Prince Fatgot Guillermo. Now the Prince was an animated Jamaican with a fondness for flashy hats and capes during Carnival time. He played maracas with a few bands in the Latin clubs and led a complicated street life. Several articles I had written were born out of collisions with the Prince. But this was no day for a jaunt.

"Go away," I said. "It's too cold. I'm going back to bed."

"Naw, naw, you listen here." He stood there in the doorway, hands on hips, wind whipping in off the street. "They cuttin' a record over at SeaSaint tonight, and you got to come see about this. Big tall boy from Texas coming in to make a Mardi Gras song and *I'm* handling maracas."

"Yeah, yeah, I'm going back to bed."

He was such an outrageous character, bending my ear in the front doorway, it took another ten minutes to get rid of him. But that is how things inevitably began with the Prince. A seed was planted, some hint of mystery. I began to wonder about the recording session when he phoned several hours later to insist I go to Allen Toussaint's studio and witness the making of a forty-five record. He wouldn't tell me the name of the artist, just "this big tall boy from Texas."

By now my curiosity was piqued. I called Tad Jones, a collector whose work had appeared in *Living Blues*. He was always a step ahead of recording sessions or events about to break. Tad didn't know the man from Texas, so we went to the studio, and the Prince introduced us to Jonathan Foose, a genial chap who played guitar and had come from Austin to fulfill a lifelong dream: the recording of his own song. As the musicians who would be his sidemen filed in, Foose explained: "I grew up on a plantation near Yazoo City, and my first exposure was to the blues. I live in Austin now, was playing congas in the French

Quarter when I met the Prince. I got hooked on New Orleans. Come here every chance I get."

Foose had a solid group backing him that night. On tenor saxophone was David Lastie, who figures prominently in a chapter of this book. Wendell Brunious, a powerful young trumpeter, came from another musical family. Fats Domino's son, Antoine, played keyboard. On tambourine was Oliver "Who Shot the La La?" Morgan, the same cheery winner who played the proms and dances of a decade ago. The drummer was called Dogman. And the Prince was on maracas.

The disc coming out of that session, "Tuesday Morning," was a spirited Carnival tune, and if it never made the top one hundred at least the tale of its conception appeared in the *Courier*, a plucky little paper published once a week in the French Quarter for most of the 1970s. Foose soon moved to New Orleans. And I suppose it is fitting that this book, which melds the research of three aficionados of New Orleans music, should have its origins in a recording studio, with introductions by no less a diplomat than the Prince.

In 1974 a small British magazine called *Blues Unlimited* issued in paperback *Walking to New Orleans*, a history of local rhythm-and-blues. Author John Broven did most of the discographical research from England, where New Orleans music has something of a cult following, and traced careers of many artists through their discs. After two brief field trips to New Orleans, he gathered interviews to balance the recording chronicle. In 1978 Pelican, a local house, issued the book in hardcover under the title *Rhythm and Blues in New Orleans*.

Through the late 1970s, as R&B artists of the fifties and sixties made comebacks—Professor Longhair, Art and Aaron Neville, Dr. John, Irma Thomas, among many—Broven's book was the only text covering the rise of black music in the city since World War II. The literature of seminal jazz is voluminous by comparison. As the decade drew to a close, with an outpouring of music on a resurgent nightclub circuit and with the Jazz and Heritage Festival showcasing artists, old and new, the idea of a large, sweeping narrative about New Orleans music began to occupy my thoughts.

In 1978 Jonathan Foose and I received a grant from the Louisiana Committee for the Humanities to produce a television documentary about musical families. Tad Jones was a history consultant. During the production, we amassed a bank of information through videotaped interviews, enriched by the Neville and Lastie families' historical perceptions. Many of the reminiscences would not fit the format of the one-hour program *Up from the Cradle of Jazz*, which first aired in 1980.

We began work on our book in 1979 during a production lull. My research associates had unique resources. Tad was able to draw on interviews and from material he had collected during the 1970s—records, clippings, photographs—on rhythm-and-blues, his special interest. Jonathan had a large library of interview tapes and friendships with musicians who had shared reflections of neighborhood life. Like Tad, Jon saw the blues idiom running deep in New Orleans music. Since publication of *Amazing Grace*, I had worked as a political and investigative writer, but by 1976 had begun forays into cultural criticism. The city was filled with musicians; in writing about them, I wanted to understand the strength of historical memory behind their varied sounds.

Jazz was alluring music: challenges of metaphor came forth, suggesting new rhythms to one's prose. The many interview voices formed a large incantation, requiring textual layers. Thus the architecture of the book, like a New Orleans song, is polyrhythmic. In casting the narrative I wanted a singular prose voice to function as the central rhythm, with poetic cadences of the musicians' words arranged like a counterrhythm to read on paper much as they are spoken.

The urban culture as musical seedbed became our dominant research theme. The tradition of musical families, the importance of neighborhoods and kinship networks, the ceremonial importance of clubs and bars in the segregation years, oral traditions and rituals of the Mardi Gras Indian tribes—these were manifestations of a distinct, Afro-Caribbean sensibility that has long shaped the city's cultural identity. From the outset, then, the idea behind *Up from the Cradle of Jazz* was two-fold: to extend the historical terrain of rhythm-and-blues by charting parallel courses of modern jazz and the Mardi Gras Indians; and to portray within this narrative the rise of postwar music in New Orleans amid the transformation of a long-segregated society.

Some sections deal with events prior to 1949—that was the year Professor Longhair hit his stride and Fats Domino cut his legendary first hit, "The Fat Man"—while others include events occurring as late as the early 1980s. Our general cutoff date was 1980 because that was the year when heroes died—Professor Longhair (Henry Roeland Byrd); Big Chief Jolley (George Landry), the grand Mardi Gras Indian leader; and Walter Lastie, one of the city's finest drummers. So was 1980 the year John Lennon died. Fess and Jolley were in their sixties, Walter but forty-two. With the passing of the older men one saw the full brush strokes of their poetic vision of the city, while Walter's abrupt death somehow seemed to punctuate the era.

New Orleans music is steeped in a long history of dancing. The songs articulate a special language that is, first of all and finally, about New Orleans. Rhythm-and-blues was a national idiom with important New Orleans influences. As a local idiom, countless tunes are really tone poems spun from local lore. Like R&B, postwar jazz was a clear departure from the classic idiom fostered by Buddy Bolden, Louis Armstrong, Jelly Roll Morton, Sidney Bechet, and others of the first jazz generation. In essence, the new jazz impulse extended the heritage of the older style and was built on improvisation. The influence of R&B on these new improvisational designs has now passed into the older jazz repertoire as well. They are distinct idioms, yet ones that often overlap, particularly in the brass band marches of the 1980s.

The Mardi Gras Indians, however, advance a rather different cultural vocabulary. The coded chants, as passed down through decades of a remarkable oral tradition, are sung to an African percussive sensibility, one long viewed as a primitive root beneath the trunk of early jazz. With the 1970s movement of Indian chants into popular songs, one saw the renaissance of this ancient spiritual tradition in rich musical coloration. In selecting these three idioms—R&B, modern jazz, Mardi Gras Indian music—we have dwelt but passingly on traditional jazz, Dixieland, and gospel music, treating them primarily as source and influence on the others. (Dixieland popularly refers to traditional New Orleans jazz; however, the term means the traditional ensemble style, as played by whites, often interpreting the style of blacks. Basically, Dixieland means white traditional jazz.)

The tendency in America, largely as a result of television, is to isolate music as entertainment—to see it solely as some spectacular commercial engine, bereft of deeper meaning. But popular music, like jazz and literature, like painting and film, springs from an organic culture: the lyrics, rhythms, and dance patterns reflect a specific consciousness, the values of a given place and time. As I write, in 1985, race relations in America have reached a bitter impasse. The passions of our nation reach out to starving African children, yet national policy has all but abandoned the basic needs of millions of black American children and impoverished families. How long ago it seems—yet less than a generation—when "urban renewal" meant progress. Today urban blight is a growing obsession. Once we accepted cities as repositories of our growing civilization; today the fate of cities is an open question.

New Orleans is hardly an exception to this disturbing phenomenon. It is poor and scarred by crime; however, it has long been marked by a unique biracial housing pattern with many neighborhoods where blacks and whites live in close proximity. The neighborhoods selectively profiled in these pages are Afro-American enclaves with lasting musical resonance. Modestly, I would argue that the chronicle within this cultural history—recent annals of an old, ethnically varied city—carries a poignant message about the larger anguish of our urban condition. For among its virtues, New Orleans music, a truly urban music, has long served as a binding force between the races, and in times such as these, as a precious antidote to the imagination of violence. And so we offer *Up from the Cradle of Jazz* as one statement on the better impulses of this nation, composed of many cultures—the struggle of artists to endure and prosper as our muses, and the role of a rare and lovely city, which through the generations has contributed so deeply to the cultural heritage all Americans share.

ONE

Origins of New Orleans Rhythm-and-Blues

Chapter One

MUSICAL FAMILIES:
THE FOUNDING TRADITION

New Orleans is a city of sounds.

She has a beat, street rhythms, her own pulse. And the evolution of music in the cradle of jazz is partly an underground history of how sounds influence artists, aural shadings, murals of sound in a good-times town. The slang-studded speech of honky-tonks, oral riffs by radio deejays, recitations of children in games they play, melodies of Scripture in the sermons of preachers—there are many spoken sounds, with dialects often varying from one neighborhood to the next. An investigation of the oral environment must begin with the city itself and what distinguishes its musical heritage from that of other cities.

New Orleans is less a city than a collection of urban villages. The French settled the area in 1718, the Vieux Carré was built, and outside the French Quarter the city began as a series of plantations, muggy flatlands whose owners gradually sold off tracts to individuals, government, companies, and the church. The "faubourgs" (suburbs) developed as villages-within-the-city. What

Lincoln Steffens wrote of Paris well describes the real New Orleans: "a loose merger of many, very many small provincial communities, each of which is pleasantly or offensively clannish."[1]

In the early years of this century, environmental sounds were rich as gold. Imagine a city without belching autos, *sans* groans from truck or bus, no airplanes disturbing the sky. Instead you heard the clickety-clack of horse hooves and rote accompaniment of the wagon wheel. The ring of the triangle announced the iceman's wagon. Vendors traveled streets calling advertisements of fruit and vegetable, a tradition lingering yet in old trucks cruising and men singing: *"I got tomatoes big and fine. I got watermelons red to the rind."*

A busy port, New Orleans was a junction where the locomotive push and wheeze and the jangling bells blended with the deep boom of foghorns on the river. One of Louis Armstrong's more jocular tunes, "Hobo, You Can't Ride This Train," simulates a locomotive departing the station with

Satchmo, the genial conductor, growling to bums on the track, "Yeah, I'm a tough man, but I ain't looking"—so hobos can hitch on. Similarly, Professor Longhair's "Go to the Mardi Gras" is one of many songs that creates the aural milieu of a train ride.

When Armstrong was a boy in the early 1900s, music itself was a pulse in the environment of sounds. Horse-drawn wagons carried musicians through neighborhoods to advertise evening dances. When bands passed, wagons stopped and musicians blew loud and long in a ritual of artistic competition. Death rites became a celebration of African shadings in the jazz funeral: the solemn dirges of the brass band ushering the coffin to rest, and after burial, a cutting loose of the spirit from earthly ties with tailgate trombones, drums and trumpets triggering the second line of street dancers.

The Mississippi River has a sound of its own, wind rushing over the waters, the lapping of waves beneath docks, the bells of the boats and barges, foghorns, the creaks and moans of lines mooring the boats to the docks. Danny Barker, elder statesman of the city's jazzmen, has advanced a theory about sound and the river. "The Mississippi bends in a crescent here, so that water, the vapor from that water, sort of was an enclosure with sound. If you know about decibels of sound. An' the river, sound carries on the river, and it circles. An' you got the lake, which is a huge body of water on ya North, ya dig? Up above ya got bayous and swamplands. That's water. So when the sound hits, it's an enclosure an' it bounces around."[2]

James Rivers—lean, suave, an accomplished saxophone player—is a generation younger than Danny Barker. He gravitates to Lake Pontchartrain in contemplative moments. "If I'm into a certain mood or I'm thinking of a certain tune, I might think the sounds of the oceans; like sometimes I used to practice and go at night to the Lakefront where it would be quiet and listen at the waves and the water. Just to be alone, you know, like to hear the different sounds of the water beating against the seawall and I could meditate. You'd be surprised at the things you can work out that I worked out; playing [on stage] you don't have all these effects. You can only think of what you did and hope that it came out."[3]

Scholars now consider New Orleans, like Miami, to be part of the Caribbean Basin, rimlands of the Gulf of Mexico that are cultural extensions of the Caribbean. Since the beginning of slavery, the inflow of Caribbean peoples has had a pronounced impact on custom and habit. Alfred Roberts, the city's premier conga player, recalls his first exposure to percussion. Next door to his home "they had some seamen and when they come in they gave a party. And they played those drums. And I never could see what the drums looked like, but I always know how the tone sound. So my father, he bought me a snare drum. And with the snares on it ringin', that wasn't the sound I wanted, so I mess around and mess around, and I took the things off that bottom. And he was kind of upset, you know, cause I did all that, but I was tryin' to get that sound I had heard from that house. And I would loosen the edge and get it low, you know. Then later, as I grew older, I found that it was congas and bongos and that's the sound I was looking for. I started playin' congas."[4]

The late Melvin Lastie, a brilliant trumpeter, loved to imitate chickens. He grew up in a rural area of what is now the populous Ninth Ward, and one of his favorite sounds went "cocka-cocka-*teeta-teeta.*" The chicken sound was popularized in a 1961 novelty hit by R&B singer Ernie K-Doe. It was called "Tee-Ta Ta" and is still a popular dance song in New Orleans. The chicken sound also found an instrumental interpretation in the late 1960s with the funky guitar work of Leo Nocentelli and bass player George Porter in the Meters.

Like most cities with large black communities, New Orleans has an animated street culture. The dozens, a game of verbal dueling, is but one part of a larger oral tradition. The semitropical weather draws people to front porches, street corners, benches, and small outside gathering spots, where groups exchange chants and harmonize to rhythms made on sticks, boxes, cans, bottles. Children toss verses back and forth to the beat of a jump rope or rubber ball thrown against the wall. Some verses entered lyrics of teenage dance songs in the early sixties. Huey "Piano" Smith, whose novelty tunes were big hits in the heyday of rhythm-and-blues, recalls: "What we used to do was sit on the steps and be kiddin' with each other and say something like, 'I saw your sister with a spoon, round the corner trying to jump the moon.' And songs would come."[5]

In his tune "Scald Dog," Huey drew on an old children's jump-rope chant to form the melody:

I'm looking for that dirty dirty crook
I'm looking for that dirty dirty crook
  I'm looking for that dirty
  That dirty dirty crook
That stole my momma's pocketbook.

He was running through the smoke and fog
He was running through the smoke and fog
  He was running through the smoke
  He was running through the fog
He was running like a scald dog.

There have even been occasions when musicians were drawn to sounds of engines. Vocalist Aaron Neville recalls: "Me and [Allen] Toussaint would ride around with a tape recorder and one day we pulled up next to a big semitruck. The motor was going 'rumble rum rumble' with a nice beat, you know, and Toussaint recorded that beat."[6]

The New Orleans sound refers to a distinct style: percussive piano rhythms; rocking, vocally suggestive horns; and a parade-time backbeat on the drums. Its root is called the second line, the waves of marching dancers who engulf the brass bands and trail behind them, moving to the beat with their bodies gyrating in the streets. Before anything else, it is dance music: sounds to make you clap your hands, move your feet.

For a city of under six hundred thousand people, New Orleans has produced a startling number of fine musicians from the rise of jazz to the revival of rhythm-and-blues in the 1970s. The reasons for this heritage are somewhat complex. But the shaping force, today as in years past, is the long line of musical families.

The musical family tradition is an important pattern of cultural history. The gift passes in bloodlines and through environmental influences: idioms arise, and instrumental lineages carry from one generation to the next. Musical families must be as old as music itself. From tribal units of our earliest ancestors came the groping to organize sound in some tonal order, a foundation for ritual. In the growth of consciousness music broadened with cultural expression, out of clans and tribes into families and homes, churches and courts.

Musical families were a cornerstone of the European tradition. Johann Sebastian Bach, a guiding light of eighteenth-century baroque music, sired twenty children by two wives; four sons became noted musicians. Mozart performed with his father, a court composer, before the age of seven. The great Viennese composer Strauss merged his orchestra with that of Johann Sr. upon his father's death in 1849. From Hapsburg courts to concert halls of La Belle Epoque, the mingling of families and classical music enriched the Continent.

The case of jazz is different. Long before the music issued out of *fin de siècle* New Orleans, cultural seeds had scattered. A unique environment took root, nourished by different ethnic traditions. Music was nurtured in these ethnic families, but more important was the city where the families settled.

Street rhythms

New Orleans, ceded by France to the Spanish in 1762, was reclaimed in 1800 by Napoleon, who sold it three years later as part of the Louisiana Purchase. The city bore the stamp of two colonial hands: the French influence ran deep. French was the city's first language, and Louisana's state civil law is modeled on the Napoleonic code. By 1830, with a population of forty thousand, the town hosted three opera companies, including the Negro Philharmonic.

The port of New Orleans lay at the bottom of America in a swampy, semitropical bowl; slow-paced, Latin by temperament, the town was run by planters and colonial administrators, while prostitutes, thieves, and roughnecks grafted their own ideas onto settlement living. The place was more hotly hedonistic than Anglicized plantation communities of the upper South and is still that way.

Slavery intensified the cultural mélange. African peoples brought with them a drumming tradition, voodoo beliefs, and West African–derived dance steps. In the early 1800s thousands of planters, slaves, and freedmen poured in from Saint-Domingue, liberated in 1804 as Haiti. Many settled in Treme, an old neighborhood behind the Congo Square area or what is now Louis Armstrong Park. Irish immigrants arrived to work the river docks and settled in a strip straddling the Mississippi that is still called the Irish Channel. Italians came, many settling in the French Quarter, where they sold fruits and vegetables. German immigrants came, too. Social intercourse was fluid among these peoples.

The spread of music was rich indeed. Brass bands played French martial music. Society orchestras played versions of polkas, Germanic waltzes, the French quadrille. Musical celebration among the slaves was evident early on. In 1802 a Saint-Dominguean refugee observed, "They dance in the city, they dance in the street, they dance everywhere."[7] Police arrested slaves for dancing at functions held by freedmen of color; tavern owners were fined for letting slaves dance; still the tide continued.

Between 1860 and 1880, the Negro population of New Orleans more than doubled to 57,617.[8] By the end of Reconstruction, blacks formed more than a third of the population. A long history of free blacks—many Catholic—strengthened the familial lines that slavery had weakened. From these families came professional musicians.

Revisionist historians of the 1970s—Lawrence Levine, Herbert Gutman, Eugene Genovese, and others—produced important books about cultural and familial bonds of the black South in slavery and since Reconstruction. New Orleans is an interesting city in this regard; against the pattern of heavy outmigration by black musicians from Memphis, Kansas City, and the Delta—hundreds followed the rails North—New Orleans's musical family tradition strengthened in the twentieth century. Such stability suggests the city was not one blacks fled; rather, to the city they came. This is particularly evident in the rhythm-and-blues generation that emerged in the 1950s. Professor Longhair (Roy Byrd) came from Bogalusa, a paper mill town. Smiley Lewis, a seminal bluesman, came from DeQuincy. Producer-bandmaster Dave Bartholomew came from Edgard, a river town servicing the sugar plantations. Singer Irma Thomas came from Ponchatoula. The list goes on. Over the years, many musicians did leave—among them: King Oliver, Louis Armstrong, Ed Blackwell, Dr. John, Wynton Marsalis—but far more have stayed, and in a city with no recording industry.

New Orleans Jazz: A Family Album is the reference work to first and second jazz generations (those born around 1860 through the 1890s). A pictorial survey with several hundred thumbnail biographies, it lists seventy-one musical families, either parent-child, or siblings, who played professionally. By our count, at least twelve new families have emerged in the postwar years.

Why have so many musical families come from New Orleans? What are the special characteristics of the city that sent forth jazz and a lineage of accomplished musicians? We are looking for a definition to embrace families of old and emergent ones of the mid-twentieth century. Our first consideration is the idea of community.

When jazz flowered in New Orleans in the early 1900s, a symbolic line divided the downtown and uptown musicians. Downtown meant below Canal Street—beyond the French Quarter and adjacent neighborhoods to the parish line. Uptown meant the poorer black sections across Canal, upriver from the Vieux Carré. As the city grew, streets were laid onto soggy earth in a fan-shaped grid, gradually joining near-river streets with Canal. Today's central city ghetto was first known as Back O' Town. Louis Armstrong was born there.

Many, but not all, of the downtown jazzmen were *gens de couleur,* Creoles of color descended from African mothers who bore children by French or Spanish colonists. Many followed a bloodline first crossed in the Caribbean; others were offspring of New Orleans interracial liaisons. Certain aristocrats supported shadow families and freed their mistresses from slavery. Think of this. A society built on slavery endows black mistresses with financial privilege, yet isolates them in a racial limbo. Like a coin of opposing faces, one black, one white, the minting was made by ethnic reciprocity. With the harsh race laws of the 1890s, a different social currency emerged: despite European customs, colored Creoles were a people whose degrees of darkness sent them closer to the blacks.

Where blacks were a generation out of slavery, Creoles formed a more educated, financially stable community. Their cooking, drawn from European and island cuisines, today distinguishes New Orleans restaurants. A school of Creole ironworkers built many of the elegant lace-grilled balconies, a hallmark of Orleanian architecture.[9] Some Creoles had owned slaves; others amassed fortunes. It was a society with its own classes and musicians knew it. Paul Dominguez, a string bassist, recalled:

> You see, we Downtown people, we try to be intelligent. Everybody learn a trade, like my daddy was a cigarmaker and so was I. . . . We try to bar jail. . . . Uptown, cross Canal yonder, they *used* to jail. . . . There's a vast difference here in this town. Uptown folk all ruffians, cut up in the face and live on the river. All they know is—get out on the levee and truck cotton—be longshoremen, screwmen. And me, I ain't never been on the river *a day in my life.*
>
> See, us Downtown people, we didn't think much of this rough Uptown jazz until we couldn't make a living otherwise. . . . They made a fiddler out of a violinist—me I'm talking about. A fiddler is *not* a violinist but a violinist can be a fiddler. If I wanted to make a living, I had to be rowdy like the other group. I had to jazz it or rag it or any other damn thing. . . . Bolden caused all that. He caused all these younger Creoles, men like Bechet and Keppard, to have a different style altogether from the old heads like Tio and Perez. I don't know how they do it. But goddamn, they'll do it. Can't tell you what's there on paper, but just play the hell out of it.[10]

One man who bridged the gap was James Brown Humphrey, a fair-skinned Negro with red hair who, starting about 1887, boarded the train each week, wearing a swallow-tailed coat and carrying a cornet case and music sheets in a satchel. The professor had many New Orleans pupils who entered the ranks of the early jazz; he is also said to have taught whites. Most students on his weekly tour of the plantation belt—twenty-five miles either way from the city—were illiterate workers who lived in shacks behind the sugar and cotton fields along the river.

Born on November 25, 1859, in the small town of Sellers, Humphrey by 1890 was a rare commodity, a black man who lived off his talents as an artist. He played all instruments, directed bands and orchestras, and became a catalyst sending rural blacks into urban jazz ensembles. His children played music, and in the 1970s two grandsons, Percy and Willie Humphrey, Jr., were active at Preservation Hall. Historian Karl Koenig writes: "Humphrey was part of the process that created jazz. There was no jazz before James Humphrey. There were the regular brass bands and ragtime bands, bands that read music off the little march cards."[11]

In New Orleans, differences were emerging between jazzmen who read sheet music (like Dominguez's Creoles) and those who improvised by ear. Humphrey's most important group was the Eclipse brass band from Magnolia plantation, owned by former governor Henry Clay Warmoth. "The legit New Orleans musicians could not 'fake.' The untrained 'faking' musicians could not read [sheet music]. The Magnolia and other country musicians taught by Professor Humphrey could do both, read and fake. Thus they made excellent band members and could, when called upon, play either type of music. . . . It was from these musicians and the young city musicians that credit should be given for crystalizing the early jazz style."[12]

As previously untrained blacks broadened musically, Creole assimilationist tendencies increased in kind. Perhaps the genius of this caste lay in its varied ethnic origins. In *The Latin Tinge*, John Storm Roberts writes: "Several important early musicians whom jazz writers have casually labeled 'Creole' were in fact of Mexican origin . . . at least two dozen musicians with Spanish surnames figure regularly in the reminiscences of early jazzmen."[13]

Lorenzo Tio, Sr., born in Mexico about 1865, was an active New Orleans bandleader-teacher in the early 1900s. Lorenzo Jr. became a teacher of such prized pupils as clarinetist Barney Bigard and the great Johnny Dodds, who played on Armstrong's classic Hot Five discs. An interesting remark in Paul Dominguez's quotation is that

Buddy Bolden, the first great jazz cornet player, caused younger Creoles, like clarinetist Sidney Bechet and trumpeter Freddie Keppard, "to have a different style altogether from the old heads like Tio and Perez." Manuel Perez was a Storyville professor and bandleader.

Keppard and Bechet, trained by musical professors, played a hotter, more improvisational jazz than the orchestrated technique. Keppard's cornet made a powerful impact in Chicago prior to 1920. His brother Louis played jazz guitar. Bechet was a virtuoso clarinetist and saxman, one of New Orleans's most esteemed artists. His brother Leonard played trombone before becoming a dentist.

Jazz—like Cuban rhumba and Brazilian samba music, like the Beatles' Liverpool rock and latter-day South Bronx break-dancing—grew out of working-class neighborhoods in New Orleans.[14] In a sense, jazz was the articulation of a new cultural language: the African genius for improvisation, tonal, and percussive communication, advancing through European instruments and melodies, drawing liberally from ragtime, marching bands, church songs, and blues, a synthesis of varied musical expressions converging at the bottom of America. The family served as the main passageway through which these sounds merged into a common current.

What were these early families like? Of his father, Sidney Bechet wrote: "He just filled his house with music, and when it wasn't being played at home, he'd be off somewhere else where it was being played. . . . He wasn't a musicianer, but he really had a feeling for it. He lived right on, too, and died in 1923. I was just hitting New York then, a musicianer traveling all over. . . . That was what he wanted for me, what he'd always wanted for me."[15]

In such early families were people who taught, played, or simply lived for music. Theirs was a city of great ethnic diversity, where musical expression cut through obstacles of race and class. It was the

North American city with the deepest African identity: voodoo and a communal drum-and-dance tradition among slaves flourished in the nineteenth century. (See chapter 17.) As the African sensibility overlapped with European and Latin musical traditions, so did New Orleans become the cradle of jazz.

Although the majority of families in our study are black, the impact of white Dixielanders has been steady since the earliest days of jazz, with clans like the LaRoccas, Brunies, Christians, Shieldses, and in later years, the Assuntos and Primas. The three Boswell sisters were successful pop singers of the 1930s. The first jazz recording, in 1917, was made by the white Original Dixieland Jazz Band. Freddie Keppard had turned down an opportunity to record a few years earlier in Chicago, fearing a disc would let others steal his music. Nick LaRocca, leader of the Dixieland band, jumped at the chance when he reached New York.

Dominick J. LaRocca (1890–1960) grew up playing cornet with white ensembles whose members included several sets of siblings. His father, Giarolamo, was a shoemaker who played clarinet on the side. "Musicians are like gypsies," the father told his son. "They play for eats and drinks, they wander around the country, they are always penniless."[16]

What a contrast between LaRocca's father and the elder Bechet! One tells his son to avoid the penniless wandering of drunk gypsies; the other "just filled his home with music and when it wasn't being played he'd be off somewhere else where it was." And so it was in numerous other black homes, the excitement and contagiousness of a new art form spreading through families. There were white families who encouraged the young, but to blacks music was a profession promising a way up from poverty, into respectability and a certain triumph over racial barriers. James Humphrey undoubtedly felt that way when he began teaching plantation blacks around 1887.

Among the important early families are the Tios, Manettas, Marreros, Bocages, Nicholases, and Bacquets. In the generation of post–World War II rhythm-and-bluesmen, the piano was a central instrument. The city has a long history of blues piano, and to religious families the piano bonded gospel to the home. Parents of many R&B artists played gospel piano. Professor Longhair cites his mother; Earl King, guitarist and composer, was an only child reared in a gospel home. How do their musical parents compare with such early jazz masters as Humphrey and Lorenzo Tio, Sr.? Then let us define. A musical family is first of all blood relations for whom music is central to their existence as a people, and with *at least two immediate kin*—parent-child, or siblings—who are professionals, that is, playing or teaching music as a source of income. Some musicians have worked day jobs to support families, but the central force of music in the home stayed steady.

R&B and progressive jazz artists came to know one another as youngsters in the forties and fifties and today form an extended professional family. So let us follow pathways of the tradition by listening to those who span the generations, observing as we go the force of kin on music, how elders pass on lessons to those coming up from the cradle.

Danny Barker was born into a distinguished musical family on January 13, 1909. His grand-uncle, Louis Arthidore (1884–1905), was a clarinet virtuoso who played with the Onward brass band. Arthidore's sister married Louis Barbarin, who played alto horn, mellophone, and clarinet and became the patriarch of a jazz family whose influence ran through four generations. In a remarkable genealogical study of his family, Barker wrote: "In New Orleans it was never a problem to have music for some social event because many of the musicians were related to one another. A party for some social event was planned and the musicians came and played. There your elders would explain to you, at length, how and why different musicians were related to you—when you greeted each other after that, it was 'Hello, Cuz.' "[17] Paul Barbarin, Danny's uncle, was one of the city's finest early jazz drummers and played with the legendary King Oliver and his protégé, young Louis Armstrong. In the following comment, Barker, who was thirteen when he got his first banjo, moves from a description of a mother telling her child to learn an instrument into the story of his own indoctrination.

Mammy would say, "Go over there and get your uncle to give you some lessons if you want to play trombone. Go see your uncle Octave, he'll show you. Take care of that horn, too, and keep it clean."

I started out on clarinet, and my uncle [Barbarin] sent me to Barney Bigard, but he left town, and I picked up ukulele and I never connected the ukulele with the banjo. Then all of a sudden I'm in the neutral ground playing the uke when a famous band passes and I started playing along with the right chords, I guess, and an old man, Albert Glenny, had seen me fooling around with the ukulele and he called me over to his truck and said the regular banjo player was drunk and would I play a little? So they watched me and kindly smiled 'cause I was keepin' a beat, and they said, "Why don't you get a banjo?" I went and took some lessons and mother bought me a banjo.

All they do in the Barbarin family is talk about music, all the time music. So, you are destined to be a musician if you want it. Some kids shy away from it, all the notoriety, the bombastic second line and all that. They don't like it so they stay in the background and don't want to be involved with music. It's people's personalities, but for me, it was a thing to be there. You were identified 'specially with poor people, black and white. It's like you saying, "My uncle plays with the Dodgers." We didn't have that in New Orleans, but we had, "*My uncle* plays with the Dixieland band, or my cousin works with Chris Kelly's band, my uncle works with Manny Perez' band." It was a thing that you were associated with some notoriety to claim a musician.

When you give a kid a musical instrument he does something with his personality. He becomes a figure, and he's not so apt to get into trouble. Later on, the kids got into grass and narcotics, but in those days families would encourage you to play music. There was something about playing music that gave you something special. You are not a waster or a bum. Now you can be a musician and still be those things, but generally you were a little something special when you were a musician. You had extra special talent.[18]

Placide Adams, born on August 30, 1929, originally came from suburban Algiers. Matriarch Dolly Adams was a pianist and second-generation member of a musical clan. Placide, a Creole, recalls:

We lived next to Henderson's undertakers and I could look out the window and see the crying and weeping and the bands organize. I was nine or ten and my mother played practically all instruments. My granduncle, Manny Minetta, taught my mother to play, but we weren't allowed in his studio when he gave lessons. In fact, he was the only one teaching black and white. My grandmother was a violinist, my mother's mother. My grandfather was a cornet player. He used to do triple-tongue duets. In those days, families would go to each other's houses and entertain, trying to outdo others from other parts of the family. The cousins in my family were all vocalists. They had quartets and my mother and her brothers would get on their instruments and play behind them.[19]

At thirteen, Placide on drums joined a family group including Dolly on piano, her brothers Irving Doroux on trombone and Lawrence on trumpet, and Placide's brothers Justin on guitar and Jerry on bass. Schooled in ensemble jazz, Placide moved easily into 1950s R&B, working with such influential figures as Clyde McPhatter, Big Joe Turner, B. B. King, and others.

The Adams family moved into the Seventh Ward, where black Creole culture had flourished. In the 1800s Bernard Marigny of the landed gentry inherited a vast estate from his father; he planned a grid stretching from the river to the lake. Streets laid out in wobbly parallel to the Mississippi he named for family and friends: Urquhart, Morales, Jean Baptiste, Saintavid, Prosper, Solidelle, Celestine. Into them ran streets toward the lake. The downtown boundaries were, fittingly, St. Bernard Avenue and Elysian Fields (in French *Champs Elysee*).[20]

But clannish Creoles soon took the district for their own. Poet and historian Marcus Christian wrote: "The genealogical strength of the Seventh Ward families are such in evidence . . . with building trades, music, business enterprise, and their attitudes of self-help."[21] The city's transformation was like the slow unfolding of a lady's fan: strip by strip the new municipalities grew, from the triangular head in the Vieux Carré westward toward the lake, eastward along a concourse of plantations and faubourgs upriver.

Creole artisans and tradesmen gave the Seventh Ward their stamp. Commerce built on family-owned funeral parlors, builders and carpenters, barber shops, corner bars, a network of social clubs. In 1915 a hurricane destroyed the local church, which Creoles promptly rebuilt. Today, Corpus Christi is the largest predominately black parish in the country. A partial list of Seventh Ward musical families includes Manuel Perez, Sidney Bechet, Joe and Buddy Petit, Chris Kelly, Lorenzo Tio, Sr. and Jr., the Renas, Barbarins, Louis Arthidore, two families of Fraziers, Dave Williams, Emile and Paul Barnes (cousins of the Marreros). The Barneses, Williamses, Fraziers, and Marreros intermarried. Then there was Barney Bigard, Albert Nicholas, Danny and his wife, Blue Lu Barker.[22]

Those were founding jazz families. Among the midcentury, jazz-to-R&B clans are the Josephs— Walden "Frog" Joseph is a distinguished trombonist whose sons, Charles and Curt, perform with the Dirty Dozen, the eighties' most exciting brass band—and the Bruniouses. John Sr., a trumpeter, did arrangements for Satchmo and Fats Domino. John Jr. played trumpet in the seventies, while brother Wendell Brunious is one of the city's finest trumpeters.

More than musical information passed through the generations. Parents served as role models; they taught children practical things about artistic economics. Albert "Papa" French (1910–1977) was a banjo rhythm man and influential bandleader. His sons George, a bass player, and Bob, a drummer, are active in jazz and rhythm-and-blues. Papa worked as a carpenter sometimes. George recalls: "He'd come in after a hard day's work, take a bath, lay down, make the gig, sleep three or four hours and go back to work that morning." Bob remembers: "I'd ask Daddy, 'How much do you charge for this and what do you charge for transportation?' I'd always ask him about the business 'cause he had been in it so long. It was a heck of an advantage."[23]

To other Creoles, musicianship meant struggle. "Deacon" John Moore, born on June 23, 1941, was the fifth of fourteen children. His forebears came from Pointe Coupee parish. John Boudreaux, Sr., his maternal grandfather, played banjo with the Moonlight Serenaders. His mother was active in the church choir, and his paternal aunt "had a dancing school and my older sister used to do toe-dancing and I used to sing in the review every year. I was about three or four. Then later, my mother would have her classical music on and we'd try to turn on rock-and-roll. She'd say, *'Turn that jive off!'*"

The family was poor, but most children went to college. One sister, Sybil Klein, is the author of *Gombo People*, a book of Creole poetry. Deacon John continues:

My second sister played violin in high school, Marie. The sister after her played trombone in the high school band and the sister after her sang in the choir at St. Mary's. There was always a lot of music around the house 'cause my mother would play piano and we'd sing; my sister was always practicing her violin, and the

LOUIS ARTHIDORE
1884–1905

Virtuoso with the Onward Brass Band
Clarinet

Isidore John Barbarin	Alto Horn
and Louis Arthidore	Clarinet
(Isidore Barbarin married Louis Arthidore's sister)	
Paul Barbarin	Drums
and Jimmy Noone	Clarinet
(married two sisters)	
Paul's wife's brother, T. J. Thomas	Saxophone
Louis Barbarin's wife's brother, Billy Phillips	Drums
Louis Barbarin's daughter married son of Louis Nelson	Trombone
Louis Barbarin's son, Louis, Jr.	Trombone
Willie Barbarin	Trumpet
Willie Barbarin, Jr.	Drums
Louis Barbarin	Drums
Lucien Barbarin, Isidore's son	Trumpet
Isidore's grandson, Danny Barker	Banjo
Danny Barker married Louisa Dupont (Blue Lu Barker)	Blues singer
Blue Lu's nephew, August Dupont	Saxophone
Blue Lu's cousin, Joseph Thomas (Brother Cornbread)	Clarinet
Blue Lu's cousin, Erthy Lazard	Drums
Blue Lu's cousin, Bibbs Lazard (Erthy's son)	Drums
Danny and Blue Lu's daughter, Sylvia Brunner	Monologuist
Isidore's cousin, Esther Bijou	Blues singer
Boy Bijou (Esther's brother) (sang Creole songs)	Piano
Octave Clements, Isidore's cousin (Big Bell Fob)	Trombone
Isidore's cousin, Lionel Tapo	Banjo
Lionel Tapo's brother, Charlie Lajoie	Guitar
Lionel Tapo's brother-in-law, Howard Mandolf	Piano
Louis Nelson's brother	Saxophone

Source: From a genealogy by Danny Barker in the William Ransom Hogan Jazz Archive, Tulane University, New Orleans.

Deacon John Moore

Danny Barker, elder statesman

David and Melvin Lastie, circa 1956

other one with the trombone, the guitars, and my brothers were beating on conga drums.

My father was a hustler—not *hustling*—he laid bricks, mixed mortar, sold scrap iron, construction work, and before that he sold ice and charcoal. He was really into the money then but they invented the refrigerator and stove, cut him out, man. He had chickens in the backyard. He'd come home with grass and feed his rabbits. He had turkeys, ducks, parakeets, pigeons, dogs. He had a goat, you know, but the neighbors signed a petition to the Board of Health, made him get rid of it. That was kind of a way of life back then. New Orleans wasn't as densely populated. People had their cows and all. Chickens in yards was common. The guy across the street from me was a gas; he had a aviary and a tank with alligators in it. He still raises parakeets.[24]

Moore's father gave him fifty dollars for his first amplifier, but at St. Augustine High, priests scolded a scholarship student leaning toward rock-and-roll. By graduation, he was earning money playing rhythm-and-blues. On the Louisiana State University in New Orleans campus, he faced an identity crisis. "The old theme, 'The wretched mulattos, despised by one race, hated by another,' made me feel, 'Hey, what am I?'" He dropped out, formed a band, took the name Deacon "from my style of singing then, screamin' and hollerin' like Ray Charles, like preachers in church." His band, the Ivories, did well on the white dance circuit with an evolving repertoire drawn from the pop charts. Later, he broke the band down to four members, with his brother Charles on bass. Today the act is simply known as Deacon John.

Up to this time, New Orleans's reputation had rested largely on jazz. In the passage of musical families through the middle decades of this cen-

tury, rhythm-and-blues emerged as the new popular idiom, planting the seeds of rock-and-roll. At the same time, a deep blues sensibility coursed through the city. The heyday of R&B, from 1954 to 1963, was an exciting time for musicians under the arch of segregation. Records were being produced; tours left for the Gulf South, East, and West. There was money to be made but how much varied with individual producers. Many dealt unscrupulously, stealing from blacks who had little knowledge of contracts or business. Nevertheless, a legion of talented artists came forth producing hits, and it is their chronicle this book records.

By 1980, with R&B in a colorful revival, new clans were emerging. The Neville brothers—Art, Charles, Aaron, and Cyril—cut albums and toured successively with a sound of R&B and intricate Carnival percussions set against four-part harmonies. The younger Marsalis brothers—trumpeter Wynton, saxophonist Branford, both in their twenties—are jazz modernists who broke on the national scene in 1982. Their improvisational designs reflect the modern idiom and a family heritage: patriarch Ellis Marsalis, an accomplished pianist, played bebop and more experimental jazz with a handful of pioneers in central city clubs of the 1950s.

Like the exploratory jazz of the postwar years, rhythm-and-blues came into its own with a distinct urban tone. With the rise of these idioms in the 1950s, a new generation of musicians took prominent places in the society that raised them. And as the old uptown-downtown dichotomy faded into aging pockets of the city, so did the spread of music leave deep imprints on the neighborhoods where families settled.

Chapter Two

PROFESSOR LONGHAIR: AT THE ROOTS

On a hot, muggy Sunday in May 1979, a camera team from the "Today" show wove through the crowd following an aging black man called Professor Longhair. With the tropical heat of the temperate zone just beginning, thousands of people were crowding up to the open air stage erected on the grassy infield of the city's racetrack. Professor Longhair and the Blues Scholars were about to start their set. The New Orleans Jazz and Heritage Festival was in full force. In the distance, the unorthodox piano player could see five other stages and thousands of sweaty spectators wearing cutoff jeans and tee-shirts, eating jambalaya, smoking marijuana, and drinking beer as musicians performed. The gospel tent looked like a big balloon, filled with people packed shoulder-tight, thumping to the Lord's music.

The whole scene was vintage New Orleans, talented musicians feeding the hedonistic temper of the town. And by 1979, Professor Longhair had reason to be satisfied. After years of obscurity, the jazz festival had given him an annual platform; fans had now come to adore the old man, a shaping force behind the city's musical rhythms.

The NBC cameras followed as Professor Longhair took the stage to an explosion of applause. Born Henry Roeland Byrd, he had taken the stage name Professor Longhair years earlier. Now, at sixty-one, Byrd had arrived. For better than a decade he had been a distant legend to the blues faithful of America, Europe, and Japan. Now national pop critics were praising Fess's idiosyncratic style, built on a thumping boogie-woogie line with fusions of Carnival parade beats and a heavy rhumba flavor. In New Orleans, in a rocking music club near the Mississippi docks named Tipitina's (after his famous song), Professor Longhair had become a living legend. When the lanky man with the stiff leg limped through the closely packed crowds on Saturday nights, the faithful parted in reverence, with murmurings of "Hey, Fess" and "Where y'at, Byrd?"

The NBC cameraman edged closer to the piano as Byrd acknowledged cheers. His fingers hit the ivory chips. The camera was moving. It was not always this way.

In 1949, Herb Abramson and Ahmet Ertegun, owners of young Atlantic Records, went talent scouting in New Orleans. They had heard about a popular piano player called Professor Longhair and set out to find him. They managed to get the name of an Algiers club where he was playing, but the cab driver refused to take them all the way "because that's a niggertown." They got across the river and, following the cabbie's directions, trudged across an open field toward a distant light and pounding sounds of music. At the door of the strange honky-tonk, the bouncer wanted to know who these white men were. Nervously, they made up a story about *Life* magazine having sent them to hear Professor Longhair, but they were mistaken for police. An argument broke out at the door, some people fled through the back, but the pair finally got in and found seats behind the piano.

The band consisted of Professor Longhair alone, and Ertegun never forgot him.[1]

He was sitting there with a microphone between his legs. He used to play an upright piano, and he had a . . . drumhead, you know, attached to the piano. He would hit it with his right foot while he was playing. He made a percussive sound. It was very loud. And he was playing the piano and singing full blast, and it really was the most incredible-sounding thing I ever heard. And he was doing it all by himself. It was one of the most primitive dance halls I'd ever been in . . . people jammed in there dancing and this wild thing going on, and they hid us in the corner there and we were listening to the music. I thought, My God, we've really found an original.

And I said, "No white person has ever seen this man." So as soon as he finished, Herb and I, very excited, said, "Look, we have to tell you, we're just astounded by your playing," you know, and shaking his hand. "We want very much to record you." He said, "Oh, what a shame. I just signed with Mercury."

The Mercury contract produced one hit, "Baldhead," in 1950. The lyrics gave hints of the street comedy and folk humor of Longhair's music:

Chorus
Look-a-there, she ain't got no hair. *Baldhead!*
My, look-a-there, how come no hair? *Baldhead!*
Oh, look-a-there, she ain't got no hair. *Baldhead!*
Hey, look-a-there, where's that girl's hair? *Baldhead!*

You know, boys, this little girl I'm tryin' to tell you about,
Supposed to be a good friend of mine's wife
Everyday at the job he tells me he made a mistake.
He wished he had a married on some other night.

(Chorus)

And everyday on the job he said she was worrying him to death,
Beggin' him to take her out to a ball,
So he got her straight, he couldn't take chances, he told her,
"If I carry you, baby, you got to stand out in the hall."

(Chorus)

So she thought if she gave him a drink or two out of a jug,
He would take her for a walk, down in Lee Circle's park.
Yes, he did, but he got drunk and wanted to make a little love,
Put his arms around her making him knock the wig off.

(Chorus)

Later in 1950, however, Longhair did sign with Atlantic and in 1953 recorded "Tipitina," which years later became one of his most famous songs. But it had only a brief flurry of success in the local charts in March 1954 and soon sank into obscurity, like Roy Byrd himself.

Byrd got his stage name in 1947, while playing at the old Caldonia Inn a few blocks outside the French Quarter. It was a popular watering hole and a bit offbeat, a haunt for black transvestites where Byrd once played for a gay wedding.

Brawls were not uncommon. "We had long hair in those days," he explained, "and it was almost against the law." The Italian proprietor announced: "I'm going to keep this band. We'll call you Professor Longhair and the Four Hairs Combo."[2] Various musicians passed through the combo's ranks. The band dissolved in the early fifties but Roy Byrd had his professional name.

In those days few places welcomed unorthodox black pianists; most played the honky-tonks and dives. And Byrd made the circuit. Rampart Street, stretching from the downtown wards across Canal Street to the uptown blocks, was a black city-within, much like Beale Street in Memphis, with small businesses, barrooms, pool halls, and music everywhere.

Byrd was born in Bogalusa, Louisiana, on December 19, 1918. After his father deserted the family, his mother moved with them to New Orleans. He grew up on a side street near the Ramp and as a kid gravitated there. His early influences came from church and dancing. With little formal education, he owed much of his musical knowledge to his mother, who was well versed in guitar and piano. "My mother took me to church when I was little," Byrd explained. "That's the best place to begin learning music for getting the soul up. We used to make our own instruments when I was a kid—like trap drums out of boxes; we got all kinds of noises out of that."[3]

By his early teens, Byrd was haunting the clubs on Rampart Street where he heard honky-tonk pianists like Kid "Stormy" Weather and Isidore "Tuts" Washington. This was during the Depression, and he shined shoes, sold newspapers, and worked odd jobs to supplement his family's income. As a teenager, Byrd began to develop his sense of rhythm by learning to dance. He was influenced by the lanky, disjointed tap dancing of Bill "Bojangles" Robinson, and together with his friend Streamline Harris, Byrd began working the clubs along Rampart Street. He often sat in on piano, trading songs and music passages with Champion Jack Dupree, Sonny Boy Williamson, and other musicians working in the Crescent City.

The rhythms Byrd danced on nightclub stages were not enough to satisfy his musical desires; he took the drum-infused movements of his feet and translated them to the piano, adding layers of melody to intricate rhythm patterns. Chief among them was boogie-woogie, the barrelhouse keyboard style popularized in the twenties and revived in the late thirties. Byrd's choice of this style was probably influenced by Sullivan Rock, a blues pianist ten years his elder about whom nearly nothing is known. "Come here, boy," Rock would shout. "Let me show you the 'Pine Top Boogie Woogie' so you'll have something to play."[4] Sullivan Rock is an obscure figure, but his influence rivaled that of other musicians who recorded sparsely, if at all, yet served as mentors to younger players with no access to formal music education.

Another mentor was Isidore "Tuts" Washington, a grand old pianist who remembers Byrd as "just a kid when I was playing them speakeasies and nightclubs on Rampart. That's where he came from. He jumped and learned how to play a few blues and things that made him famous. At that time I didn't play nothin' but blues."[5]

American popular music was changing in the late 1940s. White singers like Perry Como and Dinah Shore topped *Cashbox* charts but drew little interest from blacks. For fledgling rhythm-and-blues labels, the jukebox began as an alternative distribution to radio. Johnny Vincent of Ace Records, who recorded early New Orleans hits, recalls, "I went to Chicago with a record and a [disc] jockey told me, 'Man, I couldn't play anything like that. It's oriented black and I'm on top forty, mostly white pop.' I said, 'Listen, this trend is coming. You might as well get used to it.'"[6]

Rhythm-and-blues replaced "race recordings" in the June 25, 1949, issue of *Billboard*, a trade publication. What was rhythm-and-blues? At root, it was a fusion of the blues idiom with a variety of other forms—gospel, jazz, swing, Afro-Cubano, hillbilly. As a popular music style, R&B was a less personal form of expression than the older, rural blues. The rhythm of the new sound drew heavily on the intense, building rhythms in the churches, a gospel sound that merged into the blues sensibility.

By the 1950s, R&B was used to denote many forms of black music that were not jazz. The roots of R&B lay in different pockets of black culture. The richest wellspring of rural blues was the Mississippi Delta, where a generation of post–World War II bluesmen left the poverty for dreams of life in the cities. B. B. King migrated from Sunflower County to Memphis and then the world, Muddy Waters from tiny Rolling Fork to the southside of Chicago. In Chicago the music changed to fit an urban pace. A down-home boy could hit a dozen city honky-tonks in half as many blocks. People could travel, had more dollars in their pockets. Poverty was still great, but an urban black culture was emerging.

Rhythm-and-blues was more than a music: it was a national phenomenon—the country sounds of the South flowing into the streets of the North and the West Coast; thumping gospel choirs and lonely bluesmen; little trios and folk quartets playing harmonica, washboard, and strings; and then the "doo-wop" vocalizers, inspired by sacred music, improvising on hundreds of street corners—all spread out and like a great current charged into the cities with electrified instruments, radio, and recording outlets.

Professor Longhair was very much a progenitor of R&B; his influence, however, was largely limited to New Orleans. In a very real sense, he lay the foundation of a unique musical sound that the coming generation revered and built upon. He played with the deep heart of a bluesman, but Fess's rhythms were a complex affair: the movement of feet translated to piano, boogie-woogie stride, a sizzling left-hand—to these layers he added "a mixture of mambo, rhumba, and Calypso."[7] You can hear the fusion best in "Go to the Mardi Gras," the anthem played on hundreds of jukeboxes during Carnival. The tale of a man going to the city, it is sung to sounds of horns, rocking drums, and rippling through it all, a wave of piano. Horns burst through like the rush of a train. Byrd sings of black Mardi Gras—the parade of Zulu, the oldest Negro Carnival krewe. Members mask as mock Africans, adorned with bones and teeth, in minstrel face with gaudy white mouths: grown men wearing grass skirts, throwing gilded coconuts off floats to crowds below.

Well, I'm goin' to New Awleens,
I wanna see the Mahdi Graw.
When I see the Mahdi Graw,
I wanna know what's Carnival for.

Goin' down to New Awleens,
I've got m' ticket in mah hand.
Goin' down to New Awleens,
I've got m' ticket in mah hand.

When I get to New Awleens,
I wanna see the Zulu King.
Way down in New Awleens,
Down on Rampart and Dumaine.

Yesss, down in New Awleens,
Onnn Rampart and Dumaine,
Goin' make it mah standin' place
Until I see the Zulu Queen.

Rampart and Dumaine, in addition to being a hub for black Carnival, was also the location of J&M Music Shop, where Byrd's song was recorded in 1950, under the direction of Ahmet Ertegun.

Mac Rebennack (rock star Dr. John) states: "I think Fess put funk into music. I don't think . . . a Allen Toussaint or a Huey Smith or a lot of other piano players here would have the basics of style without Fess. . . . All those cats have absorbed a lot of other piano players, but Longhair's thing had a direct bearing I'd say on a large portion of the funk music that evolved in New Orleans."[8]

Byrd's life reflected the lonely odyssey of the blues. In the early years he often relied on his skills as a gambler or worked hard jobs to support himself while he played the piano. "They called me 'Whirlwind' when I used to box. I was 135 pounds. . . . I was pretty good, too. I gave it up, though. I quit the first time I got my ass whipped. I didn't really have that many fights, and they weren't anything fancy. We'd just fight in the alleys, back rooms, and take whatever they would throw on the floor. It was better than unloading bananas from ships. I still don't like the taste of bananas to this day."[9]

In 1970 British blues journalist Mike Leadbitter visited New Orleans on a research trip. He went looking for Professor Longhair, whose music he and scores of English enthusiasts had come to venerate. He found him on South Rampart Street, sweeping out the One Stop Record Store. His playing was sporadic at best; he was broke. Then a young promoter, Quint Davis, went searching for Byrd in hopes of resurrecting his career. "He was in a totally depreciated state physically," Davis recalls, "along with poverty and rejection. When he sat down, he couldn't get up. When he did stand up, his knee would rattle around until it set into a groove so he could walk. He had a vitamin deficiency, he had no teeth, no digestion, and he couldn't go to the bathroom."[10] Davis began managing Byrd, now all but removed from the shifting trends of rock music. At the New Orleans Jazz and Heritage Festival, which Davis and Allison Miner Kaslow helped launch, the renaissance of Professor Longhair began. He limped onto the stage in a black suit. Davis: "And when he started playing—this sounds like a cliché—everything else stopped dead on the other stages. There were four acts playing simultaneously, and the crowd just gathered and gaped. They had never heard anything like him. It was a truly magic moment."[11]

Davis saw that Byrd got solid billing at the jazz festival each spring and began booking him into local clubs. By the mid-seventies Byrd began to play festivals at Newport, Chicago, and Montreux, Switzerland. Atlantic Records released a collection of his work, further reviving his popularity and attracting the interest of writers and collectors. In Europe and Japan his reputation among blues fans accelerated. In 1976 he cut a new record, *Live on the Queen Mary,* with the help of Paul McCartney, who admired his work. Finally, in 1979, after the "Today" show appearance, Byrd set out on a North American tour with his band, the Blues Scholars. He played three packed nights at the Village Gate in New York (prompting a long, scholarly assessment of his career by Gary Giddins in the *Village Voice*) and then made a triumphant appearance in Toronto.

Off the road, Byrd made Tipitina's his home base, exciting local fans as well as visitors from around the world. A lifelong dream for Byrd, he became part owner of the club founded in 1977 by a group of young rhythm-and-blues enthusiasts. Converted from a small blue-collar bar in the uptown section near the river, the business grew, and in 1983 the editors of *Esquire* called Tipitina's one of the best bars in America.

Tipitina's featured live music nightly, hosting local and national talent with a slant toward rhythm-and-blues and jazz. The club became a haven for a cadre of fans, drawn by the bar's unpretentious atmosphere and reputation for sizzling music. Byrd's Mardi Gras eve performance became legendary.

Although he was nearing sixty-one, Byrd had never been recorded with the sensitivity that his complex music deserved. The old hits were now blues gems, but in the evolution of his career, no modern LP had done his music justice. In 1977, when Allison Kaslow took over managing Byrd, she began to seek out recording companies. A live recording, produced by writer Albert Goldman, was made during the Mardi Gras of 1978. The money advanced to Longhair was substantial, but the tapes were not used until 1983, when *The Last Mardi Gras* was produced.

Alligator Records had established a reputation for production and distribution of urban blues. Bruce Iglauer, the company's founder, had been wanting to record Byrd for several years. During the summer of 1979, Iglauer, who also worked as a booking agent, spoke to Kaslow about booking Byrd at the Notre Dame Blues Festival coming up in November. Iglauer flew to New Orleans and heard Byrd play with the Blues Scholars, and an agreement was reached for an LP.

The recording session was set for November 1979 in New Orleans, but the Blues Scholars needed a guitarist. When Mac Rebennack, then in Los Angeles, heard this, he quickly offered his services. Byrd, Iglauer, and Kaslow agreed that Rebennack would be a valuable asset, not only as a guitarist but for his wily sense of studio recording. It was near freezing the night of the first rehearsal session at the Musicians' Union Hall on Esplanade Avenue. In a bare, open room with a lone piano and several folding chairs, the musicians filed in, slapping themselves against the cold. Byrd arrived an hour later in his aging blue Cadillac. With his rhythmic limp, he entered the room, embraced Rebennack, and the rehearsal began.

Timothy White wrote in *Rolling Stone* that "Professor Longhair was a collector of rhythms."[12] His band, the Blues Scholars, was also a collection. Johnny Vidacovich had drummed with many of the city's jazz and rhythm-and-blues artists; his loose-limbed playing was marked by rapid, crisp syncopations. Conga player Alfred Roberts gave the rhumba-tinted music a distinct tropical flavor; he had been with Byrd nearly a decade and knew how to complement his complex rhythms. Bass player Dave Watson had been with the band about a year and had a good reputation. There were

three saxophones in the Blues Scholars; Jim Moore on baritone; Tony Dagradi, a skilled jazz modernist, on tenor; and Andy Kaslow, Allison's husband, also on tenor. Andy, studying for a Ph.D. in anthropology at Columbia, played a crucial role in Byrd's comeback plans.

Several days of rehearsal blended Rebennack's sharp, biting guitar rhythms into the larger sound. The album *Crawfish Fiesta* was cut at SeaSaint Studio, owned by pianist-composer Allen Toussaint and businessman Marshall Sehorn. As early as four o'clock in the afternoon people began arriving for the seven o'clock session. The NBC affiliate was there to do a short videotape of Byrd and Allen Toussaint for a local documentary. Once the cameras left, Iglauer's engineer, Freddie Breitburg, began adjusting microphones and moving the grand piano into place. The session was recorded live with few overdubs; the idea was to capture the music as played, not to produce a multilayered recording dependent on studio technology. This was Breitburg's forte. He moved the drums from the enclosed booth, setting them just to the left of the piano. After finishing an oyster po-boy, Byrd took his seat at the piano. Iglauer yelled from the control room, "What's the first song, Fess?"

"Take out your false teeth, poppa, 'cause mama wants to mingle in your gumdrops." That broke the ice, and in a roomful of laughter Byrd kicked off a spirited version of his 1957 record "No Buts, No Maybes." The album took form with relative ease, few songs requiring more than three takes. Byrd had not done a studio recording in five years, but his ease and command of the music calmed the musicians and technicians. At one point, during "In the Night," Vidacovich was having trouble capturing the rhythm; Byrd genially removed himself from the piano stool and with his hands lightly tapped the rhythm on the young drummer's chest.

The relationship between Rebennack and Byrd was special, dating back to 1959, when Mac produced and played guitar on Byrd's "Go to the

Street life

Mardi Gras" and "Cuttin' Out." For years he had wanted to record with Fess. Mac and Byrd conferred throughout the session, and if some minor problem needed correction, Rebennack, sensing Byrd's shyness, would articulate ideas to the Blues Scholars. "This was Mac's gift to Fess," Allison Kaslow later observed.[13]

The band moved through Byrd's repertoire. Songs he had played for years were now being recorded under the best conditions. These included "Baldhead," his first hit; "Whole Lotta Lovin' "; and "It's My Own Fault," with the crusty lyrics:

If I had known you had company, baby
You know I would have had weiners for my lunch
The man was twice my size
And packin' a Joe Louis punch.

The song capping the three-day session was the title cut "Crawfish Fiesta," loosely based on the melody of the Andrews Sisters' hit "Rum and Coca Cola," a tune with heavy Latin flavoring. The song was cut with just three musicians: Byrd on syncopated ragtime piano, Alfred Roberts on island conga, and Walter Payton, whose name was accidentally omitted from the album credits, on a bouncy second-line tuba. The song itself had come to Byrd in a series of dreams; twice he had mentioned the song to Rebennack, who urged him to record it.

After the album was completed, an independent television producer, Stevenson Palfi, arranged to videotape a concert with Byrd, Tuts Washington, and Allen Toussaint at Tipitina's. The idea behind the documentary was to trace three generations of New Orleans pianists, spanning blues, boogie-woogie, and the more funky, modern sound of Toussaint. The show, scheduled for February 3, 1980, foreshadowed Byrd's final emergence as a prominent musician, with the album and PBS program exposing his music to the broad audience

that had long eluded him. He was earning decent money—$32,000 by 1978—and finding his groove.

At three in the morning on Wednesday, January 30, 1980, Byrd lay quietly in bed with his grandson sleeping beside him. "He didn't moan, he didn't groan, he didn't move," recalled his wife, Alice. "His toe didn't even wiggle; he just slept away."[14] At six o'clock that morning he was pronounced dead of pulmonary emphysema, chronic bronchitis, and advanced cirrhosis of the liver. Within hours of his death, radio stations and jukeboxes in local taverns began playing his music, a tribute that continued through the weekend. Allison Kaslow drew together a coalition of friends to assist the family in burial expenses. The funeral was paid for by Allen Toussaint and Marshall Sehorn; other contributions came from the Musicians' Union and a handful of friends. Flower arrangements from Fats Domino, Paul McCartney, Irma Thomas, the Neville Brothers, and many others were delivered to the Majestic Mortuary on Dryades Street, just a few blocks from Byrd's home. The casket was opened for viewing on Friday afternoon, and long before the wake that night, a stream of people had paid homage.

Even in death, bitter irony stalked Byrd. The day he died, Alligator Records was shipping boxes of *Crawfish Fiesta* from Chicago. Bruce Iglauer said: "We'd already sold out of the first run of records. This is so sad; the guy was getting ready to take off. He played a concert at Notre Dame last November and the students, most of whom had never heard of him, mobbed him when he left the stage. The next night he played in Chicago and people were lined up around the block in the snow. Some of them had to wait for the second set and they stayed there in the snow. He could have really moved with this record, and now. . . ."[15]

Naturally the concert with Washington and Toussaint was canceled, but rehearsal sessions and interviews had been videotaped earlier in the week. Producer Stevenson Palfi, like everyone

Above: Professor Longhair at the Jazz and Heritage Festival, 1978

Professor Longhair, 1978

around Byrd, was crushed. "I sent a camera crew (from Mississippi ETV) back to Jackson. I told his wife I wanted the wake to be sacred, but she wanted the documentary completed. So I called the crew and told them to come back."

Television coverage of jazz funerals in New Orleans has been common for more than a decade now; however, the presence of two cameras and video monitors inside the funeral home created a bizarre atmosphere. A few of the many musicians who had gone to pay respects did agree to talk on-camera for the local news, but the flashing lights and cameras seemed disrespectful to others. Art Neville, keyboard leader of the Neville brothers, noted: "These cameras are sixty-five years too late. Where were they all those years Byrd was playing, but couldn't cut records?" His brother, vocalist Aaron Neville, was more philosophical: "The body is dead, but Byrd's still here."

Byrd was laid out in the formal white suit he was to have worn for the television concert on Sunday. The casket was bordered by yellow chrysanthemums shaped in a musical note. A string of preachers, neighbors, and musical friends spoke passionately of the man and his music. Vocalist Johnny Adams sang gospel, Ernie K-Doe gave a rousing sermon laced with gospel phrasings, and Aaron Neville's voice rose magnificently in "One Fine Day." Allen Toussaint played a composition written for the occasion, weaving a gentle medley of Fess's standards into a touching tribute.

When the funeral began the next morning under cold, slate-colored skies, Henry Roeland Byrd was still a throbbing heartbeat in the city whose primal rhythms he had translated into a unique keyboard style. The Olympia and Tuxedo bands, two of the city's traditional marching brass ensembles, were stationed at the front and side entrances of the mortuary. The video truck was ready to move, and cameramen began to circulate among the crowd. Close to three thousand people surrounded the old mortuary, blocking traffic on Dryades Street. The weather hovered at forty degrees. When pallbearers brought the casket down the front steps of the mortuary, a huge roar went up, almost as if Byrd himself had come in person to play. In a time-honored parade tradition, brightly colored umbrellas began to sprout like mushrooms above the crowd, the reds and silvers and yellows bobbing above the heads and shoulders of people wedging in tighter. Attendants had to burrow through the crowds to get the casket in the hearse. The Olympia band began "Just a Closer Walk with Thee," a gospel played in slow-time, as a dirge. After fifteen minutes the limousine was able to turn around and follow the procession.

"Lawda mercy," said an old black man. "Nobody could ring that piano like Fess!"

The funeral procession began to move, slowly, to the rhythms of the dirges, and still more people came, issuing out of the tottering honky-tonks and following the pumping umbrellas as the crowd paraded over scarred streets, past aging clapboard houses with black people leaning over the rusty iron-grilled balconies. This was Byrd's neighborhood and these were his people.

When the Olympia band reached Rampart Street, just four blocks from the funeral home, the crowd had grown to about five thousand and the wall of people was so thick it took another ten minutes to prod them back from the middle of the street and onto the sidewalk so the limousines could pass. The band stopped playing temporarily, and as the hearse passed, people crowded in again to get one last look at the casket, shrouded by an American flag. Byrd had been a lieutenant in his neighborhood civil defense unit.

The funeral was moving along Rampart Street, wide enough to contain the chaotic procession, and as the band broke out of the dirges, the trumpet took the lead in Byrd's classic "Go to the Mardi Gras." A cheer erupted from the crowd and people burst forward in a second line, coursing ahead, waving handkerchiefs, hats, and scarves,

Second line, circa 1950

parasols dipping and swaying to the beat of the band. As New Orleans jazz funerals go, it was one of the worst managed and most exciting ever, a fitting tribute to an artist whose idiosyncratic music almost defies description.

Of the many eulogies he received that weekend, a poignant one came from recording mogul Jerry Wexler, who recorded Byrd for Atlantic in the 1950s. "No, Fess didn't keep tabs on the Hit Parade," Wexler said at the wake, "and I feel we are the richer for it. Because he saved his attention and concentration for the blues. 'Tipitina' is just like Fess. It's always as pretty as it could be, and anytime you hear it, it hits you where you live." But in an interview in his hotel room late the next day, Wexler conceded that Byrd was "a casualty of the economics of the rhythm-and-blues world. He played a seminal role, parochial, but he never had the fortune to ride the crest of recording sales. . . . He simply wasn't commercial enough. It's tragic, but he'll become legendary now that he's dead."

Yet those who worked with Byrd believe he could have made it in his own lifetime. Quint Davis commented: "Everyone now says he's a genius, but why didn't they say it when he was alive? He had such a vast influence and his death leaves a big musical space in New Orleans, but the record companies didn't give him the opportunities."

Andy Kaslow said: "His poverty had to do with the structure of the music industry, music consumed by the white public after it's watered down from black origins. Look at the fame of Elvis Presley compared to the obscurity of Professor Longhair, the notoriety of Dave Brubeck compared to the lesser fame of Thelonius Monk. Fess was a bridge between all the different forms that led to rock-and-roll—jazz, blues, calypso, rhythm-and-blues. He was the purest expression of what rock-and-roll is all about, and he deserved one hell of a lot better."

Henry Roeland Byrd was buried in a cemetery far from the jazz funeral, in a grave that did not even bear his name. A hundred and fifty people attended the service at the grave site, and at least a third of them had cameras. After the minister finished the oration, Earl Turbinton, a longtime associate, played a soulful eulogy on the saxophone. As the last note of the sax faded into the cold wind, an old woman said, "That's just the way he'd have wanted it."

After that, all you could hear was cameras clicking.

Chapter Three

ANTOINE DOMINO: THE FAT MAN

Fats Domino lives on Marais Street in the lower Ninth Ward in a big white brick house trimmed in pink and yellow, topped by a roof of lavender terra-cotta tiles imported from Italy. The front yard, a ribbon of green, is bound by a low fence of floral-design wrought iron, the roses painted white and pink, the iron stems green. Fats has a hot pink El Dorado with gold trim, two Continentals, and a snow-white Rolls Royce bearing the initials "FD" bracketed by a pair of dominoes, all in gold.

Closed circuit cameras attached to the eaves watch the house. Front double doors open into an atrium with a big fireplace, crystal chandeliers, several couches, and in the best rock-and-roll tradition, four ivory dominoes, outlined in brass, set into the tile of the white marble floor. Off the atrium is a Steinway grand piano, surrounded by stereo equipment. Upstairs, his closets are filled with hundreds of suits in a rainbow of styles and colors, and scores of shoes. Fats Domino's house and cars—like the man himself—stand out in bas-

relief from the poor dwellings in the neighborhood.

He has quite a family, too. His wife, Rosemary, gave birth to four girls—Antoinette, Andrea, Anola, Adonica—and four boys—Antoine III, Andre, Anatole, and Antonio. The hub of family activity is the kitchen. Fats loves to cook. His approach to red beans and rice, a traditional New Orleans dish, is as grand as his piano. The beans simmer in a big commercial vat next to a large pot of ham hocks. Fats lords over them with a long, heavy spoon, stirring, tasting, seasoning with spices and herbs and hot sauce. Even when he travels, Fats Domino carries trunks filled with hot plates and cooking gear along with the wardrobe chests and musical equipment.

For three decades he spent the greater portion of each year on the road, from small gigs and one-night stands early in his career to long stints in Las Vegas hotels and highly paid performances in concert halls of Europe. He tours less these days, but the bucks are still big. And yet, for all of his wealth and baronial life-style, Fats Domino, an international star, is an almost anonymous presence in his own town. A shy man of humble origins, at home he spends most of his time in the neighborhood where he was born and raised, visiting the haunts of his youth.

Antoine Domino, Jr., was born in New Orleans on February 26, 1928, one of nine children in a Catholic family. His father, who worked at the local racetrack, had come from Vacherie, a small town upriver. The family, poor but not destitute, lived at 2407 Jourdan Avenue in the lower Ninth Ward—on the city's downriver fringes. In Antoine's childhood, the area was heavily rural. Out of the little clubs and honky-tonks came the lingering strains of a blues tradition. Unlike the raw, plaintive sounds of Mississippi guitars and harmonicas, Ninth Ward blues built off of pianos and horns. Many an old upright piano found home in the small clubs dotting the lower Ninth; people came to play them, and proprietors often encouraged youngsters to try their hand.

Antoine went only as far as the fourth grade at McCarty school, but he was already playing music. A childhood friend remembers watching him in the school auditorium, playing piano up on the stage, barefooted, kicking as he played boogie-woogie.[1] At home, his father played violin and the boy's Uncle Gustave played trumpet. His sister, Philonese, married Harrison Verrett, who played banjo and guitar. Verrett, twenty-one years older than the boy, formed a link to the jazz age, having played with Papa Celestin and Kid Ory. He took a professional interest in Antoine and functioned more as avuncular mentor than brother-in-law. "He was the first one to take me out of New Orleans," Domino recalled. "He just about raised me. He showed me the first note on the piano."[2]

Verrett helped other youngsters, too. Saxophonist David Lastie recalls:

He was a hip old man. Very neat, very clean, and very direct. He'd say, "Lastie, you played that wrong. It goes like this." He wasn't gonna have no *no*'s and *but*'s about it. We be going on a job, he come pick us up in a big Cadillac. It was nice to ride in a Cadillac. That was a gas for us then. He used to come pick us up and he'd tell us: "You ain't got time for them women; you learn your music first. Don't smoke and please don't fool with none of them drugs. Always go on your job neat and clean, get your hair cut." He say musicians should have a white shirt and black pants, black bow tie and red long tie. That was standard.[3]

The musical influences on Domino in his formative years were, besides Ninth Ward blues and traditional jazz, a melting pot of contemporary sounds. He was drawn to the riffing brass and hard-driving beat of early R&B artists from the West Coast: Amos Milburn, Roy Milton, Camille Howard, and Charles Brown. Of Louis Jordan, the most popular black musician on the mid-forties commercial charts, Domino said: "I was crazy about him. I used to listen to him all night."[4] Fats was also a big fan of Louis Armstrong.

By his late teens Antoine Domino was working hard jobs and playing music in small clubs in and out of the Ninth Ward. He worked at the Fair Grounds racetrack, on an ice truck, in a lumberyard, and in a bedsprings factory, where he nearly lost two fingers. He soon gravitated toward the big band of Dave Bartholomew, the man who would shape his career, both as producer and composer.

Dave Bartholomew is one in a long and distinguished line of New Orleans trumpet players, a line begun in the early 1900s, when Buddy Bolden blew powerful rhythmic melodies for dance halls and barrooms. As jazz rose to an international art in the twenties, there came a more personal style with delicate phrasing and a wider variety of tone. Joe "King" Oliver, Louis Armstrong, and Bunk Johnson popularized this new sound. Other locals continued the style, and the trumpet endured through the difficult days of the Depression, with strong play by Punch Miller,

Kid Rena, Kid Thomas Valentine, and Oscar "Papa" Celestin. During World War II many musicians went into the service, but after the war, swing-styled combos and orchestras reappeared. New Orleans bands of the late forties played a variety of music—swing, traditional, Dixieland, bebop, ballads, Mardi Gras music, gutbucket blues. And Dave Bartholomew led one of the best dance bands in the city.

Bartholomew, born on December 24, 1920, is a tall, stocky man, well groomed and with a confident air. There is little frivolity in his interviews. Bartholomew exudes prosperity and has a commanding presence. He sat in his office one day, discussing his professional origins.

My father had a barbershop on Thalia and South Galvez streets. A man who had taught Louis Armstrong, Mr. Peter Davis,[5] used to be in the place most every day, playing checkers. So he said, "Give me that boy." He was a very, very fine man. He always said to me, "I know one thing. A black man has a hard road to travel in this world, and if you don't know how to do nothing, it's gonna be harder." So he embedded in our mind to learn to play music so we would at least know how to do something.

I really started playing professionally with the late Oscar "Papa" Celestin. He had a big band at the time in the Count Basie mode. I traveled all over Louisiana and Mississippi with them. But the best band that I played with at that time that was paying any money was Claiborne Williams' band in Donaldsonville. It was considered a "society" band. We played for nothing but whites in those days. After I graduated from that, I went with Fats Pichon. He was organizing a band for the steamer *Capitol,* which was the sister ship of the *President* and *Admiral* in St. Louis. I was considered a brilliant trumpet player for my age. I could read and play with anybody. That was in the summer of 1938, and I went on the steamer *Capitol* and stayed there for three or four years.[6]

By age twenty-two, he was well schooled in both New Orleans and big band jazz. In 1942 he entered the army as a musician. "We shipped out of Boston and on that ship there was nothing but bands. We had our horns out day and night. I think it took us ten days to get over and we jammed all the way." Not a bad way to start the war. Bartholomew remained in the army until 1946. Once back in the States, he assembled one of the best dance bands in the South.[7] Over the next few years, his orchestra played at colleges, picnics, Carnival balls, and local clubs. By the time he took an interest in the struggling young Domino, Bartholomew at twenty-nine was an established musician clearly on the rise. His first recordings were new interpretations of "High Society" and "Stardust" for the DeLuxe label out of New Jersey. In 1949 Bartholomew had his own regional rhythm-and-blues hit, "Country Boy."

Bartholomew was playing in a black nightclub in Houston called the Bronze Peacock when he met Lew Chudd, president of Imperial Records of Los Angeles. Chudd wanted to crack the rhythm-and-blues market. He had recorded a handful of black artists on the West Coast with limited success, but in Dave Bartholomew's band he saw better commercial possibilities.[8] He offered Bartholomew a job as talent scout/producer for Imperial in New Orleans.

At that time, like most young musicians who played the wards, Fats had to hustle his own gigs. He would approach bar owners with: "Hey, man, let me get up there and play. I can get you a crowd in here." He was doing it, too; soon Domino had his own following of night people. Earl Palmer, who played drums for Dave Bartholomew, remembers Fats in those days: "We were working at a place called Al's Starlight Inn in the Ninth Ward. Fats Domino used to come in and just play the piano at this place, play boogie-woogie piano. When I was runnin' the band, I used to let him come up and play during the intermission—y'know, when we'd get down, because it would keep people in the place. And Dave wouldn't object if I let Fats come up and play, but

Dave Bartholomew, band master

Fats Domino on the S.S. *President*

Harrison Verrett

lots of times if he'd ask Dave, Dave would say, 'No.'"[9]

In late fall of 1949, Chudd flew to New Orleans to see Bartholomew, and as a matter of course, Chudd made the rounds of the radio stations. At WNOE in the Jung Hotel he met disc jockey Duke Thiele, known as "Poppa Stoppa." Poppa Stoppa told Chudd about "a fat kid" playing piano in a Ninth Ward barroom. Lew Chudd decided to have a look at the "fat kid," so he caught a cab with Poppa Stoppa. They had to lie on the floor because it was illegal for a cab driver to take a white person to a black establishment. They found Domino at the Hideaway, a lounge in the sprawling Ninth Ward.

"Lloyd Price was on the same bill," Chudd said, years later. "I was offered Price but I wanted the fat man who played the piano. He was so shy, he wouldn't come over to our table."[10] Dave Bartholomew brought the bashful youngster over to meet Chudd and they began to talk. Chudd recalls that Domino played "a primitive beat, but it was a different beat. I wanted him then and there."[11] Domino signed with Imperial.

It was late in 1949. Domino was twenty-one when he followed Bartholomew into a modest studio on Rampart Street, at the edge of the French Quarter, to cut a song fittingly titled "The Fat Man." The story behind that session is something of a legend in the annals of rhythm-and-blues, not least because it was Domino's first studio attempt. His talent was real enough, but even the rawest, most pulsating talent does not, in and of itself, guarantee success. (Professor Longhair is a case in point.) In this respect, Fats Domino was lucky. Three music professionals were interested in him, and each was a vital element in the chemistry of that rough and rocking little song. Dave Bartholomew arranged the tune, as well as Domino's subsequent hits. Lew Chudd saw the potential and made sure the disc was well distributed. And then there was the recording

engineer, who ran his operation on a wing and a prayer. His name was Cosimo Matassa, and he owned the J&M Record Shop where the recording was made.

It really was a shop, with the "studio" located in a room behind the small display lobby containing racks of records and shelves of radios and ancient phonographs. An early J&M advertisement read: "We install phonographs and pin ball machines on commission." The idea of a first-class studio was still years away from New Orleans.

Matassa was fascinated with electronics. Early on, he built his own radio and listened to the Joe Louis–Max Schmeling prizefight on it. During World War II, Matassa was a partner in a jukebox business started by his father, an Italian immigrant who founded a family grocery store and a French Quarter watering hole that catered to a bohemian clientele. Cosimo sold used records for his father and after the war, in 1945, opened the J&M. He was eighteen years old.

The J&M became a hub for musicians. Station WNOE sponsored live Sunday afternoon broadcasts from the shop, featuring the local rhythm-and-blues talent. Matassa's venture into studio recording was, like the radio he made, long on ingenuity if short on money and sophisticated hardware. "Everything I did personally was with black groups or with guys who were into black music because that was really the native idiom."[12]

In those days, Matassa used "a Duo-Presto disc recorder. We cut two [discs] simultaneously and we didn't play the one that hopefully was going to be transferred to the master disc. You made a master and a safety, and you played back the safety to see what you got. So that meant [in] all of the performances, there was no intercutting, no tape editing: in fact those were the good performances, probably some of the best. Because they were really performances as opposed to the synthesized record you make today, when you lay down the rhythm and start putting things on it; three months and twelve sessions later nobody knows what the original thing was really going to be like."[13] Tommy Ridgley, a rhythm-and-blues bandleader who started out in the late forties, remembers the disc-cutting apparatus: "They had a man catch the wax as the needle was playing. The quality of mixing was poor. Nobody really knew what they were doing; we were all learning at the same time."[14]

Domino sat at the piano. Cosimo gave the cue, and Fats kicked off with a boogie-woogie beat, driven by a pounding left hand that just kept building. And then came the voice, that magic voice, so unlike blues shouters of the day, youthful with a tone rich and warm, shaded by sweetly rolling accents of the country French patois. Despite the large technical inadequacies of Cosimo's studio, Domino was somewhat in awe. He would interrupt some of the best takes to ask, "How is it?"

They call, they call me the Fat Man
Cause I weigh two hundred pounds.
All the girls they love me,
Cause I know my way around.
I was standing, standing on the corner
Of Rampart and Canal,
Watching, watching those Creole gals.

Domino was fat, too; stood five feet five, weighed 224. Heard today, the background instruments barely leak into the song. Domino's control is total; in the slot where a sax break would typically come, Fats launches into nasal scat-singing, the "wa-wa" imitation of a muted trumpet. Even then, Bartholomew had high standards. "The sax sound was too harsh, and I really was responsible for it because I couldn't play trumpet and I was in the control room. . . . So what happened, Fats played loud at the piano . . . we didn't really want it that way but at the same time you couldn't do anything about it. Today with eight tracks or so, you could bury the piano, but Lew Chudd put the record out and they liked it."[15]

The song title was borrowed from the radio program "The Fat Man," which, Bartholomew explained, "came on the radio at night around seven or eight o'clock, and you could walk the streets and everybody would have their radios on. You could just walk a block and hear what the whole story was about. Fats was singing what is called the 'Junkers' Blues.' I thought about this program which was the most popular thing all over the country. It was a catchy name and he was called Fats Domino. We called the song 'The Fat Man.' "

If his thumping boogie-woogie lent a flavor of the barrelhouse, the deep Creole shadings of Domino's voice coated the song with a warm human flavor. The song shot to number six in the R&B charts. His early recordings included regional tunes for the local market—later he covered Longhair's "Mardi Gras in New Orleans"—the jazz classic "Careless Love," and a wild, frantic rendition of Albert Ammons's "Swanee River Boogie" called "Swanee River Hop."

With each new hit, Fats edged closer to the white market. Rhythm-and-blues was creating a musical revolution, moving from black audiences into the larger, more lucrative market of young whites. "Goin' Home" hit the number one spot in the R&B charts in the summer of 1952. Despite technical problems in the studio, the song has a floating melody and unforgettable lyrics: "Goin' home tomorrow / Can't stand your evil ways." He followed with an easy down-home blues, "Goin' to the River," that sold another million records.

Finally, in May 1955, "Ain't That a Shame" made the *Billboard* Hot 100—the first song by a New Orleans rhythm-and-blues artist to break the white charts. Domino now had a foothold in the white audience market. In 1955 a *Billboard* magazine poll of radio deejays voted "Ain't That a Shame" best song and Fats Domino their favorite artist. The song that put him center stage was a rolling dance number, "I'm in Love Again," that hit number five on the white charts. Drummer Cornelius Coleman hits a driving snare on the two- and four-beats, giving the song its rock. Lee Allen's tenor sax rounds the drive into a roll, with an instrumental "call" to Domino's vocal "response" and a blasting solo at the center of the song. The lyrics, simple and humorous, deal with unrequited love.

Yes, it's me and I'm in love again,
Ain't had no lovin' since you know when.
You know I love you, Yes, I do,
And I'm saving all my lovin' just for you.

Need your lovin' and I need it bad,
Just like a dog, when he's goin' mad.
Ooo-wee, baby, ooo-wee,
Baby, won't you give your love to me?

Eeeney meeney and miney mo,
Told me you didn't want me 'round no mo'.
Ooo-wee, baby, ooo-wee,
Baby, don't cha let your dog bite me.

From the line "Ain't had no lovin' since you know when," it is obvious the boy and girl are well acquainted. Fats's warm, mellifluous voice makes it a happy tune despite the "love gone sour" theme, and using a device of rhythm-and-blues novelty songs, he draws on children's rhymes with "Eeeney meeney and miney mo." The song has a jump-rope bounce. The lines "Need your lovin' and I need it bad, / Just like a dog, when he's goin' mad," though sexual in implication, suggest teenage frivolity. A tormented heart is no reason to stop dancing.

The emergence of an entertainment figure is not simply the rise of a single talent. A career is molded, moves charted as a business. Bartholomew continued studio work at Matassa's; between recording dates Domino spent a great deal of time on the road, his bookings by the Shaw Agency of New York coordinated with new Imperial releases of his records to the local distributors. There were no costly media saturations, so crucial to a rock band's success today. By 1957

the *Louisiana Weekly,* New Orleans's black newspaper, noted: "The roly-poly pianist, who was a day laborer making $28 a week in 1949, has grossed more than $500,000 since he hit the big time back in 1952. He draws up to $2,500 a night."[16]

Bartholomew was just as content to remain in New Orleans, for he had the entire society of black musicians to choose from, and he recorded dozens of them. Through the early fifties Bartholomew remained the preeminent bandleader in the city. Poppa Stoppa called him "the pit man" because in Dave's words:

I was always in the pits behind different bands. Whenever anyone would come to town looking for a band, they'd get mine. My band could read, play anything. That's the reason he gave me that name, because I was always in the pit, behind the star. . . . In the studio the musicians used to call me the Gestapo. Said I was the worst thing in the world to get along with. I felt that if a guy worked and put out, he would be paid. I'd see that he got the best contract possible. If he made a record that was passable, we'd give him a raise. All in all, I think we kept everyone happy on the Imperial label. If I had to do it again, I'd do it the same way. I don't play around in the studio.[17]

Late in 1954 Domino played the Rock-and-Roll Jubilee Ball at St. Nicholas Arena in New York City. The show was organized by Alan Freed, the disc jockey who coined the term "rock-and-roll." Rock-and-roll shook America to its roots and Fats was right in the middle of the revolution, singing happily and pounding his way across the keyboards, into the halls and auditoriums and soon on television. His first television appearance was September 2, 1956, on the "Steve Allen Show"; he was the first black star of the new music to appear on national television and was billed as "the newest rock & roll sensation."[18]

That appearance led to others. Twice in 1957, in February and May, he did the "Perry Como Show" and in July performed on ABC's "The Big Beat," hosted by Alan Freed, now taking his message and business onto the television airwaves. Domino was a frequent performer on Dick Clark's "American Bandstand," one of the most powerful media outlets of early rock-and-roll. Dick Clark wrote: "Fats was terrified of appearing on TV. When he came to the Little Theatre, I always had a case of Teacher's scotch waiting for him and his band. One Saturday morning he was late for rehearsal, so I went to his hotel to get him. It was about eleven o'clock in the morning. When I got to his room, he'd just gotten up. He stood there in his underwear, brushing his teeth, and drinking a can of beer. 'Antoine, come on, let's go downstairs. We'll have a little breakfast and then to the show.' He looked at me. 'No, Dick,' he said sipping his beer, 'I can't eat on an empty stomach.' "[19]

It can hardly be overstated that television helped Fats Domino become the biggest black rock-and-roll star in the 1950s. He appeared in trendy rock-and-roll films that were little more than a quick attempt by Hollywood to make a fast buck on the rock-and-roll craze—*The Girl Can't Help It*; *Do Re Me*; *Shake, Rattle and Rock*; *Disc Jockey Jamboree*; and *The Big Beat*. In each picture, he performed a lip-sync of his latest recording, but did not play a dramatic role.

A special quality in Fats Domino's music set him apart from the merging audiences of black rhythm-and-blues and white rock-and-roll—a large following among blue collar whites, country folk as well as urban workers. Even today, his range of popularity is apparent in various New Orleans bars that stock his older hits on jukeboxes. Parasol's, a hub of the Irish Channel, is not a bar where blacks go to drink, and yet Fats Domino, like Louis Armstrong, Bing Crosby, and Louis Prima, has the staying power. "Blueberry Hill," "When the Saints Go Marching In," "Blue

Monday," and many old Domino standards endure in jukeboxes of other white enclaves in town, too.

The biggest hit of Fats Domino's career was "Blueberry Hill," a western tune recorded by Gene Autry in 1941, by Louis Armstrong some time later, and by Domino in 1956. Interestingly, the urbane producer Dave Bartholomew was opposed to the tune at first. "It had been done a million times before," Bartholomew argued. But Domino was insistent. They cut the disc and sent it to Lew Chudd. Bartholomew called Chudd, told him it was horrible. "Pull it off. Pull it off the streets," Bartholomew said. "You're gonna ruin Fats."

"What do you mean?" Chudd came back. "We just sold two million records."

Twenty-five years later, Bartholomew shrugs his shoulders. "So who am I? The record now is at about thirty million sales."[20]

Fats also re-recorded songs by white country artists, like "I'm Gonna Be a Wheel Some Day," written by Roy Haynes, a singer from Baton Rouge, and first recorded by Bobby Mitchell, a black New Orleans vocalist. He sang Hank Williams's country hits "Jambalaya" and "Your Cheatin' Heart," "I like to reach all the people," he explained. "Country-western is like rhythm-and-blues; it tells a good story. That's why country-western is so big."[21]

Through it all, there was the loose Domino bounce. Part of this musical sensitivity springs from the Cajun ensemble tradition, and to a lesser extent the western-swing sound of Bob Wills and the Texas Playboys, which appealed to Domino. Ironically enough, one of Domino's most parochial and best-selling songs, "Walkin' to New Orleans," was composed by Bobby Charles, a Cajun from Abbeville in Vermilion Parish.

Between 1950 and 1955, fourteen of Domino's singles hit the top ten in the rhythm-and-blues charts, still a predominately black market in those years. The success of "The Fat Man" could easily have been the end of his career, given the unpredictability of the public taste. But with

Cosimo Matassa, 1982

Fats Domino, 1956

Bartholomew's production skills and judgment of the market, Domino's recordings had an identifiable sound. Although the recordings were not always polished, the material was good, with Domino and Bartholomew collaborating on compositions. Domino released twenty-six records during those five years, half of them winners. Lew Chudd's investment paid off. As Fats Domino began to climb the ladder of success, Imperial Records grew more prosperous.

By the early 1960s Fats Domino had matured as an artist, performer, and vocalist. Whiney vocals of "The Fat Man" gave way to a more mature, deeper vocal style. Songs like "When My Dreamboat Comes Home," "My Blue Heaven," and "I'm in the Mood for Love" showcased more complex melodies with a broader range of tone. The trend toward standard popular songs was to a great extent the sign of shifting attitudes by record executives about the pop market. Many people in the industry felt the rock-and-roll phenomenon had run its course, and a turn back to the more traditional pop melodies meant survival for rock-and-roll performers. Soon, however, the British invasion launched by the Beatles (who often acknowledged the influence of southern blues and R&B) established rock as a genre—and a big money business of its own.

In 1963 Lew Chudd sold Imperial Records; the decision showed financial foresight. After 1962, none of Domino's records climbed higher than fifty-nine on the charts. The heyday of rhythm-and-blues was beginning to fade; perhaps Chudd sensed the radical shift in the market before it came. When the Beatles exploded into American popular culture in 1964, R&B moved into a rearguard market slot, with declining salability. Domino signed with ABC Records after the Imperial years ended and reached the charts a half-dozen times during the next year. But the golden period of his recording life was through. As British rock swept into America, the tastes of popular music changed rapidly. White rock stars came

forth with lyrics reflecting currents of the counterculture—opposition to the war and racism, advocacy of drugs and new sexual freedoms—and Fats's down-home good-time music simply did not fit. His last song to make the charts came in 1968, his version of the Beatles' "Lady Madonna," which just squeezed into the one hundred slot.

As a recording artist, Domino's career waned considerably after the Imperial years. In 1982 he cut "Whiskey Heaven," which made the country-western charts, but his recording efforts since the 1960s in no way match the phenomenal success of old. Today his professional life is largely occupied by concerts and nightclub appearances. He has done long stints over the years in Las Vegas, where, according to *Ebony* magazine, he lost two million dollars over a ten-year period, mostly at the Flamingo Casino. "I was a country boy who didn't know no better," he explained. "First I started playing slot machines for a nickel, then a dime, then for a quarter, then for half a dollar, then for a dollar—I lost $180,000 the first two weeks I worked here and at that time I wasn't making but $6500 a week. But I had record money [royalties] and I paid it off with that."[22]

It was some measure of his appeal that fans in the 1970s packed the halls where he played. *Newsweek* profiled him lounging at the bar of a Lake Tahoe club before one show. A long-haired fan asked him to autograph his draft card. He had come all the way from Berkeley. "As he signed the card, Domino remarked happily, 'The old-time music is coming back again. I haven't had a hit in ten years, but when I play 'Blueberry Hill,' people act like it's a new number.'"[23]

Despite his popularity on the performance circuit, it is difficult to assess Fats Domino's career in the eighties. He still commands a great deal of money for concerts, and like one of his early influences, Louis Armstrong, has developed a distinct vocal style that he keeps alive through extensive tours. And if the songs by now are oldies-but-goodies, the Fat Man still has the punch and flavor of his zesty musical youth. Most of the fans in the expensive nightclubs are now in their late thirties and forties, and many grew up hearing his tunes. A drummer who played Las Vegas with him says the barmaids love it when he comes to town because the tips are always bigger; everybody has a good time.

And Dave Bartholomew keeps a more relaxed pace these days. He still goes on the road, but prefers European dates. His office occupies the back room of an old shotgun double house behind a beauty salon run by his wife. There is no need for a big office downtown. He keeps it close to home, where the royalty statements are sent. He sits behind a big oak desk, his walls adorned with music awards. And what of his old protégé, Fats Domino?

He was always the same person. Antoine is a very nice guy to get along with. But he is very shy. Some people tend to think that he is stuck-up. But Fats isn't stuck-up. Fats just happens to be a shy guy and all this glamor was thrown on him all at one time. He has said to me plenty times, "Bartholomew"—he always called me Bartholomew—"you know, I really can't sing. I don't know what all these people are excited about." He's just humble and he is very nice. He was always that same person. He is still the same person today. He's not excited about anything. Success didn't mean anything to him except that he didn't have to look for a job anymore. Now he's got more work than he needs. Fats is making an awful lot of money. If he wants to work, he works, and I don't blame him. When he first started working, he would stay out on the road a year. And work a whole year, and miss Christmas and all that kind of stuff. I've gone out Thanksgiving and seen him, and we sitting in the back of the car and we got a big old turkey, but that's not the way to do it. That was his life; he enjoyed doing it. Now he's getting tired and everybody wants to know why. It's because, when he first started, he stayed out there for fifteen or sixteen years—fifty-two weeks out of the year. That's why he's tired.

For a musician who has achieved so much, gone so high in a game where so many others end up broke, who can say whether Fats Domino won't one day flash back into the charts and reignite the bluesy rhythms of rock-and-roll? One way or another, Antoine Domino is still quite a man, cooking his red beans, dressing like a baron, and driving that white Rolls Royce with the golden dominoes on the door.

Chapter Four

THE LASTIES: A NINTH WARD FAMILY

The lower Ninth Ward lies at the edge of the city, rimmed by the Mississippi River and divided by Industrial Canal. On bright days sunlight glints off the steel webwork of the silver bridge, rising and descending at St. Claude Avenue. Across the bridge, the lower Ninth extends to the Orleans Parish line. When David Lastie was a boy in the 1930s, parts of the neighborhood were open fields. Children hunted opossum and rabbits in high grass where palmetto fronds and oleanders sprouted amid crepe myrtles and occasional oaks. Sounds during the late Depression were an amalgam of urban and country life, the blurred lines of converging cultures. A high shrill whistle came from the cotton press. Jackson Barracks was a red-brick military compound, surrounded by trees, where the cannon boomed twice daily. Jangling bells rose above the St. Claude streetcar line. People sitting on stoops and porches heard the moan of livestock being led to the slaughterhouse. From river docks came the rumble of loadings and the voices of men working there.

But then the city changed. The cotton press closed. The streetcar gave way to lumbering busses. There are still ships on the river with foghorns baying, and many more trucks on St. Claude than before, but the rustic slaughterhouse only packs meat now, and the echoes of dockworkers have long since waned into silence. After World War II, streets were laid onto the back-swamp terrain as more black families followed the river downstream from the old city. By the end of the 1970s, after the boom in housing renovations, hundreds of blacks had been displaced from uptown, the Irish Channel, and the Treme neighborhood, where fourteen square blocks were razed, the land eventually providing room for Louis Armstrong Park. But through all of this, the lower Ninth remained heavily black. The Lasties called it "Soulville" and "The Big Nine."

As a child, David Lastie fed dimes to the nickelodeon at Jackson Barracks to watch a film short of Louis Jordan performing "Caldonia," feet stomping, knees high, an irrepressible smile as he sang. The image stayed in David's head as he played with his brothers in a backyard "spasm" band before he ever owned a horn. His values and musical experiences were shaped at home.

The Lasties have spanned three generations, playing gospel, jazz, and rhythm-and-blues. Patriarch Frank Lastie, born on July 4, 1902, is a prominent church deacon and leads a senior citizens' gospel choir, the Silver-Haired Songbirds. Three of Deacon Lastie's sons—Melvin, David, and Walter—were playing professionally by their late teens. Daughter Betty Ann, reared on gospel piano, is a powerful vocalist. Betty Ann's son, Herlin Riley, plays drums and trumpet professionally, and another grandson, Joseph Lastie, Jr., drums for jazz and gospel groups.

The origins of this remarkable family were anything but promising. Frank's mother died in 1912. In 1913 his stepbrother Lewis Rock was sent to the Colored Waifs' Home, a reform school on the outskirts of the city. Frank soon followed "for being a little mischievous bad guy."[1] Their misdeeds were picayune by today's standards. As a ten year old, Lewis spent time in the institution for fighting. He was committed a second time for pulling the cord on a streetcar, ringing up paid entries when there were none. Frank's offense was hitting a little girl. He was eleven, without a stable homelife, so the court sent him to join Lewis and almost two hundred other "colored waifs."

The reform school was more commonly called the Jones Home, after Captain Joseph Jones, director, and Manuella, his wife. They lived on the premises and were kind to the boys. The two-story building sat in a wide field, fronting on woods and a pond. The dormitory was upstairs; on the groundfloor was a mess hall, a chapel, and a schoolroom. The boys were taught reading, writing, and arithmetic, with garden work as a sideline. Twice weekly they marched around the yard with wooden guns and wooden drums. But the focus of activity was music. Band instructor Peter Davis worked long hours with the boys nearly every day. Sometimes Davis took groups to his home for individual instruction.[2]

Louis Armstrong, thirteen, was sent to the home just after New Year's Day of 1913 for shooting a pistol in the streets. Frank remembers him as a "happy guy . . . a jokified guy. We used to go fishing behind the home, and he would get in the dormitory upstairs and blow taps on a bugle to let us know it was time to come in."[3]

"I used to love to beat on the steps with sticks," Lastie recalls, "so I went for the drums." His stepbrother played alto horn. Lastie remembers young Armstrong starting on drums before Davis gave him a cornet. Each year in late May the boys would march at a military cemetery in St. Bernard Parish.

Lewis Rock, released from the home before Frank, left New Orleans for Muscle Shoals, Alabama, where he worked in a gunpowder factory during World War I. By 1918 he had drifted away and lost contact with Frank altogether. Out of the home, Lastie signed on with a crew of laborers demolishing buildings to make room for a shipyard. On the job he found Louis Armstrong. "We was getting thirty cents an hour. But then that was a big salary—in World War I. While we was beginning to tear down those houses, Joe 'King' Oliver called, took Louis from that, and told Louis he can do better than that. And from then on, Louis went on."[4]

Lastie roamed the city's undercrust, hustling pool games, selling lottery tickets, working cabarets and music haunts of the 1920s. He told one journalist:

One of the popular places was at Basin and Iberville and was called the "Club 225." It was a big gambling joint. . . . There was another place located at Dumaine and Claiborne where all the pimps, hustlers, gamblers, and whores hung out. I went in there a lot. Nobody talked about age. I just made myself look like I belonged.

It was jumping on South Rampart, on both sides of the street. It was like it says in that song, "where the white and dark folk meet." There was as many whites as there were blacks, all looking for the same things. . . . I'd get to know the women and introduce them to the men. I got paid for doing that.[5]

By 1926 he was in Chicago. "I was a pool shark and used to bum with all the musicians and prizefighters. Jack Johnson used to hang by there. Lot of guys from New Orleans was up there, too."[6] He returned to New Orleans in 1927, broke, down and out. At this time his stepmother introduced him to the spiritual religion. He received guidance from Mother Spencer, Mother Jackson, and finally Mother Catherine Seals, a faith healer and prophet whose vision revolutionized Frank Lastie's life. "She taught me many things. How to live, what to do, and how to get along with people. . . . In 1928, she baptized me, and after baptizing me, I saw her perform so many miracles. I mean I've never seen anything like that in all the days of my life! The people she healed through the power of prayer."[7]

Mother Catherine had come to the city from Lexington, Kentucky, in 1922. Soon thereafter she suffered a paralytic stroke. From the authors of *Gumbo Ya-Ya* comes this report on her life.

A white "healer" whose services she had solicited had refused to cure her because of her color. Right then and there she resolved to pray herself into a state of grace and good health. A spirit told her that her prayers would be answered and suggested she found a religion of her own as soon as she was able.

Mother Catherine set about her task without money and without followers. She chose a tract of land out by the Industrial Canal and in some way was able to secure the services of the builders who erected her first temple and residence.

She became known as a healer. Soon she had many followers, and gifts from grateful devotees made possible the furnishings of her church. Flags of the Sacred Heart, Jehova and the Innocent Blood flew from atop her building, and the interior became crowded with holy pictures, statues and altars; five hundred oil lamps burned constantly.[8]

During Lastie's years under Mother Catherine's tutelage, he also became a grand marshal, leading brass band parades, wearing a white shirt and black tails, a wide sash, and top hat. The grand marshal sets the pace for the slow solemnity of the funeral dirge, then starts strutting after the coffin is lowered and the band cuts loose, surrounded by dancing second liners.

Mother Catherine applauded his musical urges and told him to play drums in church. That was in 1927. "Mother Catherine gave me an idea to bring drums out. They used to criticize me, said they never heard anything or never seen nothing like that before—drums in church. I endured the rebukes and scorns. Now, they're very few churches that don't have a drum."[9]

Spiritual religions among black and white Americans varied in geographic areas. But the larger faith was built on the belief in spirit visitations. Spiritual religions spread across America in the nineteenth century, attracting blacks as well as whites. Many New Orleans ceremonies reflect a syncretism that is pronounced in Caribbean religions: the African vision of many gods melded into the pantheon of Christian saints, forming rituals of great energy surges, talking in tongues, and spirit visitation.[10] Deacon Lastie cites John 4:24, "'God is a spirit and they that worship him must worship him in spirit and in truth.' Spirits are not visible. God's not visible. But you feel it when you pray and do things—God works *through* you."[11]

In 1930, at the height of her popularity, Mother Catherine told a tent meeting that she was leaving New Orleans. People implored her not to. "My time is up," she said, meaning her own life. She wanted to return to her Kentucky birthplace. She then announced that Frank Lastie would continue her work. This triggered an uproar. Gambling and lottery are not the stuff of which religious leaders are made. But Mother Catherine stood firm. Lastie drove her to the depot. As the train pulled out, tears streamed down his face. True to her prophecy, Mother Catherine died on August 9, 1930, two days after her arrival in Kentucky. The coffin came back to New Orleans on the train.

"The day of the funeral there were thousands of people, and I've never seen it rain so hard in my life. Mother Catherine always told us there'd come a day when the sun would shine in the rain. . . . When [the funeral] reached Industrial Canal bridge, the sun broke through and people started *fallin' out* on the bridge. People had *babies* in their arms, and they knew it was prophecy. That was a powerful, powerful woman and she done so much for people."[12]

Approximately one hundred Spiritual churches dot New Orleans today, many of them storefront chapels. Frank Lastie heeded Mother Catherine's call, and continued drumming in church. Aside from raising six foster children, Frank and Alice Lastie had six children of their own. Four became professional musicians. The boys began on drums; Betty Ann on piano. As each child in turn realized a desire to play, Alice Lastie would buy the instrument on installment.

The Lastie home became a haven for musicians. Sometimes wandering piano players of the lower Ninth Ward would stop by to play for Mrs. Lastie. "They would always remember to leave their wine bottles outside out of respect, and they would play old jazz and always a spiritual number for me."[13] They had names like "Peaches," "Big Four," and "Mr. Camille."

Melvin was the oldest child, born on November 18, 1930. When only four years old, he begged his mother for a trumpet. She remembers: "My aunt had died up in Mississippi. I had to go to the funeral by train. Melvin came to me and said, 'Mommee, you gonna get the horn you promised me?' And I made it down to Werlein's Music Store and got the horn, and I barely made it to the train.

I was gone for two weeks, and when I returned, Melvin was playing the horn so pretty, and I said, 'How did you learn so fast, Melvin?' and he looked up and said, 'Mommee, this is what I want to do.'"[14]

Deacon Lastie adds: "Melvin just continued to play music, and practice, and sometimes I'd hear him up in his room, two, three o'clock in the morning. I'd say, 'Melvin, you gonna bother the neighbors.' He'd say, 'Old man, I'm gonna put a mute in it.' So he just continued to play, and I let him alone. And finally he made it."[15]

Melvin Lastie matured rapidly on cornet and trumpet and began road trips before he was twenty. In 1949 at a gig in Natchez, Mississippi, he met an odd-looking man about his own age named Ornette Coleman, who became a pioneer of post-bebop jazz. He was skinny, with a long beard and straightened hair, a vegetarian and self-styled "Jesus-type image." He was a radical sax man playing an experimental vein that chafed traditionalist sentiments of many Deep South musicians. Melvin invited Coleman to return with him to New Orleans, where he moved in with the Lasties. Melvin Lastie and Ornette Coleman spent long hours exchanging figures on the cornet and sax. "I went to church with him and his father," Coleman recalled, "and I took the alto, David's horn, and I played there every Sunday. Melvin could play his heart out. He was really good. He seemed to have been—how can I say it?—very spiritual, but such an individual. He had a unique sound."[16]

Ornette followed Melvin to a gig in Baton Rouge.

And I was sittin' there listening to the band and all of a sudden a guy came in and said some musicians wanted to meet me outside. So I went outside and there were these really big guys, six or seven of them. I said, "How you doin'?" And one of them said, "Where you from?" And I said, "Oh, I'm from Fort Worth." And

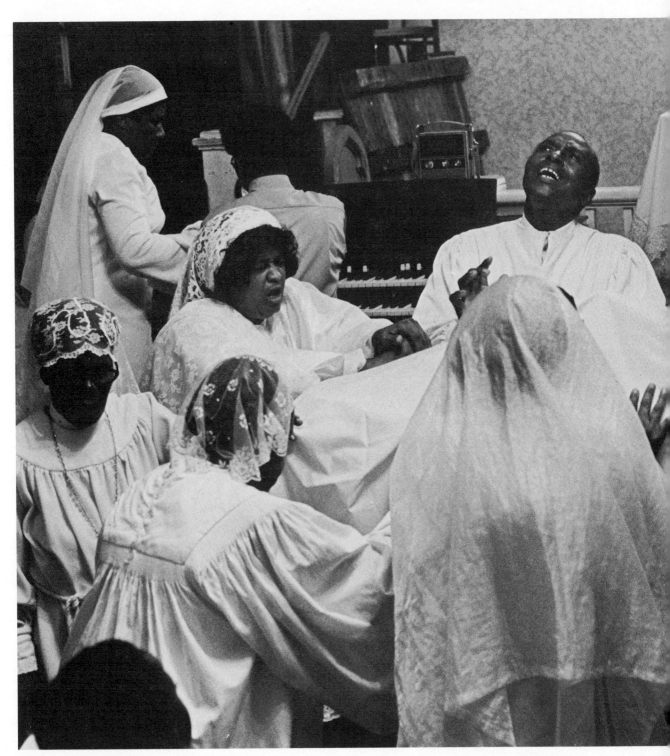

Spirits visit the faithful

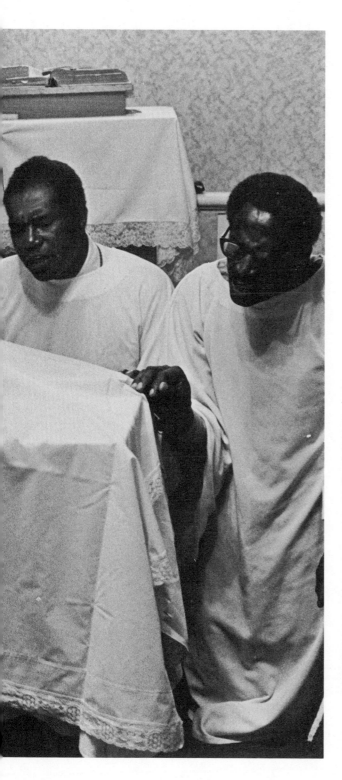

Mother Catherine, circa 1925

they were all black guys. . . . They started using "nigger" and all this, and "You're not from Texas with your beard like that and your long hair. You must be one of those Yankee kind of niggers!" And all of a sudden a guy kicked me in my stomach and then he kicked me in the ass and I had my horn cradled in my arms and I blacked out cause blood was everywhere. . . . They were just beating me to death. One guy took my tenor and threw it down the street. Then Melvin and the band came out and discovered I was beat up and they took me to the police department. The cops said, "What you doing with that long hair?" And they started calling me nigger and they told me that if them other niggers didn't finish me, *they* were *gonna*.

So I went back to Melvin's house, and I was thinking just like my mother had told me, that the tenor was bad luck. David had an alto, and he said, "I'll let you borrow my alto."

Ornette Coleman left New Orleans in 1950 to continue his often painful musical odyssey. (He is discussed further in chapter 12, "AFO and the New Jazz.")

David Lastie fell in love with the saxophone. Leroy Sergion, who played alto with Melvin and also in Roy Brown's band, showed David the key finger placements on the horn. David drew the sax keys on a small, flat board and would play along with Melvin and Sergion.

The Grunewald School of Music opened after World War II. With many black musicians returning from the military with GI Bill benefits, the school quickly became a hub for musicians of all ages. David remembers: "It was 1948 and I had just started high school . . . hanging around with some good cats, and we would go by Grunewald up on Magazine Street. I wasn't interested in nothing but music. After I found out we could go by Grunewald, there wasn't any more school."[17]

Buddy Hagen, Fats Domino's saxophone player, gave David formal lessons while David continued to play, influenced by national recording artists Jimmy Liggins, Jimmy Forrest, and the great Louis Jordan. His first band was called the House-

rockers. Alice Lastie's younger brother, Jessie Hill, played drums. He was just about David's age and more a brother than an uncle. Percy Stovall, a promoter and booking agent, liked the group and put David and guitarist Eddie Langlois in a band with Huey "Piano" Smith on keyboard. In 1950 they toured with Guitar Slim, a blues guitarist from Mississippi, playing nightclubs, dance halls, and school auditoriums. In Nashville they performed at Grady's nightclub, which also served as a front for a gambling operation. While in Nashville, the group came to the attention of Jim Bulleit, owner of Bullet Records. He saw the band and liked what he heard. A deal was struck and Guitar Slim and his band were brought to Castle Studio in Tulane Hotel to record. They did two sides, "Certainly All" and the classic "Feelin' Sad," which featured the moaning sax work of David Lastie and Charlie Fairley.

In 1953 David joined Edgar "Big Boy" Myles and James "Sugarboy" Crawford in a band called Cha-Paka-Shaweez; he remained with them briefly before teaming up with brother Melvin in the first Lastie combo, which included Reveal Thomas on piano, Lawrence Guyton on guitar, and Jessie Hill on drums.

After the band dissolved, Melvin went on to other gigs. David joined blues singer Smiley Lewis's band for a western tour in 1954. His memory of it is vivid. "I wrecked the band's car after my first night in Tijuana. I lost the car and most of my money to the Mexican police, so we had to ride in Smiley's car 'Lillie Mae.' She was a 1948 Carry-all. He wouldn't let you smoke in Lillie Mae, not even regular cigarettes, and he always carried a couple of shotguns and pistols around. I remember we would be driving across the desert shooting at jack rabbits and stuff. It was a great trip!"

Walter, the youngest Lastie, was born on September 18, 1938. He learned drumming in church under the Deacon. Walter, nicknamed "Popee," re-

Above: Deacon Frank Lastie. *Left:* Walter Lastie in Europe, 1938–1980. *Below:* The Lasties, 1979. *From left:* David, Betty Ann, and Walter Lastie

called: "My father had a very rare style of play. He played mostly with his fingers. He would use the tips of his fingers rather than his wrists to move the sticks. It's supposed to be something new, and he been doing it ever since I can remember."[18]

Another early teacher was Cornelius Coleman, who drummed for Fats Domino. "Every month they would have a children's hour at the Hot Spot," Popee said. "That's where Fats Domino used to play; and Cornelius Coleman would stand behind me with his hands on my shoulders. He was left-handed and he'd cross his hands and play beats on me, and if I played it wrong, he would slap me! So I had to learn that way."

In 1954 sixteen-year-old Popee joined the band of Freddie Domino, Fats's first cousin, a trumpeter and vocalist. "It was a real good experience for me and a whole lot of other guys who came up during the time I was coming up because Freddie hired all young people. He is the cause of a lot of musicians my age getting their start."[19]

The Domino band went to Nashville for a month's engagement. David Lastie remembers: "I was back on the road with Sugarboy Crawford and Papa Lightfoot at the time, and we all piled into a 1940 Chevrolet, six musicians and all that equipment. I had around seven dollars and the other guys about the same. We drove nonstop up to Nashville and played all night without rest, and my pay came to fifty cents—two quarters! I didn't even know Popee was on the road; then I found out he was in Nashville with Freddie. He was having money problems with his gig, too, so we pooled what little money we had and caught the Trailways with the drums and all and headed back for New Orleans."

In 1955 David played on the disc "I'm Wise" by New Orleans pianist Eddie Bo. Bo went on tour for the Shaw Booking Agency with David and Popee in the band. Popee recalls: "We worked with about every artist in the fifties because we was the house band. We made Little Willie John's first tour through Texas. After Little Willie John,

we went to Denver with Amos Milburn; we worked with Amos a year and a half. We would also play behind artists like Etta James, the Teen Queens, Ruth Brown, Fay Adams, the Platters, and Big Mama Thornton."

Walter Lastie recalls playing with a blind band. "I was one of the only guys in the band who could see. . . . And we played the Club Tiajuana. They had a fight break out one night in the bar and I was worried about the blind guys until one yelled, 'Watch it, Popee, here comes a Regal beer bottle at you!'" He also played for "snake dancers, and one fellow had a large lizard. We played for a snake wake—they waked him, and they buried the snake. Dancer was named African Queen. They put some chicks in the cage for the snake to eat—and the chicks ate the snake up!"[20]

David Lastie joined the pool of session men working periodically at Matassa's studio in the 1960s. He became a valuable sideman on early Minit recordings by Allen Toussaint. David's bouncy sax breaks helped push Uncle Jessie Hill's 1960 novelty hit "Ooo Poo Pah Do."

Melvin meanwhile became involved in a record producing company called All For One (AFO), founded by Harold Battiste, a jazz modernist. Battiste's plan was to have a profit-sharing company run by the musicians themselves. Melvin was working as "the busting man," policing record sessions to make sure sidemen were paid union scale. He joined Battiste enthusiastically.

AFO proved a short-lived dream. The company fell apart after business problems caused Battiste, Lastie, and others to move to Los Angeles, where Melvin Lastie remained, pursuing a career as a session artist. Battiste moved into other endeavors, but the bond of friendship endured. In 1970 during spare moments the two men began experimenting in a small studio with flugelhorns and saxophone, searching for new expressions, combining piano and trumpet phrases, each taking turns on different instruments, playing back the tapes, and analyzing passages. The atmosphere was relaxed. They used electronic echo effects and overdubbing on a multitrack system to produce long, floating passages with a dreamlike lyricism. The record finally appeared in 1976—*Hal and Mel Alone Together*—but Melvin Lastie was gone by then.

Melvin Lastie's death from cancer in 1972 shocked the family; he was only forty-two years old. But in the months after his passing, Melvin's spirit remained with them. His mother kept the Indian statues he had sent her from New York. She had dreamed of Indians and often related to her son small things an Indian had told her in dreams, maternal advice for Melvin in his travels. Now she placed the Indian statues on an altar in the foyer of the family home.

Harold Battiste reflected on Melvin Lastie: "His playing had such heart. He could communicate. That's the kind of person he was. He was a very charismatic man, a person who somehow commanded you to pay attention to what he was saying."[21]

As the months wore into years after Melvin's death, David and Popee drew closer to Betty Ann. At her mother's urging, Betty, born on May 2, 1941, had taken up piano and performed in local gospel choirs. In 1957 Deacon Lastie organized the Spiritual Circle, a twelve-member confederation of churches in the larger spiritual network of the city. Many of Betty Ann's formative experiences came from the Guiding Star Church, her father's chapel.

"Melvin always wanted us to play as a family group," Betty reflected. "But when Melvin was living, seem like we never could get together. But sometimes a person's death can cause a closeness in a family. And I can truly say that this happened to us. After Melvin's death, seemed like we got a little bit closer. Because I never dreamed I'd be playing with my brothers."[22]

In 1977 the Lasties' Uncle Jessie Hill returned from California and lived with the family for a while. Betty continues: "And Professor Longhair used to come by all the time for rehearsal. One day he told me, 'Girl, you might as well go on and do something. You got a nice voice. Go on and sing!' I only wish he was still around. He inspired me so much."[23] That summer Betty flew to Boston to visit David and Popee, who were performing at Lulu White's, a jazz club, with Cricket Fleming, a white trumpeter. David invited Betty to come onstage and sing a gospel number. Reluctantly she went forward and delivered a rousing "Jesus on the Mainline." The crowd gave her a standing ovation.

When they returned to New Orleans, Cricket Fleming went to work arranging gospel numbers to showcase Betty's talents. Gradually she peeled away the restraints of religious music and launched into blues and pop singing. By this time, a third generation of Lasties was coming forth. Betty's son, Herlin Riley, played trumpet and drums. "When I was a baby," he explained, "they used to roll me into the room where the musicians were rehearsing. And my Uncle Melvin would blow me to sleep. He played lullabies on a muted trumpet."[24] Herlin's cousin, Joseph Lastie, Jr., also became a drummer under the Deacon's tutelage in church. Alice Lastie bought him his first set of drums, as she had Walter's years before.

In 1978 the Lasties began expanding their repertoire into a full review of New Orleans music. David burned experimental passages on saxophone; Betty Ann sang "I Know" for a televised concert, with Riley playing Melvin's cornet solo. In the same concert, the band played Duke Ellington's "Caravan," which features a long drum solo. In the middle of his motions, Walter slipped the drumsticks under his seat, kept the beat moving, thumping his fingers on the skins, pounding them faster and faster, sweat swirling off his brow, the hands came down in perfect time, one throttle after another, the force of his fists so strong they blasted into the microphones. The club exploded in applause. There have been many great drum solos in New Orleans, but none so stunning has ever been recorded visually.

On December 28, 1980, a chilly, sunlit Sunday afternoon, Walter Lastie was playing in front of St. Louis Cathedral off Jackson Square. In the middle of "When the Saints Go Marching In," he fell off the stool, his foot kicking the pedal as he hit the ground, and was dead of a heart attack in a matter of minutes. He died at forty-two, the same age Melvin had been when he died nine years earlier.

Walter Lastie's funeral the following week was a remarkable outpouring of affection by the musicians who had known him. More than fifty turned out to play in his honor. But in the months that followed, David and Betty grew despondent. The idea of a family band seemed lost. Popee's percussion was the heartbeat of their group, an extension of Deacon Lastie's drumming that had begun in church.

Musical families are a strange phenomenon. While death is difficult for any family to accept, in a musical unit the weight of the loss lasts longer; the space, spiritually and artistically, is harder to fill. In the autumn of 1981, Herlin Riley returned from a long London engagement with the touring cast of *One Mo' Time,* a stage musical. He joined the band, and as A Taste of New Orleans began a stint at Tyler's, an uptown jazz club, the strength started to rebuild. Then in late November something wonderful happened to the Lastie family.

From the phone of a public rest home in Louisville, the caller identified himself as Lewis Rock, Deacon Lastie's stepbrother, unheard from for sixty-three years. Frank and a church bishop drove to Kentucky and brought the old man home.

Going by the name "Cricket," he was eighty-three now, blind in one eye, and walking with a heavy limp. But his memory was sharp. Betty Ann and David, now in their forties, gathered around the Deacon's table, and as the nieces and nephews and grandchildren flowed through the house, old Cricket told stories of his life—wandering in the Depression as a hobo, riding the rails, eating at firesites with other travelers in the night. He told of card games won, of ladies loved and lost—he had outlived the last one—and of the years he owned a shoeshine stand. Why had he never come back, nor even sent a letter? "Well, I was just busy."

In the spring of 1983 Frank Lastie, the pillar of his family, approached his eighty-first birthday. Alice Lastie, slowed by a stroke, continued to light candles surrounding the Indian statues on the family altar in the foyer. Betty was singing blues and gospel. David Lastie played the saxophone at the Jazz and Heritage Festival, with old Cricket front and center on a hot harmonica. And the cradle of jazz kept rocking.

TWO

The Flush Years, 1954–1963

Chapter Five

CLUB LIFE

In the decade following World War II, many musics colored New Orleans. The French Quarter was the big strip, and music varied from traditional jazz to respectable white Dixieland and the sugary accents of swing. The Quarter appealed to more than musical interests, however. New Orleans was a wide-open town where a savvy tourist with a roll of bills could find a gambling joint or slot machine if he knew how to be subtle, and willing ladies if he wasn't so subtle. In 1946 we find Chep Morrison, handsome young reform candidate for mayor, at a late-night meeting on Esplanade Avenue that would have made good drama had Tennessee Williams been interested. The patrician lawyer assured a conclave of hookers, pimps, cabbies, and underworld figures that the delicate balance between the city government and their closet economy was safe in his hands.[1]

But musicians were the cultural statement of the Quarter. During the early fifties, in the two hundred block of Bourbon Street, the Sho-Bar featured trumpeter Louis Prima and vocalist Keely Smith. At the Famous Door, the Dukes of Dixieland or tailgate trombonist Santo Pecora played into the early morning. Just up the street clarinetist George Lewis played sweet, high notes on a legendary clarinet, while Sharkey Bonano's brash trumpet poured out of the Dream Room. Dan's Bateau Lounge and Pier 600 booked Al Hirt and Pete Fountain in the early days of their careers. Singer Blanche Thomas often played the 500 Club, and in later years Poodle Patio was home for a barrelhouse pianist called Archibald (Leon T. Gross). In addition, jazz, mambo, and calypso music rippled at the 809 Club behind Miss Chris Owens, a Cuban dancer.

Away from the neon shades of Bourbon Street and other French Quarter rues, the city's major hotels featured plush clubs. The Blue Room of the Roosevelt Hotel gained a national reputation through broadcasts on WWL, the CBS radio station, and showcased lavish reviews with vocalists, dancers, and full orchestras led by Jan Garber, Ted

Lewis, and others. Smaller clubs on Canal Street were an extension of French Quarter night life. The Texas Lounge and the Brass Rail, which featured Paul Gayten's band, drew a steady tourist trade in the 1950s. In suburban Jefferson Parish, orchestras played dinner dances at the Beverly Country Club; smaller groups played at the Southport on River Road, a gambling den. In New Orleans East, the other side of town, Natal's was the stronghold of Edgar Blanchard and the Gondoliers. The Safari Room on Gentilly Highway featured R&B locals like Shirley and Lee and Frankie Ford, as well as visiting national artists like Erskine Hawkins, Jerry Vale, Sam Cooke, and the Five Keys.[2]

But these clubs did not admit black people. Segregation was the law of the South and most of the thousands of tourists visiting Bourbon Street were white. The big hotels and better-known clubs admitted blacks only as employees or entertainers. This cultural isolation gave rise to different, freer performing traditions in a network of central city clubs far from Bourbon's bright lights.

To these clubs gravitated a society unto itself, an oasis of night people—jazz players, singers, shake-dancers, an occasional movie star, drag queens, snake charmers, bohemians from the Quarter, and countless other character types who lived in a different world. Upper- and middle-class blacks came for quality music and dance. Music was the central force, the raison d'être, of the Dew Drop Inn, Club Tiajuana, and other places of the early rhythm-and-blues years. The clubs also served elemental human needs.

To saxophonist Charles Neville, the Dew Drop was "a subculture within a subculture. . . . Musicians didn't distinguish themselves from other people in what we called 'show business' like we do now. You were an entertainer, and it was thought of as show business, rather than now, you are just a band, making gigs. You were in show business and that old rule 'the show must go on' was really the main law. It was not only that the show on stage must go on—but the whole show of trying to *make it* was what it was all about."[3]

The Dew Drop grew from humble origins. The proprietor, Frank Painia, was born in 1908 in Plaquemine, a town some eighty miles upriver from New Orleans. Painia moved to New Orleans in 1935 and opened a two-chair barber shop on LaSalle Street, a dirt-covered avenue that ran through the uptown black district. Frank's Barber Shop occupied a small rented section of a building near the intersection of Washington Avenue. In early 1938 the city obtained Federal funds from the Roosevelt administration for the construction of some six hundred low-income dwelling units across LaSalle from the barber shop.[4] When construction began, workmen on lunch break would wander into Frank's barber shop asking, "Hey, man, where's a place to get a Barq's root beer or soft drink?" There was no place close, so Frank opened a small stand selling soft drinks. In short order, he expanded the operation to sell sandwiches and beer; local residents wandered in to trade stories and pass the afternoons.

As the side-trade grew, Frank brought in his brother Paul to handle the extra load. Soon he was buying property and by 1942 had opened a hotel and restaurant, the Dew Drop Inn Cafe and Bar. An ad in the *Louisiana Weekly* read: "Specials offered are seafoods, fried chicken and all kinds of sandwiches. The mixed drinks cannot be beat and the prices on packaged goods are lowest anywhere. Frank's slogan is 'deliveries are made anywhere in the city. We never close.' "[5]

Painia wanted an ambience for the nightclub, so he hired a young white artist from the French Quarter, Johnny Donnels, to work on the interior. "But it was a black nightclub," Donnels recalls, "and at that time it was against the law to go there. One of the ways [artists] got around was by doing murals . . . so whenever the police would come in, Frank Painia would just tell 'em we're his decorators. Of course, we were there to see all the floor shows and we'd go up there and there

Jamming at Club Tiajuana. *Left:* Robert Parker

Female impersonator at the Dew Drop, 1953

were quite a few people from the French Quarter. The name of the place was the Dew Drop so what I thought I would do was sorta make some free-form drops. They never did come out the same. Since it was a black club, I did 'em in shades of black and brown and purple—different shades. Then I would put an abstract shape of, say, a sax-ophone across it. It was all different instruments and all different musicians; the abstract shape of the instrument would break up the shape of the dew drop and the dew drop would actually cut across and break up the shape of the instruments. So by the time it was all over, everybody was all broken up."[6]

Today Donnels is a prominent photographer with a studio/gallery in the French Quarter. He remembers the early mural work "dragged out about a year. It was too much fun. I could have probably painted it in one day if I wanted to, but that wasn't the idea. Painia paid me, but I also ran up a bar and food bill. From his promoting and concerts, he got to where he made all kinds of money. But every day he'd drive up in his big, long Cadillac, get out and go in the barber shop and cut hair. Every day."

Charles Neville recalls the Dew Drop serving "the best red beans and rice in New Orleans. For twenty-six cents you got this big plate of red beans and rice piled up on it and there was the pigtail—and for fifty-two cents you got two big po'k chops with it. The restaurant was known all along the circuit the musicians traveled."[7]

The "circuit" was a loose network of clubs in cities where black musicians, likened by Neville to "wandering minstrels," knew they could find a stage atmosphere devoted to *quality.* There was the Bronze Peacock in Houston, Big Row in Memphis, the Barrel House in Watts, Club DeLisa in Chicago, and the famous Apollo Theatre in Harlem. These clubs belonged to no formal confederation but were prime spots for headlining black talent, and the biggest black musical stars of the forties and fifties played at most of them.

And so it was with the Dew Drop. When not featuring R&B headliners like Amos Milburn, Big Joe Turner, Pee Wee Crayton, Chuck Willis, Little Richard, Dinah Washington, or Gatemouth Brown, the Dew Drop would provide a stage for local newcomers, like Guitar Slim or young Allen Toussaint. And then there were the big band-leaders and preeminent vocalists who often dropped by for "guest" appearances. Duke Ellington, Ray Charles, Ella Fitzgerald, Curtis Mayfield, Lionel Hampton, and others passed through the Dew Drop in its heyday.

Another aspect of the "subculture within a sub-culture" was the hotel wing of the Dew Drop complex. Many of the popular black night spots in the city had hotels—like Foster's, the Robin Hood, and Shadowland—as both musicians and patrons generally were not admitted to the downtown tourist hotels. Musicians found a sprawling assortment of regular tenants at Painia's lodgings. James Booker, a brilliant young pianist, lived there for a time, as did Earl King, and other singers and dancers. Among these people a camaraderie grew of deep inner strengths. Musicians lived at the Dew Drop, ate there, and performed there.

Vocalist Gerri Hall's residence at the Dew Drop is a good example.

From the time I was real young, I always wanted to be into music. I felt it in myself, this talent. I wanted to touch it. Some things were happening in my life that were really heavy changes for me as a young woman with children, and I didn't know what to do. I was like someone being tossed around. Because I was unaware, being a peaceful child all involved with the little babies and cooking meals. My husband didn't look at me for the person I was. I started thinking that I should get away, and I loved music. I had been singing all the time. It was 1954, and by 1955 I had moved out.

I got to the Dew Drop going through a dramatic change. After I got there, I stabilized myself. I became familiar with the place and the people around me.

Guitar Slim had his thing, and Earl King had his thing, Roland Cook and Huey Smith had their things going on around the Dew Drop. They didn't have much going on for themselves yet. They were just musicians that knew how to play and came together on weekends to have gigs. And beautiful stuff would develop from it, you know.

It was like a family. Mr. and Mrs. Painia were ma and pa to me and the other girls that lived there. It was really a two-family thing that you had with the Painias and the other was the family that you had with the other people that lived around you in the hotel. Frank would choose who would live there. You had to be screened by Frank, and he let me be part of the scene. Everybody there had concern for each other's welfare and you did not violate the trust that was given by the Painias.[8]

The Dew Drop became a fixture in the local black community and an important way-station for the legions of artists who lived long stretches on the road, pushing their songs, earning money in a string of one-night stands or, if they were big names and lucky, extended stays in the bigger cities. To most musicians, however, life on the road was strenuous work.

Charles Neville's career was steeped in the lore of road life. Born on December 28, 1938, he left home at fifteen to join the Rabbit's Foot Minstrel Show, a waning echo of vaudeville. He lived in Memphis for a time, staying with a struggling bluesman named B. B. King, was drafted into service, and went AWOL so often he was finally released. A strong wanderlust played deeply into his life. The South was no paradise, however. "There were these places, the clubs, and there were routes our vagabond caravans traveled and there were these oases. And we traveled through hostile desert country where there were other elements to contend with, and the very hostile natives and other roving gangs of desperados. It was really like that traveling through rural towns in the South in the fifties; it was bad when I got in and I can imagine what it was like earlier. I talked with peo-

ple who had been in it for ten or twenty years before and it was getting progressively better. I caught it toward the end of the really open bad stuff that was happening."[9]

Few musicians were immune to the "bad stuff." Placide Adams, the veretran bassist, recalls an experience of his brother, Justin, driving through Mississippi in the fifties. The Adamses are Creoles. "Justin was on the road with Tommy Ridgley coming through Laurel or one of them places. They had played a job and they were all feeling kind of good and Justin used to wear cowboy hats and was a little lighter complected than the others in the band. They were swerving all over the highway when the police stopped them. 'Where y'all niggers thank y'all going?' I don't know where Justin got the nerve from, but he told the policeman, 'Officer, don't worry. These my niggers and I'll take care of 'em.' And the officer said, 'Okay, in that case you tell them boys to take it easy now.' Justin turned to the others and said, 'You heard what the man said. Now straighten up and let's go home.' "[10]

Charles Neville continues:

Okay, here's what we wanted to do; play music, and pit ourselves against all of this. With little places like the Dew Drop, these oases where we could regroup and recover made the music that happened there kind of special. There were things projected into the music there that was not there on the road. There was that sense of security about being there, and that sense of belonging with the strangers who were there, but who were not, in fact, strangers because they were members of this same order.

The Dew Drop floor shows were really the most artistic thing that was happening back then. In the black community this was the only place where these people who had these tremendous creative things happening could get to display their stuff. There were dancers who were geniuses at what they did . . . but black dance was not accepted in the mainstream of American dance performance. So there were these people who had these shows fit for Carnegie Hall or anywhere in the world, and the people who came to the Dew Drop were the fortunate ones who got to experience these things.[11]

The shows at the Dew Drop began with an exotic gay singer called Patsy Valdalia, who functioned as master of ceremonies at the club. He would begin: "Ladies and Gentlemen, it's *showtime* at the Dew Drop!" Variety acts, comics, a colorful singer called Mr. Google Eyes, shakedancers, novelty skits wove in and out of numbers played by the house band, which varied week to week. The Dew Drop featured many musicians: Allen Toussaint, Guitar Slim, Chris Kenner, Huey "Piano" Smith, Bobby Marchan, Earl King, the Lastie brothers, Art Neville, Placide and Justin Adams, James Rivers, Red Tyler, and Tommy Ridgley.

Patsy Valdalia was hand-picked for the job. "I remember it like it was yesterday," Patsy explains. "We developed a chorus line, out-of-sight. Everybody danced. Everybody came and did a number, singing and dancing. We opened at the original Gypsy Tea Room and from there we moved to the Club Desire, in the Ninth Ward. Frank Painia and Mr. Cook came by to catch my performance. That night Frank had a bet with Mr. Cook that I was a girl, not a boy. We were the Valdalia sisters. There were four of us, three others and me. Annette Valdalia, Jean Valdalia, Ann Valdalia, and Patsy Valdalia. We worked in front of a band. Mr. Painia was so impressed with my act and the fact that he had lost his bet with Mr. Cook that he hired me for the Dew Drop and I worked there from then on."[12]

According to Charles Neville: "Patsy served the same function as a majordomo would serve at a supper club. He was that, plus he was a big part of the entertainment. He also worked as a waitress. I've seen him behind the bar; I've seen him really dressed up at the door bringing people to the tables, and he could do that with dignity, man; then at showtime he would become the M.C. There

was no caste difference. There are a lot of clubs where people see themselves on different levels and sometimes entertainers see themselves above waiters and waiters see themselves above dishwashers, but Patsy would do anything and he brought something to the station, rather than the station having some effect on him."[13]

Earl King continues:

You must remember that Patsy was the M.C. and female impersonator. His theme song was "Hip Shakin' Mama" and he sings it comin' out of the kitchen. Instead of comin' through the stage entrance, he comes out of the back door of the kitchen and he starts singin' from the back. That's how he come on stage.

When they got comedians on, Patsy usually bring them up front, like Tops and Bottoms—this was the duo team of comedians. Then he'd have, like Von and Virgil on, and they come out doin' dramatic acts, different impressions. Then would come the Billy McAllister Review which was more or less the feature. They were all gays and it was hard to discern whether they were female or not. That's how close they were on everything. Wardrobe was *fantastic!*

Of course, you know you keep the headliners for last. He would have Ruby Calhoun come out. She was a kind of classy dancer, no strippin', and none of that stuff—the fashion, real top-quality stuff. Then he would bring on maybe a local act next to the feature act.

The trump card after the show is the *jam session.* That's when all the musicians be gettin' off all their gigs from outa town, in town, and they all meet up in the Dew Drop. And they eat breakfast there, they have drinks, and many of them get up and jam with other musicians. That had to be like about 4:30 in the morning. . . . But really that was entertaining for the musicians to go there to hear some of the outa town guys that come in and jam there. Of course you had people around here that was fantastic guitarists with more credentials, like Ernest McLean and, of course, my good friend, the late Roy Montrell, and Edgar Blanchard, Bill Jones.[14]

It was indicative of Frank Painia's commercial sense that he would not allow jazz—which was

Only in New Orleans . . .

leaning to bebop and more avante-garde expressions—until late hours after the main show was done. Rhythm-and-blues headlined most Dew Drop shows.

The place certainly didn't lack variety. Two memorable shake-dancers were Princess Lamoura and Princess Tangoula. There were also snake charmers. Saxophonist James Rivers recalls: "They kept those snakes with 'em in the dressin' rooms. Man, they had boa constrictors, and when I got up there on stage to blow behind that, believe me, I be standin' *way* back."[15]

In many ways, the Dew Drop Inn was a descendant of old vaudeville, a variety of entertainers, steeped in comedy and music, people of every imaginable stripe who knew, come what may, that the show must go on and that they were the show. Placide Adams, then playing drums, once "played behind Peg-Leg Bates up there. Now *there* was an act. Boy, that man was something. He was a one-legged tap dancer. He didn't have the artificial leg: he had a peg leg, and that sombitch would start dancing with that peg leg and his natural leg and tap dance better than any tap dancer I ever saw. In his act he would unstrap this peg leg and dance on one leg and make as much noise with that one leg as he was with both. He would do flips and everything with that one leg. That was one of the greatest acts I ever saw in my life. I had to play behind him with all the accents. It was something! That's days I'll never forget, the Dew Drop."[16]

The elaborate histrionics and costumes of the gay dancers, shake-dancers, and acts like Peg-Leg Bates forced the musicians to play with all the fire they had. Painia himself was a shrewd judge of talent. Crowds of musicians went to the Dew Drop, looking for a gig. Painia, also a successful booking agent, often put bands together by going outside the bar and sizing up the crowd of musicians with their instruments. In Earl King's words: "He'd start puttin' bands together on the sidewalk just like they do out on the river to hire long-shoremen."[17] Painia booked bands in remote townships outside New Orleans, sending them to Covington or Buras or Slidell and other points in the Gulf South. That he remained a popular, even beloved, figure is testimony to his fair treatment of the musicians.

As its popularity grew in the 1950s, the club began to attract whites. Record executives like Ace's Johnny Vincent and Atlantic's Nesuhi Ertegun made the trek to LaSalle Street, as did disc jockey Ken Elliott ("Jack the Cat") and a young Dick Allen, who years later became curator of Tulane University's jazz archive. But the presence of whites could make things difficult. Although Louisiana law did not forbid whites from entering a Negro establishment, it stipulated that blacks and whites could not be served or drink together. Frank Painia welcomed anyone to his club and basically disregarded these laws. As a result, the Dew Drop was periodically raided by the New Orleans police. The most famous case involved Zachary Scott, a movie star.

On a Saturday night in November 1952, Scott, then thirty-seven, his wife, and two friends went to hear blues singer "Papa" Lightfoot at the Dew Drop. Several black sailors seated at a nearby table invited Scott's group to join them for drinks, celebrating their return from Korea. The situation seemed innocent enough, more drinks were ordered. But as Saturday night ebbed into Sunday, a raid by the police nailed Scott, his party, and Painia.

Scott and his crowd were charged with "being seated at tables with and consuming alcoholic beverages with Negro patrons." Painia as owner was held responsible and charged accordingly. By Monday morning charges were dropped in municipal court. For his entire party Scott pleaded "guilty because of an act of ignorance." The judge stated that it was all a mistake and hoped the affair was not too much of an inconvenience. He also suggested that in the future, if Scott wanted

Top left: Exotic dancer at Club Tiajuana, 1953. *Top right:* Justin Adams at the Million Dollar Room, 1953. *Above:* Saturday night function. *Bottom right:* Dancing at the San Jacinto Club, 1954

to frequent Negro clubs, he do so as a spectator and not drink.[18] The case made the newspapers, and though the charges were dropped, there was no indication that segregation laws were softening. But handfuls of whites continued to patronize the club, and the police continued occasional raids.

Under such repression, humor became all the more precious for musicians in the "subculture within a subculture." As tales of cavortings, affairs, and exploits spread among members of the Dew Drop family, Earl King and a young singer named Chick Carbo (who sang with the Spiders) created the Dew Drop's own scandal sheet. It was called the *La Salle Street Strip*. King recalls:

Chick not only drew the pictures but, being a sign painter, he's got a fantastic hand; he'd print just like it come off a machine. And he did the whole paper. It cost you a dime to read it. And you'd give it back when you're finished readin'. Curtis Gutter used to go around rentin' the paper.

And all the groups would come to town, they would say, "Hey, I heard they got this paper in town. Who's got it?" And they might have "NEXT WEEK, BOBBY BLAND!" Like in later years, they had the *Confidential Magazine*. But they would have stuff in there like "Gay of the Week," "Closet Queen of the Week," or somethin' like that.

One time Chick says, "Hey, man, I feel like I'm gonna run Frank [Painia] up on the wall. I'm gonna print somethin' in here to see Frank's reaction." He put on there "NEXT WEEK, FRANK PAINIA!" Frank called both of us in the office. He says, "I heard y'all got that paper out, but if y'all put anything in that paper about me, I'm gonna have both of y'all sued!" Chick says, "I was just jokin'. I told Earl I put that there to see your reaction."

Man, it was comical—the people who would rent it again to show it to somebody. That's the ironic part. They would say, "Hey, man, did you see this? Man, you got to see this." And I could see Chick Carbo and Curtis Gutter squabblin' about the money one night. Chick said, "Open all your pockets up, Gutter." And he had thick pockets of money.[19]

In 1947 the Dew Drop became a subject of song writing, with Ivory Joe Hunter's tune "Jumpin' at the Dew Drop." The lyrics offer a glimpse of the club and show life.

If you go down to New Orleans,
  You wanna see things you've never seen,
Just go to Washington and LaSalle.
  There you'll find some real fine gals.

Jumping at the Dew Drop, meet you down there,
  Jumping at the Dew Drop, really send you.
They swing and they boogie and they groove some, too.
  If you don't enjoy, there's something wrong with you.

The other "big" club of the black circuit in the fifties was Club Tiajuana, still in business on Saratoga Street nestled below a section of elevated highway in the heart of central city. The place is quieter now, but it still hints of a past glory. The jukebox sports the old hits, like Guitar Slim's "The Things That I Used to Do." The crowd is older now, but many remember the days when the Tiajuana filled up each night with hungry music fans. Behind the bar is a giant portrait of Miss Gloria Bolden, owner and manager. Below Gloria's picture is a large black-and-white photograph of her parents, Oscar and Delphia Bolden. Oscar purchased the Gold Leaf Hotel and Bar in 1942; he had made his money in a dry cleaning business. He expanded the premises and in 1948 reopened as Club Tiajuana, which quickly emerged as a rival to the Dew Drop.

The Tiajuana was different from Frank Painia's club in several respects. The crowd was younger, the prices lower. While the Dew Drop leaned toward hot jazz in wee hours, the Tiajuana almost enshrined rhythm-and-blues. The decor was different, too. In contrast with Johnny Donnels's impressionistic murals at "The Drop," Club Tiajuana opened into a gently curving wall of glass bricks. The bar featured glass bricks with neon lights behind, giving the place a flashy glow. No country honky-tonk here. Behind the barroom and

A subculture within a subculture

Female impersonators at the Dew Drop

Ernie K-Doe's birthday party at Winnie's bar, 1982

through a double door was the stage area, which seated 350.

Like Frank Painia, Oscar Bolden had an eye for talent. He recognized an early winner in Guitar Slim and hired him often. Huey Smith recalls, "When Guitar Slim decided to play at the Tiajuana, Frank Painia at the Dew Drop took back the guitar he had bought for Slim. So when we walked over to the Tiajuana, Slim didn't have a guitar, so Mr. Bolden said, 'Well, Slim, how much a guitar cost?' " Slim returned with a brand new guitar and a fifty-foot cord. He told Huey, "Man, I can walk clear to the front of the building with this one!"[20]

Gloria Bolden recalls, "Guitar Slim was packing the house so much that Daddy expanded the back room."[21] During the Tiajuana's peak years, 1952 to 1959, the Boldens featured a complete review, seven nights a week, with comedians and dancers. Unlike the Dew Drop, Club Tiajuana featured stripteasers.

Vocalist Bobby Marchan performed at the Tiajuana in its glory days. It was a place he enjoyed working when he wasn't on the road with Huey Smith and the Clowns. "It had a stage in the center of the room and people could sit on either side. The Dew Drop had all the publicity, but the Tiajuana was great! I used to do shows at the Tiajuana and hop in a cab and do one at the Dew Drop the same night. Little Richard, Huey Smith, Ernie K-Doe, and I would all be on the same show and they would always have a 'shake-dancer' like Lady Carmen Tangoula, Caldonia, or Dottie Cassandra. Mr. Bolden had full entertainment."[22]

"There was a large group of female impersonators," recalls Gloria Bolden, "who would always stay at the hotel and dance for the shows. There was one girl we used to call 'Chicken Lady.' She did a strip and ended up laying an egg!"[23]

Today behind the bar is an old publicity picture of Bobby Marchan in four separate poses; three show him in a platinum wig and a metallic brocade, full-length cocktail gown. In the fourth he is dressed as a man. The Tiajuana was a retreat for the exotic, a place of few inhibitions. Marchan says, "I remember when [producer] Johnny Vincent came by the Tiajuana to get Huey and me for one of our recording sessions. I had just done a show and I was still in my women's clothes. We was runnin' late so Johnny didn't give me time to change. I had to do the recording session in *full drag!*"[24]

The Tiajuana also served food; visiting entertainers stayed free at the hotel. Thursday was talent night with a five dollar prize to the winning young artists. Many Tiajuana performers left their mark on the city's musical life—Chris Kenner, Ernie K-Doe, Huey "Piano" Smith, Guitar Slim, a group called the Tic-Tocks. The most famous touring musician who played the New Orleans clubs was Richard Penniman of Macon, Georgia—who exploded into rock-and-roll popularity as Little Richard.

For black musicians in the segregation years, the clubs served as a stage for their most complex expressions. The family tradition that sent forth a new generation of jazz and of rhythm-and-blues players extended into the secular community of clubs, where musicians came to know one another. The "subculture within a subculture" embraced those whose talent showed real promise, as well as lesser talents struggling on the fringes. In many ways, the history of rhythm-and-blues in New Orleans is rooted in the social histories of these clubs. By the late 1950s, the transition from R&B to rock-and-roll was steeped in irony. The songs and performing styles blacks refined in clubs with black patrons soon became standard fare in dances for white teenagers.

Chapter Six

MIDNIGHT ROCKERS AND SWEETHEARTS OF THE BLUES

In 1947 a fair-skinned black man named Vernon Winslow began frequenting the Dew Drop Inn on an odd mission. Winslow held a doctorate in art and taught at Dillard, a local Negro university. A northerner who came South before World War II, he was intrigued with radio, both as a vehicle for the burgeoning black popular music and as a sideline occupation for himself. Stars like Ellington, Basie, Armstrong, and Nat King Cole were heard often on the airwaves, but there were no "soul stations" back then. WJMR, broadcasting from the Jung Hotel, hired Winslow to develop a programming strategy aimed at blacks. This meant rhythm-and-blues music and advertisements geared to black listeners, a new market for advertisers.

Winslow began working part-time for the "Jam, Jive and Gumbo" show, whose host was Poppa Stoppa. (Duke Thiele was the first of several Poppa Stoppas.) Because Winslow was black, the radio management did not allow him to speak over the airwaves. Such was the logic of segregation that

Winslow wrote "scripts" for Poppa Stoppa and white deejays to read on-air, while hosting black record shows. To pick up the street talk, Vernon Winslow took a notebook and headed for the Dew Drop.

"I wasn't brought up on the streets," Winslow recalled. "But anyone who lives in the type of neighborhood in Chicago or Gary as I did, even though you read books or poetry, you would never admit it."

Despite the discriminations Winslow endured at that first radio job, he maintained a sense of detachment and went on about his business.

The Dew Drop was a good place to be. It was just the sprouting up of new terms like, "Man, she's fine," "I don't come through the door, man, I come through the window." Those phrases I would listen to and new languages just seemed to spring up. New meanings for a combination of ideas and metaphors; this rhyming pattern, which everybody took a little bit of. Things like, "Come on, Ruth, get out of that phone booth, drinking that strong vermouth."

It was, as I could figure it out, a kind of urbanity they were reflecting, not knowing too much of the prepositions and Latin derivation of words, and the Latin connection of word structures . . . they would just develop their own hip talk. I would interpret those phrases and put them into the script, like "Don't act froggy or I'll make you jump." It was laced with neighborhood inflections. It was something that was just part of my job.[1]

The WJMR show gained a tremendous following. Blacks began listening to the show—*their* music—which pleased advertisers. Tailors on Dryades Street began to buy airtime. Jax beer executives took notice, too, as they were trying to create a black marketing strategy. White teenagers and young adults, geared to the quickening tempo of urban black music, began buying records. In 1947 black popular recordings were still called "race records." *Billboard* magazine did not list the rhythm-and-blues classification until 1949. When Roy Brown's "Good Rockin' Tonight" hit the airwaves in 1948, the impact was immediate. "The fact that we played that record on the 'Poppa Stoppa Show,'" Winslow reflected, "just swept new audiences into WJMR. With the suggestive words 'we gonna rock tonight,' we'd get requests like 'Play that nigger's record that talks about at twelve midnight, I'm gonna take you out behind the barn and gonna love you so much, don't mean you no harm.'"[2]

The lyrics, in fact, are slightly different, but the overt sexual references, for the time, were a dramatic departure from commercial pop radio.

Well, I heard the news, there's good rocking tonight,
   Yes, I'm gonna hold my baby as tight as I can,
Tonight she'll know I'm a mighty, mighty man,
   I heard the news, there's good rocking tonight.

Well, meet me in a hurry behind the barn,
   Don't be afraid I'll do you no harm,
I want you to bring my rocking shoes,
   'Cause tonight I'm gonna rock away all my blues,
I heard the news, there's good rocking tonight.

Well, Deacon Jones and Elder Brown,
   Two of the slickest cats in town,
They'll be there, just wait and see,
   Stomping and jumping at the jamboree,
Crying, "Hey, man, there's good rocking tonight."

"Roy Brown was R&B's first flagship in New Orleans," Winslow continued. "It was his record that identified [the radio show]. It just broke open!"[3]

Roy Brown was born in New Orleans on September 10, 1925. His father, Yancey Brown, was a brickmason. His mother, True Love, was of Algonquin Indian and Negro lineage. A schoolteacher and organist who directed gospel choirs, she taught the boy to sing spirituals. The family moved to Eunice, a small town west of New Orleans in the agricultural belt. At thirteen, Roy was singing in church; he organized a quartet and wrote spirituals. One night they did a tune called "Satan's Chariots Rolling By." As he told John Broven in a memorable interview:

Man, oh man, I had about six or eight ounces of blackberry wine, and my boys and I, we got in the church and we started to sing. And we started doing things we'd never done before. The sisters started clapping their hands, and patting their feet, they were shouting "Amen! Amen!" and we had them rolling. And I was so very proud because my mother was there.

My mother didn't say anything on the way home. We had to walk about a mile and half back to our residence from the church. When I got home, she said, "O.K., so take off your clothes." I knew what that meant, a whipping, because she didn't get to me often. There was a peach tree growing at the front steps and she said, "Get out of your clothes and get me a few limbs!" I said, "Mama, what did I do?" She said, "I'm gonna teach you to jazz up spirituals!" I said, "What do you mean, jazz?" I didn't know what she was talking about. She said, "That wasn't a spiritual you were singing. I don't know what it was, but it wasn't a spiritual!" And she just ripped me apart.

But I guess at that day and age I had the rhythm. And I got it from her. She was a singer, you know. But anyway, to make a long story short, I think that was what you might call my inception of doing rhythmic things.[4]

True Love may have been a disciplinarian, but a strong bond united mother and son. Roy worked as a field laborer in the sugar and rice fields around Eunice. Sometimes True Love would cry because he was so thin. But the work exposed him to the field songs of other workers steeped in rural blues. He heard men sing "I'm cutting this cane . . . for the man, the man upstairs"—and he would hum along to himself. Late at night in his room he wrote notes and rhyming lyrics, influenced by his work in the fields.

True Love died of pneumonia when Roy was fourteen. Her death shattered him. He followed his father to Houston, where he finished high school, and then drifted west to Los Angeles. He wanted to become a prizefighter. At 143 pounds he was a welterweight; field work had made his body strong, and he was a good hitter. The only problem was the sight of blood nauseated him. When other fighters learned this, they broke ketchup capsules in their fists to make Brown back off. His manager suggested a new career.

Oddly, his primary influence as a singer was Bing Crosby. Brown went to Crosby films with pen and paper, scribbling furiously each time Crosby sang on screen. He would leave the theater with a fistful of tunes, head home, and start rehearsing.

In early 1945, twenty-year-old Roy Brown won the sixty dollar first prize in a talent show at the Million Dollar Theatre in Los Angeles. He sang two songs, "San Antonio Rose" and "Got Spurs That Jingle Jangle Jingle." Over the next six weeks, he made the round of amateur nights and "had a regular job, winning first, second, third and fourth prizes. Singing those same damn two songs."

Brown did a short army stint but was released because of his flat feet. Coming into his own as a balladeer, he moved to Galveston and teamed up with a combo, the Melodeers. He told journalist Bill Bentley:

I was still singing ballads, but I was also getting accustomed to the blues. Then I wrote "Good Rockin' Tonight," right out of the *blue*. I took it to rehearsal and the trumpet player sang it. It was at first a spiritual, in that form, and the characters Elder Brown and Deacon Jones were characters I'd heard of. We had this radio show, the first blacks to have their own show, and the first time we played "Good Rockin'," the trumpet player was passed out, so I had to sing it. I didn't think nothing of it, and wouldn't sing it the next night. I guess I still didn't like the blues. Anyway, over the radio the song got a big response, and we started packing the club. Then, I got into a tiff with the club owner and had to get out of town quick, so that looked like the end of my singing for a while.[5]

He arrived in New Orleans with the suit on his back, found a bed in a dilapidated rooming house, and learned that bluesman Wynonie Harris was playing that night. He remembered Harris's performances in auditoriums when he was younger and thought it would be worth a shot to meet him. He wrote the lyrics to "Good Rockin' Tonight" on a paper bag and headed to Foster's Rainbow Room. Brown wanted to give the song to Harris in exchange for cash to tide him over until he became established in New Orleans.

But Wynonie "Mr. Blues" Harris was in a mood that night and rebuffed him. Brown was dejected. But the sidemen playing behind Wynonie had grown restive; the star of the show had several girls around him. The vibes between band and Mr. Blues were getting worse. One of the musicians invited Brown to sing on stage. He belted out "Good Rockin' Tonight," the musicians clapping as he finished. A man in the club approached Roy and told him he should see Cecil Gant. Roy said okay. The two men ended up at the Dew Drop Inn, where Gant, a blues pianist with a good voice, was performing. Gant gave him the chance to sing the song, and Roy delivered.

When the band took a break about 2:30 in the morning, Gant took the young singer aside. He heard about the bad luck with Wynonie Harris, but didn't offer Brown any money. Instead, they went to a pay phone. Gant placed a collect call to Jules Braun, president of DeLuxe Records, at his home in New Jersey. It was now well into the wee hours. Braun finally answered the phone, and Gant said, "I hate to call you at this hour, but I want you to listen to a new sound and a new tune. This boy's name is Roy Brown."[6]

Mr. Braun's initial response is not known, but he agreed to hear the song. Over the telephone, Brown sang "Good Rockin' Tonight," a bit softer in view of the situation. A long silence followed.

"Sing it again," said the voice from New Jersey. Brown sang it a second time. Braun—who would be in New Orleans the following week to record Paul Gayten and Annie Laurie—told Gant to give Brown fifty dollars as an advance on the record session. After Braun went back to bed, Roy Brown was ecstatic. Cecil Gant gently scolded him for approaching Wynonie Harris to buy the song. "You fool, don't go around giving songs away. There's a lot of money in publishing."

"Good Rockin' Tonight" hit the airwaves in 1948 and made Roy Brown a star overnight. Wynonie Harris, ironically, sang it soon thereafter, and Elvis Presley made it a hit again. By then Brown had other hits and was touring nationally.

Between June 1948 and the same month of 1957, Roy Brown cut thirteen hit records. The first five made the *Billboard* charts, but before numerical standings were kept. Of the final eight, "Hard Luck Blues" was first in the R&B category in July 1950, with "Love Don't Love Nobody" reaching second place three months later. Two other hits made the top ten in the next year. For a black singer, breaking into the commercial mainstream

was a major achievement; soon he was earning handsome sums on the concert tour.

But the larger financial picture was not very good for an artist of his stature. In 1950 Jules Braun sold DeLuxe to a larger label, King Records, and with it Roy Brown's contract. King was owned by Syd Nathan; Brown's personal manager was a man named Jack Pearl. Looking back on his career and the long descent that followed the late fifties, Brown said bluntly, "They cleaned me out."[7] He began to understand the complexities of his losses in 1957 at an Imperial recording session under Dave Bartholomew, the master bandleader who had guided Fats Domino's songs through the studio mill.

"Roy Brown," Bartholomew said, "you should be a millionaire but I don't think you are."

"No, I'm not a millionaire. I'm barely getting along right now. I had a lot of difficulties."

Bartholomew countered, "All the hit records you made, man, you should have money in all the banks around here."

"What do you mean?"

"The performance royalties, your mechanical rights."

"What are you talking about?"

Mechanical royalties were paid by the record company, in this case DeLuxe, to the publishing company, which was apparently owned by DeLuxe. Performance royalties were paid by Broadcast Music Incorporated to the publisher and writer, based on the number of times the song was played on radio and on jukeboxes and performed publicly by other artists or Brown himself.

"And then we went to Broadcast Music Incorporated," Brown remarked in the Broven interview. "BMI said they had never paid Roy Brown no performance royalties or writer's royalties because he never signed a form. My manager had all the forms. He never gave them to me. They were taking all the money. . . . When you think about those guys, how they did it. . . . If you didn't make it on your one-night stands, your personal appearance, you didn't make it."[8]

Roy Brown's hard luck story has been echoed by many New Orleans musicians; artists who saw their stars rise and then begin to fade found they had not secured contractual rights. Thus a hit record composed by Roy Brown would be "covered"—cut again by other artists without the original artist receiving his writer's fees.

And so we find Roy Brown, behind on tax payments, showing up at a party in Little Rock honoring Elvis Presley (who had an early hit covering "Good Rockin' Tonight"). The doorman would not admit him. "So I got the doorman to give him a note telling Mr. Presley his yardman is here. When Elvis got it, he came right out, asking me if I needed anything and gave me enough to get straight with the IRS. That's the kind of guy he was."[9]

By the mid-sixties, Roy Brown was living in Los Angeles. With Bartholomew's help, he had straightened out the contractual matters with BMI and had begun receiving royalties. Happily married and the father of a daughter whom he treasured, he settled in the San Fernando Valley and continued selected club engagements. For a time he worked as a salesman; his wife ran a nursery school and the Brown home was comfortably middle class. He went on to record an album for Bluesway, an ABC affiliate, that was released in 1973 as a blues revival swept America, attracting young white musicians who had been influenced by stars like Elvis, the Rolling Stones, and the Beatles. But Roy Brown didn't exactly fit the bill. The young fans were drawn to the more traditional rural bluesmen, like Muddy Waters, John Lee Hooker, and Howlin' Wolf. As one writer observed, "Roy's blues singing wasn't 'gut bucket' enough for the younger public's taste."[10]

In 1970 Brown appeared at the Monterey Jazz Festival with Johnny Otis's orchestra and the hearty crowd approval gave him confidence for a comeback. He cut several tunes through the mid-seventies, wrote others that added to the voluminous compositions he had written throughout his career, and by 1978 made a grand tour of Europe, with one album making the top ten in Sweden. With the seventies' nostalgia craze taking root in America, his picture brightened. A movie contract was in the works when Brown visited New Orleans for the 1980 Jazz and Heritage Festival.

Trumpeter Teddy Riley, an old sidekick, played behind Brown that day. "I felt just like the old days," Riley said. "He was a big, strapping guy and he hooked his arm around my shoulder and we linked up with the other guys and he rocked us back and forth like we used to do. He was happy to be back in New Orleans. Blues singers from all over were there and had come to hear Roy Brown. The voice was there. He was in top shape."[11]

Ten days later in Los Angeles, Brown died of a heart attack. The last song he performed was his first and biggest hit, "Good Rockin' Tonight," in the city where it all began.

Vernon Winslow summed up his career this way. "Roy must have stood in the mirror many times before he got where he was; with his height and the image he gave, Roy was the personification of the songs that he sang. Just a midnight rocker, a midnight rider, big and well-dressed, a hand shaker. He could sing a song and almost shake hands with you."[12]

By the early 1950s, Vernon Winslow was a busy man in New Orleans. With the success of Poppa Stoppa at WJMR, the Fitzgerald Advertising Agency offered a $5,000 annual salary if Winslow could create a radio name and air presence to help market Jax beer. The Jackson Brewing Company was a major Fitzgerald client. Winslow, earning $32 a week as an art professor at Dillard, took the job. Thus began the career of Dr. Daddy-O, one of the grand figures in southern radio and entertainment. Winslow's smooth on-air voice, laced with slang chatter of the streets, sent forth the Jax beer message in New Orleans on WMRY, a clear channel station that reached as far as Beaumont, Texas. Jax then began a regional marketing drive, and under Winslow's auspices, deejays in Baton Rouge, Jackson, and Houston took the name Dr. Daddy-O and followed the script formula Winslow refined. Winslow, having the foresight to blend beer promotion with the rise of rhythm-and-blues, organized films with Fats Domino, Dave Bartholomew, and baseball star Jackie Robinson that were shown as shorts in black theaters. Dave Bartholomew cut a promotional record called "Jax Boogie." Winslow kept quite busy in those days spinning records, broadcasting the Jax ads he wrote, making the round of clubs on the local circuit as a suave master of ceremonies, as well as venturing into record production. One of the true original performers to come his way was a portly, round-faced bluesman known as Smiley Lewis.

New Orleans has an old and enduring blues tradition that has long been overshadowed by jazz. But what is "New Orleans blues," and what distinguishes it from other musical styles? The early rural blues, played on guitar and other instruments, grew from the postslavery culture of the black South. But New Orleans, even before the Civil War, was a bustling port with its own opera and a sophisticated musical awareness. By the early 1900s, when ensemble jazz emerged, blues had filtered into the city from the rural parishes. Jazz was the dominant form; the blues became a precocious stepchild. The erotic messages, the lyrics of love lost, aimless travel and sorrowful struggle—like the vocal quality of instrumental blues and rising emotional temperatures of the idiom—became the messages of jazz.

Jazz drew heavily on blues, often using the word *blues* while discarding the idiom. "Basin Street Blues," as sung by Louis Armstrong in his famous 1928 cut with Earl "Fatha" Hines, bears little resemblance to the gritty, lonesome blues of Son House, Charley Patton, and Blind Lemon Jefferson of the early down-home tradition. In fact, "Basin Street Blues" is really a jazz song with the word *blues* in it. In New Orleans rhythm-and-blues, as in jazz, the blues was a subdominant element, in many respects overshadowed by rhythmical properties. Its sound is often laced with sweet, melodic riffs, contrasting with the rougher blues styles of the Mississippi Delta, Chicago, and East Texas. For this reason scholars have failed to give the New Orleans blues form serious consideration since it neither followed certain musical criteria nor fell within any accepted definition of the blues. Thus, New Orleans blues must be defined within the perimeters of the environment and culture that gave it identity and form.

The piano is the instrument that gives New Orleans blues its definition and style. And in the blues idiom, it is the "blue note" that distinguishes the blues from other musical forms. Within the three-chord blues format—the tonic chord, the subdominant, and the dominant (I-IV-V)—there are three blue notes: the flatted third, the flatted fifth, and the flatted seventh. The flatted third is central to the New Orleans blues form. The blue note is produced by a slide from the flattened third to the major third, which is struck in hammering fashion. The chords are played in a rhythmical style, often in two-four or four-four time, in a call-response pattern with the bass line. This is evident in songs such as Huey Smith's "Rockin' Pneumonia," Professor Longhair's "Tipitina," and the Radiators' "Sunglasses On."

Structurally, blues is generally played in a twelve-bar phrase. Also popular in New Orleans was the eight-bar blues form derived from country blues and gospel. Songs like Fats Domino's "The Fatman," and Smiley Lewis's "Tee Nah Nah" showcase the popular blues style.

Top left: Smiley Lewis. *Above:* Dr. Daddy-O (Vernon Winslow). *Left:* Roy Brown, 1982

While the I-IV-V chord structure is in general use in all blues forms, there are simpler patterns played in New Orleans. The I-V phrase, two-chord blues was commercially popular. Professor Longhair's "Baldhead" in 1949 is an early example, followed in the mid-fifties by Earl King's "Those Lonely, Lonely Nights." For the most part, the rougher style blues was relegated to barrooms of South Rampart Street and diminutive taverns in remote black neighborhoods. The influence was real, though. Three popular bluesmen who frequented the Ninth Ward clubs were Polka Dot Slim, Harmonica Al, and Boogie Bill Webb. Isidore "Tuts" Washington, a pianist, started out in brothels and honky-tonks around Rampart Street in the thirties. A slender, wizened man with fair skin, Washington was playing the piano bar at the elegant Pontchartrain Hotel in 1981. He recalled the early years of the Depression: "See, those women in them speakeasies wanted blues, low-down blues, so we played the blues."[13]

Washington was influenced by Meade Lux Lewis and Red Cayou, a local barrelhouse pianist slightly older than he. In the downtown wards, he found blues pianists with names like Drive 'em Down, Papa Crutch, and Kid Clayton. One memorable contemporary was Earl Johnson, whose son, Earl King, changed his last name and grew to maturity in the Dew Drop era. Snooks Eaglin, a blind guitarist and veteran singer, was still active in 1984. Finally, no list of seminal New Orleans bluesmen is complete without pianist Champion Jack Dupree, born in 1910, who left the city as a young man.

Tuts Washington (1907–1984) was a prototypical New Orleans bluesman; he played blues on the piano but learned rags and jazz as well because the city's dancing tradition demanded a wider repertoire. He was performing regularly when the stock market crashed in 1929. But such was the lot of the local blues that Tuts did not record on his own until 1984. In 1980 he was profiled in a television documentary with Professor Longhair and Allen Toussaint, marking the first recorded solo appearance by the enduring artist. Washington remembers meeting Smiley Lewis: "He used to live Back O' Town by me, he used to fix horseshoes when I met him."[14]

No one knows when Overton Amos Lemons took the name Smiley, some irony since he had no front teeth. He was born on July 5, 1913, in DeQuincy, a small town in southwestern Louisiana near the Texas border. Facts of his personal life are sketchy; he was never interviewed. Jeff Hannusch, who located his sister-in-law, reports that Lemons and his two brothers were raised by a stepmother, suggesting that his natural mother died young. At an early age, possibly as young as ten, Lemons ended up in New Orleans. Hannusch speculates he may have run away from home. According to his first wife, Leona Robinson Kelly, Smiley was "part raised" by a white family in the Irish Channel. Years later, when he lay ill in Charity Hospital, Kelly says an elderly white woman appeared at his bedside, calling him "my baby."[15]

He married at twenty-five, soon had children to support, and forged ahead as a musician. Rural origins of the blues ran deep in his music. Smiley loved the blues and had taught himself the rudiments of guitar. He performed in the late thirties with trumpeter Thomas Jefferson, who had a quartet that played the city. Jefferson recalls:

Smiley Lewis was more like a hustler, you know. He went around from place to place, playin' and singin', pickin' up what people give him and what not. He never read no music. He was just a guitar player that sang. We played at every joint in town. We useta go from joint to joint to play. I know we made two or three hundred dollars one night. Cause we played for rich people and all the workin' people, and it was durin' hard times we made that. There weren't no salary, just what they give us. All them guys throw half-a-dollars and quarters and all that for us to play songs. . . . We'd play 'em a song and then go around the table with a hat. We useta wear derby hats, we wore frocktail coats and derbies with the high peak to it. That was our uniform. We were very popular. We played all the joints, colored and white.[16]

As a singer, Smiley could hold his own with the most popular bluesmen in town. His booming voice had great range and could fill an entire room without microphone or amplifier. As a soloist he often performed in troubadour fashion, singing from table to table as he had once done with Jefferson's combo. After World War II, Smiley formed a trio with Tuts Washington and Herman Seals on drums. They soon became the rage of black nightclubs, with Smiley known then as "Smiley Lewis, the Drifting Blues Singer."

"He reminded me of Bunk Johnson quite a bit," recalled Vernon Winslow. "Had a little bit of a rural Fats Domino in him. His repertoire didn't go too far. He relied on his few melodies and his tunes that he had—nothing extensive. He was very friendly, always anxious to perform, always anxious to tell you things that would happen to him, some of the unfortunate love affairs. Although in his forties, he liked to peel off certain layers of his life and express them, not at any level of sophistication but as someone from the country, and had learned two or three melodies that the people liked. He was more like a deacon in a church with a sense of syncopation than a star."[17]

Smiley Lewis first recorded in 1947 for DeLuxe, the New Jersey label owned by Jules Braun (who first recorded Roy Brown) and his brother David, who produced Smiley. In 1950 he was signed by Imperial, then earning good profits from Fats Domino with Dave Bartholomew as the local field producer. Lewis's first songs came straight out of the blues tradition, a deep booming voice with passion in its push. The tunes by "Smiling Lewis," in vintage blues tradition, suggested sorrowful loves or just plain hard times—"Low-down," "Growing Old," "If You Ever Loved a Woman," "Dirty-Dirty People." He finally hit the charts in

1952 with "Bells Are Ringing." But at the very time Roy Brown was moving into the white market, drawing large crowds of fans at concerts, Smiley's concentration on the blues, despite the urban quality of the lyrics, rooted him deeper in the black market and, as such, limited commercial possibilities.

Smiley Lewis's sustained concentration in the blues followed the pattern of earlier rural artists whose expressiveness shifted as they migrated to the cities. One of his best early songs was a 1950 number, "Tee Nah Nah," with Tuts Washington on piano. The song title was inspired by a song that Jelly Roll Morton made famous as "Mama's Got a Baby Named Tee-Nah Nah." It was originally something of a lullaby, but between Smiley and Tuts, it took on a more worldly quality, reflecting the folk idiom of the New Orleans blues.[18]

"'Tee Nah Nah,' he cut it for me on a lacquer disc," Winslow recalled, "and I played it on the air like that. I heard him at this little spot. It might have been the Club Desire. I said, 'Man, I want you to have my engineer tape what you got.' He made the first cut for me. Then Imperial got it and recut it."

The poetic sensibility of the blues was engrained in Lewis's world view. Fragments of his songs read like scattered pages from a life whose hard-luck times were hidden behind the mask of a nightclub troubadour. "Here comes Smiley / Please take a chance on him / I ain't from nowhere / Or nowhere I've ever been." In a humorous interpretation of love through the metaphor of a radio, he sang: "Turn up the volume / I want to hear a little more / Now your speaker's buzzin' / But your volume is too low / I want to hear a little music / Babe, before I go."

His recordings elevated Smiley to professional status in the city. And Imperial made money off his work; he recorded steadily for ten years until 1960, but performed in the shadow of the label's big star, Fats Domino, whose power and charm were galvanizing young white audiences. Smiley

Lewis played to that crowd, but with nothing close to Fats's success. In 1955, for example, he cut the memorable "I Hear You Knocking," which became a hit when covered by television actress Gale Storm of "My Little Margie."

Lewis's most famous song was "Blue Monday," which Fats Domino later made a commercial hit. Smiley originally recorded it under Dave Bartholomew (who shares the writer credits), but the lyrics, which tell the story of a common laborer, are clearly a self-portrait.

Blue Monday, how I hate Blue Monday,
    Got to work like a slave all day.
Then comes Tuesday, oh hard Tuesday,
    I'm so tired got no time to play.

Here comes Wednesday, I'm beat to my sox,
    My gal calls, got to tell her that I'm out,
Cause Thursday is a hard-working day.
    And Friday I'll get my pay.

Saturday morning, oh Saturday morning,
    All my tiredness have gone away.
Got my money and my honey
    And I'm out on the steps to play.

Sunday morning my head is bad,
    But it's worth it for the time I had,
But I got to get my rest,
    Cause Monday is a mess.

Smiley continued to play the taverns and beer parlors of New Orleans in the early sixties.[19] But his touring, which in the fifties took him through the Gulf South and to the West Coast, had fallen off sharply. Illness stalked him like a shadow in the sun. In the *Louisiana Weekly* of March 19, 1966, columnist Joe Emery wrote: "Any help for one of the grooviest entertainers would be most highly appreciated. A cat who has helped many, Smiley Lewis is at home ill. He resides at 4628 Freret Street. He has great confidence in the man above. Let's all of his friends fall in and hep' 'em out. We would like to thank all of those who have already dropped off the green stuff."[20] On October 7, Smiley Lewis succumbed to stomach cancer. But the legacy of his music—the blues of Smiley Lewis—endured as the years passed. By 1980, with a rhythm-and-blues revival flourishing in New Orleans, at least four Smiley Lewis albums were available in the better record stores. And his best songs were still sung by others.

Roy Brown and Smiley Lewis represented divergent styles of the emergent R&B idiom. The midnight rocker took the blues and, with his background as a crooner, found a vocal style with enormous appeal to whites. Smiley Lewis on the other hand was a bluesman whose work was identifiably black with a raw, comedic strain.

If a single reference point holds validity for the flurry of recordings between 1947 and 1952, it would have to be the blues: New Orleans blues. Fats Domino and Professor Longhair were now moving forward in different styles that in time would divide the city's rhythm-and-blues idiom with highly personal signatures. But both men began from a blues foundation and pioneered piano sounds from it. So, too, did blues themes line the sad-sweet lyrics of R&B bounces. The early rural blues told of lovemaking, but Roy Brown's lusty lyrics of going behind the barn for good rockin' with his babe *shook* with the imagery.

Rhythm-and-blues instrumentation began to change. Horns and pianos of the jazz tradition moved in a new direction, away from the tight ensemble sound of jazz into throbbing beats built off honking saxophones with a gospel-derived pattern of vocal responses. The five years culminating in 1952 were in fact a prelude to rock-and-roll. From 1947 to 1950 the DeLuxe label under Jules and David Braun set the course for record production. Roy Brown was their most profitable artist, but their first winner was a suave balladeer named Paul Gayten.

Gayten was born on January 29, 1920, in Kentwood, a sawmill town seventy-five miles

Above: Shirley and Lee, Sweethearts of the
Blues. *Left:* Sugar Boy and the Sugar
Lumps, 1960

north of New Orleans. His mother's brother, Eurreal "Little Brother" Montgomery, was a bluesman who migrated to Chicago. In his early twenties, Gayten moved to New Orleans from Jackson, Mississippi, where he had played piano with an orchestra led by Don Dunbar.

"Paul was a tremendous personality," said Vernon Winslow, "with an ego to match. He sensed the [R&B] change. He was the flower of the talent, but he didn't make himself of this popular R&B beat. He had tremendous arrangements, reminded me a little of Oscar Peterson. He could sit there with just a piano and a bass . . . and he didn't need too much bass."

Gayten was a fixture at the Robin Hood, a hotel-club in the heart of black central city, not far from the Dew Drop on LaSalle. Winslow adds: "Paul Gayten had what you might call this 'Black Champagne' music. Gayten was smooth; cufflinks and cuffs, blue suits. He had a pudgy, pleasant smile, a kind of dominating person on the piano."[21]

Gayten worked with a young singer named Annie Laurie and cut "True," a cool ballad reminiscent of Nat King Cole, for the DeLuxe label in 1947. Annie Laurie's "Since I Fell for You," cut at the same session, sold well and made the charts, too.

With Roy Brown under contract to DeLuxe, the Braun brothers were doing well. Then in 1950, through an arrangement with King Records, DeLuxe was sold, and Brown went with the deal. Paul Gayten and Annie Laurie found themselves on the new Regal label with young balladeer Larry Darnell. New efforts focused on Gayten's production skills; Darnell delivered "For You My Love," which hit number two in the R&B charts in 1951. Gayten and Annie Laurie performed together for a time, then parted ways. Gayten soon led his own combo at the Brass Rail and became the local artist-and-repertoire director for Chess Records. Laurie moved to New York where she continued her career.

Roy Brown, Smiley Lewis, Paul Gayten, Annie Laurie, and Larry Darnell were mature musicians whose shifting interpretations of popular music were well suited for the young men and women of the postwar years. The market was now increasingly dictated by radio deejays like Vernon Winslow, whose promotional strategies were meant to expand the commercial boundaries as quickly as they were charted. Despite Roy Brown's success, New Orleans R&B remained a predominately black music, with young dancers and high school teenagers as a ready-made audience.

All that changed in 1952 when two students from Joseph Clark High School cut "I'm Gone." It hit the number two sales slot in the R&B charts almost overnight. Shirley Goodman and Leonard Lee, who had grown up together in the Seventh Ward, became a pivotal force in the transition from rhythm-and-blues to rock-and-roll. "I'm Gone" featured Shirley's high, childlike voice, offset by Leonard Lee's deep vocal shadings. The record label promoted them as "Sweethearts of the Blues."

"Traveling was great for me," Shirley Goodman recalled years later. "But it was hard work because we had to do one-nighters. We'd sometimes do thirty one-nighters with maybe a day off. My mother traveled with me because I was under age. It was sometimes hard."[22] For the next several years, Shirley and Lee crisscrossed the country, playing theaters like the Regal in Chicago, the Howard in Washington, and soon barnstorming the rock-and-roll shows of Dick Clark and Irving Felt.

After the success of "I'm Gone," Shirley and Lee followed with a series of recordings that chronicled teenage romance. Songs like "Lee's Dream," "Shirley, Come Back to Me," "The Proposal," and "Shirley, Marry Me" were all designed to keep record buyers and young pop fans involved in the ongoing love story. In real life, they weren't sweethearts at all, just good friends.

In 1955, Shirley and Lee cut "Feel So Good," and the next year broke into the white rock-and-roll market with "Let the Good Times Roll." (The title, borrowed from a 1946 tune by the ever influential Louis Jordan, was also a popular theme in the colorful Cajun parishes of southern Louisiana; "Bon Ton Roula" was recorded by Clarence Garlow.)

But the song was never intended to be a serious offering. Leonard Lee explained it this way: "Well—we needed a 'B' side for a song, and it just so happened we were playing a dance somewhere in Louisiana. Everybody was having such a good time that the tune just came to mind, and we just sat down and wrote the words. . . . It just flowed in."[23] While many of the later rock-and-roll hits were overtly sexual, nothing was more innocent than the lyrics as sung by the Sweethearts:

Come on baby, let the good times roll,
　Come on baby, let me thrill your soul,
Come on baby, let the good times roll,
　Roll all night long.

Over the years, the song became synonymous with the duo, and in the last two decades it has become an American pop standard, recorded by Jerry Lee Lewis and even Barbra Streisand. The title was adopted as the theme for the rock-and-roll revival picture of 1973 by the same name.

The tunes after "Good Times" never matched its success, but Shirley and Lee kept performing. When Eddie Mesner of Aladdin records died in 1959, the young performers were without a label to promote them. Other firms tried to duplicate the early success to no avail. By 1962 their careers as a performing pair had ended.

Leonard Lee returned to college and Shirley Goodman moved to California where she raised a son and worked as a background vocalist in Los Angeles, singing on dozens of recordings with Sonny and Cher, Dr. John, Jackie DeShannon, and with the Rolling Stones on the LP *Exile on Main Street*. In 1974, she responded to a call from Sylvia Robinson—of the rock-and-roll duet Mickey and Sylvia—and flew East to record the hit single "Shame, Shame, Shame," a disco novelty song that charted in America and Europe.

Shirley and Lee held a brief professional reunion for a rock-and-roll revival concert at Madison Square Garden in 1972 that did not go well. Otherwise, they fell out of touch, save for occasional long-distance phone calls. Leonard became a social worker in New Orleans, where he died unexpectedly in 1976.

A fatherly smile breaks on Vernon Winslow's face when Shirley and Lee are mentioned.

They were wonderful kids. Even after they hit their peak, they would come to the studio and we would rap, a very wonderful experience. I didn't know at the time he was a preacher's son, but he would tell me that this was an experiment for him and that excited him tremendously.

If you look at Roy Brown and you look at Shirley and Lee, Roy was our first gut expression of those things that we fantasized, a good-looking chick who winks at you and takes you behind a barn and can talk to you and who could send you home on Saturday night a different way. That's Roy Brown. Shirley and Lee came along as the high schools' interpretation of what this movement meant to them; they took off largely because of the younger crowd entering the R&B cycle. It was a nice, clean bouncy duet.

At that time there was a group called the Cha-Paka-Shaweez that was doing instrumentally what Shirley and Lee were doing vocally. They were a group of high school instrumentalists, with a modulation of reeds and horns against a duet. These guys were really musicians.[24]

The Cha-Paka-Shaweez were not only charting new instrumental territory; the band was fronted by attractive singer/pianist James "Sugarboy" Crawford. Born on October 12, 1934, Crawford was raised uptown on LaSalle Street near the Dew Drop Inn. Some of his earliest musical exposure came while sneaking in the back door to witness the piano talents of Paul Gayten.

The Cha-Paka-Shaweez formed in 1951 at Booker T. Washington High School and through their appearances on the Dr. Daddy-O show a local following developed. Winslow gave them the name, which was the title of their theme song. The band recorded "No One to Love Me" in 1952 for Aladdin records. Crawford's next recording was "I Don't Know What I'll Do" on the Checker label. "We made that record in the radio station WMRY," he recalled. "We used to rehearse after-hours at the station. When I did that record, Leonard Chess gave me a five-dollar bill. That was five dollars for the whole band!"[25] The song was released under the name "Sugarboy and the Cane Cutters." Crawford had been nicknamed "Sugarboy" since childhood; Chess added the "Cane Cutters." Two more Checker releases followed: "Jockomo" and "I Bowed on My Knees." "Jockomo" was inspired by the Mardi Gras Indians and was covered in 1965 by the Dixie Cups as "Iko Iko," reaching a respectable twenty on the charts. "Jockomo" was the largest seller for Crawford and the Cane Cutters. Befitting his nickname, Sugarboy had a polished vocal style and is best known for ballads like "Morning Star," recorded for Imperial, and "Danny Boy" for Montel records, both done in the late fifties.

One Tuesday morning in 1963 the band pulled into Monroe, Louisiana, with two cars full of musicians and equipment. Smiley Lewis was along. Crawford recalled: "It was during the time when they were having these 'freedom riders,' and the police stopped me and said I was speeding and drunk. It was about eleven in the morning and I wasn't doing either. Then they hit me in my head and I was paralyzed."[26] Thrown in jail, Crawford was later hospitalized with brain damage. "I lost my coordination and I couldn't play and sing the way I used to." The paralysis lasted a year; Crawford performed sporadically until 1969, when he retired from music. Today he is a building engineer, who sings spirituals as an avocation.

Through the critical "swing years" of 1947 through 1952, as the artists emerged and receded, Vernon Winslow kept a steady hand on the local pulse. Then a curious thing happened. Just as rhythm-and-blues had come into its own, with the rock-and-roll movement visibly building, Winslow began to have a change of heart. The pulsing rhythms and often-racy lyrics that once amused him had now taken root. Whites as well as blacks were responding, in Winslow's words, "to this music we were calling R&B." But as Smiley Lewis, Shirley and Lee, Roy Brown, and others increased their messages of blues and love and rock-and-roll Dr. Daddy-O grew restive. He had a radio name marketable on its own, and when he shifted his programming to gospel music, although many people were surprised, it conformed to a thematic vision on Winslow's part. Long removed from R&B, Winslow today views his persona as a gospel messenger with ironic detachment: "Lawyers and doctors smile with half-uncertain approval. I look in the mirror and think I'm looking at my person. I've had neighbors who say, 'You're the one on the radio who plays church music. You're such a nice person.' I talk to the Tulane students, in history of religion, and I'm in a world that floats with approval all around, with gay-colored balloons and handshakes. I'm trying to treat gospel as an emotional language. It's a reinforcement of purpose in my life and it becomes a return each time I hear it. I always try to back away and see the big picture, the camp meetings and little chapels that contributed to the beginnings."[27]

Chapter Seven

HUEY "PIANO" SMITH AND GUITAR SLIM

The rise of rhythm-and-blues marked a shift in the cultural patterns of New Orleans. In the 1890s, when the seeds of jazz began to sprout, the outlying areas and inner pockets of the city were swamps or open fields. Along the New Basin Canal, which cut through muddy Back O' Town to the Dryades dock, communities were black and very poor, while in the older downtown villages, Creoles of color who read music invested jazz with an instrumental sophistication to match the blues pulse and emergent powers of the brass bands. By the 1950s, however, the canal had become an interstate and the music emanating from those once-swampy enclaves—lower Ninth Ward, central city—reflected a new identity, a distinct urban character.

There was a religious dimension to this self-image in the soaring choral passages, sturdy chords, and rocking drums of gospel music. And in many R&B horn charts, the saxophones honked like preachers. But the new R&B idiom drew heavily on secular rhythms of the blues piano, too. Lines of the country blues filtered through R&B, but the new idiom had a full, warm flavor that articulated life in the streets, in the clubs and bars, in the cultural passageways of people who lived in growing cities. The strength of rhythm-and-blues stemmed from its closeness to the daily lives of black people. In this respect, the sound was a linear extension of communal ceremonies of West Africa, of work songs in southern fields and certainly of the music in churches. Like jazz, R&B came out of working-class neighborhoods of the city. Oral traditions fueled the imagination; the singer became an organic instrument of his community and of its endurance. LeRoi Jones writes:

Blues was a music that arose from the needs of a group, although it was assumed that each man had his *own* blues, and that he would sing them. . . . But classic blues took on a certain degree of professionalism. It was no longer strictly the group singing to ease their labors or the casual expression of personal deliberations on the world. It became a music that could be used to entertain others formally. The artisan, the professional blues singer, appeared; blues-singing no longer had to be merely a passionately felt avocation, it would now become a way of making a living. An external and sophisticated idea of performance had come to the blues, moving it past the casualness of the "folk" to the conditional emotional response of "the public."[1]

By the mid-twentieth century, urban performers developed new needs to maintain performing standards. One of them was physical space where music could be rehearsed. Dryades Street, an old commercial strip, borders the central city wards of New Orleans, and in the fifties it filled daily with people looking for all kinds of things—groceries, funeral arrangements, meeting halls, furniture, Mardi Gras costumes, spirit oils, quick meals or a highball when the day was done.

Doc Wonder's Curio Shop was a hub on Dryades where musicians flocked. Doc's real name was Victor Augustine and he claimed to know talent scouts. More important, he had a back room. Earl King recalled his first visit as a young vocalist. There was "the smell of incense burning, the sound of a piano wailing out some mean boogies. The door was open so we walked in and gasped for breath from the strong vapors of incense. We noticed voodoo dolls hanging on the walls and mojo hands in jars. He introduced us to the pianist. His name was Huey Smith."[2]

Huey "Piano" Smith is one of the legendary figures of early rock-and-roll. His great hits of the 1950s—"Rockin' Pneumonia and the Boogie Woogie Flu" and "Don't You Just Know It"— were homespun tunes and widely popular at teenage dances. Huey was a first-class piano player; as a composer, his vision was delightfully simple. From childhood he had taken jive phrases, children's street poems, and jump-rope rhythms to create lyrics. The songs were light and fun, filled with innocent exuberance.

Huey remembers: "The dances always come from the children. When we was kids, they had a theater around the corner that had a talent show every week, and me and my friend got two songs together and went on. We called ourselves Slick and Doc. Slick was Slick because he had straight hair. We did a song we put together on the street called 'Robertson Street Boogie.' We lived on Robertson Street and the kids around the neighborhood used to sing:

Get hip everybody to a street that's all reet.
  It's not Canal, but it's Robertson Street.
It's the Robertson Boogie, Robertson Boogie, Robertson Boogie,
  Boogie Woogie all day long.

The kisditacality will drive you mad.
  With "Hey Little Daddy, now ain't I bad"
It's the Robertson Boogie, Robertson Boogie, Robertson Boogie,
  Boogie Woogie all day long.

"We had a little boy in the neighborhood and we used to kid him 'cause he always tried to use big words that he would make up like 'kisditacality.' It didn't have no meaning, but we put it in the song with another street sayin', 'Hey Little Daddy, now ain't I bad.'"[3]

But Huey Smith's roots also lay deep in gospel and blues. Born on January 26, 1934, he played as a youngster on the piano in his mother's house. Professor Longhair's fusion of rhumba and boogie-woogie and Smiley Lewis's full, rich blues vocals were strong influences in Huey's adolescence. Just fourteen, he formed a group called the Honeyjumpers. Ray Charles, who visited New Orleans often between 1950 and 1953, also influenced Huey Smith.

But stylistic influences were not like accompanists—musicians with whom Smith could actually play, explore rhythmic expressions, and converse in the language of a distinct musical sound. He was searching for his own sound, something to set him apart from other young pianists around town. He found an able partner in Eddie Jones, known as Guitar Slim, a gospel-styled bluesman from Mississippi. Starting in 1950, Huey Smith and Guitar Slim played often in Doc Augustine's back room, trading licks with other musicians who happened by, while in the showroom up front people shopped for records, herbs, and voodoo dolls. The early musical dialogue of these men was an exchange of different traditions, New Orleans's sophisticated piano rhythms keying off the rawer blues of Mississippi's rural river counties.

Guitar Slim was born Eddie Lee Jones in Greenwood, Mississippi, on December 10, 1926. He never knew his father and his mother died when he was five, at which time he was sent to live on the L. C. Hayes plantation near Hollandale, Mississippi, with his maternal grandmother, Molly Edwards. In his 1954 recording "The Story of My Life," he sings:

If my mother hadn't died,
  And my father left his child at home,
Maybe my life wouldn't have seen so miserable, baby,
  I wouldn't have been so alone.

Jones started out chopping cotton. When he was fourteen, his stepgrandmother made him plow behind mules, and he hated it. But nights were different; he found escape in Bluefront, the strip of black clubs and cafes across the railroad tracks from Hollandale proper. He gravitated to a place called the Harlem Club and there began to dance. One night he met a girl named Virginia Dumas; eight months later, in 1944, they married. Eddie was eighteen and Virginia was sixteen; of the four years they were together, he was in the service about half of the time.

Today Virginia Dumas lives in the Delta port of Greenville, and she remembers her early years with Eddie Lee Jones. Their home was a two-room wooden house on the plantation grounds, with heat from a fireplace and light from coal-oil lamps.

He would be at home sometimes, and he would get that comb and just get a piece of newspaper and tear it, put it across that comb, and me and him would start to dancing. If he wouldn't dance with me, I would just catch ahold of the doorknob and swing out with it! He was the best dancer there was in Hollandale. There wasn't but one girl who could dance with him, and her name was Lucille. He could pick her up and throw her across his lap and squat down and never stop movin'. We called him "Limber-legged Eddie." When he walked in the club, everybody would fall up against the wall and start callin' for Eddie Boy.[4]

She remembers him singing with some of the bands appearing at the Harlem Club and says that if he could hear a song once, he was able to sing it. He experimented with the tissue paper and comb and the drums. "There was a piano on the bandstand in the Harlem Club," she explains, "and Eddie would go there and play it. He played boogie-woogie and all that kind of stuff. He would listen to songs on the Seabird and then get on the piano and play them." (Seeburg is the trademark of a national jukebox chain. Delta blacks gave the name an idiomatic twist—Seabird!)

Then Jones became interested in the guitar. Robert Nighthawk, a blues singer and guitarist from West Helena, Arkansas, was an early influence. Whenever Nighthawk came to the Harlem Club, Jones would play around on his guitar at intermission. He also traveled to nearby country honky-tonks with Johnny Long, another bluesman who picked the guitar. In May 1944, after three and a half months of marriage, Eddie left for army basic training at Fort Benning, Georgia. In the beginning, he came home on furloughs but eventually was sent to the Pacific as World War II was winding down. Little else is known about that period of his life. He returned to Hollandale in 1946 and took a job at a cotton compress. But the army had given hints of a brighter world beyond the drudgery of plantation labor. He stayed with Virginia for a year and a half, then left town. The next time she saw him was in 1952, four years later, when he played the Harlem Club as Guitar Slim and Band. By that time, he was established in New Orleans.

A seminal figure in early rhythm-and-blues, Guitar Slim is a man whose back pages have been a mystery to solve. We know of no recorded interview with him. In 1948 the twenty-two-year-old left Hollandale; 1950 was his first appearance in New Orleans. What happened in the two years between? A 1977 interview by blues enthusiast Martin Gross with Willie Warren, a Delta bluesman living in Detroit, fills in several critical spaces. Willie Warren was playing in a roadhouse in Lake Village, Arkansas, across the Mississippi River from Greenville. Warren remembers Eddie Jones as a plantation worker who didn't play an instrument. He appeared in the roadhouse one night and started dancing with a woman. Gross writes: "The whole place cleared the dance area and formed a circle around Jones and his partner and watched them dance to Willie's music. Apparently Jones was a great dancer because the people went nuts and started begging for more and tossing money. Willie said Jones was agile, and would do splits, fall down on the floor and bounce up in one movement, drop down and all kinds of stuff."[5]

Willie Warren drove home after the gig, but he couldn't get the dancing man out of his thoughts. He got back in his truck and drove sixty miles in search of the plantation where the man was supposed to live. He found the place after the sun had risen and asked some children where he could locate the exciting dancer; he didn't know his name. The kids led him to a small shack. Willie Warren doesn't remember whether these were Jones's people; he found Jones sleeping on the back of a tractor out in the field. Warren woke

him and asked if Jones wanted to join the band he and his brother had in Lake Village, Arkansas. Jones left with Willie Warren on the spot.

Jones began as a dancer with Warren's group, but he had a good voice and yearned to sing. He got his chance at a club one night when Warren gave him the okay, and the crowd went wild. Given what we know of his early performances in the Harlem Club, he must have been a magnetic performer, gyrating and dancing as he sang. Warren recognized his talent and began showing him tricks on the guitar, how to play one chord by placing his fingers on each string and strumming. Jones practiced on the single chord, playing it over and over, singing to it, demanding that his talent come forth. Warren showed him other chords and Eddie Lee Jones's love affair with the guitar began.

Jones and Warren were partners for about two years; then Eddie announced he was going to make records and would call himself Guitar Slim. Warren didn't take him seriously at first—how many Delta bluesmen actually got to cut records?—but a sad twist of fate intervened. Willie Warren came down with pneumonia. He got so weak Jones had to take him to his family's home in Lake Village where a long convalescence began. Despite a young man's excitement about his own emerging talent, it must have been a sad parting when Eddie Lee Jones, now Guitar Slim, left the Delta.

Jones arrived in New Orleans in 1950 and started scraping, playing wherever he could. An elderly blues pianist, Cousin Joe, recalls: "I knew Guitar Slim when he was playing for wine on Conti and Burgundy at a place called Savoy. . . . Nobody knew about this boy. He was sitting in a booth, and he had his guitar with him—a straight guitar, not electric."[6]

Jones met Huey Smith at a grocery store in central city. They quickly struck up a friendship. "He had a habit of not completing all twelve bars in a song," Huey said, "or playing too many, but I could jump along with him. If he finished too

Huey Smith, junior high school
graduation

Huey "Piano" Smith, 1979

The earliest known photograph of Guitar Slim,
circa 1950

quick or too late, I would finish with him and he enjoyed that. So he told me we could get together and do this and do that and go places."[7]

It was rough going in a new town, especially one as competitive as New Orleans, but Guitar Slim kept hunting for gigs and playing his guitar long hours on his own. In the Ninth Ward he sometimes sat on a little bridge leading to McCarty school. He wore a black suit, a wide white hat, white shoes, and played his guitar for the kids coming home from school.

Gerri Hall, who teamed with Huey Smith as a singer, remembers her first exposure to Guitar Slim. "When I lived down in the Ninth Ward, I used to go to this little store. Six o'clock in the morning—he done been out all night—and he'd be playing that guitar with the amplifier so loud. Just sittin' on his step. The people in the Ninth Ward wasn't used to that, and they all be wondering, 'What the hell, who the hell is that?'"[8]

As he moved into nightclub performances, the larger expression of his musical persona came forth. A country singer from Mississippi after all needed more than just a good voice and a guitar to compete with established performers. His formal debut at the Dew Drop was on August 26, 1950, when he shared a three-night bill with an exotic dancer, a female impersonator, and a house band headed by saxman Lee Allen. He did well enough to rate an engagement the following weekend, which was announced in the black newspaper *Louisiana Weekly:*

Guitar Slim, New Orleans' newest gift to the show world who opened for the first time two weeks ago on LaSalle Street has been held over at Painia's blues department for the Dew Drop. . . . Acclaimed as an exact copy of Gatemouth Brown, the singing guitarist includes "My Time Is Expensive," "Gatemouth's Boogie" and several other recordings written by Brown, who recently played at Painia's. The New Orleans blues sensation has made a terrific musical impact on blues fans in New Orleans.[9]

Not a completely flattering assessment, the review does brush a few strokes onto the portrait of Guitar Slim starting out. Clarence "Gatemouth" Brown was a marvelous entertainer. A native of Vinton, Louisiana, he heard Cajun music as a child and established his career in Houston. A wizard on guitar, Brown was equally adept in country-style swing as in the deeper nuances of blues. Besides Gatemouth, bluesmen T-Bone Walker and B. B. King influenced Slim. But the influence of Gatemouth Brown undoubtedly helped Eddie Lee Jones mold the entertainment personality of Guitar Slim.

And what presence! His dress was given to lime-green pants and red coats, his hair dyed any number of colors. The intimacy of audience connections he had learned in the Delta was magnified under New Orleans lights. He was packing in crowds on the black nightclub circuit—the Dew Drop, Club Tiajuana, Hotel Foster, San Jacinto, Caffin Theatre, the Moonlight Inn—and with the aid of booking agent Percy Stovall, one of the grand old men of New Orleans music, he made road tours to other southern cities.

"So we got to travelin'," recalled Stovall, now deceased, "and we had another little boy with us. His name was Eddie Langlois, we called him Little Eddie. [Slim was Big Eddie.] He and Slim worked together in the band. They had fifty feet of wire on their guitar, each had that. So they would walk on top of the bar, walk on tables. Then business started comin'—like pourin' water from a pitcher. Everybody wanted to book that band, see that little boy and that man walkin' tables, walkin' the bars."[10]

Earl King remembers: "I saw him one night and he had done burst his head on a pillar in the place. He had on a white suit and you would think he would stop playing, with blood runnin' down his head. He keeps on playin' outside the door, and he's bleedin' to death. Nothin' would stop him."[11]

By late fall of 1951, Guitar Slim was supporting

himself as a musician. As a headliner at the Dew Drop, he found a friend in a little known blind pianist named Ray Charles. Al Young offered Slim a recording shot with Imperial Records and supervised a session at Matassa's J&M Studio, but the discs sold poorly. Guitar Slim kept pushing. He found his break in the back room of Doc Wonder's Curio Shop, where a short, stocky, fast-talking white man from Mississippi introduced himself as a record producer. He was known as Johnny Vincent and he became a pivotal figure in the careers of Huey "Piano" Smith and Guitar Slim.

The producers of early rhythm-and-blues, in the South at least, were a curious lot. Like Cosimo Matassa, they were interested in the emergent technology of records, the commercial prospects of getting discs in jukeboxes and then on the airwaves. It was a consuming process; you had to record the music in a studio, have the master pressed into discs, distribute them like a salesman, and finally, if you had the right contacts, the song might air on radio. In the late 1940s, R&B was still "race" music and white southern disc jockeys were not always receptive to discs by black artists.

John Vincent Imbragulio is one of the extravagantly colorful producers of early rhythm-and-blues. From 1955 to 1963, his Ace label was a major outlet for the "New Orleans sound." Vincent's exposure to records began in his hometown of Laurel, Mississippi, in the late 1930s. "I used to help a jukebox operator change records and count his money. I came out of the service in '45, I bought me ten jukeboxes, ten Rockolas."[12] When records "changed," they didn't just die in a box. Vincent began recycling discs, selling used ones to blacks who cared little if the grooves had worn down a bit under needles in a Seeburg. These were seventy-eight records, which today are collector's items. Vincent remembers:

In Mississippi in those days, a lot of people wouldn't let you put a R&B record on their jukeboxes, but when the kids would hear the records, they did want them, and they especially went for Roy Milton's "RM Blues" and Goree Carter's "Rock Awhile." And the spirituals were back then, too; there was Sister Rosetta Tharpe and then Marie Knight came up with beat gospel records. We could sell 50 to 100,000 of those old gospel records in those days."[13]

Vincent worked as a retail record distributor, opened a record shop in Laurel, then moved to Jackson and opened a shop on Farish Street, the black thoroughfare with a blues culture akin to that of Rampart Street. Vincent earned the biggest sales from the blues, couldn't keep enough of them stocked in his shop. He decided to produce his own discs and eliminate the middleman.

He started the Champion label and recorded several bluesmen from Jackson. He was making a go of it in 1952, when Art Rupe came calling. Rupe was a Los Angeles producer with the Specialty label. He had seen Lew Chudd's success with Fats Domino and realized there was a black market to be tapped in the South. Rupe bought the Champion label from Vincent, and hired him to work in the South as a Specialty talent scout, selling records and recording new ones.

At Rupe's suggestion, Johnny dropped his last name and became known as Johnny Vincent; Rupe reasoned that *Imbragulio* was too difficult for most people to pronounce. As Vincent told writer Jeff Hannusch:

I used to listen to records constantly, night and day. Ask Art Rupe. He said, "Man, I ain't never seen anybody work as hard as you!" I used to go to the record shops and play every record that was a hit. I'd buy it and take it to my house or my room at night and play it over and over, for as long as fifteen hours! I wanted to find out what sold it, what made it a hit! Hell, a record is like a sandwich; you can't just put lettuce and tomatoes on it. God gave it the flavor, but you had to put the mayonnaise on it to bring it out! I found Frankie Lee Sims, Mercy Baby, Earl King, Huey Smith, a group called Henry Smith and the Five Notes, and Guitar Slim.[14]

Guitar Slim had cut "Feelin' Sad" for a small label in Nashville. Vincent liked what he heard; he booked a recording session at J&M on October 27, 1953. On piano Vincent wanted Ray Charles, then living at the Dew Drop, but Charles was in jail for a minor offense. Vincent posted a hundred dollar bond to get him out. The session began at five in the afternoon and lasted until seven the next morning. They cut four sides; the best was a tune called "The Things I Used to Do." Slim later told friends the song was given to him by the Devil one night in a dream. Whether truth or fiction, the song was inspired by something. It is a pure emotional experience with a memorable first line, "The *thinggggsss* that I used to do, Lord, I won't do no more!" Sung in a crying gospel style, the disc featured slow, melodic horn riffs and a piercing guitar break by Slim. Some who remember the session say the song was played thirty times before it was recorded correctly; others say some eighty takes were necessary. Slim had trouble keeping time with the band, often missing notes. By any standard, it was an epic session. At the end of the song, Ray Charles can be heard shouting, "Hey!"—jubilation because they had finally got it right.

Vincent air-shipped the tape to Art Rupe in Los Angeles, who listened to it and called back disturbed. Vincent recalls Rupe saying, "I don't want to hurt your feelings cause you're doing such a good job out in the field, but that's the worse piece of shit I ever heard. None of these records will ever sell. I hate to put it out, but I'll put it out just for your sake."[15]

Undaunted, Vincent took to the road to peddle the song. He went to Memphis and as far north as Cleveland, where an influential disc jockey named Alan Freed gave the song substantial airplay. "The Things I Used to Do" went on to sell a million copies. Rupe then realized the blues market reached well beyond the South.

It wasn't a typical blues that Guitar Slim and band had set to wax. There were blues lyrics and the sounds of the genre, but the additional horns and Charles's piano gave a gospel pulse to the song. And this was the kind of music Vincent wanted—tunes that hit black folks where they lived. By now Johnny Vincent was very busy. He knew a great many New Orleans musicians, had proved himself with Specialty, made the rounds of clubs and bars, and thus decided to start his own recording company, Ace. It is unclear whether he quit or was fired by Rupe; in any event, their parting was hardly a no-fault divorce. Vincent had apparently begun setting up his own operation while in Rupe's employ, and he raided the talent stable he'd developed for Specialty, convincing Earl King and Huey Smith to record on Ace.

Johnny Vincent was not a saint, but he was intent on developing New Orleans talent. And he always had an eye on his own hip pocket. Still, Vincent was a complicated figure; skillful at motivating musicians in record sessions, a hustling salesman, yet a businessman cursed by disorganization.

Ace emerged over a period of several years as a label strong in New Orleans talent; Huey Smith began working under Vincent's auspices. One of the earliest sessions was in a small studio in Jackson with Smith playing piano while Earl King played guitar and sang "Those Lonely, Lonely Nights." The record moved slowly at first, but eventually sold eighty thousand copies. When Huey saw the final record, he was shocked. The label read: "Featuring Fats on Piano." Vincent later conceded that this "gimmick" was something a small record company had to do, reasoning that "we couldn't wine and dine the disc jockeys the way the big boys [labels] did."[16]

One of the first recordings Huey Smith did on his own was a bouncy little number called "We Like Mambo." He was coming into his own as a pianist, playing boogie-woogie with a distinct

Bobby Marchan

New Orleans flair; he signed each melody with a rocking keyboard style. But Smith was not an exceptional vocalist; Gerri Hall sang the lyrics. Vincent used the song as the flip-side of a feature by a bright young pianist-composer named Eddie Bo—Edwin Bocage, a nephew of the great jazzman Peter Bocage. Bo, too, was a singer—and a good one. But Bo and Vincent had parted ways by the time Smith recorded "We Like Mambo." Huey's song became the better half of the disc and pushed its sales. But Huey Smith's name was not printed on the record, and when he asked Vincent why, the producer offered the lame excuse "a mistake at the printers."

Scores of "mistakes" plagued R&B artists in the formative years in New Orleans. Contracts were offered and eager musicians often signed away copyrights unknowingly. The cultural gap between shrewd record producers and musicians who knew music but little business often ended in bitterness. Unless an artist was represented by a good lawyer or financial advisor with the musician's best interests at heart, his talent was something like a chip thrown into a poker game where producers held the aces. Unfortunately, there were few concerned lawyers or advisors in those days.

Vincent was a wheeler-dealer, but in some ways better than others. There was a depth to the man, and a measure of concern for musicians. However unfair his early treatment of Smith, Vincent nevertheless helped mold his talent, and the records he produced in the late fifties earned royalties for Huey Smith. But the two men bickered, often over money.

The rise of Huey "Piano" Smith began in 1957 with "Rockin' Pneumonia and the Boogie Woogie Flu," which reached fifty-two on the *Billboard* R&B charts. Huey was featured prominently on the label—no mistake at the printers this time—and was backed by a group called the Clowns. The song, today a dance classic, opens with Huey's right-handed ripple and the frolicking lyrics:

I wanna jump, but I'm afraid I'll fall.
  I wanna holler, but the joint's too small.
Jump and rhythms got a hold of me, too.
  I got the rockin' pneumonia and the boogie woogie flu.

It was Huey's song all the way, but recognizing his own vocal limitations, he used a young singer named James Black (not to be confused with the drummer of the same name). Within a short time Smith found a vocalist with greater range and a galvanizing stage presence: Bobby Marchan. A deep friendship grew quickly between the two men, and around Huey there formed a rollicking association of attendant singers whose vocal energies he fused into the magic of his happy, rocking sound. They were known as Huey "Piano" Smith and the Clowns and no group was better named. Smith says, "I had seen a movie about a court jester with the funny hats for the king. In my mind I thought, 'The Jesters was a good name for the group,' but I decided to call 'em the Clowns."[17]

Marchan recalls: "We hit the road and had a ball, made plenty of money, ate good food, and had a stomp-down party good time. I remember in New Orleans on the big 'Roy Hamilton Show' I wanted to do something different so I told Huey, 'Let's come out in some Bermuda shorts suits.' So we took tuxedos and cut off the pants and we came out in the Municipal Auditorium and tore the house down."[18]

A parade of musicians moved through the ranks of the Clowns. An early vocalist, "Scarface" John Williams, was also a Mardi Gras Indian. But the nucleus of the Clowns came down to Smith, Marchan, Gerri Hall, and Roosevelt Wright. Bobby Marchan was the most electric personality. Long after the group's dissolution, he was still one of the city's better vocalists and a brilliant comedian.

Gerri Hall

Earl King and Johnny Vincent, 1982

A gay who often performs in drag, Marchan has a falsetto reach, a radiant smile, and bright eyes. His stage presence is something to behold—he winks to the crowd, with hands on hips and shifting shoulders, peppering the audience with a string of one-liners: "I see you comin' in late, Big Boy, now inch up front and sit down here with the big tippers." Marchan's wide, clean vocal range and bubbling histrionics fit perfectly into the simple, often nonsensical lyrics by Huey. Bobby served to keep the madness in focus.

Gerri Hall, with dark hair and deep Indian features, high cheekbones, and pale brown skin, was an attractive girl who sang well and joined the stage antics with a relish. She later cut the single "I'm the One" for Vincent and teamed with Huey to sing his novelty tune "Little Chickee Wah-Wah." Gerri Hall's vocals blended smoothly with the Clowns' harmonizing, and visually a female Clown embellished the party atmosphere Marchan and Smith strived to create.

Roosevelt Wright was something of a straight man, if such a term can be applied to the Clowns. Tall and broad-shouldered, he sang bass in an apparently bottomless voice, booming out catch phrases in call-and-response fashion, a solid antipode to Bobby's weaving falsetto.

The Clowns was not a static group at all. Various combinations of the Clowns formed and drifted away, making it difficult to pinpoint who was where and when. The recording atmosphere, like their performances, was loose. Huey reflects: "Each individual was at liberty to decide what he would do to act foolish and that's what tickled people so much. We had the songs down so each one would break out and go to clownin'. That's what it was all about." The sessions for Ace were explorations into a sound, and Vincent encouraged them with his production style.[19] A sideman at the time, Mac Rebennack (Dr. John) analyzes it this way: "Johnny had a real gift of gab. . . . He pronounced everything so funny that he overused his country Jackson accent and had everybody falling about laughing."[20]

The group's biggest hit was "Don't You Just Know It," which reached number nine in the *Billboard* charts in March 1958. The song was conceived on the road between Baltimore and Washington. The band's chauffeur, Rudy Ray Moore, would respond with "Don't you just know it, child," to everything said in the car. "I'm gonna make a record out of it," Huey announced. The group started working out lyrics in the car and cut the song when they returned to New Orleans. Gerri Hall says, "I knew it was a hit when we put it together in that car. We all knew it. And, boy, when Johnny Vincent heard *that*, he said, 'Let 'um do what they wanna do!' "[21]

With the antics of the Clowns to propel the fun, Huey Smith's songs were pure merriment. Bobby Marchan states: "He wrote simple stuff and it caught on. After all, you have to be very silly to say you got rockin' pneumonia and boogie-woogie flu. Nobody wants rockin' pneumonia and boogie-woogie flu, but it caught on like wildfire and everybody came down with it. Then he came up with another 'sick' song called 'High Blood Pressure' and I been had high blood pressure ever since, still got it today."[22]

By the late 1950s, Huey Smith was doing extensive recording work as one of the city's most valuable session pianists. He continued composing, but road trips had lost their appeal. "I was tired of rippin' and runnin'," Smith recalls.[23] The irony of Huey's relationship to the Clowns is that he was the quietest of them all. He was the creative force behind the music, but his persona was a flicker compared to the theatrics of his mates, who loved the lights and reveled in their own gaudy antics.

He turned the Clowns over to Bobby Marchan, who had organized the early tours. Marchan handled the money and functioned as the group's manager, so the move was a natural one. He explains: "We went out so much without Huey Smith, they thought I was Huey Smith. . . . I was doin' all the lead singing and we would take little James Booker, who could sound exactly like Huey Smith, so [audiences] didn't know the difference."[24]

Meanwhile, Johnny Vincent was producing scores of records for Ace and developing the rock-and-roll sound with rhythm-and-blues artists around town. But things were changing for Guitar Slim. In 1954 "The Things I Used to Do" brought him national recognition; Milt Shaw, a New York booking agent with a stable of black talent, flew to New Orleans in late January to sign contracts. Shaw had done well with Fats Domino and viewed Guitar Slim as promising. Slim's band, led by Lloyd Lambert, drew good crowds in Texas and California, then swung east for an appearance in late April at New York's famed Apollo Theatre.

Since the 1940s, Jack Shiffman's Apollo had attained legendary status among black entertainers. A week's engagement at the Apollo meant a musician had arrived. Lloyd Lambert recalls: "We drew more people at the Apollo Theatre than Sammy Davis, Jr., and the Will Masten Trio at that time. That's how hot that record was."[25]

After the Apollo, Slim played in Washington at the Howard Theatre, again to sellout audiences. By summertime, Guitar Slim was a steady player on the Shaw circuit, but the press of performances in one-night stands was not helping his music. Songs like "Late for You, Baby," "Sufferin' Mind," and "I Got Sumpin' for You" were blues songs at heart. They didn't sell well enough to keep Specialty interested. "It was a low period for the band," recalls saxman Clarence Ford. "The band had changed, and he had went to five pieces [from seven]. We were playing mostly smaller clubs. The band was working so little till I just decided to stay home."[26] Something had to give. In early 1956 Hosea Hill, a nightclub owner from Thibodaux, Louisiana, became Guitar Slim's manager. Hill persuaded Slim to move to

Thibodaux in Cajun country, where the rural pace was more relaxed.

In March 1956 Slim signed a new recording contract with Atco Records, a subsidiary of Atlantic. Over the next few years more than a dozen tracks were recorded, but few matched the early Specialty cuts in fiery guitar solos. In an attempt to broaden his audience, Atco's producers softened Guitar Slim's sound, giving his recordings more arrangement and less spontaneity. Songs like "Hello, How Ya Been, Goodbye" and "If I Had My Life to Live Over Again" imitated Fats Domino.

Guitar Slim had been a drinker since his earliest days in the city, and by 1958 he had begun to have difficulty breathing. In January 1959 the band began a road tour from Jacksonville, Florida, to Buffalo, New York. Guitar Slim made it as far as Rochester and then became sick. He went to a local doctor who told him to stop drinking. The next day the group arrived in New York City and checked into the Cecil Hotel on 118th Street. He was so weak that members of the band had to carry him from the lobby to his room. "We were on the elevator," recalls drummer Harry Nance, "and we thought he was still drunk. And one guy from Thibodaux was holding him by one arm, and I had him by the other arm. All of a sudden it felt like we was holdin' up six tons." Attempts to revive him were fruitless. "So we took him to a Doctor Shapiro—I think that was his name—and this doctor gave him a shot in his chest, but no results. So then they declared him dead."[27]

It was February 7, 1959. Eddie Lee Jones was thirty-two.

New Orleans was in the middle of Mardi Gras season. Small notices appeared in the daily press and *Louisiana Weekly.* New York's *Billboard* magazine printed a small tribute, but the industry in general was preoccupied with the deaths on February 3 of rock-and-rollers Buddy Holly, Big Bopper, and Richie Valens in an Iowa plane crash.

Virginia Dumas recalls: "I was livin' in

Greenville and Eddie's cousin come and told me Eddie was dead in New York. The funeral home man had him and all his equipment, so I called him. He said send $250 and I could get him back. But I couldn't get the money 'cause I wasn't in no shape. . . . I finally got it together and called back to New York and the man said, 'I'm sorry. Eddie Lee Jones is ridin' now.' "

The body was returned by train to Thibodaux, Guitar Slim's last home. His manager, Hosea Hill, covered the expenses.

Chapter Eight

HAIL, HAIL, ROCK-AND-ROLL

There are periods in a nation's history when cultural patterns suddenly go haywire. Attitudes, hit with tidal force, swirl together as if caught in the rising suction of a tornado, shredding customs in the maelstrom, jolting society long after heavy winds have winnowed down and the center of gravity is restored. Such was the impact of rock-and-roll on middlebrow America in the 1950s, a decade of contradictions. Willie Morris called it "a quiescent time . . . [with a] softening of disaffection on most campuses."[1] The civil rights movement began in 1955, but the larger campus conflicts, the rivers of revolt over civil rights and the Vietnam War, merged with greater force in the sixties. So too have the fifties been deemed innocent, a time when the shadow of atomic destruction was itself overshadowed by tangible energies of rock-and-roll unleashed. The revolutionary literature by Beat writers like Allen Ginsberg and Jack Kerouac urged changes in society, but the deeper course of shifting mores in the popular culture issued from those pools where rhythm-and-blues music became popular. Culturally, the most revolutionary change of the fifties was the embrace of traditionally black music by youngsters from the white middle class.

Not much was radical about the black musicians, though. The world view of New Orleans artists in the 1950s stemmed from shared experiences, a common musical heritage. As R&B emerged in other pockets of America, New Orleans artists were extending a cultural language passed down from an earlier generation. Langdon Winner writes that the city "has given us the oldest, richest, and most influential continuing tradition of rock-and-roll playing the music has ever seen."[2]

Rhythm-and-blues was the foundation of rock-and-roll. As Fats Domino and Roy Brown became popular, the behavior of young whites began to change. One writer observes that "listening to R&B itself conferred deviant status, at least in some communities." One such community—the relatively isolated middle-class suburb of La Canada, California—"developed an entire deviant life-style around rhythm-and-blues, drinking in the high school parking lot and dressing in low-slung jeans and motorcycle jackets in the manner of James Dean and Marlon Brando. . . . When someone threw a party, the rowdies were not invited, since parents would not approve; but word was always leaked to them, so that they would crash the party, bring their records, and liven things up."[3]

Nearly a decade would pass before northern whites journeyed South to march for civil rights. After the 1954 Supreme Court desegregation decision, the White Citizens Council disseminated pamphlets warning Delta parents that black music was a danger to their children. Yet in Mississippi and New Orleans, white women entered stores to buy such "evil" records, allegedly for black maids and housekeepers—who sometimes taught white youngsters black dance steps. As rhythm-and-blues spread through the cities, complex response mechanisms figured into the lives of some white adolescents. One of them, Duke Dugas, today hosts an oldies show on WWOZ, the New Orleans community radio station. "The Duke of Padooka" is one of the most colorful, unabashedly parochial voices in American radio. His early exposure to R&B is a case study of the "deviant culture" of the fifties. Born in 1936, Dugas as a child fell in love with "nigger music."

So invariably I would sit at night, and I'd hide in my bedroom with a little crystal radio with the antenna going to a screen, and I'd listen to the music on the radio, and it really instilled me. It wasn't really "rock-n-roll," it was blues, really. Things really started changing, I would say, in '51. It started picking up a little bit more in '52. Willie Mae Thornton made "Hound Dog," Lloyd Price made "Lawdy, Miss Clawdy," and then Fats Domino made his phenomenal "Goin' to the River." These three songs in themselves mark a transition period in my life when it came to notoriety for artists. White radio started playing black music. So we could turn to two or three places on the radio dial and hear what we used to have to hide to hear. I'm gonna tell ya just like it was. From 1951, my freshman and sophomore year in high school, I was tabbed as a "nigger lover" in some circles. But by '52 it was becoming acceptable; rhythm-and-blues was catching on. By the time I had gone into the service in '55, it was a wide-open ball game. Everybody had a radio on at the park listening to "nigger music" which I had been listening to for quite some time . . . Fats Domino, Ray Charles, Bobby Mitchell.[4]

An alluring element of early rhythm-and-blues was the youthfulness of its artists. For example, Bobby Mitchell, born on August 16, 1935, was one of seventeen children in a poor family. He wanted to be a football player at Landry High, but his music teacher persuaded him to try out for talent shows. A tape was recorded and given to Vernon Winslow, who at the time was programming the "Dr. Daddy-O Show" from WMRY. By 1953 eighteen-year-old Bobby Mitchell was recording for Imperial. "On our contract we had 2½ percent royalty," Mitchell recalls. "That worked out to a penny a record."[5]

Mitchell, along with his group the Toppers, was the first to record doo-wop music in New Orleans. Between 1953 and 1963, he recorded some twenty singles for Imperial and made road tours with Chuck Berry, Ray Charles, and Big Joe Turner. Several of his early numbers were seminally important: "Try Rock n' Roll," "You Always Hurt the One You Love," and "I'm Gonna Be a Wheel Some Day." The latter songs were recorded by Frogman Henry and Fats Domino, respectively, who turned them into hits. But artistry and business occupied very different realms, as Mitchell learned. "You see, we were young guys who didn't really know the music business. We went into recording blindfolded. So many things were stolen from us. If I wrote a tune and they changed one word, they could put someone else's name on it. They used to do it to people who didn't know the business."

Bobby Mitchell's entertainment career leveled off in the mid-sixties. The same fate befell other early rhythm-and-blues performers, but Mitchell prepared for a second career by studying electronics and radio engineering. Today he is a medical lab assistant in New Orleans and entertains on weekends, keeping the old hits alive. He reflects on the early days of rhythm-and-blues: "The idea was to learn what the public wanted, see how they danced and what they listened to."

The popularity of jazz had long been a force of moderation between the races in New Orleans; black bands performing for white social functions was a tradition. Vernon Winslow's Jax beer ads and Dr. Daddy-O shows moved beyond tradition, however, by sending black slang into the white market. New Orleans had always been a melting pot of languages, its residents combining dialects and idioms of various cultures to produce that distinctive "N'Awlins" accent, somewhat akin to Brooklynese. When two guys meet on a street, the greeting is "Where y'at, podna?" Women leave for the store to "make groceries." Girls, boys, men, women are variously called "dawlin'."

Perhaps the "y'at" accent is an historical accident. One theory holds that the speech inflection was imported by northern immigrant laborers. Others say New York nuns teaching in parochial schools had influence. But for years, the city's biracial housing pattern meant whites grew up playing with blacks, or in close enough proximity to hear how they spoke and to pick up or transfer inflections. The subtle interplay melded into a homespun dialect with many softly sinking *r*'s and lost *g*'s. The most legendary example of the y'at accent came when Mayor Robert Maestri entertained Franklin Roosevelt over lunch at Antoine's. The mayor said, "How ya like dem ersters?" The dish was oysters Rockefeller. FDR's response is not known.

And so, in the midst of the segregationist 1950s, along came R&B. Fats Domino charmed people not only by his music but by the *sound* of his

words, the dialect heard with varying degrees of inflection and bad-or-better enunciation throughout town, from crusty white enclaves of the Irish Channel to diminutive taverns of Gert Town. Fats had a down-home accent and, like Satchmo, people of both races loved his music because it spoke straight to them.

By the time Lloyd Price came along, the ears of white teenagers were tuned to the "new" music. Price's "Lawdy, Miss Clawdy," produced by Dave Bartholomew for Specialty, hit the R&B charts in 1952 and was named record of the year in *Billboard* and *Cashbox*. Lloyd Price found himself named the best new singer of 1952. The immense success of that sound, that song, widened the trail for others to follow. The evolution of early rock-and-roll made a quantum leap.

Lloyd Price was born on March 9, 1933, into a family of ten children. His mother played piano, his father the guitar. He sang in the church choir, which provided a sturdy base on which to build his clear, resonant vocal style. With his records selling well, Price toured extensively in 1952 and 1953. Then he was drafted. The army put his career on ice for four years, but a more mature Lloyd Price was discharged. He settled in Washington, D.C., where he formed a record company and later wrote "Just Because," a song that put him back in the lights. ABC Records issued the tune and began grooming Lloyd Price for the pop market of 1957. His voice easily appealed to white teens. "Personality" and "I'm Gonna Get Married" were perfect adolescent fare—and some distance from the more thumping, blues-based roots of the New Orleans tradition. If a girl had the "Walk, Talk, and Style," then she had "Personality," a high school code word that meant she was not just cute, but fun to be with. When that personality finally got to the boy, there was no way to live without the girl. "I'm Gonna Get Married" was the logical fifties conclusion. Parents might try to reason by saying, "Johnny, You're Too

Young," but a defiant "my name she'll carry" was Johnny's heartfelt reply.

Lloyd Price, like Roy Brown, made the transition from R&B to rock-and-roll, but with a distinct style obviously geared to white youths. Price continued to record through the early sixties; however, the hits came less frequently. He then turned his energies to producing, helping launch the career of Wilson Pickett. He eventually retired from music and ventured into different enterprises. Although removed from New Orleans for most of his career, Lloyd Price still must be considered *of* the city and a primary figure in the rise of rhythm-and-blues.

As producers came to New Orleans, more songs made the national charts. The city was building a distinct "sound." The crowning achievement came in the second week of February 1954 when four of *Billboard* magazine's top ten records were produced at Cosimo Matassa's studio. Number one was Guitar Slim's preaching blues "The Things I Used to Do." In fifth place was "Honey Hush," a sturdy jump blues by the Kansas City shouter Big Joe Turner. "Something's Wrong," a plaintive ballad by Fats Domino held at number nine, and at ten was a new vocal group, the Spiders, with strong gospel shadings, "I Didn't Want to Do It."

The Spiders, originally a gospel quintet called the Delta Southernnaires, were led by the Carbo brothers, Chick and Chuck. Organized in the late forties, the group gained popularity in churches and at social functions. Through a chance encounter with Phyllis Boone, Cosimo Matassa's secretary, they were offered an audition. "We were under the impression we'd go audition for gospel songs," Chuck Carbo remembered. "We tried the gospel songs, but they wanted what they called 'rhythm-and-blues.'"[6] Weeks later they returned with a new dance number, "I Didn't Want to Do It." It caught the ear of Dave Bartholomew, who produced their first session.

With "You're the One" as the other side, the record became a surprising best seller. The songs featured the Carbo brothers singing in cool vocal tones, delightfully soothing to the ear. While sales figures were brisk, some radio stations found the lyrics a bit suggestive.

Fine little mama comes knockin',
  Knockin' on my front door,
Hip-shakin' mama was a rockin',
  Rockin' and a-reelin' so.

But I didn't wanna do it, no, no,
  I tried not to do it, no, no.
I didn't wanna do it,
  But she sends me so.

The Spiders continued through the mid-fifties with a string of hits: "Am I the One," "Bells in My Heart," and "Witchcraft." When internal conflicts caused the group to disband, Chic and Chuck pursued solo recording careers; however, neither was able to match the artistic quality of the Spiders.

The most outrageous example of R&B unleashed came in late 1955 in a song called "Tutti Frutti" by one of the wildest figures ever to appear in pop music: Little Richard. More than any previous tune, "Tutti Frutti" bridged R&B with rock-and-roll. Like nobody before him (and precious few who followed), Little Richard came to New Orleans a one-man sideshow of energy and dazzle.

Little Richard's background, like his later life, is a study in struggle and painful divergence from the norms of his own community. Twice in his career he abandoned rock-and-roll for gospel music and preaching. In the 1980s he was traveling the country, giving dramatic testimonies to born-again believers, confessing in graphic detail to drug addictions and the "sin of homosexuality" that possessed his earlier life.

Little Richard is a curious figure on the fundamentalist circuit. Unlike the slick preachers who use television to make money and advise on matters from real estate to politics, Little Richard is a brilliant comedian for whom the seeming constraints of ministry hardly restrict self-deprecating tales. At times, they seem a parody of his former self. As with his rock-and-roll music of the fifties, Little Richard pushes the boundaries of preaching about as far as they can go. In a sermon delivered to a New Orleans congregation in May 1981, he speaks of his past:

I went from marijuana to angel dust. How many of you heard of angel dust? The angels had nothin' to do with it! Your body is the temple of God. God is the holy God. His angels are *holy.* His word is *holy.* His people are *holy.* God said any man shall defile this body, him shall God destroy, for the temple of God is holy. . . .

I went from angel dust—I was payin' thousands of dollars a month for dope—to cocaine. I took so much cocaine so they shoulda just changed my name from Little Richard—to Little Coke! I used to fill my album covers so all my friends would come by because they knew I was gonna have somethin' good there. They would come by and get high! I have an album cover that's *packed* with cocaine, *thousands* of dollars a month. I took so much cocaine, to when I would blow my nose, all you would see on my handkerchief would be flesh and blood, where the cocaine was just eatin' out my membranes. *Isn't that pitiful?* Not realizin' that your body is a temple of God? *Not realizin'* that God's power is available? *Not realizin'* that His mercy has been extended? Not realizin' that He can change you, and that He's ready, watchin', willing and able.[7]

A dispassionate analysis might view Richard as one who speaks the Word with tongue in cheek, a satire of the old Little Richard performed in gospel histrionics. But the *angst* of certain reminiscences punctuated by cries of *"Isn't that pitiful?"* inject caution in one's analysis. Born Richard Penniman on December 5, 1935, in Macon, Georgia, he was one of a dozen children; two uncles and a grandfather were preachers. "I came from a family where my people didn't like rhythm-and-blues,"

he is quoted. "Bing Crosby, 'Pennies from Heaven,' Ella Fitzgerald was all I heard. And I knew there was something louder than that . . . and I found it was *me.*"[8]

Life at home was difficult. "When I was a lil boy, a man led me into homosexuality. I was a real boy. It is contagious. Somebody can teach you how to do that. By beholding, we become *changed*! . . . I met this guy, they useta call him Madame Oop. He useta work on the railroads. I would go over to the man's house and he would give me three dollars. You know money can do a lotta things."[9]

By adolescence he was showing signs of the flamboyant gay who would burn fifties' concerts and sixties' television appearances. But the boy's dress and bizarre antics offended his father—what a child Little Richard must have been!—so he left Macon with a snake oil salesman and sang Louis Jordan's thumper "Caldonia" to draw crowds, soon finding club work as a vocalist.

In his biography Richard credits an exotic New Orleans pianist called Esquerita as an early influence. Richard was nineteen when they met in Macon. "I used to sit around the all-night restaurant at the Greyhound bus station in Macon, watching people come in and trying to catch something—you know, have sex."[10]

Esquerita arrived in town, playing piano behind a preacher named Sister Rosa, "whose line was selling blessed bread." Richard recalls: "She said it was blessed, but it was nothing but regular old bread you buy at the store. . . . So Esquerita and me went up to my house and he got on the piano and he played 'One Mint Julep,' way up in the treble. It sounded so pretty. The bass was fantastic. He had the biggest hands of anybody I'd ever seen. . . . It sounded great. I said, 'Hey, how do you do that?' And he says, 'I'll teach you.' And that's when I really started playing. I thought Esquerita was really crazy about me, you know. . . . I learned a whole lot about phrasing from him.''

Richard was an outrageous character but he came from a state with a deep and lasting gospel tradition intermingled with the blues. Gospel composer Thomas A. Dorsey was called "Georgia Tom" as a young bluesman. Ray Charles, born five years before Richard in Albany, Georgia, began on gospel piano. When Richard was a child, the gospel tradition was moving closer to black popular music; his musical origins were in the church, but by the 1940s other influences were at work. The chief forerunner of rhythm-and-blues was Louis Jordan, whose sax play and infectious singing won a large following, particularly in New Orleans. Jordan prefigured the intersecting lines of racial popularity in postwar R&B. As he told Arnold Shaw in a memorable interview: "I worked with Chick Webb and Ella Fitzgerald, and I played jazz. And then I switched over. I didn't think I could handle a big band. But with my little band, I did everything they did with a big band. I made the blues jump."[11]

A great deal of switching over and blues jumping took place when Little Richard went to Atlanta in 1951 for an audition taping at a radio station. He won a contract with RCA and cut eight sides over the next two years, a series of combo-styled jump blues. Then New Orleans beckoned. "Lloyd Price came to my hometown with Patsy Valdalia," he told the church audience. "[Price] had a black and gold Cadillac and I wanted one. So I came here and made 'Tutti Frutti' and 'Long Tall Sally' and I was known all over the world instantly."[12]

Well, not quite. While still in Macon, he met New Orleans saxophone player Lee Diamond, who became Richard's bandleader. They worked together for about two years, mainly in rural Georgia. Bobby Marchan recalls their early trips to the city. "The Club Tiajuana was the first place Little Richard played in New Orleans, with a group called the Tempo Toppers. They played the Tiajuana nightly. Richard had his face made up

and all his long hair done up and everything. He acted very sissified on the piano. He wasn't singing rock-and-roll at this time. He was doing slow ballads."[13]

Richard went to Houston in 1954 and cut discs for the Peacock label owned by Don Robey, proprietor of the Bronze Peacock Club. But the Houston cuts failed to generate good sales. Richard's personality did not mesh well with Robey's. "He jumped on me," Richard recalled, "knocked me down, and kicked me in the stomach. It gave me a hernia that was painful for years. I had to have an operation."[14] During Richard's peregrinations across the South in search of the "big record," Lee Diamond went off to work with James Brown, then launching his career as a soul singer. Down on his luck, Richard cut an R&B demo tape and sent it to Art Rupe in Los Angeles. At first, no word came from Specialty. Richard went back to Macon, where, he has said, for eight months he washed dishes in the Greyhound station.

In time, Bumps Blackwell, a black producer, heard the audition tape, liked Richard's gospel-tinges, and told Rupe it was worth a try. The Specialty date was set for late November 1955; Little Richard wanted Lee Diamond to lead the session with his band. But by this time, a tight cadre of artists had become established as *the* sidemen for New Orleans recordings, and Bumps Blackwell pragmatically turned to them. Dave Bartholomew's mainstays were largely responsible for the emergent "New Orleans sound": Earl Palmer, Frank Fields, Justin Adams, Alvin "Red" Tyler, and Lee Allen.

New Orleans music is built from the bottom up: drums first, bass second, then guitar and horns. Since the dawn of jazz, New Orleans has produced a distinguished line of drummers, and with the rise of R&B, Earl Palmer came to the forefront. His heavy backbeats, pounding footwork, and crisp snare lines laced hundreds of recordings. Palmer was born in New Orleans on October 25,

Above: Alvin "Red" Tyler and Lee Allen, 1982.
Left: Richard "Little Richard" Penniman, 1954

1924. His mother worked in vaudeville. "I was practically born in the wings," Palmer recalls. "One of the backstage babies. I started tap dancing when I was four years old."[15] He played in parades as a youngster and after World War II enrolled in Grunewald School of Music under the GI Bill. One of his first professional jobs was with Dave Bartholomew, who gives this estimation: "He was just like a clock. Earl Palmer *was* a clock. If you set a tempo, you never had to worry because Earl was gonna hold it."[16] As his reputation grew, Palmer began freelancing his own recording dates—the drummer most in demand for local sessions. Besides Domino and Little Richard, Palmer left his percussive signature on tunes cut by Shirley and Lee, Lloyd Price, the Spiders, and many more. In later years, after settling in Los Angeles as a highly paid studio musician, Palmer achieved a high status among rock musicians.

The bass player on "Tutti Frutti" and many Bartholomew sessions was Frank Fields, who was born in Plaquemine, Louisiana, on May 2, 1914. Fields began playing guitar, banjo, and ukulele, learning the basics from his half brother Joseph Butler, a saxophonist who graduated from a music conservatory in California. He joined the service out of high school and played in the Algiers navy band. "Ninety percent of the band was from New Orleans," Fields recalls, "and we played a *lot* of jazz. I was playin' tuba, guitar, bass violin as well as bass. You had to play more than one instrument in the navy band."[17] After the war Fields joined Bartholomew's band, patterned after Louis Jordan's Tympany Five. When Bartholomew disbanded the group in 1949 to become a scout-producer for Imperial in New Orleans, Fields moved with him into studio work. He played bass on nearly all the Domino and Smiley Lewis recordings and was also a mainstay on Huey Smith sessions.

The guitar player was Justin Adams, born into a well-known musical family. He was playing at the Million Dollar Room with his mother, Dolly, and his brothers when Bartholomew approached him. "Man, can you play rhythm-and-blues?" Justin said, "I can play anything."

Dave Bartholomew made his mark as a producer by employing reedmen who were stellar jazz artists. Alvin "Red" Tyler was born in New Orleans on December 5, 1925, grew up in the Ninth Ward, and was drawn to the big band sound early on. Jazz to R&B was a smooth transition. Drafted during World War II, Tyler played in the navy band in suburban Algiers with Frank Fields. Once out of the service, Tyler joined Bartholomew's dance band and continued with him into recording sessions. He earned $41.50 for a session that could last anywhere from three hours to six or seven, with no overtime pay. "We did the arrangements right in the studio," Tyler recalled. Those "head sessions" were a direct outgrowth of the city's long improvisational jazz tradition. Of the Little Richard dates, Tyler remembers: "A unique aspect was that they had me playing baritone more as a rhythm instrument with Lee Allen on tenor. None of the arrangements were written; he would just sing it, and we would make the rest of it up. We were going so fast by the end of the fifth take, we knew we had to stop and that was it."[18]

The irony of Red Tyler's stature is that he is most remembered outside the city for the early R&B sessions; his enduring reputation locally is that of a jazzman. His deepest love was always jazz and through the 1950s, besides the session work with Little Richard, Domino, Bartholomew, Huey Smith, and others, Red Tyler did steady work in improvisational jazz. By the seventies Tyler was an articulate voice of the modern idiom.

Lee Allen on tenor sax was the only sideman not originally from Louisiana. He was born in Pittsburg, Kansas, in 1927 and was raised in Denver. Drawn to recordings of Coleman Hawkins and Dexter Gordon, Allen played like them as best he could in a high school combo. With a music and athletic scholarship to Xavier University, Allen moved to New Orleans in 1944. He eventually gave up sports and left school before graduation to work with Paul Gayten, and joined Bartholomew in 1948. "Lee Allen gave the songs soul," Bartholomew reflected. "In other words, when you gave Lee a solo, he was gonna sell that record!"[19] On recordings, Lee Allen's sax solos are easily identifiable; a big horn sound with the solos woven closely around song melodies, almost effortlessly on the beat. Singer Frankie Ford recalls: "He played those solos right off the top of his head. Some players get paid extra just for a solo. But Lee would play his part, then step back and riff with the rest of the horns."[20] By 1981, living in Los Angeles, Lee Allen had become a successful studio artist. He performed with the Rolling Stones on their 1981 tour and, more recently, as a featured member of the Blasters.

And so they were five—Palmer on drums, Fields on bass, Adams on guitar, Tyler and Allen on saxophones. Through the early fifties, the "clique," as they were known, dominated sessions at Cosimo Matassa's studio. When Little Richard entered the studio on September 14, 1955, it was just another job for the sidemen.

Little Richard had come from gospel to work as a balladeer; the R&B cuts that day were not distinguished ones. As the session drew to a close, Richard was singing a ditty during the breaks, repeating the scat phrase "Whooo tutti fruttiii"— elasticizing the last vowel with great flourish. Producer Bumps Blackwell had heard the chant all day long and thought it might be worth recording, but not in such a raw state: Richard was singing "Tutti Frutti, good booty / If it don't fit, don't force it / You can grease it, make it easy."

Dorothy La Bostrie, a poetic young Creole, was in the studio that day and at Blackwell's urging the lyricist went off to a corner of Cosimo's studio, cleaned up the words, and with time running out, the musicians went in for a final cut.[21] Little

Richard's voice exploded the now-famous opening scat: "WOP BOP ALOO BOP ALOP BAM BOOM!" Beneath Little Richard's bursting voice and unvarnished keyboard came Palmer's driving drums and the rising temperature on the saxophones, an overall sound that was extravagantly *unleashed*. The lyric was equal to the music: "I've got a gal named Daisy / She almost drives me crazy / Whooo—" It was the same *Whooo* that the Beatles would incorporate into their early hits.

Two months later the song was at the top of national charts, and the manic, wildly comedic quality fit perfectly into the grooves of the times. It was a bad-ass song, sexually suggestive, but a funny one, the singer's persona rising off the disc and overpowering the message of the lyrics, which didn't make much sense anyway. But it was a superb song to jump to, to dance to. The career of Little Richard had begun.

The hits fell into line swiftly. "Long Tall Sally," "Slipping and Sliding," "Rip It Up," and more. Richard had his own touring band now, led by Lee Diamond, his sidekick from the early Macon days. "He never tried to hide his gayness," Diamond said in 1981, adding that Richard neither drank nor indulged in drugs in the early stages of his career. "He would tell people on the microphone, 'I am what I am and I love what I am.' The funny part about it was he would try to convince the people that his whole band was gay and that would knock us out with the girls. He'd get on the microphone and say, 'No need in lookin' at them, darlin', cause they're just like me.' It was funny. He would pull some fantastic things. Every place we would play, the gay people would come."[22]

Little Richard was riding the crest of his popularity in 1957 when Diamond and the band accompanied him on a concert tour to Australia. As the plane crossed the Pacific, Little Richard found God. Diamond recalls:

We had just passed the point of no return, out of the Fiji Islands, and that night around ten o'clock we are over the ocean and you could see the moon shining over the water, and the guitarist looked out and saw the engine was on fire. He said, "What the hell is going on here!" And I looked out and said, "Oh, my God!" And here the stewardess is supposed to be calming people and you could hear her voice just trembling, saying, "Don't be alarmed. We may have to make an emergency landing and, if we do, the plane stays up on the water ample time, which is three minutes, to get your life jackets. We have already radioed the Coast Guard!"

She was shaking, man, and dishes were falling all over the place. And everybody is looking, thinking, *this is it*. I know the world is over and I can just see the papers saying, "Little Richard and the Band Crashes in Ocean." I can see my mother crying and everything. Some kind of way they extinguished that motor and we made it in on the three other ones.

Now this is when Richard comes up with the big idea that he has seen some angel holding the plane up, and God had told him to come out of show business.

During the perilous flight, a spiritual sensation gripped Little Richard. High in the sky nearing Australia, the burning engine evoked a frightening vision; he saw images of the Apocalypse and his own damnation. The plane touched down at the Melbourne airport, but Richard's behavior had changed radically by the time of the concert. Diamond continues:

Richard is telling us that God has told him to preach. And everybody is telling him that God has given him this talent. "You don't think He gave it to you to quit? You're making people happy." Richard said that he wished the band would come along with him out of show business. The tenor player, Clifford Burke, said, "Yes, but you're going to God with your pockets full, but what we gonna do? We're going to Him with nothing. We got to work."

Richard didn't budge. So Clifford called his bluff. You know, he used to wear all those rings like Sammy Davis, Jr., diamonds all over everywhere? He said he was gonna get rid of all his diamonds and things. He didn't want any of this material, and all of this bit. He said this in front of everybody on the show, and we are in the bus and going across this bridge. So Clifford said, "Okay, you say you're gonna quit. Why don't you throw your rings away now?" So now everybody is looking, and he's gotten everybody's attention. I don't think he had intended to do this. But he said, "Clifford, you don't believe me? I'll show you they don't mean anything to me." He took off all his rings, and he had some nice diamonds, and threw them in the water.[23]

True to his word, Little Richard, at the zenith of career in 1957, abruptly quit performing. Lee Diamond took the band to Los Angeles for an engagement just after the Australian tour. When he announced Little Richard would not appear, angry fans heaved bottles onto the stage. Fortunately, no one was hurt, and Diamond, who went on to cut records of his own, managed to salvage the performance. Little Richard was serious about his conversion. He went to Huntsville, Alabama, and enrolled in Oakwood College, a Bible school, where he pursued scriptual studies. He began preaching and singing in churches. Specialty at first sought to dispel the rumor that Richard had abandoned rock-and-roll for Jesus, but to no avail. By the mid-sixties, Richard had a change of heart, and after sporadic gospel recordings, hit the rock-and-roll trail again. Rock critics generally agree the old fire was gone, but there was still quite a flame glowing. He appeared on television shows, sang in drag, and made one dazzling, uproarious appearance on "The Dick Cavett Show." By the late 1970s, Little Richard had returned to the ministry again. His denunciations of rock-and-roll and homosexuality were perfect fare for the burgeoning fundamentalist circuit. By 1981 he was touring extensively, testifying, confessing, soul-searching, and then some.

Little Richard exploded into popularity in 1956, the same year as Elvis Presley. More than any other rockers of the seminal period, these two divided the idiom between them. Outlandish performers, they were sheer spectacles on stage, tailor-made for the hot new medium of television—the first exponents of the exotic histrionics that now form a staple of rock music marketing. He appeared on NBC's "Tomorrow," and when Tom Snyder asked if he thought rock-and-roll was the work of the Devil, Richard answered: "I believe that rock-and-roll is the work of another master, not Jesus Christ. Now, it was a steppin' stone for me to be famous, and God spared my life and had mercy on me. But God didn't tell me to write 'Tutti Frutti, oh-rootee.' I didn't even know any Tutti. He didn't tell me to write 'Long Tall Sally.' The Sally I knew was short. . . . But after the fame and fortune, after I 'wakened out of the dream, God said, 'Richard, let's come to reality.' "

Thus spoke Little Richard on NBC, July 29, in the year of Our Lord 1981.

Chapter Nine

DEEJAYS AND TEEN IDOLS

Rock-and-roll began as a teenage phenomenon. And the shaping of those tender hearts, the innocent minds of the postwar baby boom, was in large measure at the hands of disc jockeys. They did more than play records; they pushed the personas of their favorite performers and read advertising copy for local businesses that sniffed profit over the airwaves. At night, they released eclectic chatter to kids at home and sent sizzling messages to lovebirds in steamy cars. The deejays were brokers in the new market of rock-and-roll. Long before most adults took the music seriously, producers and distributors recognized the economic power that these men had and competitively courted them, for it was the tunes the deejays pushed that became hits.

If a single trait was shared by most early disc jockeys, it was a true affinity for black music. If a second trait was common, it was the medicine man's first rule of the road: walk in, set up, and wing it. What a collection they were. The names alone suggest the growing crossrhythms of white and black musical tastes. By the end of the 1940s, black radio voices like Dr. Daddy-O were established in urban areas. Sugar Daddy was in Birmingham, Professor Bop in Shreveport, Jockey Jack Gibson in Atlanta, the Mayor of Harlem Willie Bryant, and elsewhere in Manhattan, Tommy Small, who kicked off his WWRL show with, "Sit back and relax and enjoy the wax, from three-o-five to five-three-o, it's the Dr. Jive Show!"[1]

White deejays began drawing from slang-studded rhythms of black speech and from lyrics of the songs, casting new slogans into the white popular consciousness. The granddaddy of rock-and-roll deejays was Alan Freed, who began the "Moon Dog House Rock-'n-Roll Party" from a Cleveland station in 1952. Freed, generally credited with coining the term *rock-and-roll,* soon expanded his interests into concert promotion. At one concert, twenty-five thousand youngsters turned out at a hall built for ten thousand. Freed, wearing a loud checkered coat, introduced acts like a carnival barker, pumping the audience with chants of "Go, man, go!" By 1955 Freed had moved to New York and station WINS, making a profit pushing the mid-fifties musical revolution.

The sight of euphorically unleashed adolescents sent shivers up the spines of many parents entering middle age, many of the fathers war veterans. Was *this* what they had fought for? But the cutting edge of the rock-and-roll revolution was racial. If early rhythm-and-blues fans nestling with their radios projected a "deviant status," the roar of Little Richard, the good-time sound of Fats Domino, the general force of black entertainers at big dances shattered the color barrier even more. The *New York Times* of March 20, 1956, carried the following story:

A segregation leader charged today that the National Association for the Advancement of Colored People had "infiltrated" the Southern white teenagers with "rock and roll music."

Asa Carter, executive secretary of the North Alabama White Citizens Council, said the group was starting a survey in the Birmingham and Anniston areas and would ask jukebox operators to throw out "immoral" records in the new rhythm.

Coin distributors said this could mean eliminating most of their hits. Mr. Carter said other records featuring Negro performers also should be "purged."

Two months later we find Fats Domino fomenting rebellion. Again, from the *Times:*

November 4, 1956
Gas Ends Rock & Roll Riot
[Fayetteville, N.C.] Several persons were injured when the police fired tear gas to break up a rock & roll riot here last night. They fired tear gas grenades into ventilation ducts at the dance hall where the Fats Domino band was playing. Mr. Domino said the fight was caused by "the beat and the booze." He and three band members received minor cuts. George L. Ahumade and Roy E. Williams, both of Fort Bragg, were stabbed.

The final entry in our *New York Times* ledger is from February 23, 1957, a front-page headline: "Rock'n'Roll Teen-Agers Tie up the Times Square Area." A news article of forty-four paragraphs, it is rich, descriptive journalism: feet pounding, a glass door shattered, and Alan Freed saying, "These are not bad kids, they are just enthusiastic." But nowhere does the article mention the name of a single musician. By 1969, the Woodstock performers had become protagonists in a mass media music drama. As for the fifties, what was all the ruckus about?

Deejays played on emotional chords of young fans. The image of white teens dancing to "infiltrated" music scattered mental demons in the minds of white reactionaries. Deejays and black artists had become agents of an idiom reflecting the intersection of white and black cultural tastes. In its embryonic stage, rock-and-roll was fundamentally dance music, a modified version of rhythm-and-blues that went back to the blues itself. The heightened fifties' rhythms built on energies similar to those of the down-home Saturday night functions at which blacks let loose. In *Stomping the Blues,* Albert Murray treats this as ritual.

What is at issue is the primordial cultural conditioning of the people for whom the music was created in the first place. They are dance-beat-oriented people. They refine all movement in the direction of dance beat elegance. Their work movements become dance movements and so do their play movements; and so, indeed, do all the movements they use every day, including the way they walk, stand, turn, wave, shake hands, reach or make any gesture at all.[2]

The foundation of rock-and-roll was communal dance and movement, rooted in the culture of Afro-Americans. Few young whites realized the transfer of habit and custom as it occurred; the music, tapping psychic energy, simply demanded movement. But the rhythm-and-bluesman had advanced from the role of black musical protagonist to a biracial one.

In 1955, with rock-and-roll booming, Jim Russell arrived in New Orleans. Now Russell is no ordinary source. A lean, balding man with a penchant for asking questions so he can answer them, Russell recycles old records in a warehouse-size stereo shop on lower Magazine Street. "You wanna know who started rock-and-roll in New Orleans?" he asks. "All right now. You ever been to a graveyard with lights?"[3]

In Canton, Ohio, Russell was fired from his first job as a deejay for locking himself in the control room of a country-western station and spinning race records. Then he met Alan Freed, whom he followed to New York before staking out his own new territory.

I'll tell you what a graveyard with lights is like. Seven o'clock at night, October 6, 1955. I walked six or seven blocks down Canal Street. There wasn't twenty people. . . . And there was not any *noise,* man. I didn't hear no music no place. Only place there was music was in the French Quarter—which, where I came from, was a quarter of a dollar. It didn't take me fifteen minutes to get outa there, 'cause all I heard was jazz. That wasn't my bag. But what I did observe, real fast, to make me come down here and stay—*no rock and roll!*

Russell made the rounds of radio stations, got to know the deejays, and began organizing record hops for eighteen radio personalities he represented. With no hint of understatement, Russell says: "I did eighteen record hops Friday night, eighteen Saturday night, and eighteen Sunday night. For ten years. Fifty-four different record hops each weekend. I'd find a place for it, get people to okay it, and set up equipment at each place."

Russell engineered promotional stunts to push the men who were pushing the records.

What we did for Bill Novak was to have him kidnapped one weekend. Jim Dunbar we put up on a telephone pole and wouldn't let him come down til the sales reached over a certain amount, and we'd feed him with a bucket goin' up. Bob Robbin, one of the most influential men in public relations and publicity for record companies, we had him throw money out the window at WTIX, brought him down in a straightjacket and taken away, as a gimmick.

In every radio station I had a basket with my name on it, and I went around five days a week and collected records from every distributor. Do you know how many distributors there were when I walked into this town? There was RCA, there was no Mercury, there was Columbia who shared a little office—Columbia, now—with Interstate Electric who had a block long of electric parts and all hangin' up and also in the corner in a little room about 9' × 12' was Henry Hildebrand [who later founded All-South, the city's largest independent distributor] as a clerk, takin' orders for these records. That's all!

And all these companies wanted their records played, but there was only so much time on each station to play 'em. So where do you think all of the records would finally come? When they were in the baskets of the disc jockeys, all the records went into my basket. I sorted them out and I said, "Play *that* one . . . *Forget* this one . . . *Lay* on *this* one . . . *Kill* that one! Break that one up . . . Play this one every fifteen minutes! And so on, *for ten years.*

Russell points to a stall in the rear of his store, filled with vintage discs. "That's how Ernie K-Doe, Irma Thomas, Bennie Spellman, Huey Smith, all these cats, Eddie Bo, Lee Dorsey, that whole stable is full of 'em all—everyone would go to record hops and sing over the record that was made. Lip-sync. Ten years with no bands. That's what took place at the record hops. If I hadn't had eighteen disc jockeys who had faith, who believed in me, and who knew that everything I knew was for them, they would not have given me this liberty. But they were *so* poor . . . Larry Regan, $47 a week at WTPS; Poppa Stoppa, same; Larry McKinley, $52. Okey Dokey [James Smith] was the strongest black man the city's ever known."

Russell took a special interest in Okey Dokey, who played volumes of R&B in his programming slot on white-owned WBOK. Russell went to the station owner, one Stanley Ray, to lobby for Okey Dokey. Russell explained:

"The man needs a raise. I want $25 a week more—." "That's a hundred bucks!" [Ray said.] "Man, I can put him into a car for $70 a month notes, that's all, he needs some wheels to take him around to these dances." [Ray] says, "I don't know, the phone rings off the hook all day long, but I don't know about the money comin in."

"Well, raise your *billing*," I tell him. "No, let's prove it tonight." He says, "Whaddya wanna do?" So I said, "Let's say tonight we're gonna give away on this show, *free albums* at midnight on the Huey P. Long bridge!" He said, "My God, you're gonna have a traffic jam." And I said, "Well, certainly! I'm tellin' ya how popular the guy is!" And we had a traffic jam coming down both sides of that bridge! So the guy gets his $25 a week more money.

Anyhow, the scene was like this and I went over these changes for ten years and I never thought of the power that we had, but the kids never went to a dance in their life until we came here. These dances we created—just as many black dances as white, and we mixed it up so well that we taught officials in this city and they started scratching their heads about it. Now, who then, created the New Orleans scene? That should be very simple. If you take a car right now and load it up with gas and don't stop from here across the nation, you will never have anybody managing *eighteen disc jockeys at one time!* Do you know how many people we played before in that ten-year span? *More* than Elvis Presley, Bing Crosby and all the big stars combined, Allman Brothers, Rolling Stones, you could take 'em all, Woodstock—*six million admissions*. That's where the kids were born!

Well, maybe not six million.

Larry Regan, now a late-night talk show host, arrived at WJMR after Vernon Winslow had moved on. The "Jam, Jive and Gumbo Show" featured Duke Thiele as the seminal Poppa Stoppa. "Duke Thiele was the rage in those days," Regan says. "I was surprised at the number of whites listening. Thiele would say, 'Get your jiver's li-cense.' There was a lotta rhyming with words, new to whites."[4]

Thiele had a falling out with station manager Stanley Ray; Okey Dokey was put in Thiele's old slot, and Clarence Hayman became the new Poppa Stoppa at WJMR. According to Regan, "Clarence Hayman *made* Fats Domino in the crescent city. He'd play an hour a day on Fats, and Fats Domino was like Glenn Miller would be to the whites. He wasn't too raunchy, more or less Mickey Mouse rock-and-roll. Black kids didn't like him; he was too Mickey Mouse for them. But for the white kids, he was a real groove. They were just learning rock-and-roll. To blacks, he was square."[5]

Programming strategies began to change. Clarence Hayman recalled: "In 1953, the 'Poppa Stoppa Show' was immediately followed by the '990 Hit Parade.' In those days what they called 'popular music'—such as Sinatra, Peggy Lee, Bing Crosby, etc. So one day I said, 'What would happen if I played one of my top rock 'n roll records along with one of my top pop ones? Intermingle them.' These were both my top programs and I might ruin it. We did it anyway. We'd play the cream of the crop. And play it back to back as much as we could. For twenty minutes to half an hour without saying a word. We were right on the borderline between pop music and race music.

"This was in '53 when songs like 'Lawdy, Lawdy, Miss Clawdy' started catching on with the white people. And they said that white people didn't listen to those things."[6]

The record hops spread to high schools, CYO halls, and college campuses. Russell and Regan began to explore television. Joe Banashak, a local distributor who later formed the Minit label, agreed to sponsor a half hour record hop on a VHF channel with the same call letters as WJMR radio. The show aired from four-thirty to five in the afternoons, five days a week, preempting the last half hour of Dick Clark's dance show, syndicated from Philadelphia.

But the segregationist mindset of the programming department created problems. Russell and Regan could not put black artists, or black youngsters, on the air. Larry Regan elaborates:

Banashak and I said, "This is ridiculous!" The producer of the show, I don't know if he was a Klansman or in the White Citizens Council, but one day Ray Charles came to town. I said, "I got Ray Charles." He blew his stack, "*Ray Charles* is black!" "But this is Ray Charles," I tell him. Producer says, "I'll make a deal with you. If you don't shake hands with the guy, okay." So I said, "Okay, you got a deal." So Ray came on, he lip-sang a couple of numbers. You know he's blind, so when he got through, I went up and shook his hand. Okay. Producer says, "*You broke your promise!*" That's the way television stations were run in those days.

We used to play a lot of black record hops. The kids loved the TV show, wanted to come on the show, naturally. I said, "Man, we ought to let 'em come on, have their own show one day a week." What happened, one of the salesmen told me that Dick Clark's manager called up, to offer more money if they'd carry the last half hour, instead of us. Dick Clark and all these big stars. Somebody told me, he'd name three or four artists, then say, "You in New Orleans are going to miss the rest of it."

The manager said, "Why don't you fight him, man?" I said, "Fight him? You're not gonna back me up. I don't have any talent. I can't just walk out here with rockabilly singers."[7]

In the absence of black artists to lip-sync as the whites who came through on tour would do, Russell and Regan played R&B hits.

We used to say, "My God, it looks like an epileptic convention." They went from Little Richard, Chuck Berry, to every artist you could think of. See, the white kids had the buying power. They could buy like an album a week, and half a dozen records. That's why the black artists started selling like crazy. We used to give Fats Domino pictures away at record hops. Kids would come back the next week, give the picture back, say, "It's not that we don't like him. My momma doesn't want a black guy's picture in the house." That's when Elvis came along. The white kids needed a white idol.

The television show lasted thirteen weeks before Dick Clark's managers won out. But by the end of the fifties, the powerful CBS affiliate—WWL, owned by Loyola University—started its own "Saturday Hop," with black and white youngsters on at different times, and cashed in on the struggles of Russell and Regan.

Another grand figure in the rise of New Orleans rock was Ken Elliott, known as "Jack the Cat." Born in New Castle, Pennsylvania, in 1919, Elliott came to New Orleans in the late 1930s. In 1942 he was stationed in Okinawa as a radio operator on a B-29 bomber. In his spare time, he would spin records for dances to entertain the troops. Once back in New Orleans, Elliott settled at WWEZ and adopted the radio persona Jack the Cat.

"He saw the R&B trend coming before any of us," remarked Keith Rush, now a talk show host at WSMB. "He said the white kids would be dancing to black music, and he sure was right. He was in a position to create records, to break records. He'd break 'em in New Orleans, and companies would use New Orleans to get other cities like Chicago to play them."[8]

WWEZ was an independent radio station—having no affiliation with the major radio networks CBS, NBC, ABC, and Mutual Broadcasting System. Independent stations were usually low-powered operations with limited hours for broadcasting. While the affiliated stations carried soap operas, quiz shows, and the radio dramas from the network, the independents saw music as an inexpensive alternative for attracting audiences wanting blues, R&B, country and western. These stations established the concept of playing top forty records on radio, which promoted record sales.

Jack the Cat became an overnight sensation. The show began each night with Elliott saying, "This is Jack the Cat"—broken by a music riff,

Deejay Clarence "Poppa Stoppa" Hayman with Mac "Dr. John" Rebennack, 1973

dum dee dumm—"All right, you cats and kittens, put on your jivin' mittens!"[9]

Elliott married Ann Bodenheimer, a secretary at the station, and the duo became a big hit on the record-hop circuit run by Jim Russell. As Ann's popularity grew, she became cohost of Ken's show "The House That Jack Built." As the counterpart of Jack the Cat, Ann became Jacqueline the Kitten. The show came on weeknights from eight to ten, and oddly enough, originated from their home in suburban Harahan. The Elliotts had three young sons, Mark, Keith, and Ricky; the home broadcasts became a mildly chaotic family affair, something like the atmosphere on the "Ozzie and Harriet" television show, with Jack and Jacqueline conversing with the kids between records and occasional sibling quarrels erupting in the background.

WWOZ deejay Duke Dugas recalls, "Jack the Cat used to come on at night, saying, 'This is Jack the Cat, sayin' where y'at, from the house that Jack built, right here on the banks of the muddy Mississippi.' And you could drive down lovers' lane on Saturday night behind the Coast Guard station off the seawall by Lake Pontchartrain, and all these couples were parked in their cars, and every car had on Jack the Cat."[10]

Following the lead of Russell and Regan, Jack the Cat and Jacqueline the Kitten began hosting a Saturday night television show, "New Orleans Bandstand," patterned after Dick Clark's show, for WJRM-TV. But as with any popular fad, Jack the Cat's stature soon diminished. The marriage broke up, and by the end of the fifties, Ken Elliott was making an effort to disassociate himself from the past image, working under his own name. He left New Orleans in 1963, disenchanted. "A lot of the shifts in programming he felt were unnecessary," remarked his son Ken Jr. "He finally came back home in 1968. He worked as news director at WNOE, but he wasn't very happy. Too many things had changed."[11] The following year, at fifty, he died of a heart attack.

But there was staying power in the old records. Clarence Hayman, the second Poppa Stoppa, spanned the entire decade of the fifties, did public relations work, then resurfaced with a colorful oldies show in the 1970s. In 1986 Hayman is still Poppa Stoppa—broadcasting from WSDL, a station in Slidell, thirty miles east of New Orleans. He spins the oldies with a relaxed conversational style, no fast talk.

If deejays were celebrities among the new rock-and-roll fans, the performers themselves became teen idols. As Fats Domino began his remarkable ascent in the late 1950s, a string of white rock-and-rollers appeared locally. In their careers, we find a pronounced divergence from the early blues sensibility. Like the blacks, however, they knew humor was first spice in the gumbo of Deep South rock. Bobby Charles's work is a case in point.

Bobby Charles was born Robert Charles Guidry in 1938, in a quaint town called Abbeville about two hundred miles west of New Orleans in Vermilion Parish. Lying at the bottom of the state—a mass of marshlands, farms, and bayous—Vermilion Parish is the heart of Cajun country, where French patois has endured alongside a rich folk music tradition marked by two-step waltzes set to accordion melodies. As a youngster, Bobby absorbed the Cajun idiom but was attracted to the pulsing rhythm-and-blues sounds pouring out of airwaves by the early fifties.

Bobby formed a high school band, the Cardinals, and played at local clubs and for high school dances. One big hit, which created a slang expression that spread nationwide, came after one of these engagements. "We were walking out of a restaurant, and I turned around to my piano player and told him, 'See you later, alligator.' They had two couples sitting in a booth in front of us. They were pretty loaded, and a girl said something. I walked back and asked her what she had said. 'You said, *See you later, alligator,* and I said,

After while, crocodile.' I said, 'Thank you very much'—and that was it."[12]

Charles went home that night and wrote one of rock-and-roll's early gems, "See You Later, Alligator." With his band, Charles began performing the song and the Cajuns loved it. A demo tape was sent to Leonard Chess in Chicago, resulting in a contract with his record company. Years later, Charles whimsically recalled, "When I got to Chess Records, the only reason they signed me, they thought I was black. And when I got off the plane, it kind of shocked 'em a bit." "See You Later, Alligator" came out in 1955. It sold only moderately for Charles, but covered by Bill Haley and the Comets in 1956, it became a million seller.

In New Orleans Charles signed with Imperial Records and wrote songs Fats Domino scored well with—"It Keeps Raining," "Before I Grow Too Old," and the famous "Walking to New Orleans." The scene captured in Charles's lyrics was made-to-order Domino material, a vision of the city from the eyes of a country boy. "I got my suitcase in my ha-and, Ain't that a shame. . . . It looks so good to me, ooh-oooh-wee. . . ." By the end of the 1970s, Charles had returned to the tranquility of Abbeville to continue his career as a lyricist, composer, and performer.

Another teenager who came to New Orleans in search of fame was Jimmy Clanton. Born in Baton Rouge, Clanton cut his first demo in New Orleans as an eighteen-year-old. He had been told that for twenty-five dollars he could record at Cosimo's studio. "One of the songs that we did," Clanton explained, "I had written about my old girlfriend. I did it one afternoon in about twenty minutes when I didn't have anything to do. It was called 'Just a Dream.'"[13] Johnny Vincent, the shrewd scout for Ace Records, was interested in Clanton, but according to Earl King, he didn't like the song. King thought it had potential. After all, Clanton had recorded it with Huey Smith, Red Tyler, and Lee Allen. But Cosimo Matassa, who owned the studio and had presided over many hit recordings, thought the tune was solid and offered to manage Clanton. Johnny Vincent changed his mind and released the song on Ace. Clanton got a break early on; he was invited to sing on the Dick Clark show in Philadelphia. "I lip-synced," Clanton recalled, "and the next day Ace Records got orders for over 100,000 from distributors around the country." By July 19, 1958, "Just a Dream" had hit number four on the charts and eventually sold over a million copies.

Johnny Vincent began to have second thoughts about his label. Up to then, the heart of the Ace sound had been black rhythm-and-bluesmen like Huey Smith and Earl King. With the emergence of rock-and-roll, Vincent shifted his strategy toward the new market, with Jimmy Clanton as a teen idol. Clanton's sweet nasal voice was perfect for the sugary love songs he recorded. He was a good-looking young man with blue eyes, wavy brown hair, fair skin, and an innocent air which bore a porcelain resemblance to Pat Boone and Tab Hunter. Clanton's early songs had a slight blues tinge, reflecting the R&B idiom whose sidemen played on his tunes. Johnny Vincent, convinced that Clanton would continue to mount up the hits, made a reckless decision to release a double album of new songs—not a "greatest hits"—and the result, according to Clanton, was 35,000 unsold records.

The loss came when Clanton's contract with Ace was near expiration. "I was still very big, record-wise," Clanton said. "And Johnny asked me to re-sign, and I didn't want to at the time, because I felt he was just going so far, and [would] not spend X amount of dollars to go all out to keep Jimmy Clanton alive. Of course, 'Venus in Blue Jeans' brought back things very much because we did over 400,000 of that record. I didn't receive a cent of it. The usual thing that is done nowadays, when you re-sign with a company, you also erase all debts and you start fresh.

But not being a businessman in those days, I signed again and all those double LPs immediately became my responsibility. So the $32,000 that I was supposed to receive for 'Venus in Blue Jeans' was erased. This broke my back and it broke my heart, and it kind of killed everything I felt, not necessarily for Johnny Vincent, but for the structure of Ace Records."[14] Clanton drifted away from Louisiana. In 1973 he was a deejay on a station in Lancaster, Pennsylvania, and in 1981 he appeared on a religious show, singing about Jesus.

Frankie Ford was one of the other white pop singers on Vincent's label. Born Frank Guzzo on August 4, 1940, he spent his childhood days playing in the backyard of his home in Gretna across the river from New Orleans. Encouraged by a neighbor who heard Frank singing in the backyard, the Guzzos enrolled the boy at Schram Studios for lessons. By age six, Frank was singing in children's matinees on Sunday at the plush Blue Room of the Roosevelt Hotel and was entering talent contests around town. He once sang with the Ted Fiorito Orchestra, Carmen Miranda's band, in the Peabody Hotel in Memphis. He won thirteen contests while in grade school and free dance lessons for his efforts. His vocal coach introduced him to the piano.

Finally he won a chance to appear on the coveted "Ted Mack Original Amateur Hour" in New York. Vincent and Anna Guzzo made the trip with him. "My mother and father were nervous as cats, but I was a little trooper by then so I wasn't nervous. I sang Rosemary Clooney's song, 'Bacha Mi.' It was in Italian. And I sang 'Wheel of Fortune.'"[15]

He joined his first band, the Syncopaters, in 1952. The musicians began to move from stock arrangements of mellow standards of the day to R&B music they discovered on the "Poppa Stoppa Show." "When I joined the Syncopaters, we would go outside the Laborers' Union Hall and listen when they had Ray Charles or Little Willie John or someone like that. Of course, whites couldn't get in, so we had to stand outside. I would listen to the vocal things they were doing, and the horn players would listen to the horn parts. We would also learn every record we could get our hands on. We used to sneak into the Joy Lounge across the river to hear Sugarboy Crawford. The manager would run us out; we would just go outside and keep on listening on the sidewalk."

By the late fifties, a loose group of Italians had moved into record productions. Johnny Vincent (Imbragulio) had the Ace label; Cosimo Matassa had the J&M Studio, Joe Assunto owned One-Stop Records, Joe Ruffino owned Ric and Ron Records, and Joe Caronna was a talent manager. Caronna and Vincent were interested in Frank Guzzo, but no hint of ethnic pride entered their decision to change his name. Guzzo would not do. The promoters wanted Frankie Lee Ford because it sounded like Jerry Lee Lewis. Frank didn't like the Lee, and Matassa agreed. So they settled on Frankie Ford.

White artists were gaining entry in the city's music marketplace. Frankie Ford was good-looking, and he could sound like a black singer. But he was a novice in the recording studio, a white boy among black veterans of rhythm-and-blues. "Here I walk into that studio with people like Red Tyler, Robert Parker, Frank Fields—and my arranger and pianist was Huey Smith!"

By this time Matassa had moved his studio to Governor Nicholls Street, at the far end of the Quarter. Musicians were always around, the vibes were good, and nobody seemed to mind that Frankie Ford was white. In early 1958 he cut his first disc, "Cheatin' Woman," which sounded black, suiting Vincent's designs. Soon thereafter came the recording date that turned Frank Guzzo's life around.

Huey Smith had cut a song called "Sea Cruise" and knew it was a winner. But Vincent and Caronna had second thoughts. For all of his talent, Huey Smith hated road trips. Frankie, on the other

Frankie Ford, 1959

Lloyd Price, 1958

hand, had promise and wanted to travel. When Vincent said he wanted Ford to do a new vocal track for the song, Smith exploded. "No, no! This song is too good. I wanna be the one up there on the stage when people go to yellin' for 'Sea Cruise.'"[16]

Johnny Vincent said no, and removed Smith's vocal track from the disc. Huey swallowed his pride and went to work with the young singer. "I just loved the song," Ford explained. "Huey taught it to me. In fact, somewhere I have the original chart with his handwritten remarks. The record lay around for about seven months. Then one night we were driving home from a job in Jackson, listening to the radio. We had Hoss Allen on [WLAC Nashville]. Joe hit the wheel and screamed, 'It's on Hoss Allen!' and woke me up in the back seat. They started playing it in Miami and Cleveland and around. One afternoon they called me up and said, 'Turn on Channel 13. It's on Dick Clark!' And I liked to fainted."[17]

"Sea Cruise" is vintage New Orleans R&B. The children's songs woven into early compositions are still evident, but the lyrics represent a more mature Huey Smith. "Sea Cruise" was Huey Smith at his best.

Old Man Rhythm gets in my shoes,
  There's no use sittin' and singing the blues,
So be my guest, you've got nothing to lose.
  Won't you let me take you on a sea cruise?

Ooo Wee, Ooo Wee, Baby,
  Ooo Wee, Ooo Wee, Baby,
Ooo Wee, Ooo Wee, Baby
  Won't you let me take you on a sea cruise?

I feel like jumping,
  Baby, won't you join me, please?
I don't like begging,
  But now I'm on bended knees.

Got to get movin', got my hat off the rack,
  Got the boogie-woogie like a knife in the back,
So be my guest, you've got nothing to lose.
  Won't you let me take you on a sea cruise?

Frankie Ford walked into "Sea Cruise" through no fault of his own. Like other white rockers who covered tunes, he rode it successfully. But in 1962 he was drafted, and when he was discharged in 1963, he found a changed city. The heyday of R&B had passed. The following year the Beatles arrived in America, and an exodus of New Orleans musicians began. "When I left, there were recording sessions every week, and when I returned, there was *nothing*! Pow!" Frankie Ford developed an eclectic piano act and started drawing crowds in local hotels and clubs. Except for a brief stint in California, Ford has remained in New Orleans, playing the circuit as a soloist. He has managed his money wisely and is comfortable with his present niche.

Frankie Ford is quick to smile. "My father advised me financially, and so, quite luckily, I ended up with a lot more than some of the people who had bigger hits. There's a line from *A Chorus Line* which goes, 'Who am I, anyway? Am I my resume?' Sometimes when I look back, I know who this person is today, but it was happening so fast that I didn't know who the person was back then. Kids storming the bus and stealing your clothes. . . ."

One spring day in 1980, Huey Smith, now retired from an active career, asked Jonathan Foose to join him on a drive to Jackson, Mississippi, to visit Johnny Vincent. When they arrived, Huey and Johnny exchanged warm greetings; an hour later they were yelling at each other. Talk ran hot and cold, anger and sentimental memories mingling like oil and water. Such scenes were apparently common between the two. Johnny told Huey about a house that he had bought with the aim of giving it to Huey, but alas, it had burned. Vincent insisted on taking the two men to see the place, which fire had left just a shell. Ashes, charred wood, forty-five records littered the yard. The floor was covered with melted Ace Records. Records crunched beneath their feet as the men inspected the ruins. Vincent had used the house to store his back stock. Jimmy Clanton's teen-idol face smiled up from ashes of the LP that had lost him $32,000. Frankie Ford, Little Booker, "High Blood Pressure" appeared in the mush. A large piece of R&B history, ashes and dust.

A flicker came to Vincent's eye. "Look, man, why don't ya come up here, spend a few days. We can clean all this up, get some of these records in shape, start selling 'em." Huey gazed out at the street. A silence fell over the men. It had been a long time since 1957.

Chapter Ten

ALLEN TOUSSAINT AND THE MINIT SOUND

Allen Toussaint is something of a legend. Pianist, composer, singer, producer, and partner in SeaSaint Studio, he is a prosperous man with the stamp of genius to his cast. His *Southern Nights* and *Motion* albums won critical plaudits and gave hints of greater talent. With composition royalties and studio profits providing a comfortable income, Toussaint is indifferent to road tours. His best powers surface in studio production. It's arguable whether he has held back as a performer, yet by all accounts the shyness is real. An accomplished showman when he wants to be, Toussaint makes infrequent public appearances.

Toussaint was born on January 14, 1938, in Gert Town, a tiny industrial neighborhood on the western, uptown fringes of the city. The name evolved in the 1890s after a German grocer, Alfred Gehrke, settled in the town of Carrollton and purchased land. Upon his death, the area became known as "Gehrke Town."[1] But as more blacks moved into the area, pronunciation of the German's name became a little looser: Gert Town.

Today, widened vowels of the folk dialect render the name "Goit Town."

Gert Town holds a special place in jazz history. In 1902 Lincoln Park provided a stage for Buddy Bolden, the first great player of jazz, who electrified audiences on a powerfully melodic cornet. By the 1920s, after Bolden was gone, scattered developments dotted Gert Town. Today the thoroughfare Earhart Boulevard is lined with warehouses, a cement plant, and a lumberyard. College Court, a narrow street just two blocks long, has rows of single-framed shotgun houses in dingy browns and grays. "I remember there were gramophones in the neighborhood," Toussaint recalls, "and records were thick seventy-eights. Few people had new-fangled record players. So mostly it was radio more than records."[2]

His brother Vincent played guitar, and Joyce, his sister, studied classical piano. Allen was the youngest. "Our grandmother got the piano for Joyce," Vincent said. "Allen, who I guess was about seven then, just kept on a-ducking in on it whenever she wasn't playing. It was weird how he got good so quickly, but then he was a serious kid, and didn't mind hard practicing."[3]

Joyce taught Allen notes, even passed on a few of the classics, like the Grieg A-Minor Concerto. But most of Allen's early education came by ear, from songs on the radio that he worked hard to imitate. He went to Xavier University's Junior School of Music, but studies lasted only a few months. Classical education was too confining. He went back to the living room to practice his favorite songs and improvisational pieces.

In his early teens, Allen discovered Fats Domino and the gospel-tinged piano of Ray Charles. But the shaping influence in those formative years was Professor Longhair. In the television documentary *Piano Players Seldom Play Together,* Allen recalls his first encounter with Byrd: "I saw him one time at a record hop in earlier days, about 1958 or '59, from a distance, didn't get a chance to talk to him, just stood there dumbfounded for a while."[4] From Fess, whom Toussaint later called "The Bach of Rock," he derived his own eclectic rhythms, beginning with the left-hand percussive flavor.

At sixteen Allen had a neighborhood band, the Flamingoes, with a battery of horns, a drummer, and blind guitarist "Snooks" Eaglin, who became a prominent bluesman in later years. They played high school dances and college parties. "Then I was called to do a gig with Earl King in Pritchard, Alabama," Toussaint continues. "Huey Smith couldn't make the gig. That was the first gig I worked other than the Flamingoes."[5]

Toussaint went to Booker T. Washington, a high school that produced a distinguished line of musicians—saxmen James Rivers and Earl Turbinton, trumpeter Sam Alcorn, Earl King, and vocalist James "Sugarboy" Crawford. Toussaint developed at his own pace, a little slowly at first, playing different instruments in the school's junior band. Music became the central force in his life; classroom interests lagged. In midsemester of his final year, he dropped out of school to take a road tour with Shirley and Lee, replacing Huey Smith, who quit the road show and returned to New Orleans because "Rockin' Pneumonia" was breaking nationally.

The Dew Drop was still the proving grounds for any young artist, an initiation into the ranks of seasoned players. Toussaint started by playing piano and organ, sharing billings with Roland Cook, drag queens, comedians, and others. But to Toussaint, the grind of stage performances—three sets a night till wee hours—was only a means of gaining experience and paying the rent. He felt a magnetic pull to the studio. Dave Bartholomew sought him out for session work and in late 1957 hired him to fill in for Fats Domino. "Well, I think [Fats] was in Australia at the time when Dave called me to play like Fats would have on the record. He had a very definite style, and it was very easy to play. We did 'I Want You to Know,' 'Young School Girl,' and a couple of others." Domino returned, laid the vocal tracks, and both tunes made the charts.

Toussaint became a regular at Matassa's studio. "I got called in again and again to play like people, and to play background piano. . . . I became almost permanent party as far as makin' studio sessions." Besides Bartholomew, producers like Johnny Vincent and Joe Ruffino realized the freelance keyboard player brought a commercial dimension to productions.

Toussaint's talents were not limited to simple background work. He was coming into his own as an arranger. Working in "head sessions"—walk in, set up, organize the musical structure on the spot—he displayed an instinctive sense for directing others, balancing bass and drums to steady the tempos, layering melodic horn lines to accent the rhythm, blending instruments and voice into a sound suitable for selling. Al Silvers, president of Herald/Ember records in New York, recognized Toussaint's talent early on. Silvers traveled the country, visiting his distributors by day, scouting talent at night. In New Orleans he became friends with saxman Lee Allen. Silvers recalled:

One day, I got a call in New York from Lee Allen, who told me he had some fantastic material for recording. The next time I was in New Orleans, I set up some studio time at Cosimo's. Well, we go in, and despite what this cat told me, he didn't have a thing prepared. That was a rough town, and the union delegate was right here. I had to pay the musicians for a full session, and I had to pay the studio—here I'm frustrated. The clock is running and it's costing me money for nothing. In desperation, I went to Toussaint. "Help me out of this mess," I pleaded. He fooled around a bit and then came up with a riff that sounded pretty good. It was simple and melodic. When I told him I liked it, he called over the guitar player and drummer. After they had the rhythm section set, they brought Lee over and he picked it up. We tried several rough takes and then cut a master. It went along for four sides like that . . . all from the head.[6]

Although never given formal credit, Toussaint in fact produced the session. Of the four tracks cut, "Walking with Mr. Lee" was a charted hit and sent Lee Allen to the Apollo Theatre and to later appearances on the Dick Clark show.

Toussaint auditioned for Johnny Vincent, who thought him not commercial enough. In 1958, however, a pair of hustling young independent producers, Danny Kesler and Murray Sporn, came to town looking for new talent. After days of auditioning dozens of singers and groups, Kesler and Sporn were frustrated. The talent was mediocre. Toussaint in his role as accompanist sat quietly in the studio through days of auditions, backing singers, and improving arrangements. Finally one partner said: "We're wasting our time with all these people. How about a session on this guy Allen Toussaint?"[7]

Toussaint was apprehensive at first. The thought of writing, arranging, and recording a dozen of his own songs was a little unnerving—but he knew a break when he saw one. He called veteran saxophonist Red Tyler to assist. Kesler and Sporn were in a hurry to return to New York, giving Toussaint little time to prepare for the session. He began with only a few completed compositions and half a dozen melodic fragments from which to work. "We went into the studio cold," Tyler explained, "and started making up songs so fast we didn't have titles for them. And when the tapes were taken to New York, we had no idea what those songs were going to be titled."[8]

The album was recorded in two days. Kesler and Sporn went back to New York, sold the twelve instrumental tracks to RCA, and in the spring of 1958, *The Wild Sounds of New Orleans* by Al Tousan was released. (The name Allen Toussaint didn't sound commercial enough to them.) While only a moderate seller and produced under strained circumstances, the album showcased Allen Toussaint as a composer. Heard today, the songs have a sparkle and solid melodic quality, bright and rhythmic, with repetitive passages that linger in the memory. "Whirlaway" (influenced by Professor Longhair), "Happy Times," and "Java" have an identifiable New Orleans sound with solid syncopation. In 1963 the great Dixieland trumpeter Al Hirt turned "Java" into a million seller.

Toussaint was far from starstruck by his recording debut. But it meant a few extra dollars from record sales and potential royalties for song publishing down the road. For the most part, Toussaint continued freelance jobs at Cosimo's studio. His break came in 1959, when Minit Records was formed by Joe Banashak and Larry McKinley.

Joe Banashak, a low-keyed, straight-talking businessman adept in business organization, is a decided contrast to Johnny Vincent. Born in Baltimore in 1923 of Polish ancestry, Banashak moved to New Orleans in 1949 to manage Gramophone Enterprises, then later went to work for Lew Chudd at Imperial.

Allen Toussaint, keyboard maestro, 1973

Unhappy with the excessive travel the job demanded, he went to work for A-1 Distributors on Baronne Street in 1957. Marketing strategies appealed to Banashak's entrepreneurial instincts. He wanted to produce his own records and found a partner in Larry McKinley, a young black deejay who had come to the city from Chicago, where he had won recognition with a civil rights program, "Destination Freedom." Programming rhythm-and-blues in New Orleans, McKinley saw a good business opportunity. "We put up $250 each," he recalls. "We named it Minit because Joe was on his way home one day and they had these Meal-a-Minit restaurants, and we felt that we could play on those words, like 'Take a Minit and listen to it.'"[9]

McKinley had no moral qualms about his partnership and conflicting role as a disc jockey. "I played everybody's records," McKinley states. "All I asked was that a record be good." The relationship between radio stations and record companies was very loose in the early days of rock-and-roll. For record companies, slipping a bill to the loyal deejay made good business sense. It was illegal, however, and by the end of the fifties, a "payola" scandal rocked the industry nationwide, contributing to the demise of Alan Freed, the original rock-and-roll promoter. In an interview with Tad Jones, Banashak discussed the "payola" factor at Minit in 1959–63.

Did you ever have to pay a little something?
Oh, yes indeed! Plenty times.

Was it standard procedure?
Every station.

What form? Was it always green (money)?
Well, sometimes you'd send records, and send 'em to somebody else and tell them to convert [to cash]. . . . Or you'd send an airplane ticket, tell 'em to cash it in. . . .

Take a vacation.
There was money until the scandal. You used to send cold cash. *Cold cash!* And when the scandal broke, you tried to devise different ways—I used to have guys say, "Hey, man, I played this record three weeks and there's nothin' happenin'." And if I believed in the record I would say, "Well, what is it going to take to get it played a few more weeks?"[10]

Meanwhile, disc jockeys in different cities were trading favors, playing each other's pet records, all of it a common business practice. McKinley recalls: "I had good contact with other jocks around the country and so we would help each other. If someone in Chicago or John R. [Richbourg] at WLAC Nashville would say, 'I've got a new Joe Simon record, and I need it played,' I would play the hell out of it. We would never try to send anyone a dog. New Orleans, Chicago, Philadelphia, Detroit, Houston, Nashville, and Baltimore, we could get a record, and if the record was good, the whole country would jump on it. We could influence the whole nation. All we did was cross favors. Never was any money exchanged. That was our network."

Minit Records started slowly with a few blues releases, no big sales. In the winter of 1960, McKinley and Banashak announced an audition in the brick building where WYLD was housed. An array of singers, musicians, and songwriters showed up—Lee Diamond, former bandleader for Little Richard and James Brown; Irma Thomas, a young vocalist with an infectious smile; Joe Tex, a Dew Drop regular and feisty soul singer. Jessie Hill, a fast-talking drummer for Professor Longhair, came with a rough demonstration tape with the imaginative title "Ooo Poo Pah Do." Aaron Neville, a handsome balladeer with remarkable falsetto powers, waited his turn, accompanied by older brother Art and sidekick Larry Williams (of "Short Fat Fannie" and "Bony Maronie" fame). As the night wore on, singer Benny Spellman arrived, and a vocal group called the Del Royals.

It was an impressive gathering—all would have hits of their own in the next few years. But that night McKinley and Banashak discovered Allen Toussaint. He cut quite a figure—slender in a fashionable suit with a diamond stud to the tie. There was elegance in his bearing, all the way down to the French cuffs. He had not come to audition but to accompany singer Allen Orange.

At twenty-two, Toussaint was given sole responsibility for Minit's musical direction. He received a royalty on each artist and in time developed a strong rapport with those who came his way. His own reticence buffered the more intense egos of those bent on making it as musicians. "I was personally involved with every artist we had," he explains. "Daily, the artists would come to the house [on College Court] and we'd just hang out in the front room all day long, playing music and singing—Ernie K-Doe, Irma Thomas, Aaron Neville, Benny Spellman—we'd jam all day. When it was time to go on a Ernie K-Doe tune, I would write a tune for K-Doe. I'd usually go in the back of the house and run over the tune with K-Doe, and everybody would sing it, and we'd get it down. Then about a half hour later, after we've done that, I'd go in the back and do another tune, and come back and give Irma [Thomas] her tune, and Irma would look at it and start singin' it, and we'd iron out a few little spots."[11]

Of the many artists to come under Toussaint's influence, Ernie K-Doe was one of the most flamboyant and talented of the rhythm-and-blues generation. Born Ernest Kador on February 22, 1936, he was raised in a gospel music environment, singing at the New Home Baptist Church. He recorded as an early adolescent with the Zion Travelers. His childhood pals included the three oldest Neville brothers—Art, Charles, and Aaron, then living in Calliope housing projects near Ernie's home in central city.

K-Doe's style was steeped in gospel with dramatic movements, jumps and shouts, long falsetto reaches of a voice that well into the 1970s had such strength and control as to shoot chills up your spine. In 1954 he was playing the Dew Drop, Club Tiajuana, and smaller spots. He recorded several tracks that year with the Blue Diamonds, an R&B group, for Savoy Records of Newark, New Jersey. His first session with Toussaint was in 1958, when he recorded "Tuff Enuff" for Ember Records. He was a balladeer first and foremost, and the early Minit tunes established a pattern of solid production quality under Toussaint's auspices. "Hello, My Lover" and "Tain't It the Truth" sold well through 1960 and into 1961.

Jessie Hill recorded one of Minit's biggest hits, a raucous call-and-response novelty called "Ooo Poo Pah Do." Jessie rode the song for the next twenty years, long after his brief star faded, working crowds up to an expectant pitch, grinning beneath the sunglasses, releasing vollies of "oooohhhh" and "ohyeahhhhhhahh" before the first lines: "I wanna tell you about ooo poo pah do . . . an' I won't stop cryin' til I create a disturbance in your mind." On the original cut, nephew David Lastie's sax coats the song with heat.

Toussaint was indifferent to the song. "I just didn't think it made enough sense. I thought things had to be a bit more meaningful. . . . I almost hated it, in fact. Then, after I saw people raising their hands and popping their fingers, I said, 'Oh, no. What now?' Nowadays I hear it a bit more objectively."[12]

Meanwhile, the vocalists kept coming to rehearsals at Toussaint's. Allen, a perfectionist, often crumpled songs and threw them away. One day K-Doe found a discarded item that had visceral appeal. "I was going through family problems. . . . My mother-in-law had something to do with it." K-Doe convinced a reluctant Toussaint to let him record "Mother-in-Law," a tune literally retrieved from the trash basket.[13]

As the same session progressed, Toussaint became annoyed with one of the background singers.[14] Benny Spellman, a husky, handsome guy who was standing in the corner, recalls: "Originally, I was at the studio merely to have a few beers. They would give everyone free drinks. Allen was not satisfied with the young man who was singing the low notes. So he called me over to the mike, and I came up with the sound that he wanted, like [in *basso profondo*] *Muthuh-in-Lawh!*"[15] The song was a 1961 novelty item and deejays picked up on it immediately. (Having Larry McKinley as his manager didn't hurt K-Doe either.) The song climbed to the number one position in the *Billboard* hot 100 charts. Ernie K-Doe took to the road.

Ernie K-Doe's fondest memory is of a 1962 concert before five thousand people at the municipal auditorium in New Orleans. He was on the same bill with soul singer James Brown, a whirlwind on stage. K-Doe had a repertoire of songs he had cut for Minit, including "Certain Girl." He called the performance "the biggest battle of my life."

Larry McKinley was the announcer, and he called me out there first. You see, it was a dressin' thing, New Orleans against Macon, Georgia, ya dig? I was not gonna let my hometown people down. I had a royal blue smoking jacket on, but under that, nobody knew what I had on underneath. They could see ice blue pants. . . . So Larry called me out first. Then James Brown came out in a brown suit, white shirt, brown polka dot tie. But while Larry was talkin', everybody went to screamin'. You see, when I pulled off that smoking jacket, everything else was ice blue. And on "Certain Girl" I changed suits nine times! I had a clothes rack backstage. Everytime I'd get to a certain part in the song, I'd just run straight around to the side, change my suit and come back out to the other side. . . . Now those tricks I do with the mike stand, I learned how to do them by practicing with a broom. . . . See, to get good, working that mike like that, it has to be part of you. Not just your mike stand,

but everybody's mike stand. You see, it's a rhythm—you can tell when you got the rhythm. I can turn around and do my splits and I know the microphone will be right to me.[16]

Always the showman, K-Doe was still doing splits in 1982, even if his voice had begun to crack a little. A year later he began a popular radio show on WWOZ.

The success of "Mother-in-Law" opened the doors for Benny Spellman, a former college football player from Pensacola, Florida, who began working with Toussaint. "He knew the limited talents I had," Spellman continues. "I could sing low notes, but I didn't have tremendous range going high. He would become Benny Spellman at the time he would be writing the songs. It was a comfortable thing to be around the cat. The notes that he gave you were comfortable."

Two songs made Spellman a popular figure on the regional touring circuit—"Fortune Teller" and "Lipstick Traces," the latter selling well enough to make the national charts. The song featured some of Toussaint's more romantic lyrics and a hauntingly beautiful trombone solo by Wendell Eugene.

Your pretty brown eyes,
　Your wavy hair,
I won't go home no more
　Cause you're not there.
I'm telling you now
　Like I told you before,
I'm so in love with you—
　Don't leave me no more.

Lipstick traces on a cigarette,
　Every memory lingers with me yet,
I'm telling you now
　Like I told you before,
I'm so in love with you—
　Don't leave me no more.

With the British music invasion of the midsixties, many Toussaint songs were covered by the new rock-and-rollers. The Rolling Stones did

Joe Banashak, 1982

Irma Thomas, Queen of the Blues

Burn, K-Doe, burn!

"Fortune Teller," Herman's Hermits did "Mother-in-Law," the Dave Clark Five covered "I Like It Like That," and in the early seventies, Ringo Starr did "Lipstick Traces." A large measure of Toussaint's talent was knowing how to write for each individual vocalist. One of the most gifted vocalists was Irma Thomas.

For nearly half her life, Irma Thomas has been billed "Queen of the Blues." Thousands of high school youths in the sixties grew up with her music. By the late seventies, they were flocking to Tipitina's, to moonlight cruises on the riverboats, and to seasonal dances where she opened many a set with a gleaming smile and nostalgic interrogation. "Awright now, who remembers St. Henry's CYO?" Hands up, cheers. "F&M Patio?" "Yeahhh!" "How 'bout Laborers' Union Hall?" And so it went, the fans now adults, and radiant Irma, still cutting records, even appearing on TV commercials. She didn't look like a woman in her forties—or a grandmother! But to borrow a line from Langston Hughes, life for Irma Thomas ain't been a crystal stair.

"I've been singing as long as I can remember," Irma reflects. "I can remember standing on the front porch singing in the country, but everybody sung and it wasn't any big thing."[17] An only child, Irma was born on February 18, 1941, in the small town of Ponchatoula, sixty miles north of New Orleans. Her parents, Percy and Vadar Lee, moved to New Orleans when Irma was three. The family moved around uptown neighborhoods before settling on Melpomene Street in 1951. Irma started singing in the Home Mission Baptist Church and grammar school plays. In the sixth grade she sang Nat King Cole's "Pretend" and won first prize at a talent show in the Carver Theatre. In junior high school two faculty members encouraged her to take voice lessons with an aim at opera singing. She recorded the class song with Henry Carbo (brother of Chuck and Chick Carbo who led the Spiders) at Matassa's J&M Music Shop. Music was beginning to offer a new world for Irma Lee when, at fourteen, she became pregnant and had to leave school.

"A pregnant young lady was a no-no. No matter what society you come from, you were a bad girl. It made me a fighter. It made me have more determination. You can imagine a fourteen-year-old girl not having any true direction. I had old-fashioned parents and my father insisted on marriage, which didn't work, of course."[18]

While her parents kept the baby, the young mother went to work at the Copper Kitchen, washing dishes on the graveyard shift for fifty cents an hour, but she was fired for annoying customers with her singing. She married a second time to Andrew Thomas, had two more children, and was working at the Pimlico Club as a waitress when she was fired again, this time for sitting in with Tommy Ridgley's band. But Ridgley saw the talent and asked her to join his group. Ridgley then took her to see Joe Ruffino of Ron Records, who liked her voice. She cut two songs written by Dorothy La Bostrie of "Tutti Frutti" fame. One tune, a lusty blues called "Don't Mess with My Man," hit the R&B charts, but Thomas claims she did not receive full royalty payments. Still, the song gave her a year of steady road work. When the Ron contract expired, Allen Toussaint invited her to join Minit.[19]

The convivial rehearsals in Toussaint's living room—by then moved to Earhart Boulevard—were a healing force. Through the struggles of early motherhood, Irma, by age nineteen, had experienced more than her share of hard knocks. She found a group of men serious about making careers. Toussaint went to work writing lyrics he sensed would evoke Irma's passions, songs akin to her own life. He gave her ballads, blues, and bouncy tunes suited to her expressive range. She sang clearly, made each word count. "It's Raining" features background singers chanting "drip-drop, drip-drop" and Toussaint's feathery keyboard work. The arrangement simulates the sadness of a cold drizzly day. Irma Thomas was no stranger to the mood.

It's raining, so hard.
   Looks like it's gonna rain all night.
This is the time
   I'd love to be holding you tight.
But I guess I'll have to accept
   That fact that you're not here.
I wish this rain would hurry up and end, my dear.

It's raining, so hard
   It brings back memories
Of the time
   When you were here with me.
Counting every drop,
   About to blow my top,
I wish this rain would hurry up
   And stop.

"We did most of the rehearsing in Allen's front room. We had everything down the minute we got to the studio. There were a lot of split sessions then, and we didn't have any time to waste. He was a perfectionist, but he worked with you in a way where he had your respect. He knew you could do it, he expected it, and he got it. Whenever he wrote, he would tailor a song for you and then he would tailor you for that song."[20]

The rehearsal sessions drew the artists out of themselves; the interplay of lyrics and musical ideas, the flow of melodies under Toussaint's guidance stirred the vocalists in personal ways. One day Ernie K-Doe wrote a song that Toussaint arranged innovatively to back Irma Thomas. "I Done Got Over" is blues on paper, but Toussaint organized the horn section in a call-response dialogue with her voice. He added a tailgate trombone, unorthodox for an R&B disc, giving the tune traditional jazz quality, with background singers punctuating Thomas's lead lyrics to give the sad song a push, perfect for the dance floor.

Although many Irma Thomas standards deal with blues themes, Toussaint's deft handling of jazzy rhythms and melodies imbued the sound with warmth. No singer in New Orleans sang blues to such adoring dancers as Irma Thomas. The months of work with Toussaint gave Irma Thomas a deeper sense of the blues, allowing her own poetic impulses to come forth. In 1963, after her contract had been sold to Imperial (along with Minit), she wrote and recorded her biggest seller, a powerful song of sorrow, "Wish Someone Would Care." It was straight autobiography.

Sittin' home alone,
   Thinkin' about my past,
Wondering how I made it,
   How long it's gonna last.
Success has come to lots of them,
   And failure's always there.
Time waits for no one
   And I wish someone would care.

Some folks think you're happy
   When you wear your smile,
But what about your tribulations
   And all your trials?

The good,
   The bad,
The hurt,
   All of this goes, too,
And I wish,
   How I wish someone would care.

Irma reflects matter-of-factly: "You figure, here I am a fourteen-year-old mother; by the time I'm seventeen I've got three kids; by the time I'm twenty-one I'm on my second marriage, and I'm having trouble with my husband. He was giving me hassles about the stage and my friendliness with people. The song was about how I felt at the time. I wanted someone to give a damn about what was happening to me for a change, to stand behind me, push me along, give the support I wanted. Just someone to tell me that they care.

Lie to me if you wanted to, but make me feel that I had someone behind me. It's a true song. . . . That's probably why it sold so well nationally."[21] She took to the road again, touring England in 1965. She stayed with Imperial until 1966, then went to Chess Records, and later, Canyon, but none of her later songs made the charts. "Wish Someone Would Care" became her anthem.

Irma Thomas developed a loyal following in New Orleans and worked a number of clubs on the Mississippi Gulf Coast. In 1969 Hurricane Camille devastated the coast and wiped out a full year of bookings for Irma; her spirits sagged. She moved to Oakland, California, ending up in a sales job at Montgomery Ward. She moved back to New Orleans and later married Emile Jackson, who became her manager. Tall, silent, a strict businessman, Jackson is quite the opposite of his wife's gregarious warmth. Through the seventies, he was instrumental in rebuilding her career, now on solid ground. She does many charitable benefits, has continued recording, and remains a first-class talent.

As the Minit artists developed under Allen Toussaint, Banashak and McKinley realized they needed a distributor. To earn decent profits they had to promote their records nationally. Lew Chudd, who had established Imperial in New Orleans with Bartholomew/Domino productions, approached them. "We didn't have any money," McKinley recalls, "so we let Chudd in for 50 percent. We felt it was better to own 25 percent each of a million-dollar company than it was to own 25 percent of not shit. If it had not been for our contact with Lew, we would have never gotten the distribution nationally. Lew had nothing to do with productions, only the distribution."[22]

Between 1959 and 1962, Minit released sixty-six single recordings (forty-fives) by some twenty different groups and solo artists. The songs were recorded at Matassa's studio, the masters shipped

to Chudd in Los Angeles, and duplicates stored in New Orleans. Chudd pressed the records, packaged them, mailed them to deejays, and sent his salesmen to stores to promote the product.

Although Minit was earning money, Banashak became disturbed. He hadn't heard from Chudd often enough—and had assumed that Chudd would educate him on the workings of the industry. This had not come to pass. Frustrated in his isolation, Banashak decided to start a subsidiary label. In 1961 Irving Smith, a local music shop owner, approached Banashak. His small Valiant label was sagging; he wanted out. Banashak convinced him to form a partnership. Toussaint would operate as he was doing for Minit on the new Instant label. Banashak first chose "I Like It Like That" by singer-songwriter Chris Kenner for Instant release.

Chris Kenner was born in a suburb of the city, ironically named Kenner, on Christmas Day in 1929. Like K-Doe, Irma Thomas, Roy Brown, and the Lasties, his formative music training was in church. He sang in choirs and performed with a group called the Harmonizing Four. He was not an overpowering vocalist but had natural gifts as a lyricist. Chris Kenner's first break came when Bartholomew saw him at the Dew Drop. "He told me he liked the way I sang," Kenner recalled. "We got together and recorded 'Sick and Tired.' A girl inspired me to write it. She was my woman."[23]

I get up in the morning and fix you something to eat,
  Before I go to work, I even brush yo' teeth,
I come back in the evening, you still in bed,
  Got a rag tied 'round yo' head.
Oh, baby, what you gonna do?
  I'm sick and tired of fooling 'round with you.

Fats Domino turned the tune into a hit in 1958, but Kenner's stay with Imperial was short-lived. He signed with Ron Records, Joe Ruffino's local label and recorded a gospel-based blues tune, "Life Is Just a Struggle." So was the Ron arrangement, which fizzled shortly. Banashak signed Kenner in 1961, and his first song on Instant, produced by Toussaint, was "I Like It Like That." The tune opens with a piano stride by Toussaint, reminiscent of Huey Smith, and quickly settles into a floating bounce, as background singers chant, "Come on, come on, let me show you where it's at."

I know a little place across the tracks,
   The name of the place is "I Like It Like That."
Now, you take Sally and I'll take Sue
   And we gonna rock away all our blues.

The last time I was down there, I lost my shoes.
   They had some cat shouting the blues.
The people were yelling out for more,
   And all they were saying was, "Go, cat, go."

Ike Favorite, who worked as road manager at different times for Domino and Kenner, says of Kenner: "He was a nice fellow, but he loved to eat and drink a lot. As long as he was eating and drinking, he was happy. He wasted a lot of money. Like they say, 'Easy come, easy go!'"

Drinking became a problem for Kenner, whose fortunes fluctuated greatly. He was a loner who drifted around the city, rarely living in one place very long. For Kenner to compose, Favorite recounts: "He would stay to hisself for two or three days. Then he would come out and say, 'I'm finished.' He put a lot of time and effort into it. That's why he was so great. Nothing came before his songwriting. Nothing."[24]

Kenner worked with Toussaint whenever possible. One of his best songs, "Something You Got," featured Toussaint's brief piano figures, echoing Kenner's gospel foundation in the vocal arrangements. His father had been a preacher, and Kenner's compositions were structured from hymns he had sung as a boy. In 1963, "Land of a Thousand Dances" put him on the national map again. "It came from an old spiritual called 'Children, Go

Where I Send You,'" Kenner said. "I just sat down and listened to this, and I got an idea and went to work on it. They cut the first part of it off, because it was too long. When I first recorded the number, I say, 'Children, go where I send you.' And the background singers, ask, 'Where will you send me?' And I say, 'I'm gonna send you to the land of a thousand dances.'"[25] And send us he did. The song was covered by Wilson Pickett and Patti Smith, generating good royalty checks for Kenner. The best-known version was by Cannibal and the Headhunters (whom Kenner later referred to as "Cannonball the Headhunter"). The tune was Kenner's last hit.

Because of his heavy drinking, Kenner drifted in and out of music. His voice, while strong, was not captivating and he had little stage presence. His relations with women were strained, at best; he wound up in the state penitentiary at Angola, Louisiana, in 1969 for a sexual offense. Released three-and-a-half years later, he continued writing songs and appeared at the jazz festival, but made few records. His 1955 song "Don't Let Her Pin That Charge on Me" was chillingly prophetic.

My trial came up and I began to scream,
   The judge told me to sit down.
It was just a scheme.
   My lawyer got up and began to shout.
The judge told him to sit down—
   He didn't know what it was all about.
Then that woman took the stand.
   The things she said, it was a crying shame.

Chris Kenner died of an apparent heart attack, on or about January 25, 1976. The body was discovered four days later. He was buried with little notice.

When Kenner's "I Like It Like That" began to soar in 1961, an angry Lew Chudd called Banashak from Los Angeles. Banashak reasoned: "I've been asking you over and over to tell me more about the business. I want to sell to distributors and know what the reactions are out there. You haven't told me nothin'. So I'm gonna find out." Chudd didn't view Kenner as a profitable item. "You're not going to do any good with that," he said in a huff.

Banashak continues: "We went with the record ourselves. All the way, mostly for the experience. What was it like to owe a pressing plant a fortune? And what was it like to try and collect your money? Tough. But we did quite well with that record—like 700,000 total."[26]

As the relationship between Chudd and Banashak chilled, McKinley ran into problems of his own. "Someone turned me in to the Federal Trade Commission for being a stockholder in a record label and a deejay as well. I had to either quit my job at the radio station or sell my stock. Being new in the record business and enjoying my radio thing, I sold out. I came in with $250, and I sold out for $40,000. I was still in my twenties and that was a lot of money. I should have kept my part of the publishing. That was stupid because I had twenty-five [percent] of 'Something You Got,' 'Ooo Poo Pah Do,' and 'Land of a Thousand Dances.'"[27]

Imperial was not exactly flourishing after the Instant affair. Banashak comments: "I started having two or three records happening at once, and Imperial wasn't doing nothing. And I don't know if he would let his men concentrate on my stuff since his was cold. Later on, when we talked about the [payola] scandal breaking, [Chudd] told me that he told Larry McKinley's boss that he was involved in a record company. And he was asking *me* to buy Larry's interest out. So, he provoked the situation, and the outcome was, we both got to the point where we dropped everything on him [Chudd]."[28]

Chudd now held controlling interest of Minit—including the artists under contract, the record catalog, the stock, and Toussaint's role as music director. Banashak meanwhile cut his own deal with Toussaint for Instant. Then in 1963 Toussaint was drafted into the army. Chudd by this time was having second thoughts about his own Imperial label and sold his interests to Liberty, getting out of record production altogether.

As a subsidiary of Liberty, the Minit sound developed by Toussaint went into eclipse. Although Banashak would continue issuing Instant forty-fives into the 1970s, the creative force dwindled with Toussaint's departure, and the stable of artists he gathered went their separate ways. By late 1963, the curtain slowly descended on the prolific R&B recording scene in the crescent city. Change was in the air. The Beatles, carrying influences of southern blues, hit the States with tidal force—long hair, a different brand of rock-and-roll, a revolutionary image whose shadow lengthened across the homespun idiom.

In New Orleans, the flush years were over.

THREE

Struggling Out of the Sixties

Chapter Eleven

DECLINE AND EXODUS

By 1964 the music industry in America was in the throes of a revolution. The Beatles, the Rolling Stones, and then their many imitators swept in from England like a tidal wave. New Orleans rhythm-and-blues was drowned in the deluge. For black musicians the change was shocking. Deacon John recalls: "With my band, the Ivories, we kept changing musicians. Right after the twist went over, then came the Beatles, and that's when the whole scene changed. They didn't want no horn players."[1]

As the music changed, so did radio. Deejays like Poppa Stoppa and Jack the Cat, who loved black music, faded from the scene. And after the payola scandal during 1960 and 1961 deejays no longer made decisions on the music they could play. Program directors now screened new releases.

At the Dew Drop, Frank Painia booked fewer acts. Black tastes were changing. Gone were the lavish reviews of the fifties; big shows were expensive. Moreover, police continually harassed Painia for noncompliance with an ordinance re-quiring a partition between blacks and whites on the premises. The problems became acute, and Painia filed suit in Federal court in 1964 challenging the constitutionality of the ordinance. The Civil Rights Act passed by Congress that same year removed the restrictions before the case was heard. By the late sixties, however, the Dew Drop had become a neighborhood tavern. Painia's death in 1972 marked its end.

Nightclubs elsewhere ran into problems. In 1961 New Orleans District Attorney Jim Garrison began a crackdown on gambling, B-drinking, and prostitution. Licenses were lost; some clubs closed. Mac Rebennack (Dr. John) remembers: "The club work that useta be so plentiful evaporated between sixty-one and sixty-three. It seemed to me mosta da clubs he was padlockin' was da joints that was somewhat available for gigs."[2]

Worse still was the decline of Cosimo Matassa's studio because of a feudalistic relationship between officials and members of Local 496, the black musicians' union. Union representatives visited recording sessions, often fining session players. Nonunion sessions were not unusual, causing the union to blacklist Matassa. "The union looked on the recording people as the enemy," Matassa said sadly. "The Local had no real experience with record people, other than guys coming in from outside. I got lumped in the same bag as those people. So a lot of my experience with the union was as adversary; they were antagonists. It's unfortunate. They never really had a supportive view of the recording thing."[3]

Earl King had his own assessment: "The black local was responsible. We never had problems with the white local. They [the black union] was nothin' but crooks and swindlers. They were so busy stealin' and what have you, they gave the musicians a hard way to go. It's one of the primary reasons that New Orleans crumbled. They made it difficult to record in New Orleans, and the major companies got tired of this and went elsewhere to record."[4]

Earl King lived through the musical revolution and shifted with the changing tides. When Guitar Slim died in 1959, Earl King was advancing to the foreground, influenced largely by Guitar Slim and Huey "Piano" Smith. Born Earl Silas Johnson on February 7, 1934, King received his early musical training from his father, Earl Sr., "a stomp-down honky-tonk pianist" who later turned to the ministry, and his mother, Ernestine, who wrote and sang gospel songs. Earl began singing in church at the age of six. As he grew older, he was attracted to gospel singers like Sister Rosetta Thorpe and to country yodeler Jimmy Rogers. Also, the music of Professor Longhair filtered into the streets from neighborhood jukeboxes. One day, while young Earl was harmonizing gospel tunes with some friends on a street corner, a middle-aged black man stopped to listen. "Gospel music won't pay you much," he advised. "You ought to be singing the blues. You could make a lot of money." Victor Augustine gave Earl his card. Several days later the young singer visited Doc Wonder's Curio Shop, where he met Huey Smith.[5]

Huey and Earl became close friends, soon forming a trio with Willie Nettles. Earl learned songs quickly. One club owner wanted a guitar player to sing so Earl strapped a guitar around his neck, pretending to strum chords as he sang. The ruse worked, and Huey subsequently began showing him chords, matching notes on the piano. By his late teens, Earl was spending time at Matassa's studio, writing songs. When a Savoy producer hit town, Earl and Huey fell in line for an audition. "I was scared to death. He was turning people down right and left. Musta had twenty guys get rejected. If they didn't like your material, they just say, 'Next!' Then he told me, 'You stand on the side!' "

That day Earl recorded his first discs for Savoy; however, the tracks sold poorly. Meanwhile he was performing with a group called the Swans. At the Dew Drop he found a father figure in Frank Painia, who helped buy Earl's first guitar and occasionally loaned him money. At the Dew Drop, he also met Guitar Slim, ten years his senior, who would influence his guitar style and songwriting. "I remember going up to his room one day at the Dew Drop. There musta' been six girls in the room, and he said, 'Now, girls, Earl is here. We have to take care of some business, so y'all just run along now.' He walked into the corner and got The Devil, that's what he called his guitar, and he put volume on his amp all the way up. Then he said he was going to play a song that came to him in a dream. It was 'The Things I Used to Do.' "

Johnny Vincent saw Earl King as a young Guitar Slim and signed him to record for Specialty. Borrowing melodically from "Things," Earl's recording of "A Mother's Love" told of a tender bond.

I once was happy in mother's arms,
 Then one day I went out on my own,
Now I'm sorry that I left my mother alone.

The song was a hit on the Gulf Coast and with this success he took a new professional name, Earl King.

"The Things I Used to Do" was hot on the charts when Guitar Slim had an auto accident that put him in the hospital. Frank Painia had bookings for Slim and knowing King was versed in Slim's material, sent him in Slim's place. In the days before instant media, substitution was relatively easy. King's first date was an Atlanta show with Ray Charles. "They had Slim's name on streamers across Auburn Avenue as far as you could see," Earl recalls, "like they do here for Mardi Gras. Of course, it frightened me half to death." The auditorium was jammed with fans. Ray Charles opened with "Greenbacks" and the crowd exploded. Earl sat nervously in his dressing room, stealing glances at the crowd. "Man, they had guys out there that looked like they'd take your throat off." When the announcer said, "Ladies and gentlemen, the star of the show—Guitar Slim!" Earl stepped to the mike, strummed the opening chord and began "The Things I Used to Do." "The lid blew off the house, man. Money went to flyin' everywhere. The band put all of their instruments down and helped me collect the money, and some lady pulled my necktie off, like to strangled me half to death."

Back in New Orleans—"Who's the first person I see, but Guitar Slim. He's walkin' out of the hospital, overnight case in one hand and his guitar in the other. He walks dead into me screamin', 'I hear you been imitatin' me. Man, if you wreck my name, I'm gonna sue you! I'm gonna kill you!'" Slim calmed down long enough for King to assure him he would receive a portion of the twenty-five dollars he had been paid each night. The friendship stayed firm.

After Johnny Vincent left Specialty to form the Ace label, taking King and Huey Smith with him, he gave Earl the chance to sharpen his songwriting talents and define himself as an artist. The days of imitating Guitar Slim were over. "I began to formulate a country-type bluesy thing. Vincent and I talked many times about stayin' in one bag, just hang in one groove and that's that."

The "country-type bluesy thing" colored "Those Lonely, Lonely Nights," a simple two-chord song in a style that became popular throughout southern Louisiana. Recorded in a primitive Jackson studio, the tune featured Huey Smith's lightly rolling piano, riffing horns, and an out-of-tune guitar. The disc didn't place in the R&B charts, but West Coast singer Johnny "Guitar" Watson covered it in 1956 and charted a smash hit. Country singer Mickey Gilley and rock-and-roll idol Dale Hawkins also recorded versions of the song.

Earl King signed with the Buffalo Booking Agency in Houston and set out on a tour with Gatemouth Brown and Smiley Lewis. Then came a string of one-nighters with B. B. King. But cheap hotels, banal food, and logging hundreds of miles a day took their toll. "I was in the middle of a wind and sand storm in Texas. The sky got black, and I couldn't stand the dust, man. I left my car with the band and caught the bus. And that was it. I've never been back working on the road for any agency."

But he did continue recording for Ace. Among his discs was the plaintive ballad "My Love Is Strong," a house-rocker called "You Can Fly So High," and the whimsical tune "Everybody's Carried Away." King gave each recording a distinctive character, experimenting with numerous combinations of sidemen and arrangers, never repeating the same approach. Vincent recognized King's ability as a producer, allowing him to produce Jimmy Clanton's "Just a Dream." King was never given credit.

King left Ace in 1959 because he says Vincent failed to pay royalties or furnish him with statements. The local union blacklisted Vincent. King signed for a short Gulf Coast tour with Sam Cook and Dave Bartholomew's orchestra. He was in an Imperial recording session with Dave Bartholomew when Vincent barged into the studio, shouting that King was under contract to Ace. Bartholomew shouted back, "I'm giving Earl a $1,000 advance on the session. You match this or get out!" Cosimo Matassa escorted Vincent out of the studio and that was the last they heard from him.

The Imperial contract marked another decisive change in King's career. His compositions were rhythmically complex, but with simple chordal structures. Bartholomew's studio band by the early sixties showed new faces. Drummer Bob French and his brother, bassist George French, gave King's material a more punctuated groove. Songs like "Mama and Papa" and the famous "Trickbag" highlight his Imperial catalog.

Twelve o'clock at night
   You walked out the front door.
You told me, baby,
   You were going to the drugstore.
But in my mind I know you were lyin',
   The drugstore closed at a quarter to nine. . . .

I said I saw you kissin' Willie across the fence,
   I heard you tellin' Willie I ain't got no sense,
The way you been actin' is such a drag,
   You done put me in a trickbag.

The sale of Imperial in 1963 ended Earl King's most productive period. In 1963 he incorporated Shirley's Music, one of the city's first black-owned rhythm-and-blues publishing firms. He wrote "Hum Diddy Do" for Fats Domino, and "Loan Me Your Handkerchief" for Danny White. He also wrote several tunes for the Dixie Cups—Rose and Barbara Hawkins, and their cousin, Joan Johnson —who had grown up in the Thirteenth Ward with the Nevilles. The Dixie Cups hit the charts with "Chapel of Love" and covered Sugar Boy Crawford's "Iko Iko" with flair.

Earl King also wrote "Big Chief" for his idol, Professor Longhair, who recorded it in 1964. "The gas of the session was Professor Longhair didn't realize we were going to use all those pieces. He thought we were going to use a bass, a drummer, and maybe a horn. He came in the studio and looked around, and was wonderin' why all the people were there. We were puttin' everything on at once, no over-dubbin'. We had eleven horns on that, and when Fess heard all that stuff go off, he stopped playin'. He was just shocked. We had to take an intermission so Fess could compose himself."

By 1973, after seven years under contract to Allen Toussaint and Marshall Sehorn, only a few of King's forty-fives made it to the market. A subsequent LP for Sonet records in Sweden, produced by author Samuel Charters, featured "Let's Make a Better World," King's showpiece for the seventies.

The world we know is built on skills,
   But that alone don't count.
Stop your sweat and toil of mind,
   It wouldn't be worth a dime.
You got to live and give, share and care,
   Really put love in the air.
When your neighbor's down,
   You've got to pick him up,
Nobody can live in despair.
   So everybody let's sing, sing, sing,
Let freedom ring.
   Let's all pitch in and do our thing.
Let's make a better world to live in.

Earl King enjoyed a comeback on the local nightclub circuit, working with the Rhapsodizers and the Radiators in the seventies and performing at the New Orleans Jazz and Heritage Festival and at the San Francisco Blues Festival with Deacon John. He is still going strong in the 1980s.

The Beatles had a disastrous impact on black music in New Orleans; however, one colorful vo-

Clarence "Frogman" Henry, 1960

Aaron Neville, 1967

Earl King at the Jazz and Heritage Festival, 1979

calist who profited from Beatlemania, Clarence "Frogman" Henry, enjoyed a breezy comeback when the Beatles chose him as an opening act for their first American tour in 1964.

Born on March 19, 1937, Henry at sixteen "started playing around 1953 with Bobby Mitchell. I was playing trombone and piano. In 1955 I got out of high school and formed my own band."[6] The following year he cut his first record for Chess, thanks to Paul Gayten, who was artist-and-repertoire man for the label in New Orleans. Henry's nickname stemmed from a line in his song "Ain't Got No Home"—in a gravelly rumble, "ah can sing lahk a frogg."

Frogman explains: "Poppa Stoppa, well, he took the song and everybody liked it. But they didn't know the name of the song. So he'd say, 'Here's the frog song by the Frog Man.'" The tune hit number thirty in the charts on the Argo label. "I started singing like a frog in high school," he recalls, "and I could sing like a girl and a chicken too."

He received good royalties on the song and in 1961 scored again with "I Don't Know Why But I Do," which reached the fourth slot on the charts that February. "You Always Hurt the One You Love" features Frogman's rich, sonorous singing at its best. The response line—"the one you shouldn't hurt at all"—is drawn out with much feeling. In May 1961 the tune reached the twelfth spot in the charts. He pushed his songs on tour, returned to New Orleans, and for the next two decades played five nights a week on Bourbon Street. A perennial favorite at the Jazz Festival, Frogman left the neon strip in 1980 for a more relaxed schedule. A polished showman whose performances are marked by vocal strength and a good banter with the crowds, Frogman Henry is a kind of walking repertoire of the R&B era. His Fats Domino renditions are priceless.

Frogman's jolly hold on life maintains a steady course. When the Rolling Stones reached the Superdome on their 1982 tour, they gave a party on a riverboat, with music by the Nevilles, the Dirty Dozen, Frogman, and others. After a grand set, Frogman Henry retired to a table near the buffet, catered by several of the finest local restaurants. Pleasurably, he supped on Chef Paul Prudhomme's alligator bisque, and after a third helping turned to one fan, a little in awe at the breadth of his palate, and pronounced with a wink: "I like that alligator, baby."

By the middle sixties many New Orleans musicians had left to pursue studio work in Los Angeles and New York. Of those who stayed, a small group rose through the layers of electronic rock with distinct musical identities. The pattern, as we have seen, was for a singer to move from an exclusively black following to a predominately white audience. Johnny Adams was an exception. He sang his gospel-tinged blues from the 1950s straight into the 1980s. Born in 1932, Adams began singing gospel with the Spirit of New Orleans and Bessie Griffin and the Consolators. He launched into secular music in 1959, when Dorothy La Bostrie convinced him to record her composition "I Won't Cry" for Joe Ruffino's Ric label.

Adams remained with Ric until Ruffino's death in 1962. For SSS International he recorded a substantial number of tunes in the 1960s, charting three times with the singles "Release Me," "Reconsider Me," "It Can't Be All Bad," and the album *Heart and Soul.* A thin, razor-sharp dresser with a quiet manner and good looks, he performs amid waves of sighs from ladies in the clubs. One of Adam's memorable recordings is "Losing Battle," a gospel-based ballad written by Mac Rebennack and Leonard James.

You know it's hard to love another man's girlfriend,
  You can't see her when you want to,
You got to see her when you can.
  You may be fighting a losing battle,
But you'll have so much fun trying to win.

By 1965 the wave of rock stars and the shift to soul music spelled trouble for New Orleans artists. In the absence of a viable recording industry, the choice for individual artists was either to leave or to build a local career based on previously established hits. Ernie K-Doe, Irma Thomas, and Tommy Ridgley kept their careers alive playing for high school and college dances, parties, and in a handful of clubs.

One singer to carve a new niche in this otherwise fallow period was Oliver Morgan, an agile dancer with the odd hit "Who Shot the La La?" Born on May 6, 1933, Morgan grew up in the lower Ninth Ward, a childhood friend of the Lasties and Fats Domino. He started singing in the Spiritual churches but learned piano from a pair of uncles, nicknamed Catchee and Big Four, blues singers who played the Ninth Ward taverns. His career began with little fanfare. "I was sittin' in a place called Sander's down in the Ninth Ward. It was a Friday night and Professor Longhair got drunk. Jessie Hill [Fess's drummer] knew I could play a little. He used to call me Coon Dog. He said, 'Coon Dog, Fess is drunk, and I need a piano player.' I said, 'I don't know if I can hold the gig that long.' He said, 'Yeah, you can do it.' I was so scared I drank a pint of Ancient Age whiskey. . . . I said, 'Man, give me that mike. I'm gonna try and sing.' I started and I looked back and people were dancing and carrying on, and I said, 'What?' "7

Morgan had several discs behind him when "Who Shot the La La?" took form in 1964. "I wanted to come up with something different. Something that would keep people's attention, so I said, 'Who Shot the La La?' A mystery, you know?"

Hey, Fellows! I want to know.
  What?
Tell me, Who shot the La La?
  I don't know.
Who shot the La La?
  I don't know,
I know it was a forty-four.

Whoever shot him ran out the door,
  All I know it was a forty-four,
But everybody turned and they looked at me,
  I shook my head and said, "No Siree!"

(Repeat first stanza)

Now the only three fellows do a thing like that,
  High Head, Joe Mouth, and my brother Jock,
If I hear anything, I'm gonna let you know,
  I don't believe in shootin' no forty-four.

"Now High Head is my first cousin. We all used to run together. Joe Mouth's real name is Joe Laten; he used to talk plenty. And my brother's name is Jock-O. I just put their names in it. They were characters, you know, used to drink plenty wine and eat that sausage and bread, heh heh."

By 1969 Morgan had toured the Gulf South, playing solo engagements and fronting shows by Otis Redding, Jackie Wilson, and Joe Tex. On Bourbon Street he was often seen driving a maroon-and-white Cadillac. "I used to pull up in front of the 544 Club and park on the sidewalk. I paid a guy to open the door and park it. They started calling me the 'King of Bourbon Street,' and they had a ceremony where they crowned me. I wore a cape."

Today Morgan works as a supervisory custodian at City Hall to support his large family. His appearances are less frequent now. Yet Oliver Morgan in the early eighties was the same cheery winner who played the proms and dances of the late sixties. Every time he got on stage, the old incantation began: "I wanna know . . . *who* . . . tell me, *whoooo—*."

The music industry never formed a firm base in New Orleans. In the 1960s most records were produced by local labels, small operations searching for lease arrangements with national distributors. And by the mid-sixties the independents of national stature—Specialty, DeLuxe, Aladdin, Imperial—had faded. The rise of rock-and-roll marked corporate growth for the big labels, against which the small independents could barely compete.

Cosimo Matassa was deeply frustrated. "Record producers were comin' from other parts of the country. They'd sign an artist, record him, but there wasn't any base of production, only performing. The nearest thing to it was the stuff Banashak and Toussaint had. But just as soon as it got a little bigger, they were distributed by another company. The real impetus gradually got shifted away. I just felt if nobody else did, I was going to start a *New Orleans* record company."[8]

Matassa had tried earlier with Dover Records but had to sacrifice the name under legal pressure from a publishing company. He kept the logo and corporate structure, renaming it White Cliffs. Besides producing, he was interested in leasing discs made by others. In the spring of 1966 saxophonist-vocalist Robert Parker, who had played with Huey Smith and the Clowns, brought Matassa a tune called "Barefootin'." Matassa leased the record, began distribution, and was promptly sued. A local label, NOLA, had produced the disc. "Clinton Scott and Ulysses Davis had a deal with Atlantic for first refusal of their productions. And Atlantic was giving them a few bucks a week and just kind of stringing them along. They were producing a lot of stuff that Atlantic kept sitting on for two, three, four months at a time, and then just sending it back, turning it down and all. As a result, they were kind of hanging on ropes. They were recording themselves into the poorhouse."[9]

When "Barefootin'" started selling, Ahmet Ertegun and Jerry Wexler called Cosimo, claiming that "Barefootin'" was a signed Atlantic disc. Matassa continues: "This guy brought it to me. Nobody ever had it. I maintained the thing was mine and went on selling it and ultimately sold close to a million copies of the thing. It never became a simultaneous hit at any one time across the nation, so it didn't rise in the charts as high as it might have."[10]

The song, a steady, driving rocker, hit the market at the right time. It was spring; people were shedding their shoes. "Barefootin'" gave them a theme song.

Everybody get on your feet,
    You make me nervous,
When you in yo' seat.
    Take off your shoes,
Pat yo' feet.
    We're doing a dance
That can't be beat.
We're barefootin', *(six times)*

Little John Henry,
    He said to Sue,
If I barefoot,
    Would you barefoot, too?
Sue told John,
    I'll stir yo' stew,
I been barefootin'
    Ever since I was two.

Matassa leased his biggest hit in late 1966. "Tell It Like It Is," as sung by Aaron Neville, a brawny balladeer with a golden voice, is one of the great love songs in modern American pop music. It also wrecked Matassa's business and left Neville with a bitter aftertaste. The tune was written by Lee Diamond, former bandleader for Little Richard, and was recorded on the Parlo label, owned by George Davis, saxman Red Tyler, and a schoolteacher named Warren Parker. On a chance meeting with Diamond, Davis mentioned that they had scheduled Aaron Neville to record and needed some compositions.

Born in 1941, Aaron Neville, the third son of a prolific musical family, had an astounding falsetto reach and deep, moving inflections that could transform average lyrics into stirring ones. According to Lee Diamond, "I wrote 'Tell It Like It Is' in about fifteen minutes. I thought it was a lemon, personally. When I got to the studio, Aaron did not like it." But Aaron's voice created a beautiful, timeless ballad.

If you want something
　To play with,
Go and find yourself a toy.
My time is too expensive
　And I'm not a little boy.

If you are serious,
　Don't play with my heart.
It makes me furious,
　You might as well do
What you want to,
　Go on and live, go on and live.

Diamond, paid modestly for his labors, forgot about the recording session until Davis called him to come hear the results. "Tell It Like It Is" was the best of the lot. The producers leased the song to Cosimo Matassa for distribution. Larry McKinley promoted the song on his own station and also made calls to disc jockeys in other markets, and by December 1966, the song was rising quickly in the charts. Lee Diamond, surprised at the tune's success, received several thousand dollars from the sales of "Tell It Like It Is" before he and Davis became involved in a contractual dispute with Warren Parker.

Lee Diamond remembers: "Where I made my mistake is not getting the original contract. I signed one duplicate contract. The duplicate was basically the same except for the part where Davis and I had the right to request an audit, a statement of royalties due. It gave the publisher sixty days to honor it or all rights revert back to the original writers."[11] Meanwhile, Cosimo Matassa was pouring everything into "Tell It Like It Is." Years later he reflected ruefully: "I wasn't as good a businessman as I should have been, and I over-extended myself in money borrowed. 'Cause simultaneously I built a record factory, started a distribution company, and a national record company. I spread myself too thin and the middle fell in on me. . . . I okayed credit I shouldn't have, and I moved records out that I shouldn't have, and I set myself up for the fall."[12]

To keep up with retail demands for the disc, Matassa made larger pressing runs at the plant he had just opened. But before money from record sales came in, he was beating off creditors. He struggled financially for another three years before tax problems shut him down in 1969. As composer of the song, Diamond was paid automatically by virtue of national industry policies. On the bottom of the pay scale was Aaron Neville, whose voice gave "Tell It Like It Is" the magic. Disillusioned, he went to work as a stevedore, playing gigs when he could, and did not resume a full-time music career until the 1970s.

With the decline of Matassa's studio, a huge void existed in the city. No decent studio existed in which to record. The magic of old R&B still worked at nostalgia dances, and some performers found work locally. But overall, it was a low period. Many musicians left and those who stayed had to struggle.

Chapter Twelve

THE NEW JAZZ AND AFO

For all the humor, romp, and histrionics of rhythm-and-blues, the idiom was structured with an identifiable sound, one that producers molded to fit each vocalist or group. As R&B reached its zenith in the early sixties, a school of experimental jazzmen worked patiently in the shadows. Many played R&B for commercial reasons, but they took the jazz idiom in imaginative new directions by plumbing the deep wellsprings of improvisation.

These modernists were a curious lot. Generally better educated than rhythm-and-bluesmen, they had more difficulty finding clubs receptive to their innovations. They were more musically fluent, exploring a range of harmonic, chordal, and rhythmic expressions, taking risks few R&B artists considered. The modernists held a profound belief in the essence of jazz as improvisational art. Two became distinguished educators.

The new pulse of the city's postwar jazz first circulated in a relatively small area surrounding the Magnolia housing project in impoverished central city. But the larger, national progression away from traditional and swing jazz was a biracial phenomenon, and in New Orleans skilled whites extended the new idiom too. The most successful, Al Belletto, was born on January 3, 1928.

For Al Belletto, jazz began with bebop. He got his first clarinet at age twelve while working weekends at his father's vegetable stand. His formal education began with marches and semiclassical fare, but in spare moments he hung out on the corner outside a black bar on Rampart Street, down the block from his home. Underage and white, he couldn't go in. "That jukebox blared all day long," Belletto recalls, "and us kids [would] listen to the blues music coming out of that saloon."

By fifteen Belletto was playing saxophone. "The first time I heard something by Charlie Parker, I couldn't believe what these people were doing. This is incredible! I mean, listen to that harmony, listen to the lines, and I really spent a lot of time listening—Lester Young and eventually Dizzy Gillespie, and that's how I started getting into harmonic playing."[1]

Charlie Parker's revolutionary sax style was in part a progression from pianist Art Tatum's sudden shifts in tempo during the thirties. Starting out in Harlem in 1939, the young Kansas City reedman cut a swath through New Orleans and swing jazz with trumpeter Dizzy Gillespie, who played behind the beat while Parker soared and descended. The broad tone of Charlie Christian's single-note runs on amplified guitar and Thelonius Monk's angular keyboard stitches rounded out the sound of seminal bebop. Parker's astonishing speed and long reaches broke through conventional chord changes, liberating harmonic movements. Other songs he infused with slower, bluesy currents. But as James Lincoln Collier has observed, bop's revolution was essentially rhythmic—by virtue of accelerated tempo, counterphrases off the traditional beat, and Parker's sax lines ranging "as far away from the beat as anybody in jazz."[2]

Nevertheless, it is not surprising that to a young New Orleans saxophonist, bebop's appeal was harmonic. In a city where the parade beat provided a rhythmic floor and horns conversed via standard melodies, improvisation by the 1940s had become somewhat circumscribed. Moreover, the saxophone was a late arrival to ensemble jazz, and in New Orleans the trumpet reigned supreme. Parker's rapid-fire sax passages—with the Gillespie trumpet lagging and circling behind Parker's ascents—hit Belletto right where he lived. "Bebop, yeah, I felt, 'Oh my goodness, this is it!'"

But he found few places to play bebop. When Belletto and trumpeter Benny Clement went to the Texas Lounge, where drummer Earl Palmer and pianist Edward Frank were exploring bop, "they let us sit in a couple of times." But police ejected Belletto and Clement for playing with blacks. He studied classical music at Loyola University but found the only place to play bebop legally was in striptease bars. "They would give

[us] maybe five dollars and we'd play seven hours. When I got out of Loyola, I was coming apart at the seams. I just wanted to play. So I got in a car and went off to Chicago with one of the strippers." By 1951 he was in Baton Rouge, studying for a master's in music at Louisiana State University. At his trial audition, a professor said: "Boy, you play with such spirit. I don't believe it. You play like a whore!"

One friend at LSU was Mose Allison, a white Delta pianist who is today an international star. Late at night, the only place Allison could find for trumpet experimentation was in his car. "It used to wig us out," Belletto laughs, "'cause he played such marvelous rhythms out there for hours at a time. I don't know if you've ever heard how a horn sounds in a car. It just sounds ridiculous." Upon graduation, Belletto formed a sextet, including trumpeter Clement, and secured an extended booking in Biloxi, Mississippi.

"We tried for the sound of a big band," Belletto recalled, "using a six-piece line-up. We played shout choruses with a high trumpet lead that sounded like the brass section of a big band; things with a trombone that sounded like the 'bone section; and the sax lead come off like a sax section."[3]

While passing through Biloxi, jazz singer Mel Torme heard the group and took an interest in them, helping to improve song arrangements. He then signed the sextet with a New York booking agency. While working through that agency, the group was introduced to bandleader Stan Kenton. Kenton's bands drew on a range of sources. In the mid-forties, he produced impressionistic pieces influenced by Stravinsky and Ravel; later came screaming trumpet sections and Latin American sounds. Kenton was a pioneer of progressive jazz with orchestral arrangements and long reaches toward European music; he was developing a series for Capitol Records when he flew to Lima, Ohio, to see the Al Belletto Sextet. Under Kenton's auspices, he signed his first contract in 1954 for *An Introduction to Al Belletto*. Kenton booked the group in the Blue Note, Chicago's famous jazz emporium. In New Orleans, disc jockey Dick Martin, programming a late-night jazz show on radio station WWL, started pushing the homeboy's records.

But going home was out of the question. Studio and recording outlets in New York meant survival. When the band traveled, it was a rag-tag affair. "The guys weren't making much money [so] to keep everybody happy, their families would go. We wound up having five cars." They pulled into Denver in the winter of '57 with money running out. The legendary bandmaster Woody Herman saw the group and congratulated Belletto. "I'm glad you got to hear it," Belletto said, "because it's probably the last month." Herman asked why and Belletto confessed that he had spent withholding taxes from the men's salaries "just to keep this thing rolling"—the cars and wives and families. Herman arranged a small loan and then astonished Belletto by inviting the sextet to join his own Thundering Herd. "My first night [with Woody] we had nine people on stage and seven of them frozen somewhere in Kansas."[4] In 1957 Belletto toured South America with Herman's band on a state department cultural mission through nineteen countries.

By 1960, however, jazz had begun suffering commercially. Clubs were folding. Record companies were pulling back jazz discs and moving heavily into rock-and-roll. But Belletto's music had ripened, and intelligent jazzmen appreciated it. While he was playing at the Playboy Club in Chicago, the company told Belletto of plans to open a club in New Orleans. Later, he toured the French Quarter facility and the Playboy corporation offered him the job as musical director. Disbanding the Al Belletto Sextet, he turned to the lucrative Playboy job and went to work booking the kinds of jazz acts he liked. When the club opened in 1961, he found a pool of modernists, both blacks and whites, and began hiring them.

Modernists of both races faced similar obstacles in the two idioms, Dixieland and rhythm-and-blues. Club owners kept a close eye on the tourist dollar, which paid for recognizable music. By the early sixties, clarinetist Pete Fountain and trumpeter Al Hirt had established reputations in the industry. Fountain's appearances on the "Lawrence Welk Show" led to a long recording career with Coral Records. He has had numerous appearances on the "Tonight" show on which, as late as 1982, he played several times yearly. Hirt's powerful trumpet was steeped in lyrical flourishes. By the early seventies Hirt and Fountain were national figures, each with his own nightclub.

White modernists played in the shadow of such Dixieland stars. Few clubs played host to the more cerebral impressions of modern jazz. Rhodes Spedale, longtime jazz critic, recalls: "There were some good [white] players, but a lot ended up leaving. Frank Strazzeri was a fine pianist; a trumpeter named Mike Lala was strong. Mouse Bonati played sax; he's in Vegas now. Bill Huntington played bass. Jack Martin played French horn and cut one of the few records of the time on a local label called Patio. I guess the main difference between the white and black modernists was one of influence. More of a West Coast sound influenced the whites."[5]

Collier writes that the West Coast school was "devoted to the cool, controlled manner that embodied elements drawn from European music."[6] Spedale's West Coast reference is echoed by James Drew, a jazz pianist and modern orchestral composer. Born in Harlem on February 9, 1929, Drew, who is white, learned piano as a teenager from the famous stride pianist Willie "The Lion" Smith and from boogie-woogie great Meade Lux Lewis. From New York School of Music, Drew graduated into a career as working jazzman and classical composer-educator. He arrived in New Orleans in

1962 as a graduate student in music and played modern jazz before moving on to Washington University in St. Louis for his doctorate. Drew reflected on the white and black modernists in New Orleans during the early sixties.

There was a difference—but not everyone can be lumped into categories. Bill Huntington was a strong bassist. But the West Coast influence was apparent [among whites]. It was a softer, less aggressive style of playing. People from the East Coast find it's different, like the lifestyle. The music I came out of was more hard-edged, fiery, with a more dramatic pronouncement of ideas. The other lacked fire, struck me as lackadaisical.

I worked black clubs that invited straight-ahead jazz, the Playboy and a few of the white clubs that allowed improvisation. The [racial] difference had to do with what was rooted in the popular music of a culture. Here it was not New York school at all. In New Orleans, it seemed to be more blues-oriented.[7]

Reminiscences of the black improvisational jazzmen recall a substantial bebop influence, but the phrase "not New York school" is only partially accurate. What's intriguing about Drew's analysis is the reference to a "blues-oriented" modern idiom. The formative experiences of black modernists were both an extension of bebop and a deeper search through the possibilities of ensemble improvisation anchored in a blues sensibility.

The year 1961 was an important one for modern jazz in New Orleans. Belletto's booking policies at the Playboy Club provided a rare outlet for jazzmen to articulate new improvisational statements. And by then a nucleus of black modernists had come together for Playboy engagements—pianist Ellis Marsalis, clarinetist Alvin Batiste, drummer James Black, saxmen Earl Turbinton and Nat Perrilliat, and bassist Richard Payne, among others. The city's modern jazz movement had emerged in the 1950s through a loose association of artists, at the core of which was Harold Battiste.[8]

Born on October 28, 1931, Battiste was encouraged by his father, Harold Sr., a tailor who played a clarinet as a sideline. "He showed me how to hold it, how to make sounds out of it. . . . He put my fingers on it." His mother, Pearl, played piano and sang in the church choir but didn't want Harold to become a musician. When the boy was nine, the family moved into the Magnolia housing project across from the Dew Drop. "From my porch, I could hear various people playing," Battiste recalls. "The name I remember most was Lee Allen, because I could hear his saxophone coming out of there and someone would say, 'That's Lee Allen!' Lee was really an idol of mine."[9]

In late adolescence, Harold met a pair of struggling young players who had also grown up in the densely packed neighborhoods surrounding the Magnolia project. Alvin Batiste played clarinet and Ed Blackwell drums. In the late forties, when the three began performing, their explorations into improvisational jazz were a reflection of the shifting mores, the changing folkways of the black urban culture. Bebop was one voice; the blues was yet another.

Central city, a name coined by urban planners, was originally a swamp. In the 1850s, canals and frontage roads were carved out to link plantations fronting the river with the New Basin Canal, which cut through the backbottom. The poorest blacks were herded into this demiland, fraught with mosquitos, where animals got stuck in the mud and sometimes decomposed in it after unyielding rains.[10] By the 1920s, concrete had filled the canals to make streets. When the Magnolia and more massive Calliope housing projects were built in the 1930s, many blacks viewed them as a step up from the decaying wooden tenements owned by slumlords. It was only the failure of one mayoral administration after another, starting in the 1950s, that led to lopsided development elsewhere in the city at the expense of decent housing for the poor. By 1978, ten thousand people were on the waiting list to move into the crime-ridden, overcrowded projects.

The human process of ghettoization was another matter. The old frontage road alongside New Basin Canal became a dumping site for car parts and worn machinery. Blacks called it Silver City because of the metallic sheen. Silver City and Dryades Street were poles of the interior, like reflections in the distant mirror of the city's progress. When the projects were built, the neighborhoods seemed to have a chance.[11] In the streets around the projects, taverns kept the blues alive on jukeboxes; clubs like the Dew Drop provided stages for R&B and late-night burning jazz. An ethos endured in shadows of the city; it ran through the bars and clubs and churches, the values of a culture that prized music. The clubs were an extension of the corner bar or honky-tonk; they functioned as secular churches with music the ceremonial function of a people.

Rhythm-and-blues was a rising voice of the city. But to Harold Battiste, Alvin Batiste, and Ed Blackwell, the idiom was too simple, too confining. They played rhythm-and-blues for money, but bebop drew them together artistically. In 1949 Ornette Coleman, living in New Orleans with the Lastie family, joined this circle of musicians. Melvin Lastie introduced him to the small coterie of local jazzmen who, like Ornette, were intent on advancing improvisational statements beyond bebop. In a 1966 profile of Coleman, A. B. Spellman wrote: "Ornette recalls only two who were open to what he was doing: clarinetist Alvin Batiste [regarded as an underground giant of the clarinet] and drummer Ed Blackwell, whom Ornette met again in Los Angeles and who later joined him in New York."[12] Spellman's description of Blackwell clarifies Coleman's appreciation of his talent.

Blackwell had done a lot of studying, both of traditional New Orleans drums when he had lived there and of African and Bata (Afro-Cuban) drumming, and he had brought all of this study to his own style of playing. He has a reverential approach to drums, and building his own set is typical of him, concerned as he is with every aspect of percussion. . . . He had cultivated the New Orleans march sound so that he was able to impart the pedestrian quality (in the nonpejorative sense) to the modern sound. With Blackwell's technique and with his knowledge of the sonics of drums, he was able to play overtones that few drummers were aware of.[13]

Unable to find a niche, Ornette Coleman left New Orleans, but he and Blackwell would meet again in later years and work together in Los Angeles and New York.

Alvin Batiste had gone to Booker T. Washington High School and, with a firm grasp of the classics, performed at a young age with the New Orleans Philharmonic Symphony Orchestra. Ed Blackwell was experimenting with a loose African beat on drums, an extension of the second-line percussion in the street parades. He was a disciple of Paul Barbarin, a drumming master of the old school. But the greatest influence on his music was the parades in New Orleans. He later reflected: "They were so beautiful that even now I still feel the rhythmic inspiration that I got just from being able to run along behind the parades, coming from the funerals and things."[14]

Alvin Batiste entered Southern University in Baton Rouge but returned to New Orleans frequently enough to keep the modern jazz association alive. Musicians from downtown and further uptown made the rounds of night spots where modernists might play. One such spot was a small bar on the side of the Dream Room in the French Quarter. Edward Frank, a pianist, explains: "I had Blanche Thomas, Chuck Badie, and Ed Blackwell, and we did an after-hours thing for the barmaids, musicians, dancers, and waiters. We'd be feeling good when we would get off at seven [in the morning] and we would go by my house and

Ellis Marsalis, 1983

Al Belletto

keep playing. This was in the Magnolia project—only a couple of blocks from the Dew Drop. There was a bench right in front of my house and guys would come sit on the bench and drink beer and listen to the music we played. We would put on a pot of beans and sit around all day and play.''[15]

Harold Battiste's mother wanted him to acquire a profession. When he entered Dillard University in 1947, his profession was clearly music. He was writing serious jazz compositions but kept a shrewd eye on the burgeoning R&B market. In his senior year, he met a freshman named Ellis Marsalis. Marsalis was born on November 14, 1934, in Gert Town, four years before the neighborhood's other distinguished pianist, Allen Toussaint, was born. Marsalis began on clarinet and in high school switched to saxophone, "which was very much the instrument of the peer group. There were a few rhythm-and-blues bands. They hadn't quite gotten around to rock-and-roll yet.''[16]

In the late 1940s, the Booker T. Washington High School auditorium held jazz concerts. In the spring of 1949, Ellis saw Dizzy Gillespie play, "and it really turned me around, because I didn't know what he was doing, but I knew that was some excitement in it and I knew there was something that I wanted to do. I didn't have any way of getting at it, except to go out and take records and stand in the corner at home and play saxophone."

By the time he reached Dillard, Marsalis was playing R&B with a group called the Groovy Boys. At Dillard, Harold Battiste showed him how to read chord symbols and "was very, very influential in my earlier development of getting into jazz. Harold was a prolific writer. He wrote some very beautiful arrangements, and extremely challenging. He had a lot to do with me deciding to become a piano player because the first group that we formed, Harold was playing tenor saxophone, and Alvin Batiste was playing clarinet; Edward Blackwell was playing drums. And we started to play Charlie Parker tunes and [Harold] wanted to play saxophone, so that meant I had to play piano. And I didn't really object because I just wanted to belong. You know, play the piano—fine—play the kazoo, anything. Just let me play!''

The jazz improvisations, building on bebop, that Harold Battiste and his comrades were refining had taken hold by the mid-1950s. Younger musicians began to follow their work. Perhaps the most intense member of this younger group was James Black, born on February 1, 1940, and raised in Treme, a stone's throw from the French Quarter. Black's first impression of the drums came from a tiny old man "who played tom-toms, with the nails around 'em, and the scene painted on the bass drum and the lights on it, like it was a palm tree—and this old man looked like he was having so much fun, and the way it sounded, I must have been eight or nine, made me decide to play.''[17]

The Black family lived around the corner from the colorful Caldonia Inn, where the wide-eyed boy caught glimpses through the window of Professor Longhair. Neighborhood parades began at the Caldonia, and the young James Black would follow the Yellow Pocahontas, a Mardi Gras Indian tribe, and join in the second-line marches behind funerals. His family was one of two black families on the block during James's childhood years. "Most of my childhood playmates were white. . . . Environment influences your personality, tastes and distastes, and in the intellectual development among black and white people, the white people have been a shade higher, into reading and all this." He discovered novels such as *Les Miserables* and *A Tale of Two Cities* from his white playmates.

"And I'd go around the corner to the black kids and they'd say, 'We don't wanna read that! We wanna do something else!' So consequently, I was caught in the middle right here, between two worlds. And I had to fight the white cats, and go around the corner and fight the black cats. I was torn between two cultures, thinking, 'What's the matter with you people?'"

Drums were not his only instrument. His mother paid for piano lessons at Clark High School; the music teacher told him there were too many drummers, so James began playing trumpet. He played early R&B gigs, but by his junior year in high school, Black wanted more challenging music. The impetus of his first jazz work was Stan Getz and the West Coast school. "I liked the harmony they were playing, and I wondered if we could play that. And nobody was writing. I said, 'Well, let me see if I can write it.' I found out what the notes were, found the chords on the piano, and I just did some experimentation, got some horn players over from school, played our little West Coast jazz." Pianist Edward Frank recalls: "Red Tyler, Earl Palmer, Chuck Badie and me, we were tilted more to the West Coast type of jazz. Harold Battiste was more into the East Coast sound, more of a black scene, and the West Coast was thought of as white."[18]

The apprenticeship of James Black advanced several steps when he encountered the group led by Harold Battiste playing at Foster's near the Dew Drop. Alvin Batiste was on clarinet, Richard Payne on bass, Ed Blackwell on drums. "The first time I ever heard Ed Blackwell," Black states, "I was completely amazed and motivated, just uplifted. 'Cause I didn't know anybody who could play like that on drums. The first time I heard him, it just hit me: 'James, you got to go home and practice.'"

Black was something of a loner, given to long solitary sessions in the woodshed behind the house. Jazzmen like Blackwell were five to ten years older than James, and when he approached them, he wanted to be ready. "They were further advanced. We were bluesing and boogying and carrying on, but they were talkin' about jazz, the cerebral part. It was like the third part of a trinity; you got your emotional, you got your physical, now you can *think* about what you were playing.

It inspired thought about the music. I was down here in Treme, sheltered, practicing."[19]

Ellis Marsalis continues: "To play the nightclubs, you had to be able to play shuffles on the piano, you had to play the R&B solos, you had to back up singers, and I never refused to do any of that, cause I just wanted to play. But ultimately, the more I became involved in jazz, I was a confirmed bebopper, and I began to concentrate more of my energies and time on trying to figure out where I could play this music."[20]

Harold Battiste meanwhile was teaching music in a public school in rural DeRidder, Louisiana, but quit in anger when permission was denied to organize a parade down the main street. He returned to New Orleans to teach, but found administrators, intimidated under the segregationist school board, unreceptive to his requests for better instruments and a serious approach to music education that included teaching the students to read notes.

In 1956, Marsalis and Blackwell journeyed to Los Angeles for a reunion with Ornette Coleman, who was winning few fans with his wild, fragmented saxophone voicings that had offended traditionalists in New Orleans. But to Marsalis: "It was interesting to play with Ornette 'cause I didn't know what he was doing, so I just had to play what I could play. At that time he was still formulating." Structurally, Coleman's music had no preset chord sequences: he was given to sharply cut tones, which often sounded rough or gritty, and his ideas of harmony later developed into a stripping down of it, scattering shards of melody over a plane of shifting modes.

Marsalis recalls: "The musicians would stand in the back and laugh. And when he was in New York [in 1962] and Leonard Bernstein proclaimed he was a genius, then they stopped laughing." But in Los Angeles, the experiments were not paying off. Battiste knocked on doors of record companies, trying to shop demo tapes, but found in an industry obsessed with rock-and-roll that an experimental jazz group had little hopes of a contract. Discouraged, the group disbanded. Back in New Orleans in 1958, they regrouped as the American Jazz Quintet, which included Blackwell, Alvin Batiste, Harold Battiste, and Richard Payne and William Swanson as alternate bassists. Ten years after Harold's early bebop explorations with Alvin, the nucleus of the central city modernists was still intact. "It was almost like a survival group," Ellis recalls. Finally, Blackwell left for New York to rejoin Ornette Coleman, whose radical designs had filled into a shape critics and other jazzmen were taking seriously. Free jazz, or "the new thing," was built on Coleman's notion of improvisational latitude. As he told Jonathan Foose, "Any instrument can play the lead as long as it does not resolve itself to the melody."[21]

The music ultimately recorded by the American Jazz Quintet bears no resemblance to free jazz, with the possible exception of certain drumming solos by Ed Blackwell. In fact, the improvisational music recorded by the Quintet is marked by tight harmonies and spontaneously composed melodic lines. Coming out of America's oldest jazz tradition, these men had also played enough rhythm-and-blues to understand the provocative usages of both idioms. Theirs was a large songbook with many rhythms; as beboppers they believed in well-wrought intonations and used honks, growls, and slurred phrases sparingly if at all.

The instrumental duets, like the harmonic variations of the *Original American Jazz Quintet* album (included in *New Orleans Heritage Jazz, 1956–1966*), reflect the polished talents of urbane jazzmen. In the tradition of New Orleans jazz, they placed great importance on the relationship between the drum and the piano for its harmonic strengths, all the while embracing the bopper's faith in each soloist's innate perception of how far to stretch comfortably. The ensemble work is often seamlessly rhythmic; the improvisations executed with a control that always resolves the solo variations to the base melody. The composer listed on each song, according to Harold, is the artist who laid down the basic melody, etching these ideas spontaneously within the improvisational space, sometimes in a straight solo, sometimes in harmonic combinations. Alvin Batiste is listed as composer on four of the ten songs: "Nigeria," "Capetown," "Morocco," and "Chatterbox." Though the first three titles suggest impressionistic portraits of Africa, the music is more a gathering of piano shuffles, drumming with crisp syncopations and parade beats, and elegant duets between Alvin's clarinet and Harold's tenor. Finally, the distinctive clarinet of Alvin Batiste surfaces.

"Morocco," for example, opens with an abbreviated clarinet-tenor duet, staggered figures punctuated by splashes of Blackwell's cymbals, with Marsalis's left-handed chord progressions anchoring the harmony. The lead passage is repeated with Harold's tenor played softly to accentuate Alvin's clarinet, which then begins to roam melodically—quick ascents reversed by playful, almost satirical, plunges into the lower register, then shifts back up with Blackwell's drumsticks forming a backbeat. Alvin's plunge-rise motif breaks into a ripple of high notes strung out like a chain of stars and then the song begins to change, the clarinet embarking on swift passages brought to a low halt by elongated notes, then delicate, bursting phrases and the return to duet play with Harold's tenor in rising unison, the two reeds driven by Blackwell's hits on the metallic drum casing. Delicately, Alvin draws tight little melodic circles which ebb out, then revive to the groundbeat on drums.

Although the Quintet served to bind these innovators musically, their individual lives moved in and out of the city. Harold realized record production was weak in New Orleans and on trips to Los Angeles kept calling on producers and distributors. One day at Specialty Records, he ran into his old friend Bumps Blackwell (producer of

AFO executives, 1961. *From left:* Melvin Lastie, John Boudreaux, Red Tyler, Harold Battiste, and Chuck Badie

James Black, drummer

Little Richard's "Tutti Frutti"; no relation to Ed Blackwell), who was handling a new singer, Sam Cooke. Blackwell asked Harold to supply arrangements for Cooke's next date. Of the songs selected, "You Send Me" hit the *Billboard* top ten in the fall of 1957, the first of many hits by Sam Cooke.

Art Rupe, president of Specialty, asked Battiste to return to New Orleans as a producer/talent scout, much as Dave Bartholomew was functioning for Imperial. Thus, as the 1950s drew to a close, Harold Battiste was playing modern jazz and, from a one-room office on North Claiborne Avenue, auditioning artists for rhythm-and-blues recordings. The Specialty discs he produced were among the most innovative R&B hits of the period: the Monitors' "Rock-and-Roll Fever," Art Neville's "Cha Dookey Doo," and Jerry Byrne's "Lights Out." But by late 1960, Battiste was disappointed on two scores. Little modern jazz was being recorded, and worse, he saw too many black artists, uneducated or ignorant of business practices, signing with record companies and being paid poorly for their efforts. The city had no managerial class to shepherd careers through the money-jungles of New York and Los Angeles recording deals.

Battiste decided to form a label, All For One. AFO was a simple enough idea, but the economic and political implications were staggering in light of the times. In a way, the concept is still visionary. Battiste devised a plan whereby profits would be shared among company members. For years, whites had controlled local recording. Battiste explained: "See, that is what we needed to do. They say we can sing and dance. Let's own it! Why should some cat up in the Shaw Booking Agency sit on his ass, on the phone, and run Ray Charles around the country, and he gets rich? Or take a cat like Art Rupe. Why should he sit on his ass, can't even keep time to the music, and he becomes a wealthy man—and all of us are beggin' for rent money? *Just own it yourself.* And the only hitch was how do we satisfy the union?"[22]

Enter Melvin Lastie. By 1960, the prodigious Ninth Ward trumpeter was an agent for the local black musicians' union. Lastie attended recording sessions to ensure the musicians were not forced to work overtime without compensation. Battiste wanted Lastie for his musical talent, but beyond that, he wanted a diplomatic relationship with the union. Battiste continues: "It wasn't a matter of avoiding what the union must do, but how do we elevate ourselves from employees being paid forty-one dollars for a record date? How do we move from that point to becoming owners where we are using our talent and reaping the benefits? My solution was to form a cooperative and buy stock with session money. Melvin was very instrumental in that. He had a strong urge to do business."

All For One became a reality in the summer of 1961. The founding members were Lastie, saxophonist Red Tyler, drummer John Boudreaux, guitarist Roy Montrell, bassist Chuck Badie, and Battiste, who became president. As the recording sessions picked up, other musicians joined AFO: saxophonist Warren Bell, James Black, Ed Blackwell, Ellis Marsalis, bassist Richard Payne, saxophonist Nat Perrilliat, female vocalist Tami Lynn, and Alvin Batiste.

AFO's biggest hit came about in a circuitous fashion. Mel Lastie's Uncle Jessie Hill brought a young singer named Barbara George for an audition. Battiste liked her style immediately, and AFO bought her contract from Hill. The day of recording, she came with the Ninth Ward singer Prince La La (Lawrence Nelson, whose brother, Walter "Papoose" Nelson, was Fats Domino's guitarist). Battiste liked Prince La La's work and decided on a split session. Prince La La's "She Put the Hurt on Me" made a respectable showing in the R&B charts, but Barbara George's "I Know" hit paydirt. In November of 1961 it reached number three in the pop charts, one of the city's biggest hits. The tune was influential because of Lastie's beautiful, extracted cornet solo—based on the gospel standard "Just a Closer Walk with Thee"—which Battiste had written to bridge Barbara George's bluesy lyrics.

With "I Know," Battiste and AFO moved ahead. Battiste realized rhythm-and-blues would pay expenses for sessions of modern jazz work; thus the R&B releases continued. Earnings from the Barbara George disc gave AFO a solid start—and allowed studio time for improvisational jazz by the AFO principals. Over the next eighteen months, a string of remarkable jazz works were cut. Marsalis did an album entitled *Monkey Puzzle,* on which the title cut and several others were composed by drummer James Black. Nat Perrilliat contributed a lyrical sax line to the title song, with Black's melodic percussive work the perfect foil to Marsalis's fluid keyboard harmonies. Harold viewed the song as "a moderate waltz that captures the spirit of children at play."

The AFO artists recorded more than one hundred songs; to date, only thirty-five have been released in the anthology *New Orleans Heritage Jazz, 1956–1966,* which Harold issued many years later. It is an appropriate title in light of the range of idioms represented on these discs—bebop, cool and progressive improvisations with lengthy solos by various artists, pop songs, R&B, and blues by Johnny Adams. The heritage behind this music was prototypically New Orleans—in effect, different musics played from the deep heart of jazzmen.

The *AFO Executives* is a good example of how concessions made to the pop market were used for jazz designs. The music divides between the A and B sides of the disc, the former featuring such standards as "Old Man River" and Gershwin's "The Man I Love," layered with bluesy horn passages. Side B is closer to the New Orleans sound, with its witty use of R&B fragments, and so foreshadows the jazz-rock fusions of the seventies. "Old Wyne" is vintage AFO fusion music. Drummer James Black composed the base melody, with Harold playing piano. Mel Lastie is the cornetist, Red Tyler plays tenor, and Chuck Badie is on bass.

The tune has a distinct rhythm-and-blues melody with Harold's chord progressions on piano keeping time with the second-line parade beat established by Black's percussive work. The horn duet, Mel and Red, advances a simple, repetitive melodic figure, and out of this Tyler's tenor issues a long, rolling line of middle-register notes laced over the parade beat. As Tyler fades, Lastie's cornet begins to rise, somewhat muted at first, then breaking ahead in pulsing phrases that end abruptly, like a singer in a shout chorus, each time letting the drumbeat and keyboard chords accelerate to the point where the song seems to be lapsing into redundancy and then the new outline becomes clear: the horns break into a series of call-response passages, with Lastie at first articulating slightly muffled lines to Tyler's broad, warm, bouncy tenor refrains. Then Melvin launches into a series of blues peals with a throaty, rasplike quality, and the horns dissolve away altogether. The beat continues and we are hearing a prototypical second-line beat when the voices come in: "Tee na-na-na . . . na-na na-na na. . . ," then snatches of voices singing "Wading in the Water."

Tami Lynn, a fine female vocalist who joined AFO, recalls an appearance at a St. Louis disc jockeys' convention.

Sam Cooke and many others were at the hotel. This is the beginning of my career, see—Jerry Wexler was there. We brought albums to showcase. AFO consisted of funk, jazz, blues, pop; the ability to see the band itself as versatile, the singer was versatile. We went to this convention where Dionne Warwick had "Don't Make Me Over"—and we turned some heads around. People noticed us. Because AFO was like the Jazz Crusaders—advancement and jazz. We're playing funk jazz where people could be happy, not just progressive jazz where you sat and listened. It was the kind of jazz you could stomp your feet, get up and feel things with.[23]

But AFO jazz remained financially dependent on the marketing of R&B songs, targeted for the pop market. Battiste cut a deal with Juggy Murray, the black owner of Sue Records in New York, to distribute the AFO discs. But Murray crossed Battiste by luring Barbara George away from AFO. "He started buying her a Cadillac, her clothes, the whole works," Battiste said. John Broven wrote: "Murray didn't tell her he was buying the 'works' with funds from her own royalties. He soon persuaded her to sign with Sue."[24] After signing a contract with Murray, Barbara George's career sank in a matter of months. Her departure also destroyed Battiste's arrangement with Murray as AFO's distributor. Battiste and Melvin Lastie moved to California; a number of AFO regulars followed in time. They hoped that a Los Angeles base would facilitate a distribution arrangement. But the tide of Beatlemania was now sweeping the country, and by 1964 the roof had caved in on AFO. The AFO jazz recordings done after Barbara George's departure and Al Belletto's Capitol albums constitute the New Orleans modern jazz legacy of the 1960s.

Why did AFO fail? The distribution bust with Sue Records was a major factor. And some local musicians, outside the AFO family, resented the organization. Marshall Sehorn, a white producer who later formed a record studio with Toussaint, went so far as to say AFO artists "got greedy."[25] But Harold Battiste's assessment seems closer to the mark. "Instead of [black] artists coming to AFO, everybody then began forming record companies. Instead of a little company that had some clout on the national level, we had fifteen New Orleans record companies, none of which had any clout."[26]

When AFO collapsed, the principal artists followed divergent paths. Melvin Lastie went to New York. Drummer John Boudreaux remained in California. Tami Lynn eventually moved to London in the 1970s for a nightclub career. Marsalis continued in New Orleans, extending his interests into classical music, playing with the Al Hirt band from 1967 to 1970, and later performing at a special White House concert. Al Belletto put in many days on the college circuit, judging band contests and encouraging new talent. He helped launch the careers of vocalist Angelle Trosclair, who had two albums to her name by the late 1970s, and Johnny Vidacovich, a brilliant young drummer. When the Playboy Club folded, Belletto cut another album, *Coach's Choice,* and in 1981 was performing with Al Hirt in a quartet including bassist Bill Huntington.

Richard Payne, an excellent bassist, was still active in modernist circles in 1982. James Black took to the road in the 1960s, drumming for Lionel Hampton and Yusef Lafeef before returning to New Orleans, where he continues to perform and compose. Alvin Batiste went to work at Southern University and established a jazz program that today is one of the nation's finest. Ellis Marsalis also became an educator, teaching jazz at the New Orleans Center for the Creative Arts, a public high school for artistic students. In 1981 James Drew and Tami Lynn returned to New Orleans. Drew pursued a career evenly divided between jazz records and modern compositions for symphonic orchestras. *West Indian Lights* was performed by the Boston Symphony. In the early 1980s Drew was playing jazz gigs, many with Tami Lynn, an accomplished vocalist.

Harold Battiste did not return to New Orleans. After the AFO experiment, he became musical director for Sonny and Cher. As the rock duo rose to stardom in the 1960s, Battiste kept a hectic pace in recording circles. When Melvin Lastie died in 1972, Harold went through a period of deep introspection, wondering what the friendship and years of work together had meant. The album *Hal and Mel Alone Together* showcased Lastie as no other record has, albeit posthumously. In 1976, Battiste selected the AFO master tapes he thought best and produced a four-LP set, *New Orleans Heritage Jazz, 1956–1966,* on his label Opus 43. The records represent the foundation blocks of

New Orleans's postwar improvisational idiom, which by the 1970s was flourishing. The music of *New Orleans Heritage Jazz* is an eloquent statement by artists who had the tenacity to explore jazz regions beyond bebop at a time when the local market was dominated by R&B. The AFO pop songs were solid, often laced with satirical lyrics about street life. But in their fidelity to jazz, the AFO pioneers broadened the city's musical vocabulary. The blues heart of the core culture beats steadily through many songs, while others rise to a level of classy, urbane sophistication. In the final measure, these artists saw jazz as an evolutionary art form at a time when the white market was opening up to rhythm-and-bluesmen. They held to that vision, against the odds, and we are much the richer for it.

Chapter Thirteen

JAZZ AND BLUES KEPT COMING

The early 1960s was a period of great struggle, but the exodus of talent was never so heavy as to retard the city's musical growth. In the wake of AFO, new players appeared, deepening the improvisational currents, spilling beyond the embankments of bebop. In this respect the studio work of Harold Battiste and Alvin Batiste constituted an odd legacy. As individuals they left key impressions, but their recordings did not circulate. By 1966, the modernist trend was established, though its two most seasoned exponents no longer resided in the city.

The next five years saw a decided change, and the decade following was radical by comparison. The sax sound rising out of the late 1960s was more hard-driven, burning with blues phrases, a poignant voice set against the collapse of segregation in New Orleans. The softening of racial edges in the first few years of the 1970s ushered in a revival of rhythm-and-blues and provided a new audience for modern jazz.

The towering figure of the middle 1960s was John Coltrane, who moved from bop circles into a plane distinctly his own. "Sheets of sound" is the famous phrase ascribed to Coltrane's early tenor work—torrents of notes, cascading one upon the next as if in waves. His passion for harmony had many manifestations, including moody movements in the lower register, while in his later work, the tenor sweeps achieve a quality of incantation, a voice so personal rising from the reed as to suggest mystic elevation, man become art.

The New Orleans saxophone player most heavily influenced by Coltrane was Earl Turbinton, who felt "a sort of spiritual kinship" in sharing Coltrane's birthday, September 23; though born in 1941, he was fifteen years younger. By the time the two met in 1962, Earl Turbinton had gone through several stages of his musical growth.

Turbinton was born in central city and received early exposure to such musical figures as Guitar Slim, B. B. King, and Bobby Bland. A man who lived next door played records by Charlie Parker and Dizzy Gillespie, but bebop was viewed by many blacks "as dope fiend music." Earl's younger brother, Willie, was pounding the piano at age four. Earl Turbinton, Sr., occasionally played trombone; Mrs. Turbinton sang. Neither was a professional musician. Earl's first teacher was Professor Victor.

He had a house which must have had a thousand instruments; tuba, maybe twenty or thirty saxophones, twenty or thirty trumpets and trombones. You'd bring your own mouthpiece and Professor Victor would say, "Go in there and get an alto 'til you find one that feels good to you. Play all these horns."

He had a way of arranging; I mean, this is gonna sound unbelievable, but after I had been playing about two months, I could play melodies to a lot of popular tunes. He had a system where he wasn't teaching me to read music written on manuscript paper, but whatever the *number of fingers* for that particular note was.

After I'd been taking lessons two months, we'd go to old folks homes and play for free—I mean for hours—things like "April in Paris," "Stardust," and I didn't know that I didn't know how to read music.[1]

Earl was thirteen and Willie was eleven in 1954 when the Turbintons moved into the Calliope Street housing project.

In the projects there were quartets, singing doo-wop music. Little bands got together. Erving Charles, Willie, and I played together. Erving's family stayed right across the street. His father, Buddy Charles, played guitar, too.

It was not an atmosphere where there was a lot of drugs, not like today, anyway. Cats would shoot up in the alleys. Thalia and Dorgenois was a big hang-out for the junkies. But we weren't exceptionally aware of it. Things took us away from that. St. Monica's Catholic Church had dances and those kinds of things that pulled you away from the lawless kind of things.

The drug culture then didn't reach out to old folks gettin' robbed. Occasionally a kid would get robbed by junkies. Most of the squabbling was done within [the addicts'] own spheres. We were warned to stay away from them. Periodically you'd see junkies lined up against the wall [by police]. Everytime that happened,

the old folks pointed it out, warned you. Music, and the pursuit of learning an instrumental repertoire, kept us out of stuff other kids we played football with later got involved in.[2]

In junior high, Turbinton studied under Clyde Kerr, Sr., one of the city's finest music professors. When Kerr asked him to play scales, Earl didn't know what they were. Kerr starting humming and Earl, who had been exposed to "ear training," showed his stuff. Kerr, befuddled and somewhat amazed at the youngster's ability to carry melodies, started teaching him to read music properly. When Turbinton confronted Professor Victor about the nonreading method, "he evaded it, in a sense; I don't know if he was crippling a lot of kids, or whether he was just a person with an ingenious method of teaching—but it developed my ear to the point that most songs I heard on the radio, I could hear and play them."

From 1956 to 1960 Turbinton studied privately with Alvin Batiste and took classes at Southern University from 1959 to 1961. In 1962 John Coltrane came to New Orleans for an eleven-day engagement at Vernon's in central city. "That was like God was in town. The whole musical community turned out." When Turbinton and Coltrane discovered the common birthday, they took a closer look at each other. It fostered in Turbinton "an affinity to him, a closeness. I spent three days with Trane. He let me play for him, and gave me encouragement. . . . He showed me how to construct pentatonic scales. They were playing all kinds of inversions and they'd go outside the mode, inside the mode. That influenced me to play. It was more of an Eastern sound, African and Indian, as opposed to conventional Western harmony."[3]

Turbinton toured with the Bill Doggett Combo in 1962, then with the Jerry Butler Orchestra. During this period, younger brother Willie Tee was carving his own reputation as a singer, pianist, and composer. In 1965 Earl joined Willie Tee and the Souls and toured with Willie's R&B hit "Teasin' You." New Orleans, however, was not developing an entertainment or recording industry; Earl taught school for a time to supplement his income.

By the late 1960s, more national jazz figures were visiting the city, as Coltrane had. Nat and Cannonball Adderly approached Turbinton about a recording for Capitol, which he did, but the tapes were not released. "They recorded us extensively in Cosimo's studio in 1968, and naturally almost anything that was recorded at Cosimo's could not compete with the market sound of sophistication that other studios had. Unfortunately, that was the only studio that you could go to in New Orleans."

Capitol proved a key link for Wilson Turbinton (Willie Tee), whose *I'm Only a Man* LP was produced by Cannonball Adderly and David Axelrod in 1968. That year Earl recorded in a New Orleans Jazz Festival production. He was also thinking about a way to reach youngsters. Jules Cahn, an avocational photographer with an abiding interest in music, was sensitive to his concerns and for a nominal rent provided a building on Decatur Street to be used as a workshop. Werlein's and Educational Gateway contributed secondhand instruments. "I knew kids, like around central city, were just beating on pasteboard boxes or humming or singing or dancing, but I knew there was no way they could get an instrument."

Turbinton hit the streets, talked to kids, carried them in carpools to the Jazz Workshop, where the memory of Professor Victor's house filtered through his thoughts. At Decatur Street, Earl and Willie played in a quartet with other professionals, then broke off into smaller groups to instruct the youngsters. But the dream soon died. Turbinton could not attract other musicians without financial incentive. The idea did attract public school officials, who invited the Turbinton brothers to

several long meetings to discuss ways the Jazz Workshop might provide a focus for music curricula in the schools. "Basically, we just gave the idea away," Earl remarked. By the late 1970s, it had reached fruition in the New Orleans Center for the Creative Arts, which drew artistic students from various high schools for formal instruction.[4]

In 1970 Earl Turbinton left for New York, where he met Josef Zawinul, a Viennese keyboard wizard who had been playing with Cannonball Adderly. Turbinton played saxophone on the LP *Zawinul* and views those tracks as among his finest recorded statements. At the time, he was living in a rent-free apartment owned by musician Walter Booker where Miles Davis and other modernists often rehearsed. The place was filled with excellent equipment and was his as long as he wanted it. But before *Zawinul* was released, B. B. King offered him a job on a tour to Japan. Zawinul wanted him to stay; a new band was being formed to play the kind of music Turbinton loved. But the chance to see the world was too seductive and Earl joined B. B. King's band.

As the chain of road dates lengthened, Turbinton grew disenchanted. The work was artistically confining. King's instrumentalists played brief, circumscribed solos, with the focus at all times on the Mississippi blues master. Meanwhile, *Zawinul* appeared to great critical reception. Josef Zawinul went on to form Weather Report, which in the 1970s emerged as the preeminent jazz-rock fusion band. By then, Turbinton was back in New Orleans. "I'm not bragging, but the fact is, if I'd stayed in New York, I'd be playing sax with Weather Report today."[5]

Instead, in New Orleans, Turbinton depended on his versatility as a rhythm section professional to continue playing in the stretches between full jazz work. He performed and recorded with Gatemouth Brown, Professor Longhair, and the Nevilles. Earl's attack on tenor was perfect for Gatemouth and Fess—a husky, gritty wavelength resonating heat for the bluesmen. His own sound

Earl Turbinton

as a lead instrumental voice ripened in the late seventies; playing with a variety of local artists, he roamed, literally, across the terrain of jazz improvisation, the blues base always sturdy, the Coltrane debt evident in the arching legatos and thin, piercing modes Earl articulated in several celebrated concerts embracing Africa as a conceptual motif. By the eighties Turbinton's career was in midpassage, with increasing concert and recording work; he also gave a number of performances for prison inmates in Louisiana, Georgia, and New York.

By the late 1960s a competing set of dynamics began to surround New Orleans musicians. On the one hand, there was the impact of "outside music," songs of political protest that raced the blood of peace marchers and flower children. Inner-city blacks and hip-tuned whites jumped to intensified rhythms of soul stars like James Brown and Aretha Franklin. Amid this came drug-powered hard rockers, with strobe-lit electronics conjuring surrealist impressions of acid trips. Compared to such sounds, New Orleans music was a remote outpost, if hardly immune to lurching national changes, political killings, and the Vietnam War. By the early 1970s, however, a different consciousness began to emerge locally. A profound change was taking root. With the erosion of segregation, fans in their twenties and thirties embraced anew rhythm-and-blues, and simultaneously a new jazz audience emerged.

The catalyst in this phenomenon was the New Orleans Jazz and Heritage Festival, a grand affair offering scores of artists a chance to renew careers. The festival became a spring rite, a cohesive force drawing fans closer to the musicians, attracting blacks and whites in large numbers. For experimental jazzmen, the problem of how to make a living still existed. But the heightened interest in R&B broadened nightclub opportunities; the city was starting to open up. James Rivers came along at the right time.

Born on April 18, 1937, James Rivers lived in Treme. His family had six children; his sisters were active in gospel choirs, as was James as a boy. His childhood friends included James Black. Louis Armstrong was an early influence. "I like his trumpet and singing work on 'Sleepy Time Down South.' 'Mack, the Knife' was another; I was really inspired by his work. The tone was real good."[6] Rivers started out on clarinet, taught by Louis Cottrell, but listening to records prompted him to try soprano saxophone. In the early 1950s, he went to Booker T. Washington High School, attracted by the music program that had appealed to Alvin Batiste, James Black, Sam Alcorn, and others. "During that time, the symphony used to practice in our auditorium daily. The New Orleans Symphony . . . used to sit in on a lot of our sessions and sometimes they would correct things that we did wrong—constructive criticism."

Late in high school, he discovered Charlie Parker and Sonny Stitt and took up tenor sax. "It was self-taught. Once you play the clarinet, you can play the alto, tenor and soprano [saxophones] with a few minor changes in the keys. It has a different sound and the instrument is made a little different. The clarinet is straight. The saxophone is curved."[7]

He learned the flute in his early twenties, after hearing Rasshan Roland Kirk's "Three Fluted Festival." "I was so inspired; I thought it was impossible for two people to think and play the same note, the same beat, hold a note for the same length of time. I didn't know that he was doing that by himself. After I found that out, I bought a flute. Then no matter what it took, I was going to do it."

The bagpipes came a little later, after he saw the television quiz show "To Tell the Truth." A black man and two whites posed as a bagpipe player. "Nobody thought it was the black guy. I said, 'No, it has to be one of the whites.' But it turned out to be the black guy! And that made me run down to Werlein's and order me a bagpipe." Rivers laughed.

"That's when the trouble came. After getting the bagpipes, there was nobody to teach. So I taught myself. I bought some albums, and I studied what bagpipes are supposed to sound like. I'm doing a lot of improvising now. I'm trying to form my own concept. I like to be different, you know. You have to teach yourself."

Rivers did a brief stint with Huey Smith and the Clowns in the late fifties and cut the blues single "Blue Eagle." He played with Deacon John and the Ivories until 1969, when Deacon shifted to psychedelic rock. "He brought all the bright lights and pink lights and it was like getting blinded. I used to walk off the bandstands, man, I'd be bumping into people. Then the noise; this was ridiculous, so I decided I had to get my own thing."

In the early seventies, he played long stretches at the Royal Sonesta Hotel leading the James Rivers Movement. He was moving more deeply into modern jazz, but had to appeal to the crowd. R&B tours left him with a sense of how to read an audience. For young fans he turned on the rock-and-roll, played more traditional jazz for the older tourists, but let loose with the new stuff when he thought the audience could handle it. As soon as the Sonesta sets ended, Rivers took the Movement to a small, black uptown club called Sylvia's and played until dawn. The club became so hot that Rivers would walk outside and head up Freret Street for several blocks, wailing away on sax with people tromping down the pavement behind him. Bus drivers grew accustomed to his sets and paused their vehicles in front of the club. One night Rivers serenaded one driver and in a moment of extravagance took a seat on the bus, blowing to the driver's delight. The bus lumbered on a few blocks with Rivers blasting. He got off and marched back to Sylvia's, where the second liners met him midway for the return.

Such charisma was destined for better visibility. In 1973 the Berings, a young black couple, opened Lu and Charlie's just outside the French Quarter. The place soon became a hub for players and followers of modern jazz. Charlie Bering booked modern jazzmen who had risen in the 1960s and younger ones just emerging. For Rivers it meant visibility in the white community. As pianist James Drew observed, "By the end of the sixties, a lot of young people who had came up on rock-and-roll were looking for something different, music with more depth and range of expression."[8]

Lu and Charlie's became the spiritual center for the 1970s modern jazz. But with a growing community of artists, the club could not guarantee anyone full-time work. By 1975 Rivers had a steady job at Mel's Lounge, a cozy black club in the Faubourg Marigny, during which time the place went from no-cover and seventy-five-cent beer to red-carpeted, renovated nightclub with a two-dollar cover. Rivers made the move uptown in the late 1970s to Tyler's Beer Garden and a large white following. He was also restless to record.

His first LP, *James Rivers: Thrill Me,* was released in 1978 on a local label and was produced by Senator Jones, who is not a politician but perhaps should be. The music, a mix of disco and funk, doesn't feature Rivers at his flowing, unrestrained best; however, the Mardi Gras parade standard "Second Line" is full of power and one of the best versions recorded. *Olé,* released in 1979, is a substantial improvement. On the title cut, the rising tempo on synthesizer captures aurally the ceremonial movements of the matador and recreates the Spanish bullring. There are suggestions of Miles Davis's famous *Sketches of Spain;* however, Rivers's interpretation is high-spirited and made for dancing. The sax lines introduce the matadors, and the synthesizer creates rising passages with crowd sounds dubbed in to embroider the mood. Other songs come from Rivers's standard repertoire—Gershwin's "Summertime," Jimmy Reed's "Baby, What You Want Me to Do," and the two original compositions "Smokey, the Funky Soprano" and "Whenever You Want My Love." But Rivers's real musical strength is derived from his interaction with the audience. More than any single New Orleans modernist, his work best suits a live concert production.

Black musicians were not the only ones to experience the transition of jazz and blues in the early seventies. The saturation of rock-and-roll and the invasion of the British groups created changes for white artists as well. Luther Kent and Trick Bag, a successful big band with hot, bluesy horn charts, surfaced during the years marked by transition.

Born Kent Rowell on June 23, 1948, Luther Kent is a bearish man with a thick beard and a voice steeped in the blues. His friend and professional partner Charlie Brent, born on August 31, 1948, has dark hair and clear features. In 1982 Brent was playing lead guitar and arranging Trick Bag's music, which both men called a "fusion" of blues, big band, New Orleans jazz, and R&B. A sturdy pair, Luther Kent and Charlie Brent. Both come from musical families. Luther Kent reminisces:

I had an older brother that played on the hit, "Graduation Day." He was guitar player, Bill Rowell, with Stark Whiteman and the Crowns, okay? So I was greatly influenced by the music they were playing—Ray Charles, Fats Domino, Muddy Waters, the R&B things in the early fifties.

I played drums in grammar school, never knew I was gonna be a singer, messed around with the piano and sang. My father was a pianist, but never played professionally. Had an ear that was unbelievable. Could go to a movie on Friday night, come home and sit down at the piano and play the music score. One of those kind of cats. My sister is a classical pianist. Luther was a nickname given to me years ago by dear musician friends. And Luther Kent evolved from that.[9]

Charlie Brent remembers his family: "My great-great grandfather, from what they tell me, played every instrument. And I play every one but violin." Charles Brent, Sr., "played piano with the original Basin Street Six. I remember George Girard playing trumpet and Pete Fountain singing 'The Sheik of Arabi' in drag at the Famous Door. They had me tap dancing when I was three, singing 'I'm a ding-dong daddy from Dumas / You ought to see me do my stuff.'"

Luther Kent's father died when he was thirteen and the family moved to Baton Rouge, where he began singing rhythm-and-blues with local groups. At fifteen, Kent won a talent show, and in 1965 joined the Greek Fountains, a popular rock group that played at college fraternity and high school dances. The group's single "Blue Jeans" was cut for Phillips, a national label.

Charlie's musical path was more orderly. His father took him to the musicians' hall for jam sessions with other youngsters, one of whom, Johnny Vidacovich, "had to sit on a phone book so he could reach the cymbals." Brent was "four or five" when his father took him to visit the ailing George Girard in the hospital. "He was my daddy's best friend. My father brings his trumpet. [Girard] took the trumpet and played 'I'm Goin' Home'—took his mouthpiece, threw it out the window, and *died.* I couldn't believe it. It freaked me out. We never did find the mouthpiece."

Years later, as a young musician, Brent "used to sneak down to a place that had a cat house on top. I'd go down there with my alto—I was in college [Loyola] now—and they had a piano player and organ. And this place really tripped me out with girls hanging around, and I'd jam. It was a black club. And we'd play 'Caravan,' and this 350-pound black woman would strip and let a snake crawl around. I wasn't afraid of cops. I was afraid, for the section I was in, of somebody stealing my horn." At Loyola, Brent majored in woodwinds and worked with a big band. One night at Al Hirt's Club he met singer Wayne Cochran, who liked his arrangements. Brent moved to Las Vegas to play saxophone in Cochran's show band and to write arrangements.

Luther Kent was pursuing the blues and R&B with Baton Rouge bands. He remembers the sixties with no fondness. "I couldn't even get a job at white clubs. When the Beatles came in, that type of music really took over. So I played black clubs."[10]

In 1970, Brent recommended Kent to Cochran's people. To manage his career "they put a band together, and put me on a nightclub circuit in the Midwest, Vegas, Miami, that whole trip." The venture ended because Kent did not like the management setup. He moved back to Louisiana, and in 1973 moved to Bogalusa, a paper mill town seventy miles from New Orleans. Studio in the Country, a million-dollar recording center designed and then owned by Bill Evans, was just opening shop. Evans and Kent were about the same age and shared a love of black music. Kent moved into a cabin in the woods and spent the year writing songs and cutting demo tapes. In 1974 his career took an upward swing when Blood, Sweat and Tears hired him as a singer. He spent two years touring with the band, his talent showcased as never before. Charlie was in Los Angeles then "doing film scores, records, and arranging."

In late 1977 Kent cut his first LP, *World Class,* for RCS Records in Baton Rouge. The recording was done in Colorado and at the Abbey Road Studio in England; the sophisticated edge came from string charts played by members of the London Philharmonic. *World Class* was well received but was no chart-breaker. "The thing about albums," Kent said, "is you pay your dues with the first one, sometimes even the second. But you gotta keep puttin' 'em out. If you have the fire, you'll hit."

In 1978 Charlie Brent returned to New Orleans. Luther asked him to provide horn charts for a new band, Trick Bag, named for a famous Earl King song. The group made the rounds of French Quarter clubs, building a legion of fans. In 1981

with local backers, *It's in the Bag* was issued with a solid rhythm section, including James Rivers and pianist David Torkanowsky. Kent's "Tennessee Waltz" is coated with bluesy sadness. But the LP's best tune is a Charlie Brent composition, "Long, Long Day."

You know I work hard all day,
    And I toss and turn each and every night.
A poor man's work is a mighty heavy load
    Like walkin' all day down a hot dusty road.
Old folks keep on dyin',
    Babies, they keep on crying,
And that old sun keeps on shining,
    I gotta keep on trying,
Trying to find a better way.

The one musician to succeed—remarkably so—with his first recording is Wynton Marsalis, who was just nineteen when his solo LP was released in 1982. With his brother Branford (a year older) on saxophone, Wynton literally took the jazz world by storm. Not in years had a New Orleans artist, much less one so young, emerged to such acclaim. Leonard Feather, the distinguished jazz critic, called him "a symbol of the new decade." Another critic compared him to Louis Armstrong *and* Miles Davis. Al Belletto, well before the album appeared, called him "a genius."

Wynton Marsalis may be all of those things, but he is first a product of New Orleans and an education as solidly grounded in European music as in jazz. The family name is synonymous with sterling keyboard work. Ellis Marsalis completed a master's in music and as mentor and role model gave his sons a sturdy sense of music history. In Wynton it percolates through interviews. The musical association of two brothers reflected superior craftsmanship, and by the mid-1980s, distinct professional identities. Branford emerged in Wynton's shadow, yet with an individual sense of his own musicianship. In an early interview, well before his own 1984 debut album, Branford mused, "The position of follower is always underrated. A band has to have great followers: you can't have five great leaders."[11] Some of the finest passages on *Wynton Marsalis* (1982) are the brothers' improvisational dialogues, in which Wynton's fluttering lines from middle register into high C's echo elegantly in Branford's descending notes on tenor sax.

Ellis introduced Wynton to Miles Davis's records when he was fourteen, but his son showed more interest in playing baseball. As a classical student, he began making long strides, winning summer camp competitions, performing with the New Orleans Symphony, practicing double-tonguing and triple-tonguing on his horn. "There's a commonness between the boys' experience that overlaps," Ellis reflected. "Wynton was the more disciplined, but they arrived at the point where they are now early on."[12] Their music training began at the New Orleans Center for the Creative Arts, a public school offering a range of artistic courses where Ellis taught music. Wynton and Branford went to different high schools but attended NOCCA for music classes. For the most part, those years were devoted to technique, as Wynton explained in an interview with writer Kalamu Ya Salaam:

My daddy used to say all the time, "Practice the piano." I couldn't play the piano and would never practice. He'd say, "Listen to Louis Armstrong." I would never listen to Louis Armstrong. "Listen to Monk, Ornetee." I would never listen. Somebody standing there telling you something is not going to get you to play—I was always interested in playing jazz but I couldn't play. . . . I used to play like Freddie [Hubbard] then. I mean I wasn't as good as Freddie, but I would learn all his solos off records. I had technique, but I really couldn't play jazz.

You started listening to records to develop your jazz playing. What else did you do?

I started listening to people. I started thinking about music. I had never thought about music. . . . When I was in high school I played jazz because I wanted to be like my father and because nobody else was playing it, everybody wanted to play funk. We'd be playing funk tunes in the jazz ensemble. My daddy would be talking to the class and when he stopped, everybody would play funk, right in the middle of the jazz class. So, I was always saying, "let's play jazz," just to do something different, but I didn't understand the music.[13]

From New Orleans, the Marsalis brothers continued their education in the North, Branford at Berklee School of Music in Boston, Wynton at Juilliard in New York, which he has since said he "couldn't stand—an uptight rich vibe; a lot of people with money."[14] By then, however, the younger Marsalis brother was refining a trumpet technique in jazz and European classics simultaneously. Only seventeen, he convinced Gunther Schuller to let him audition for the Tanglewood summer music festival in Massachusetts, even though eighteen was the limit. Schuller agreed and Wynton went to Tanglewood.

Wynton's professional career began with Art Blakey, the veteran drummer whose Jazz Messengers had a distinguished tradition dating back many years. Wynton's trumpet drew critical notice on Blakey's 1981 bop homage *Straight Ahead* and in the following year on *Album of the Year*. The debut LP *Wynton Marsalis* appeared in 1982 as well—to an avalanche of critical praise and nodding approval from established artists. The sudden rise of such a young trumpeter sent waves of excitement through legions of serious jazz followers. His music was new—moving in its melodic innovations, marked by clear virtuoso powers and laced with humor. The image he affected was very different from casually attired boppers of old; he wore handsome suits and projected a sophisticated aura. He was intelligent, articulate, and displayed a feisty spirit in reflections on history.

Wynton Marsalis, 1983

Luther Kent

Saxophonist James Rivers and
percussionist Bernard "Dr. Snake"
Dixon

I studied classical music, because so many black musicians were scared of this big monster called classical music. I wanted to know what it was that scared everyone. I found out it wasn't anything but more music.

As far as both musics are concerned, I think—I *know*—it's harder to be a good jazz musician at an early age than a classical one. In jazz, to be good means to be an individual, which you don't necessarily have to be in classical music performance. But because I've played with orchestras, some people think I'm a classical musician who plays jazz. They have it backwards; I'm a jazz musician who can play classical music. Besides, if you love the trumpet, you have to love jazz because jazz musicians have done the most with the instrument. They have given it the most depth and the widest range of expression. I'm not saying that classical trumpet players aren't expressive artists. That would be dumb. What I'm saying is that jazz musicians have given the most to the trumpet's vocabulary in this century. What I'm trying to do is come up to the standards all those trumpet giants have set—Armstrong, Gillespie, Navarro, Brown, Miles, Freddie Hubbard, and Don Cherry. And that's not an easy task.[15]

The question of influences stalks a new jazz artist: Whom did you listen most to? What kind of music exerted the magnetic pull? In one sense, these interrogations by critics (and by extension, the many serious followers) constitute a ritual, an attempt to understand the vocabulary of improvisational music as it broadens. To musicians, the questions can get pretty old. And to a young trumpeter, the shadow of Miles Davis looms large. At fourteen Wynton rebuffed Ellis's advice that he listen to Miles's records; later, however, he did so. Ellis maintains that Miles's music of the late sixties was the conceptual framework out of which Branford and Wynton began maturing as jazzmen when they left New Orleans. It is a reference worth examining.

Miles by 1969 had gone through several distinct periods, each marked by a stylistic signature increasingly removed from the late 1940s bebop work establishing him as a modern master. His horn became legendary for its economy, the tight,

controlled lines emerging like a warm, sensual moan, yet others like hard, serrated edges slashing in and ebbing out at will. Miles used the "spaces" created by suspended trumpet lines brilliantly. Before launching into jazz-rock fusions of the seventies (which later came to dominate his work, disappointing many jazz fans), the architecture he had worked out for ensemble improvisations revolved around alternating modes, different variations of notes strung out in passages Miles would abbreviate or elide, giving wider rhythmic range to his accompanists. Herbie Hancock on piano and Ron Carter on bass began to play competing tempos; the overall sound was more eloquent than the electronic fusion crescendos to follow.

On his debut album and several that followed, Wynton's trumpet has echoes of Miles Davis in the pinched notes and warm slurs spilling into stunning lyrical passages hovering above the beat. But the solo runs emerging from warm melodic exchanges with Branford's tenor sax resonate an improvisational talent anchored by dialogue as opposed to sustained, suspenseful spaces. Overall, the group sound is tight, with less self-conscious distance between the trumpet and ensemble. The more direct link to Miles Davis on *Wynton Marsalis* is Herbie Hancock, who produced the disc and plays keyboard on key tracks, and Ron Carter, whose bass lines undergird Hancock and in a Carter composition, "RJ," lay down a snakelike beat off of which the horns depart and return. The analogy to Miles Davis need not be strained, but the first album reflects great strength in the range of Wynton's solo passages and the eloquent improvisational figures with his brother; in a sense, Wynton and Branford close those haunting spaces Miles opened via warm passages in call-and-response.

The more telling influence on Wynton Marsalis is one of tone—the beautiful, lustrous tone with big, round suggestions going all the way back to the full-bodied riffs of young Louis Armstrong in the 1920s. This is a clear inheritance from Ellis. Among his virtues as a pianist and educator, Ellis Marsalis's attack on keyboard is the most distinctive of his generation in New Orleans, a tone precious in its elegant, bell-like clarity and chiseled precision.

Wynton's composition "Father Time" is the lead cut on *Wynton Marsalis* and a commanding improvisational statement. What is time if not a river, timeless until the flow is gone from sight? Kenny Kirkland opens with a cascade of drums out of which Herbie Hancock draws a quickened treble keynote; Ron Carter's bass line courses between the percussions and the melodic wave is shaped for the surge of horns. The tenor-trumpet duet repeats the melodic figure and the horns begin to sing—Wynton's smears and billowing runs curling over the sough of percussions with Branford issuing deep echoes, and opening places for Wynton to soar. The albums following *Wynton Marsalis*—*Think of One* and *Hot House Flowers,* a gathering of moody ballads—revealed greater gifts. "Playfulness is a constant in Marsalis's music," writes Gary Giddins. "His trumpet playing is varied by his ability to sculpt each note; in the course of an improvisation he will growl and flutter and purr (as on the blues 'Later'), or bounce between registers, alternating long and shorter phrases. . . . But ballad playing often comes late to a jazz musician—it was the one area that still troubled trumpeter Clifford Brown at the time of his death—and Marsalis's overall control is on an ascending glide."[16] In 1984 Wynton made history by winning Grammy awards in jazz and classical music.

Although Branford's reputation was initially hinged to Wynton's, his debut album in 1984, *Scenes of the City,* shows a strong impressionist bent. His tenor sax pushes a blues thrust through "No Backstage Pass," swinging off Carter's melodic bass line with a loll. If Wynton's trumpet descends from Miles Davis, then Branford's tenor follows the path forged by John Coltrane. "Solstice" kicks off with Trane's lead figure from "Equinox," but from there the ride is Branford's, shifting fluidly between registers, switching to soprano sax after the bridge. Another influence is at work here—and, one suspects, in Branford's larger artistic urges: the title cut is a Charlie Mingus sound montage of the 1950s, the poetic tale of a wanderer on New York streets for whom jazz music is like a warm woman. In resurrecting "Scenes," Branford paid homage to a composer who used episodic fragments to enrich many scores with a narrative sensibility.

Wynton and Branford perform magnificently together, but one major difference surfacing in the mid-eighties was the latter's embrace of rock music—he did a stretch with Sting, who is no shrinking violet—while Wynton's interviews are marked by an attitude of purity toward jazz and little use, even scorn at times, for the pop world. Wynton's virtuosity assures the legendary status already earned; how well he translates those gifts into new stylistic signatures is the unwritten chapter. By contrast, Branford's impressionism as reflected in *Scenes* hints at more catholic ideas about jazz. And his excursions into rock music suggest Branford is willing—eager—to take chances.

Ellis and Delores Marsalis have six sons. Branford and Wynton are the oldest. If there is a single trait among father and sons, it is a muscular confidence in their talent, and if there is a second, it is unmasked individuality. They have strong opinions. Wynton's remarks about the injustices borne by blacks inevitably return to slavery. Branford makes no secret of his dislike for Reagan. Ellis is less gratuitously political; however, his argumentative strain lights up like a Christmas tree when the talk turns to labels, like progressive jazz, which he derides as the wordplay of critics.

One afternoon he sat in his classroom at the New Orleans Center for the Creative Arts, waiting for students to arrive. Asked if his sons' remarkable rise reflected a family tradition, he said, with a deadpan face, "No. It was the teaching."

Chapter Fourteen

PIANO PLAYERS

"You take the poorest family; they would have a piano. That's what was happening back then. That's all anyone did, was go to other people's houses playing pianos, pianos, pianos."[1] This is how Dave "Fat Man" Williams, veteran blues pianist, remembers his youth during the Great Depression. But New Orleans's piano tradition is much older. From 1795 until 1825 there was a groundswell of theater interest in the port town. The first theater was established in 1796. By 1817 a permanent opera company was in place. And the piano served many functions. It was a necessity for operas and symphonies. Ladies of affluent families viewed it as a status symbol; a home should have a parlor, the parlor its piano. Theater owners wanted pianos, and in time, so did the tavern owners. By the 1880s, in outlying areas of Louisiana, lumber and mining camps arose. Towns developed around them, and with them came barrelhouses—taverns where beer was sold from big wooden barrels. Often these ramshackle places were built as extensions to grocery stores

where hardworking men came to drink and relax after long hours of strenuous work. Pianos, often castoffs, occupied the center of entertainment in these run-down honky-tonks. These were the beginnings of the "barrelhouse piano," and by the 1930s players like Little Brother Montgomery were local exponents of this style.

Prostitution figured into the boomtown culture. In 1897 Storyville, a red-light district, was officially designated in New Orleans. Pimps who solicited customers for the prostitutes often doubled as piano players. Jelly Roll Morton, who indulgently billed himself as the "inventor of jazz," was a phenomenal pianist and, as a friend recalled, one of the "half-way" pimps.[2] The sporting houses usually employed a solo piano player to entertain guests. Those with extensive repertoires became known as "professors"—forerunners of the piano-bar players of today.[3] They left an enduring legacy, and as jazz spread in the early

1900s, pianists continued to develop the art. In the 1920s and 1930s a solid line of blues pianists emerged from remote neighborhoods; most never recorded.

A certain street or nook became identified with its own keyboard master. "Winehead" piano players made daily rounds of the honky-tonks, fashioning the blues to suit their own tastes. Little is known about these men, only the names they went by. "Buckeye," "Fish," and "Minnie Jack" are said to have come from the Seventh Ward.[4] "Lovey," "Long Tom," and "Woo Woo" were small-time heroes of the lower Ninth Ward.[5] In many ways, the piano was the musical spine of black neighborhoods, the focal point of home entertainment.

Dave "Fat Man" Williams played hundreds of pianos in his long career. One of four children, Williams was born on August 20, 1920, to Dave and Viola Frazier Williams. "I had some great musicians to come out of my family. I had an uncle, he wasn't discovered right, but I think he was as great as a piano player can be. His name was Mitchell Frazier. Alex Frazier, Simon Frazier—they are all my mother's brothers. My mother is a great piano player. My family married into other musicians. The Fraziers, Marreros, and the Barnes, all them are in my family."[6] Paul "Polo" Barnes played in the Original Tuxedo Jazz Band and later toured with King Oliver. His brother Emile, also a clarinetist, had an active career from 1908 to 1966. Cie Frazier began in cousin Lawrence Marrero's Young Tuxedo Orchestra, formed in 1920; he recorded with Papa Celestin in 1927. The Marreros spanned three generations.[7]

Williams matured quickly on the keyboard. He remembers when he was twelve, "Them old timers like Paul Barbarin and Ulysses 'Uly' Jean would come get me and tell my mama, 'It's all right. We'll take care of him. Let him go with us, and we'll bring him home and bring the money to you.' I got to where I was making three or four quarters a week. Then Mama would let me keep one, and I would go buy a nice little shirt. That quarter was a great help in those days."[8]

Williams played jazz then, but the blues idiom was inseparable from the piano. Raised near the French Quarter in the lower Seventh Ward, Dave Williams roamed surrounding neighborhoods, meeting other piano players and trading musical licks. One of Williams's favorite areas was Lincoln Court. "There were many great blues piano players right up in there. 'Minnie Jack' is a living cat today. He could play the blues on piano and that cat could sing the blues. They had a boy called 'Buckwheat,' a good little blues player, and there was a boy named Steve. They were older than me, and I used to hang around those cats and play and sing the blues." Dave's song "Way Back O' Town Blues" refers to the neighborhood pockets.

Well, they call these blues
 The way Back O' Town blues,
Way back in Boscoville, Paillet Lane,
 Gert Town, Lovers Lane.

During the economic hardship of the 1930s, black families in New Orleans held social functions, similar to "rent parties," at which a pianist played and visitors donated as much money as they could afford. In New Orleans, the piano parties were called "Saturday night fish fries." Folks came with whiskey or beer. "They'd hang a red kerosene light on the gate so everybody would know that was a fish fry. The people would sell fish and potato salad and, if they knew you, alcohol and water. Prohibition was still going on. They would have a piano, and I would be there banging the blues." The fish fries were a solidifying force among blacks. They strengthened the community and buffered residents against the difficulties of money and survival during the Depression. Louis Jordan recorded the memorable song "Saturday Night Fish Fry."

Have you ever been down to New Or-leens?
  Then you can understand just what I mean.
All through the week it's quiet as a mouse
  But on Saturday night they go from house to house.
You don't have to pay no main admission
  If you're a cook or a waiter or a good musician.
If you happen to be just pasin' by,
  Stop in at the Saturday night fish fry.

Another outlet for piano players was the network of black social organizations. Dave Williams played often at the old Perseverance Hall. "They had many families used to specialize in potato salad and ham sandwiches and, boy, they would have more flying around with that bad wine and that home-brew!" For musicians, Monday was the traditonal day off, although not exactly a day of rest. Williams continues: "The biggest things were the blue Mondays. People would have big pots of red beans, and they would get together and have jam sessions. Nobody would go to work, and the musicians would come over and play the blues. They would start around noon and last all day."

Dave Williams had an unusual method for composing. "I dream my songs. I dream the melody, just as plain as day, and the words come along with it. I get up in the middle of the night. Once I'm at the piano, I got it." Lyrically, his works are simple and warm. Williams's LP *I Ate Up the Apple Tree* contains his ballad "The Same Old Love," a delicate joy.

The same old love is in my heart,
  The same old heart that broke for you.
The same old ache, the same old break,
  I don't know what to do.

The same old blues has got me down,
  I'm like an old go-round-and-round.
Just like a fool but I don't care,
  The same old love is in my heart.

At sixty-two, Dave Williams was the youngest member of Kid Thomas Valentine's band, which performed regularly at Preservation Hall. He traveled from Europe to Vietnam with jazz groups and in the 1970s made biannual trips to Copenhagen. His songs were not national hits, but Fat Man Williams made a nice living by taking the neighborhood sounds of his youth into the world. His piano was a direct link with those anonymous city blues players of yesteryear. His death on March 12, 1982, was a sad break in the chain of that tradition.

One of the most prolific composers of 1950s rhythm-and-blues was a versatile pianist named Eddie Bo. Edwin Bocage, born on September 20, 1937, came from a family steeped in music. His uncles, Peter and Charles Bocage, and cousin Henry were respected ensemble jazz players who enjoyed long careers during the first half of the century. "All the Bocages were cross-overs from Algiers, and they were all musicians except for my father, Alvin. When I was young, I used to hear them play. They were monsters. My mother [Iona Tucker Bocage] played the blues and the little charts they were doing at the fish fries."[9]

Many "little charts" were epic folktales put to the blues piano in a tune called "The Junker." There were endless versions of "The Junker," played in a range of styles by different pianists. They sang of the dreams and pitfalls of a convicted heroin addict. Mac Rebennack explains: "It was a New Orleans classic, the anthem of the dopers, the whores, the pimps, the cons. It was a song they sung in Angola, the state prison farm, and the rhythm was known as 'the jailbird beat.'"[10]

"At those fish fries," Eddie Bo recalls, "the style they played was called the barrelhouse or the junker. That was all you heard. A lot of winos played 'The Junkers' and they would whip that sucker down in the ground."

In 1958 he formed a rhythm-and-blues band with Walter and David Lastie and guitarist Irving

Bannister. The group worked for the Shaw Booking Agency out of New York, touring as the show band with Amos Milburn, Charles Brown, Little Willie John, and Ruth Brown until 1964. His education and road tours gave Bocage solid footing as a stage performer and studio artist. "I was influenced by George Shearing, Oscar Peterson, and Art Tatum. I think if I hadn't gone to Grunewald and studied, I would have just played what I heard around the city. I found out there were other melodic lines laying out there, and I thought maybe I could make them blend in. I tried to mix the two together." Professor Longhair was a primary influence. "I was too young to get in, but I would stand outside and listen to him at the Caldonia. I don't know if I can find words to describe his talent. Professor Longhair was not from the earth. I think he came from another planet. I've never heard anyone from this earth play like that."[11]

Through the fifties and sixties, Eddie Bo recorded for various labels—Ace, Ric, Scram, Apollo, Rip, Seven B, Blue Jay, Chess, and At Last Records. In 1959 Etta James recorded Bocage's "Dearest Darling," which stayed high on the R&B charts for seventeen weeks. Most of his recordings were for Ric Records under owner Joe Ruffino and have a distinctive keyboard signature, as do those he produced for others. Like Huey Smith, Bocage drew on slang phrases of the times.

Bocage's similarities with Huey Smith are evident, too, in his awareness of children. "I think the kids with their dancing sets the stage for music," he explains, "if you watch the rhythmic pattern of their dancing."[12] Smith and Bocage were drawn to the popularity of Popeye the Sailor, the cartoon character whose adventures with Olive Oyl and the villain Bluto captured the imagination of millions of youngsters via television. Smith's "Popeye" and Bocage's "Check Mr. Popeye" (1962) pushed the dance craze, named for the salty sailor, that swept the nation.

Eddie Bo withdrew from performing in the early seventies. A skilled craftsman, he established a construction company and began renovating houses, including his own Victorian structure on North Broad Street. With the profits from his day job, Bocage saved money to record. His wife Toni, a talented singer, encouraged him to return to his music. To the side of his house Bocage built a large room with a sunken dance floor, and he and Toni opened the club El Grande in 1979 and announced Eddie Bo's formal return to music. His first LP, *Another Side of Eddie Bo,* appeared that same year. A mixture of impressionistic jazz, disco, and pop, the record demonstrated the durability of his talent and, like so many of the old forty-fives, was well arranged. But the club soon became a burden; Eddie and Toni closed it to move ahead with recording work. A second album, *Watch for the Coming,* appeared in 1980 on Bocage's own label, Eboville.

The quality of music on the second album is far better than that of its immediate predecessor, but the LP was not distributed nationally. Several of the songs might have succeeded in the charts. "What the Mon Say" features Toni Bocage in a calypso-based tune with the refrain "Love is sweet for the soul / Love is the reason you never grow old." The production of the LP represented vintage Eddie Bo. For the horn section he gathered a group of young artists from Xavier University. Their professor, Johnny Fernandez, Bocage's old friend from rhythm-and-blues days, assisted with the charts. On guitar was Guitar Slim, Jr., following in his father's footsteps in New Orleans. The Brooks brothers, Mark and Detroit, played bass and guitar.

Like his idol Professor Longhair, Eddie Bo's piano style is unorthodox. His recordings are flavored with offbeat chordings and syncopation. He absorbed Longhair's rhumba accents and mixes them with bebop figures. Bocage's music was

Papa Jellie Bellie

moving into a new phase in the early eighties. Whether he will continue the jazz improvisations and new compositions remains to be seen, but his reputation has been established.

Tommy Ridgley, another piano player influenced by the blues standard "The Junker," was born on October 30, 1925, in an outlying area of New Orleans known as Shrewsbury. Seventeen children were in his family. "I came up the hard way," states Ridgley, a lean man and veteran bandleader with lithe stage movements. "I've seen times when I didn't have nothing to eat. I used to have to go out and look for scraps of aluminum and brass and hunt for crystal bottles to sell. I shined shoes. There was no stealing, though. We were very disciplined and very religious. My grandfather and two uncles were ministers. My mom kept all of us in church on the front bench." Ridgley had no access to a piano in early years but was surrounded by music. "My grandfather, the minister, played trombone and everybody on my mother's side sang. Bebe Ridgley, my great uncle, was a great jazz musician."[13] (William "Bebe" Ridgley, born in 1882, played trombone and was founder of the Original Tuxedo Orchestra.)

In 1942 Ridgley quit a construction job to join the navy. While stationed in Massachusetts, he passed leisure hours playing the piano in the base recreation hall. He had heard "The Junker" as a child, and the sound stuck with him. It was his musical beginning. After the service, Ridgley attended the Grunewald School where he learned to read music and began to discover his vocal ability. His early endeavors were "the type of singing that was strictly heavy blues—Roy Brown, T-Bone Walker, Big Joe Turner. I always could sing ballads pretty well, so I had a good variety."

In 1949 Ridgley was singing in a Gert Town hotel when Dave Bartholomew signed him with Imperial Records. In late 1949 he cut his first record, "Shrewsbury Blues." Seeing little in the way of record sales, however, he switched to the Decca label in 1952. With Atlantic in 1953 Ridgley recorded his most popular instrumental, "Jam Up."

Ridgley viewed recording as promotion for his live performances. Local record sales were good, and his band kept a busy schedule. He developed a reputation for having one of the most dependable, well-organized bands in town, "The first thing I look at when I hire a new musician is personality. Then I look at their drink habits. After that, I listen to them play. I'll accept a little less from the music if the guy can fit in otherwise."

In 1957 Ridgley, recommended by Lee Allen, joined the Herald/Ember record label of New York. He recorded "When I Meet My Girl," a regional hit using the music from "The Irish Washwoman," a traditional melody suggested by Red Tyler. Allen, Tyler, and Melvin Lastie made up the horn section; drummer Charles "Hungry" Williams paced the tune with a syncopated beat.

From 1957 through 1964 Ridgley toured the southeastern fraternity circuit. In New Orleans, he played large concerts. "I can remember when Bobby Darin and I were on the show together at the Municipal Auditorium in 1957, and back at that time you had the white show and the colored show. The white show would come on, and we would always close the show. Well, Bobby Darin had 'Splish Splash,' so at the end of his performance, he had four encores. When we came on, we had *five* encores. And then for the grand finale, *everybody* came on stage. That was a beautiful moment for me."[14] In 1960 Ridgley signed with Joe Ruffino's Ron Records and cut some of his most memorable songs. For the last twenty years, Tommy Ridgley has been an eminent New Orleans bandleader.

As the central instrument spanning midcentury decades, the piano played a pivotal social role. Middle-class homes enshrined it. A young Allen Toussaint played in his parents' living room to tunes on the radio. Fat Man Williams, Eddie Bo, and Tommy Ridgley discovered it more communally, amid social gatherings with blues rhythms

Tommy Ridgley

Eddie Bo, 1973

beneath the glow of kerosene lamps. The son of a piano teacher, Edward Frank remembers the piano at the fish fries: "Tuts Washington would come over and play. He and my step-grandfather were friends. Tuts was so tiny, and I used to love to watch him play. Before he would play what they wanted him to, he would just fiddle-daddle all over the piano—use those big tenths [one hand spanning ten keys], and he'd butterfly all over the piano. And after everybody realized what a great piano player he was, he'd take off on some blues and let them belly-bump and stuff like that. When that would start, at eight or nine, they would whisk all of us kids across the street to stay with neighbors, but we could still hear the piano."[15]

Edward Frank, born on June 14, 1932, was raised in central city and moved to the Magnolia project at age nine. He learned piano through a series of music educators and went to Grambling College on a scholarship before dropping out to get married. He began recording with Smiley Lewis after Tuts Washington, his old idol, quit the band. Dave Bartholomew then hired him for studio work. All was going well when at twenty-three a ruptured blood vessel in his head partially paralyzed his left arm and hand. Determined to continue, Frank went back to the studio after four months of rest. With Bartholomew's help and the sensitivity of others, Edward Frank worked around his handicap.

In 1960 Frank went to Houston for session work on the Duke/Peacock labels of Don Robey. He worked with Bobby Bland, Junior Parker, and others, returning to New Orleans in 1964. In 1975 his wife died. To support his five daughters, Frank drove a taxicab on the side. Today his daughters are grown and Frank performs regularly. It takes a special man to play music through the tragedies Edward Frank has known. The measure of his talent is that he endured.

In his own way, James Booker endured, too. A brilliant pianist, he was a man of bizarre eccentricities whose life was a study in struggle. His liver was dysfunctional when he walked into Charity Hospital and quietly expired in a waiting room on November 8, 1983, at the age of forty-three. The man who alternately called himself the Black Liberace, the Emperor of Ivory, the Piano Prince, was not tied to a particular reality. Thin, kaleidoscopic in moods, he appeared larger than he was by sheer force of personality. He was blind in one eye and when he wore sunglasses and trenchcoat looked mysterious.

Booker was an outrageous, extravagantly funny man, yet a loner whose handful of friends were bar owners and booking agents who never quite knew how to handle him. His interview for this book was a round-robin affair beginning at the Toulouse Theatre in the French Quarter. "There is nothing I don't like about rhythm-and-blues," Booker announced grandly. "The rhythm makes you dance and the blues makes you think."[16]

He stood abruptly. "Take me uptown. I want to go to the record store." Off went the car in the rain, tape rolling. "Everything sounds theoretical to me, everything. And if everything is theoretical, what can you really say you know about the truth? I don't know much about truth, honestly." Searching for truth, we reached the record store, but the rain fell harder. "Hell, man!" barked Booker, "I ain't getting out of this car to buy a James Booker record when *I'm* James Booker. It's raining! I want to play the piano. Take me to Tyler's bar."

Oyster shells were piled outside the door of the bar. Booker made a quick hop through the puddles. Inside, there were fresh oysters packed on ice, but the rain, yesterday's oyster shells in sacks, and the scent of last night's beer hung heavy in the empty club. Birdlike, Booker perched himself on the piano stool. His right fingers exploded in a crescendo of blues, the left hand jabbing a gospel

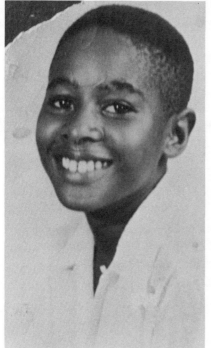

Above: James Booker, Piano Prince, 1979. *Left:* James Booker, childhood photograph, 1947

bass line. He was smiling. Dancing through a dozen rhythms he suddenly anchored a line into "The Junker Blues." Slowly, the ghost of Professor Longhair rose from "Baldhead"—then a stab at "Staggerlee" twisted into "Having a Good Time" from his old friend, Huey Smith. Echoes of Allen Toussaint receded into a chamber of Bach. Then out popped Fats Domino in triple time! Strains of Gershwin's "Rhapsody in Blue" became "Witchcraft" and that became "Black Magic." Smoke practically rose off the keyboard. Booker ordered another drink and played for an hour and a half, smiling mischievously, like a pixie. "Now did you get all that?" He laughed and laughed.

He was born to James Booker, Jr., a Baptist minister, and Ora Cheatham Booker, a beautician, on December 17, 1939, in New Orleans. His sister Betty Jean was six years older. Because of family problems, the boy at age two went to live with his maternal aunt and uncle in Bay St. Louis, Mississippi, a resort town on the Gulf of Mexico sixty miles from New Orleans. Betty Jean arrived two years later when Reverend Booker suffered a stroke. The old upright by the window of Aunt Betsy's house was the focal point of Booker's youth. With no children of their own, the Lizanas accepted James and Betty Jean lovingly. He began piano lessons at six, went crabbing and fishing with his Aunt Betsy's employer. "I have never seen a child so good," she recalls. "He was smart as a whip."[17]

At fourteen, Booker returned to New Orleans to live with his mother. At Xavier Preparatory School, he outpaced the music program, taking lessons at Xavier University where he was considered a child prodigy. In 1953 he formed a band, Booker Boy and the Rhythmaires; they played R&B tunes popular on the radio. Through his sister he met WMRY deejay "Ernie the Whip" and the group appeared on radio.

Edward Frank remembers the young Booker. "He had great technique and a good blues feeling even then. He was different, very gifted, not so sure of himself because he was so young, but everywhere he would go, he would play. He had to because people would insist on it. Dave Bartholomew asked me about James because he had heard about him, and one day Dave called me down to the studio and James was there."[18] He recorded Bartholomew's "Doing the Hambone" for Imperial. It did not sell, but at fourteen, James Booker had a record.

He was out of high school for most of his senior year, making club gigs with Earl King, Smiley Lewis, and Shirley and Lee, yet did well enough to graduate. Teamed with guitarist King, Booker became a pioneer organist in New Orleans in 1955. A road tour with Joe Tex led to an introduction to Johnny Vincent. Booker recorded the organ instrumental "Teenage Rock" for Ace. When he discovered Vincent overdubbing Joe Tex lyrics, Booker exploded. Vincent backed down, releasing a single with Tex on one side, "Little Booker" on the other.

In the late fifties he toured with Shirley and Lee and played the part of Huey Smith on the road with the Clowns. He increased his studio output at Matassa's. But he was a complex young man, sensitive, often high-strung. He began experimenting with heroin. At twenty, he entered Southern University, feeling that the structure of school would help. But when Dee Clark came to town needing an organist, Booker dropped out of school to join the tour. Because of financial difficulties, the group split up in Houston. Edward Frank found session work for Booker at Robey's studio, where he worked with Duke/Peacock artists Junior Parker, Bobby Bland, and others. His own recording "Gonzo," a rocking organ instrumental, surprised many people by climbing to number ten on the rhythm-and-blues charts in 1960. The title, suggested by Edward Frank, was

Booker's nickname, taken from the lead character in the movie "The Pusher." The flip side was called "Cool Turkey." The heroin references, which Booker and Frank took as a fine joke, eluded producer Robey.

James Booker was a bit of a gypsy, as reflected in his restlessness of the early sixties. He toured the West with Roy Hamilton's show and B. B. King. Then he toured with Lloyd Price, Joe Tex again, and Wilson Pickett. "I went down to Bourbon Street and played at one club called Papa Joe's, and the guy heard me play and he bought three organs because he had two other places, Madame Franchine's and Poodle's Patio. I played all three of those places every night, and when it got to taxing my body, I called on Dr. John and taught him how to play organ and let him be my understudy. That's how he started playing organ."

Booker's deepening dependency on drugs put him at odds with the law. He was arrested and found himself in the company of Chris Kenner at the state penitentiary in Angola, Louisiana. After his release, there was more session work. Fats Domino was on the road a great deal then, and Bartholomew hired Booker to record piano tracks for "Fats Is Back" in 1968. An exceptional Domino-style piano can be heard on Booker's "I'm Ready," released on the Reprise label. But when his drug use continued to cause problems with police, Booker left New Orleans for New York. In the early seventies, he did session work for producer Mike Stoller, who sent Booker to Nashville to work at Starday/King studio as a session pianist. His reputation on keyboard spread among musicians around the country, and he recorded with Maria Muldar, Ringo Starr, Aretha Franklin, the Doobie Brothers, and the Grateful Dead. In 1975 he played at a music festival in Barcelona, Spain, dazzling the audience with his rocking boogie version of "Malaguena." He was then working to rid himself of his addiction. Of those years, he said: "It started like a nightmare and ended like a dream. It's every junky's dream

to square up. Some pursue it, some don't. I found every reason to pursue it because I had so much to look forward to, and it seemed to be a stumbling block. I found out after I did kick it, I had a few other problems, personality-wise. When I was coming off of methadone in seventy-six, I found I was very paranoid. I got placed in Charity Hospital on the third floor mental ward. I had two nervous breakdowns between January and March. Then I came to the Euterpe Center, and I was on the tail end of detoxing the methadone, and it was quite painful. It was quite a drastic experience. I wasn't sure I could do it."[19]

He did do it, and late in 1976 rhythm-and-blues historian Norbert Hess arranged a European tour that resulted in two albums recorded live. The first LP, *James Booker: The Piano Prince of New Orleans*, features several Booker compositions. "One Hell of a Nerve" has an interesting history. New Orleans has long had fruit vendors who drive small trucks through the neighborhoods hawking their produce. Booker drew on that tradition. "I remember listening to the watermelon man: 'I got watermelon, I got cantaloupe, I got okra and shrimp.' That influenced me to write a certain style of music. I wrote 'So Swell When You Well' from that. And there's another I have, 'One Hell of a Nerve,' and it really gives you the sound of the man going behind the watermelon truck [selling produce]. The only thing that's missing is the cowbell that the horse used to have." Booker achieves the effect with an octave-spanning yodel. The other song, "So Swell When You Well," has been Booker's most successful composition since "Gonzo" and has been covered by Aretha Franklin and Fats Domino.

His second European album, *James Booker Live*, was recorded at the Boogie Woogie and Ragtime Piano Contest in Zurich, Switzerland, in late 1977. It won the Grand Prix de Disque de Jazz for best live album of the year. Booker accepted the award at the Montreux Jazz Festival in 1978. In the

United States, Rounder Records released the album as *New Orleans Piano Wizard: Live!*

Booker lived in New Orleans in the late seventies and was one of the most popular musicians on the nightclub circuit, if not always a predictable one. When the crowd was right, when the music surged, he was a wonder to behold. Other times he was cold and aloof. But Booker's brilliance was tempered in the flame. His painful struggle with heroin addiction literally embodied "The Junker." Booker's "Junko Partner," an updated version of the old piano anthem, was a part of almost every performance, grounding his eclectic style in the city's musical past. Challenging melody and rhythm, the "Piano Prince" pushed the instrument to far limits, and since his departure, James Carroll Booker III remains the legend that he was in life.

Chapter Fifteen

DR. JOHN'S GUMBO ROCK

In his time, Mac Rebennack has left large tracks through the pathways of popular music. As Dr. John he was that rare item, a true original. Dr. John!—sunglasses and radiant colors, feathers and plumes, bones and beads about his neck, the crusty blues voice rich in dialect cadences, and then the man himself in motion: scattering glitter to the crowds, pumping the keyboard, a human carnival to behold.

Today there is less exotica to his act. His Mardi Gras performances still excite the crowds, but a more seasoned composer and reflective pianist has emerged. He lived in New York in the early eighties, playing clubs like the Lone Star Cafe and Bottom Line with periodic visits home. As an artist, Dr. John has immeasurably advanced the language of New Orleans music, tapping dark myths of the past in a repertoire that won him national fame.

He was born Malcolm John Rebennack, Jr., on Thursday, November 20, 1941. He was nearly a month overdue and weighed ten pounds. His mother, Dorothy, called him "my Thanksgiving turkey." His older sister, Barbara (nicknamed Bobbie), was born in 1932. Both parents loved music. Dorothy Cronin Rebennack, born in Mobile, Alabama, was of Irish and French ancestry and studied dance as a young girl. Malcolm John Rebennack, Sr., was a third generation Orleanian who owned a radio and appliance shop.

Little Mac had a round face, pink cheeks, soft brown eyes. When Bobbie began posing for local advertisements, Mrs. Rebennack took Mac along to a photo session. "They wanted him right away," she recalled. So nine-month-old Mac graced pictures celebrating baby shoes and Ivory soap. At three, he was picking out melodies on the family piano. One day his Aunt Luella sat on the stool and asked if he had a request. He said: "My three favorite songs are 'Long Ago and Far Away,' 'Give Me That Old Time Religion,' and 'I Found My Thrill on Blueberry Hill.' "[1]

He became an altar boy in the church and at

thirteen was a page in the Children's Carnival Ball. On Saturday he helped out at the appliance store. In addition to appliances, Malcolm Rebennack stocked the latest records. Little Mac would listen to seventy-eights for hours on end—country singers Roy Rogers, Hank Williams, and Gene Autry; blues singers Roosevelt Sykes, Champion Jack Dupree, and Memphis Minnie. He quickly grew bored with piano lessons. A nun complained, "If I play what his next lesson is going to be, he will play it right behind me, note for note." At home his aunt Andre taught him a few blues licks and the tune "Pinetop Boogie Woogie." "My aunt was a groovy old broad," Mac reflects. "It was the only tune I knew. I used to drive everybody mad playing it."[2]

"I sent him to Werlein's Music," Mrs. Rebennack continues, "to see what instrument he'd like to play, and he selected guitar." But Mac balked at serious note-reading. He began picking and strumming in his room, imitating records by Lightning Slim and Lightning Hopkins; he loved the blues. One day his teacher Mr. Guma dropped by the house. He heard blues from the back of the house and remarked approvingly, "I'm so glad he's listening to records." "Oh, he's not listening to records," his mother chirped. "That's Mac playing."[3]

He entered Jesuit High, a school with a tradition of academic excellence dating back to the 1840s. Entrance requirements were stiff. Students wore khaki uniforms and had military drills. Latin and Greek were mandatory for honors classes. At first, Mac did well in his studies. In 1954, his freshman year, rhythm-and-blues was shifting to rock-and-roll. Mac listened to deejays Poppa Stoppa, Okey Dokey, and Jack the Cat. After school he'd head to the Bop Shop on Rampart Street and buy records. At home he spent hours practicing his guitar and piano, borrowing licks from new records; little time was left for translations of Caesar's history of the Gallic Wars.

Mac Sr. was a friend of Cosimo Matassa, who let the boy watch recording sessions. Shirley Goodman (of Shirley and Lee) recalls: "He'd run errands for Cosimo, listen to the playback and bug the musicians to show him things on their instruments. Everybody liked Mac, but sometimes Cosimo or Dave [Bartholomew] would chase him out of there."[4] During breaks he talked to the musicians, in time becoming friends with Red Tyler, Lee Allen, and others.

On weekends Mac helped his father, who began repairing radio and television sets in a small shop near Lake Pontchartrain. Mac reflects: "My father was one of those big-hearted, sweet guys, but he wasn't much of a businessman." As a sideline, Mr. Rebennack installed and repaired public address systems. One afternoon they drove across the river to a creaky black club called the Pepper Pot. "The group was on break because the system was broke, and that's when I first saw Professor Longhair," Mac recalled. "They wouldn't let me sit in the club 'cause I was too young. So I stood on this log outside the window, and I looked in; I could see Fess's hands on the piano."[5]

On another outing to the Cadillac Club in the Ninth Ward, he saw Walter "Papoose" Nelson, guitarist with Fats Domino's band. Everyone but Fats was there that day. "Papoose was my idol," Mac beamed. "He'd let me go on and stand right in front of him and look at how he put his hands on the guitar. Then he finally took me on as a guitar student [some years later]." Papoose played jazz and blues licks, forcing Rebennack to play straight chords behind him. "He would never let me take a solo. He got me disciplined to where I was just playin' chords for hours and hours. That had a great bearing on my music in general."[6]

Jesuit High was caught up in the whirlwind popularity of rock-and-roll. The student paper ran reviews of discs by Elvis, Little Richard, and Jerry Lee Lewis. Mac formed a band, the Dominos, to appear at the annual talent show. They wore white shirts with black string ties and black coats emblazoned with large white dominos. Henry

Gueraneaux, a childhood friend who played in the band, says: "This was the first time anything but Glenn Miller music or Dixieland was played for a talent night. We came up and did Fats Domino tunes, which are mild by today's standards. At the time, it was complete heresy."[7]

Mac made quite a hit with a wild, rocking guitar, holding the instrument behind his neck, between his legs, wiggling and shaking across the stage. Al Farrell, a musician several years younger than Rebennack, recalls: "He was *the* big man on campus. He was always surrounded by a bunch of guys asking him questions about rock-and-roll. I was the youngest one in the group, and I'd stand on the side and listen. And he'd play these Chuck Berry licks while he was talking. He could answer all the questions." With music occupying more of his time and the sessions at Matassa's a further distraction, Mac left Jesuit in early 1957, midway through his junior year. Grades were not the main reason. Farrell explains: "The Jesuit priests never did say, 'Don't listen to rock-and-roll,' or burn records in the school yard. But they frowned on his presence to a degree that made him uncomfortable."[8]

Taking a correspondence course to finish high school, Mac continued visits to the studio, listening to the playback, talking with session players, meeting producers, making his presence known. At fifteen he began to receive calls for session work. "It had a lot to do with the instrument I played [guitar]," he explains. "Justin Adams had a four- or five-night-a-week gig, whereas cats like Papoose would be on the road; I had an open field to work whenever they couldn't be reached. And as I started doin' sessions and proved that I had some value, then cats would rehire me."[9]

He doesn't remember his first recording date. He had not joined the musicians' union, so money was passed under the table. He does recall working for Victor Augustine, the talent scout who discovered Guitar Slim, and doing early blues records

for the Ace label as well as a few hillbilly dates and some demonstration sides.

Rebennack stayed in touch with his music buddies from Jesuit. Leonard James, a saxophonist, was his soul mate through the early 1960s. Leonard epitomized the "cool" culture of the fifties, wearing pointed shoes and suspenders, with his greased hair combed back. Mac began wearing sharp suits with his hair slicked back in a "kiss curl." James and Rebennack, with bassist Earl Stanley and drummer Paul Staehle, made up the nucleus of a performing band. Under James's name they cut the instrumental LP "Bobin' and Strollin'."

The group had little trouble finding work. As rock-and-roll became the craze, demand exceeded the supply. Mac's group played nightclubs, proms, and CYO dances and backed Frankie Ford and singer James "Deadeye" Herring. The group played rock-and-roll but also added some unorthodox numbers. "We used to do the old low-down blues," Herring recalls. "There weren't too many white bands that could do it. Back then, man, if you sit in with the black band, boy, they'd jump on your ass when you come outside. People took a dim view of that, but we did it anyway."[10]

Road tours followed. Rebennack remembers: "We useta work like forty, fifty days on da road . . . Baton Rouge, Alexandria, Monroe, Shreveport, go up in Arkansas, work all da cities there. Then we'd go through Oklahoma, come back through Texas, work the Gulf Coast into Florida, and come back home. Just workin' one nighters, except in those days we was drivin' to all them gigs."[11] At various times he had his clothes stolen, guitar filled with beer by a rowdy customer, and shirt torn off by a mob of girls in Cut Off, Louisiana, while backing Jimmy Clanton. Back home, the phone kept ringing. He played concert shows backing Fabian, Frankie Avalon, and Ray Stevens and sat in with an all-black orchestra, led by Wallace Davenport, backing Clyde McPhatter and Roy Brown.

In March of 1958 seventeen-year-old Mac Rebennack joined Local 178 of the musicians' union. In his early teens he began writing songs, sitting at the family piano for hours, singing and playing into a tape recorder until a suitable melody emerged. It is much the same method he uses today. The back room became a refuge for his songs with sheet music scattered among records, under the bed, atop boxes, in drawers and hanging out of them. "I wouldn't dare clean it up," his mother said, "I might be throwing away another 'Stardust'!"[12]

Mac and a friend, Seth David, composed songs, and through Harold Battiste, placed several with Specialty Records. The best composition was a risqué tune in the style of Little Richard, "Lights Out," recorded by Jerry Byrne, a vocalist in Mac's band.

Standing on the front porch,
  I grabbed her and kissed her.
Boy, was I surprised
  When I saw her little sister.
Lights out!
  Lights out!

I'm glad to know that the lights were out.
  Sister knows more about
What to do
  When the lights go out.

Lovin' on the front porch,
  Sittin' on a swing,
I could almost hear
  Those weddin' bells ring.
Lights out!

Between 1956 and 1963, more than fifty Rebennack compositions were recorded in New Orleans. Some were regional hits; others got no farther than the city limits. "Losing Battle" was an R&B hit for bluesman Johnny Adams. But these songs earned Rebennack little money. Local record companies often ignored royalty payments to

composers, and to add insult to injury, he was often forced to share credit with artists, producers, and label owners. In 1960 he sent a song to Lloyd Price. Some months later "Lady Luck" made the R&B top ten with Price's name as writer. Legal action was taken, but Price held the copyright. Rebennack could do nothing about it.

He spent weeks at a time in Matassa's studio writing, arranging, playing, mostly for union wages with a few "outlaw" sessions. For sixty dollars a week (and a few session fees), Mac worked for Johnny Vincent, building a list of rock-and-roll singers for Ace. His R&B gigs included work with Big Boy Myles, Joe Tex, and Sugarboy Crawford. He played novelty tunes such as "Chinese Bandits" for the LSU football team and "Morgus the Magnificent" for a local television horror-movie show. He also played many racially mixed recording sessions; his guitar work by then was authentically black in sound and style. Rebennack developed a rapport with blacks; his easy-going manner had a soothing effect on those around him, and he was always the first with a joke or kind word of encouragement.

"He never shun nobody," trombonist Eddie Hynes states. "There was no such thing as segregation. He didn't bother what color you were; he was going to talk to you in front of everybody. . . . I remember going to some of the most foul-smelling apartments where they had a piano up in the corner and three guys singing. Mac would bring his tape recorder in, we'd listen for forty-five minutes, and he'd tell 'em, 'Yea, man, I'll go home and listen to this, and I'll let you guys know.' He'd go anywhere [for Vincent] if he thought somebody was worthwhile. He was always willing to listen."[13]

Through such associations Mac Rebennack acquired a dialect infused by black slang; it was far removed from that of his family environment, yet a speech pattern not without eloquent rhythms. Singer Tommy Ridgley recalls: "We useta always say that Mac acted like a black dude, his actions,

Mac Rebennack starting out, 1957

Mac Rebennack (to left of king) at the Children's Mardi Gras Ball, 1944

his talk, 'cause he was a real hip talker."[14] But when he started picking up checks for session work at the black union, some musicians resented him. Mac called it "race prejudice in reverse."[15] Harold Battiste viewed his situation sympathetically. "He got treated pretty badly by some blacks. He paid a lot of dues to earn that amount of black image he wanted."[16]

Rebennack's career looked promising when on Christmas Eve of 1961 the first in a series of disasters struck. In Jacksonville, Florida, Mac and Ronnie Barron were dressing for a nightclub gig when the motel manager told them to leave. They went to the office; harsh words passed, and the manager drew out a pistol. A struggle ensued and the gun discharged, hitting Rebennack's left index finger—"The finger I used to make all them blues licks."[17]

New Orleans doctors were able to reconstruct the finger, but a year passed before he regained full use of it. He would never play guitar again with the old brilliance. Finger in a cast, he played bass in Dixieland bands on Bourbon Street. He found the music monotonous, the pay poor. He brooded and lapsed into depression. He soon shifted his energies to the piano and, with James Booker's help, learned to play the organ. Then in November of 1962 his father died unexpectedly following a fall from a ladder. Dorothy Rebennack bore up as best she could, but without her husband's income she had to sell what little there was of the repair business and move to Cincinnati to live with daughter Bobbie and her family.

The years 1963 and 1964 brought more problems. The union harassed Mac with exorbitant fines of $1,100 for illegal session work—playing with nonunion members and committing minor infractions. In and out of work, he turned to drugs, ran up debts to club owners, and encountered the police on several occasions. A bright spot, his marriage to Lidia Crow, ended, and in November of 1964 the distraught musician committed himself to a Fort Worth, Texas, hospital for drug rehabilitation. Upon release in 1965, he flew to Anaheim, California, where his mother, sister, and family had moved.

California was a new beginning. In Los Angeles, Harold Battiste, by then a producer for Sonny and Cher, hired Mac for road dates with the rock duo. Battiste ushered him into the ranks of Los Angeles session players. Over the next few years producers H. B. Barnum, Phil Spector, Leon Russell, and J. W. Alexander all sought his talents. The turning point came in 1967. For years Rebennack had been intrigued by the legendary voodoo character Dr. John. The idea had germinated many years before while his sister was a bookkeeper at Rothschild's Antiques on Royal Street in New Orleans. A chest containing books on Haitian voodoo arrived from Europe. Bobbie Rebennack gave them to her brother, who devoured them and in time other books on voodoo; he even attended spiritualist ceremonies. Rebennack made trips to the Cracker Jax Drug Store on South Rampart, which sold sacred candles, black cat bones, John the Conqueror roots, and love potions.

The real Dr. John was a huge black man who owned slaves himself and lived in New Orleans in the 1840s. Claiming to be a Senegalese prince, he told fortunes and specialized in healing and selling "gris-gris" hexes. Thousands are said to have sought him out—lovers, parents wanting protection for wayward children, women wanting youth, the sick, the old. He possessed some medical talents, knew astrology, and placed and lifted curses for a fee. Mac had long harbored the idea of making a series of records based on the voodoo myth.

The catalyst that transformed Mac Rebennack into Dr. John was Harold Battiste. Since AFO, the bearded, balding jazzman had prospered with Sonny and Cher. Battiste and Sonny Bono had a recording venture through Atco, a subsidiary of Atlantic, and Ahmet Ertegun, the label's president, with Jerry Wexler gave Battiste freedom to work

Dr. John at Tipitina's, 1981

up some projects of his own. At first Rebennack felt his own voice wasn't strong enough for the Dr. John role. He wanted to write and share producing and asked Ronnie Barron to provide vocals. But his friend balked, thinking the idea "too inside—nobody would be able to relate to it."[18] Mac was undaunted. "When I saw what Bob Dylan and Sonny [Bono] could do, even when they couldn't sing, man, I figured it was time for me to try something."[19]

Battiste recalls his marketing strategy. "The California kids, they're always looking for something to believe in. So we'll make Dr. John the new guru. We'll make him this mysterious character, and these people out here will go crazy for him. And they'll be ready to worship him. We had a big plan to sell gris-gris in stores, and all the paraphernalia that went with practicing the art of witchcraft."[20]

First came the craft of producing a record. On October 24, 1967, Rebennack and Battiste assembled New Orleans exiles at the Gold Star Studios in Los Angeles. Old friendships were renewed with reminiscences of home. From AFO days came singer Tami Lynn, drummer John Boudreaux, and Battiste on bass and soprano saxophone. Jessie Hill and Shirley Goodman joined Lynn for background vocals, while Ronnie Barron played keyboard. Rebennack played guitar and sang live in the studio. The sound, later referred to as "voodoo rock," was built on his colorful vocal shadings, street chants, and words half-spoken, half-sung. The LP was released in 1968 as *Gris-Gris* by Dr. John, the Night Tripper. Atlantic executives, unsure of a marketing plan, decided the disc would find its own audience.

The album appeared amid a great shift in radio programming; FM stations had begun a revolution in record airplay by presenting less talk and more music. The alternative stations featured new or unknown rock performers. Such stations gave impetus to the Grateful Dead, Janis Joplin, the Jefferson Airplane, cult figures like the Fugs,

Captain Beefheart—and Dr. John. The album cover was enough to make anyone take notice. Rebennack wore a snakeskin vest with a stuffed serpent for a collar, an Indian headband, and old bones festooned around his neck. He stood over a hot cauldron. (The costume owed inspiration to Ninth Ward singer Prince La-La; Lala is a devil according to voodoo legend.) The lyrics conjure visions of steamy bayous, witches, and demons. From "Gris-Gris Gumbo Ya-Ya":

They call me Dr. John,
  I'm known as the Night Tripper,
Got a stachel of gris-gris in my hand,
  Got many clients that come from miles around
Runnin' down my prescriptions.
  I got medicines, cure all y'all's ills,
I got remedies of every description.

Records alone do not make a celebrity; Mac hit the touring circuit. The times favored an exotic act. *Psychedelic* was the word for those late sixties hard rock events: high volume music, lights and projectors flashing multicolored images, fans tripping through the high theatrics. At the 1967 Monterey Pop Festival, the Who dropped smoke bombs and destroyed their equipment; Jimi Hendrix torched his guitar in front of thousands. The times were appropriate for Dr. John.

Mac took the role seriously. Costuming became a backstage ritual. He burned candles and incense to set the mood and, like a warrior preparing for battle, suited up in stages. On his head he wore a turban or crown laced with plumes of red, orange and aqua; he put yellow, blue, and red grease paint on his face, with sprinklings of glitter dust. He wore long robes with tassels, and around his neck hung necklaces, bones, crosses, and a small drum on a cord. He cut a striking figure in all those feathers and colors—throwing glitter dust into the audience.

Most critics agreed Dr. John had an uncanny ability to transmit the macabre image through otherwise solid music. But Albert Goldman of *Life,* one of the first to recognize his legitimacy, expressed some misgivings. "Mac Rebennack feels that he is only a temporary sojourner in this time and country. He regards contemporary America as remarkably similar to other civilizations which have vanished without a trace. . . . He created a character that has now swallowed up his own personality."[21] His mother had reservations too. "Religious-wise, being Catholic, I was thinking of the spells and witches, the part of it that was demonic. I didn't want him for his soul's sake to be doing this. But actually, I could see the creativeness of what he was doing."[22]

Gris-Gris sold over fifty thousand copies. What began as a one-shot recording arrangement led to a second album. But *Babylon,* weighted down with mundane sociopolitical lyrics, sold poorly, "I belong to the KKK and the NAACP," Dr. John sang, "a missile erector, a propaganda collector, a woman selector, a Castro defector."

Before his third LP, *Remedies,* Rebennack left Battiste for a high-powered, fast-talking manager, Charlie Green. Green and Brian Stone were also managing Sonny and Cher, the Buffalo Springfield, and Iron Butterfly.

Ironically, *Remedies* drew more deeply on New Orleans music. "Wash, Mama, Wash" was reminiscent of the rhythm-and-blues produced by Battiste for AFO. "All on a Mardi Gras Day" is a wonderful Carnival song, fraught with references to street parades and festival set behind a big bass drum beat.

The big bass drum lead the big parade (*three times*)
　All on a Mardi Gras Day,
And all you could hear the people say
　Was omm-ba-ay
Tou-way-packa-way.

The trombone was playing that ole tailgate (*three times*)
　All on a Mardi Gras Day

And all that you could hear the people say
　Was omm-ba-ay
Tou-way-packa-way.

The new record triggered problems, however. Rebennack claims that before it was completed, Green delivered tapes to Atco without his knowledge. Vocals were resung, lyrics on certain tunes left out entirely. When Mac arrived in London in 1970 to produce tracks for a new work, an ugly argument with Green erupted before the session. Rebennack ended up with no manager, only a drummer and several background vocalists. But he had a reputation by then, and the call went out for help. To his aid came Mick Jagger of the Rolling Stones, guitarist Eric Clapton, Bobby Keyes on saxophone (from Delaney and Bonnie), and a dozen cream session players—eighteen in all. Mountains of material were recorded at that session. Through overdubbing and editing, Mac pulled together a respectable disc. *The Sun, the Moon and Herbs* featured some of his best work. "Black John the Conqueror" had a swelling, gospel-like chant, pounding and swaying over and over like the Beatles' chorus in "Hey, Jude."

There's an old man, he lives on Decatur Street,
　He's got a little word of wisdom
For every single soul he meets.
　Everytime he gets next to me.
He try to tell me that I really can be
　One with everything.
Free—living in eternity.
　Lord, and I never forget him
Cause I can tell you that
　Black John the Conqueror, root in his hand,
Black John the Conqueror, is his name.

Because of the problems with the London session, Rebennack was deeply in debt. His career was foundering when in stepped Jerry Wexler of Atlantic Records, sympathetic to his plight—but more so, an admirer of his music. Wexler had developed a love of New Orleans music while recording Professor Longhair in the early 1950s. In the sixties he directed the careers of soul singers Solomon Burke, Wilson Pickett, and Aretha Franklin. Wexler helped Mac find new management, first Albert Grossman (who had worked with Bob Dylan) and later Phil Walden. The album that resulted in 1972 was *Gumbo,* one of the finest New Orleans albums ever done. Mac continues: "Jerry Wexler and Leon Russell came by the studio. . . . I was drunk and started reminiscing about old New Orleans music. They'd say, 'Remember this song, remember that one?' So I'd play them a little of each one. Jerry made a tape that night and got the idea of making an album with just me playing piano. I said, 'Why don't we get Harold [Battiste] and the boys and do a whole band thing?' "[23]

A radical departure from the Dr. John exotica, *Gumbo* was simply a tribute to the songs he had grown up with, to the artists he loved. The reunion with Battiste was warm; the recording tracks flowed effervescently. The LP contained an all-star cast of New Orleans musicians then in California: saxman Lee Allen, the Lastie brothers (David on sax, Melvin on cornet), and drummer Freddie Staehle. It was a down-home R&B session like the old days, spirits high, limbs loose. Mac sang "Big Chief" and "Tipitina" in homage to Fess, "Those Lonely, Lonely Nights" by Earl King, a Huey Smith medley, and Sugarboy Crawford's "Iko Iko."

Charting in *Billboard, Gumbo* became Rebennack's most commercial production. The album marked another shift; he dropped the exotic stage garb for more conventional dress. (The photo on the inside jacket of the LP features Rebennack in a cutaway morning suit, with top hat, spats, and cane.) A promotional tour took him to Carnegie Hall, Europe, and first exposure on American television. His career was at an apex.

Although Dr. John was merely a persona, fans did not distinguish between man and myth, so well did he enact the role. To his stage door came followers bearing gifts for the doctor: shrunken heads, cadaver bones, a boa constrictor, even a human hand!

After the success of *Gumbo,* Mac arranged a studio date with old friend Allen Toussaint. The LP *Right Place, Wrong Time,* well-conceived and executed, had solid instrumental backing from the Meters. Lyrics addressed new topics. "Such a Night," an old soft-shoe number, features a slide trombone and sentimental lyrics.

And it's such a night, it's such a night,
   Sweet confusion under the moonlight.
Your eyes met mine, and at a glance,
   You let me know this was my chance.

But the song that gained the most exposure and channeled Dr. John into the mainstream was the title track "Right Place, Wrong Time." The tune, built off a simple three-note riff, is deceptively complex, with a weaving instrumental polyrhythm, the clear mark of a Toussaint production.

I been in the right place,
   But it must have been the wrong time,
I been on the right trip,
   But I must'a used the wrong car,
Head is in a bad place,
   And I wonder what it's there for.

In the summer of 1973 the song charted in the *Billboard* top ten. His career was now moving at a frenetic pace with appearances on NBC's "Midnight Special," Don Kirshner's "Rock Concert," and later in the year, "Sound Stage" (PBS). He toured Europe with the Meters and Professor Longhair and played to packed halls in London and Paris, as well as at the prestigious Montreux Jazz Festival in Switzerland. In September Rebennack and the Meters were back in Toussaint's studio. The strategy was the same; Mac's songs encased in the Meters' funk rhythm backing, with Toussaint's artistic brush strokes. But the outcome was different. The album *Desitively Bonnaroo* showcased good material, like Earl King's "Let's Make a Better World," but it lacked commercial spark.

Rebennack's studio career flourished in the late seventies. As a producer he has a calming effect on other musicians in the studio. His credits read like a Who's Who in pop music: Aretha Franklin's "Spanish Harlem," Carly Simon and James Taylor's "Mockingbird," and a surprising collaboration with Kate Smith. He also produced Van Morrison's *In a Period of Transition.* In 1977 he joined Levon Helm and the RCO All-Stars for an album and appearance on NBC's "Saturday Night Live." Later in the year he appeared in the Band's farewell concert film *The Last Waltz.* Between 1974 and 1978 Rebennack recorded only one LP as Dr. John, but *Hollywood Be Thy Name* was poorly promoted by United Artists after a corporate shakeup. In 1978 with Horizon Records, he recorded one of his finest LP's, *City Lights.* The songs display a mature Mac Rebennack, with lyrics of lasting resonance.

Too many city lights,
  Too many midnights made me die some every day,
Too many never-was-never-will-be partners,
  Never gave me time to find

A real friend along the way,
  Never time to find a good wife,
Never time to find a real friend.

Now in his forties, Mac Rebennack lives in Manhattan's Chelsea District. The Dr. John of the 1980s is the epitome of versatility. He teamed with veteran songwriter Jerome "Doc" Pomus to write B. B. King's *There's Got to Be a Better World Somewhere.* Then came sound tracks for films such as *Cannery Row* and commercials—for Wendy's Hamburgers and Popeye's Fried Chicken—broadening his financial base. In 1981 a small Baltimore record company released *Dr. John Plays Mac Rebennack,* a solo piano album, both a tribute to keyboard artists he emulated and a collection of songs he was unable to record for larger labels. "Big Mac" is a homage to his father, "Dorothy" a gift to his mother. "I remember the song very well," Mrs. Rebennack recalls. "I think he wrote it in high school. I remember him playing it on the piano at the time." Now in her seventies, Dorothy Rebennack lives in Orange, California, with Bobbie and her family. She is a fashionably dressed lady with a quiet, pristine elegance. She spends much time with her grandchildren. And what is it like being the mother of Dr. John? "All my sisters married doctors," she says with a twinkle, "but I'm the only one who had a Dr. John!"

Chapter Sixteen

ALLEN TOUSSAINT AND THE METERS

Allen Toussaint has done well since the old Minit days. Plush and well furnished, his office at SeaSaint Studio is a reflection of his taste. His partner, Marshall Sehorn, is a bearish man with a thick beard and a down-home accent laced with warmth. In time, however, one finds beneath such congeniality a shrewd, tough-talking businessman with a talent for making record deals that some-times end in controversy.

The son of a Charlotte, North Carolina, cotton weaver, Sehorn began managing musical acts in college during the early fifties. After graduation, he went to New York looking for a job in the music industry and was hired by Bobby Robinson, the black president of Fire and Fury Records, as southern promotion man. Sehorn doubled as a talent scout and on a 1959 visit to his hometown discovered blues singer Wilbert Harrison, who subsequently recorded "Kansas City"—the first in a string of million sellers by various Fire and Fury artists.

Lee Dorsey was the first New Orleans musician

Sehorn signed. In 1960, Sehorn heard the tune "Lottie-Mo" while in the city and sought out Lee Dorsey. Toussaint had produced the disc; Dorsey was then under contract to Valiant/Instant Records. When the contract expired six months later, he signed with Fury. Sehorn wanted Tous-saint to produce a new song, but the Minit con-tract prevented that. "He put it down on piano," Sehorn recalls, "and gave us the name of Harold Battiste, who listened to the tape and wrote the arrangement."[1]

The song, backed by Battiste and AFO regulars, was called "Ya Ya." It broke into the R&B top ten charts in the fall of 1961. Dorsey recalled its ori-gins: "I heard these kids playin' in the street, singin' [the dozens]. They sang, 'Yo mama's sittin' on the slop jar, waitin' for her bowels to move' . . . and they had a nice rhythm. So instead of what they were saying, I just said, 'Sittin' here la la, waitin' for my ya ya."[2] Dorsey followed "Ya Ya" with another novelty ditty written by Earl

King, "Do Re Mi." "Do re mi fa so la ti," sang Dorsey, "forget about the dough and think about me."

Born on Christmas Eve of 1926 in New Orleans, Dorsey is a colorful character who stands just five feet tall. A lightweight prizefighter in his youth, his early nickname was "Cadillac Shorty." Today, some Cadillacs find their way to his body repair shop in the Seventh Ward. Dorsey enjoys cruising in a white El Dorado convertible and dresses fashionably, with diamonds on his fingers. But success never spoiled him. "I love to sing, but if they don't give me the money I want, I'll just go back to body and fender work. I love that just as much. That's where I was first discovered—at Ernie the Whip's on Melpomene and Clara, singin' and beatin' on a fender. Guy came in and asked my boss who was that. He said, 'That's my body man.' 'Do you think he'd like to make a record?' He left fifty dollars and told me to be at the studio for six o'clock."[3]

In 1963 Fire and Fury ran into cash flow problems; Sehorn struck out on his own. Toussaint, who had gone into the army in 1963, was discharged in 1965 and began producing for the Instant and Alon labels, owned by his old Minit colleague Joe Banashak. Dorsey, unrecorded since the sessions for Fury, welcomed a new Toussaint composition, "Ride Your Pony," which tapped the "pony" dance craze sweeping the country.

Ride your pony, get on your pony and ride,
  Ah, you're ridin' high,
Now stay in the saddle, stay in the saddle,
  Now *shoot! Shoot! Shoot!*

As Dorsey sang "Shoot!" a gunshot was heard. As late as 1980, Dorsey still fired a blank pistol at the appropriate time in the tune.

Sehorn approached Toussaint about forming a partnership in the spring of 1965. Besides Banashak, other labels, like Motown and Liberty, had made overtures. Although he respected Banashak, Toussaint felt Sehorn would be a more aggressive partner. When Toussaint informed Banashak of his decision, the older man, surprised and hurt, sold them the master of "Ride Your Pony." He did, however, retain its publishing rights. Banashak continued issuing records in the seventies, maintaining friendly ties with Toussaint.

Sehorn took the "Pony" master to New York and secured distribution through Amy Records. The song broke nationally that summer, and Toussaint signed a partnership contract with Sehorn. Despite Dorsey's success, the first years were not easy. Sehorn suggested that they relocate in Atlanta or Los Angeles, but Toussaint insisted that New Orleans was his home.

Thus began the return of Allen Toussaint, writer and producer. His productions carried jazzy rhythmic shadings and aural simplicity, a musical character deeply rooted in New Orleans. Toussaint theorizes on what made his productions so different: "I think I had a few things goin' on, rather than a whole lot of everything. In an arrangement there would be a few things to pay attention to, rather than crowding it with a whole lot of garbage. Whenever I had horns, they had *a* spot to play, and when it was time for horns, you heard horns. Then you didn't hear horns bothering anything after that. The piano was always right through all that. Guitar did certain little things and no more—*chink, chink, chink, chink* at the beginning of the tune, and be doin' that when the tune faded. I guess little things like that have established my identity."[4]

Through late 1969 there was hardly a time when Lee Dorsey did not have a record on the R&B or pop charts. "Get Out of My Life, Women," a rather serious theme for Dorsey's light-headed voice, followed "Ride Your Pony." Then came "Workin' in a Coal Mine" and "Holy Cow." In the seventies, Dorsey recorded "Sneakin' Sally Through the Alley" and "Yes, We Can Can," both Toussaint compositions later popularized by Robert Palmer and the Pointer Sisters, respectively.

Sansu, the Sehorn-Toussaint firm, began adding other artists to their roster. There was Willie Harper, Benny Spellman, and Betty Harris, who scored a hit with "Nearer to You." Then in 1968, Toussaint heard an instrumental quartet led by Art Neville. The group consisted of bassist George Porter, drummer Joe Modeliste, guitarist Leo Nocentelli, and Neville on keyboard. Billed as Art Neville and the Neville Sound, they played with a distinctively rhythmic pulse that further defined New Orleans "funk" music. In 1976 *Rolling Stone* magazine would call the group, by then the Meters, "the finest performing American band."[5]

Art Neville, the eldest of the Neville children, was born in New Orleans on December 17, 1937. His father, "Big Arthur," and his mother, Amelia, didn't play music, but there was always music in their home. "My father was what you call a shower singer; sang in the bathtub a lot. He used to like Nat King Cole, and my mother liked John Lee Hooker. She used to sing this tune Ella Fitzgerald had out, a thing called 'A Tisket, A Tasket.' My father and mother knew Smiley Lewis. My father used to go fishing with Smiley."[6]

Neville's parents stressed education—and encouraged their children's musical interests. Five of the six Neville children played instruments or sang. Charles, the second son, became accomplished on flute and sax. Aaron developed as a singer and learned piano. Cyril, the youngest, sang and played percussion and piano. Athelgra, a daughter, sang with the Dixie Cups. The family lived uptown on Valence Street in Art's youth, then moved to the Calliope project in central city. In Art's early teens the family moved back to Valence Street, where he began practicing on the piano. "Professor Longhair was the major cat that influenced me. When we were kids, we would hang out at the sweet shops and listen to Fess and Lloyd Glenn. Fess influenced everybody in New Orleans. Anybody who played piano, I don't care who they were, he had to influence them."[7]

In high school, Art and Charles Neville and the French brothers, Bob and George, formed a group called the Turquoise. "We used to get together just for the fun of it. From there I got into the Hawkettes. Something happened to their lead singer and piano player. We hadn't been doing any serious work with the Turquoise, so the guys hit on me to work with the Hawkettes."

The Hawkettes worked out of the Ninth Ward. With Art Neville as lead vocalist and keyboardist, the group was in demand for high school dances and club dates. They played the latest rhythm-and-blues hits, especially those of Fats Domino. "I used to eat, sleep and drink Fats Domino. In the Hawkettes days the thing I had going for me was I could sound just like the cat."[8]

As their popularity grew, the Hawkettes became friends with deejay Ken Elliott, Jack the Cat. In 1954 he took them into a small studio of WWEZ radio and recorded a song called "Mardi Gras Mambo." The song was written in 1953 by Lew Welsch, a Canal Street clothier, and Frankie Adams, a friend of his. Welsch ran a small label called Sapphire and had country singer Jody Leviens record "Mambo" in time for a Mardi Gras. It played well locally; Elliott felt a rhythm-and-blues version could sell, so he adapted a new set of lyrics, modified the arrangement, then brought the Hawkettes in to record. The record featured Art Neville on vocals, John Boudreaux on drums, and George Davis on alto saxophone. The master was leased to Chess, and by the Mardi Gras of 1955, the song was the newest Carnival sensation.

"Mardi Gras Mambo" gave the Hawkettes new status in the musical community. They began working shows with Ray Charles and Roy Brown and appearing at the Dew Drop and on the college fraternity circuit. On an engagement near Baton Rouge, the Hawkettes met rock-and-roll star Larry Williams, popular for his songs "Short Fat Fannie" and "Bony Maronie." A 1957 tour with Williams gave Art Neville a taste of the limelight. He then

Allen Toussaint and Marshall Sehorn, 1975

Lee Dorsey, 1972

The Meters, 1973. *From left:* Leo
Nocentelli, George Porter, Joe "Zig"
Modeliste, and Art Neville

met Harold Battiste and began recording for Specialty. In 1958 he cut "Cha Dooky Do" but was drafted into the navy shortly before its release.

While stationed at Norfolk, Virginia, as an aviation mechanic, Art picked up gigs in the area and sometimes sat in with touring rhythm-and-blues bands. "Once Huey Smith and the Clowns came through the area, and I stayed out all night singing and carrying on with the band. The next morning I had an inspection, and I stood at attention; I was so tired my knees locked and I fell straight forward and broke a few front teeth."[9] After the navy, Art resumed work with the Hawkettes. Dozens of musicians came and went, including Snooks Eaglin and the Lastie brothers. In 1961 Art signed with the new Instant label and was teamed with producer Allen Toussaint. For Neville, Toussaint wrote "All These Things," a provocative love ballad tailor-made for Neville's warm, rich voice.

The touch of your lips next to mine
　　Gets me excited, makes me feel fine.
I've got it bad, but that's alright
　　Long as you're near me every night.

Your love's so warm and tender,
　　Your thrill is so divine.
It is all these things
　　That make you mine.

By the mid-sixties Art Neville was searching for a new direction with his music.

George Porter, bass player for the Neville Sound, was inspired by Benjamin Francis. "I always wanted to learn to play bass because I just dug the instrument and this individual person. I said, 'I wonder if I could get an axe that would fit me like this particular axe is fittin' with this cat?' So I figured that the bass must be the instrument."[10]

Porter, born on December 26, 1947, was ten years younger than Art Neville. His mother, Henrietta, sang in the church choir while George

Sr. was a devotee of bebop and a fan of Duke Ellington. The Porters lived downtown, and at age ten George struck up a friendship with neighbor and second cousin Joe "Zigaboo" Modeliste. "I started playing when I was ten. . . . Zigaboo's cousin played violin and piano, and he was teaching me and Zig how to play piano." The Porters settled uptown in the Thirteenth Ward. "I found out we were two blocks from Zig, and three blocks from the Nevilles."[11] George and the younger Nevilles played informal jam sessions as teenagers. "We'd practice in the yard behind Zig's house," Cyril Neville recalls. "George played a box guitar, and Zig had a parade drum. Sometimes we made so much noise that neighbors called the police."[12]

Still in his teens, Porter sat in with Earl King and played a road tour. "When I came back, I was working with Irving Bannister, the guitarist. Art Neville came on the gig one night. He said, 'Hey, man, I'm getting ready to start another group; you want to play?' I said, 'Sure, brother.' That was the beginning of the Meters."

People in New Orleans call drummer Joe Modeliste "Zigaboo." Somehow the name fits. His personality is a unique blend of jocoseriousness within a professional demeanor. "Well, in the Thirteenth Ward, everybody had to have a handle," Zig remarked. "'Ratty Chin' was Cyril Neville's handle. Art was 'Art, the Mighty Ro,' and Aaron was 'Apache Red.' All these cats had their thing. Mine was 'Zigaboo,' some people call me 'Ziggy.' "[13] Born on December 28, 1948, Zig was the eldest of six children. He was raised by his godmother, Lula Blouin, who put up the money for his first drums, a modest three-piece set. In the Thirteenth Ward lived drummers Clarence "Juny Boy" Brown and Leo Morris (Idris Muhammed), but Zig's idol was Joe "Smokey" Johnson, a session player at Cosimo Matassa's who worked with the Hawkettes. "I admired Smokey a lot," he remembers. "He had a style; his personality meshed with the drums. At times he was a wild man, fun cat. He took a liking to me. When I was coming up, the thing was to 'keep the tradition going.' I wasn't thinking about being a star."[14]

Modeliste was in the seventh grade when Art Neville stopped by unexpectedly. "He asked me to come play with the Hawkettes because his drummer had left on short notice."[15] Zig played a few jobs with the Hawkettes but admits he wasn't ready to play with the caliber of musicians Neville had in his group. He continued practicing. In the early sixties, he picked up one-nighters with the Hawkettes and played review shows backing Irma Thomas, Benny Spellman, and Tommy Ridgley. In 1964 he joined Deacon John and the Ivories. Several years later, he joined the Neville Sound.

Guitarist Leo Nocentelli was the only member of the Meters not from the Neville neighborhood. Born on June 15, 1946, Leo grew up in the Seventh Ward and Irish Channel. His father, Jack, a burly Creole of partially Sicilian descent, was a warehouse worker and a larger-than-life kind of man. In his youth, Jack played ragtime banjo with the Louisiana Black Devil Band. He was also a versatile poet who wrote long ballads and could recite them from memory years later. Like Sidney Bechet's father, Jack Nocentelli infused his home with music. Leo Nocentelli's two sisters sang; his younger brother Angelo learned bass.

"New Orleans is not noted for guitar," Leo reflects, "because people tend to think of New Orleans for Dixieland. In terms of guitar, you didn't hear them locally until amplification."[16]

By the 1950s, Leo was hearing songs on the radio by the Platters, Professor Longhair, and the Skyliners. "We had an old piano . . . I started banging on 'til I was ten. Then my father bought me a $4.98 ukulele, a little plastic guitar." When he was twelve, Jack Nocentelli bought his son a six-string guitar. His father urged him on, sometimes unexpectedly. "I'd take a ride with him. I

wouldn't know the guitar was in the back of the truck. We'd go in a club. I never did like playing in front of people. I was kind of shy. Then all of a sudden, he'd go in the back of the truck and bring out the guitar and stick it in my hand. That was an important time for me, even though I didn't realize it. It prepared me to play in front of people without being shy."[17]

At thirteen, Leo joined his first professional group, led by drummer Charles "Honey Boy" Otis and trumpeter Melvin Lastie, a high-caliber combo. But Leo Nocentelli was too inexperienced at the time and left the group to concentrate on instrumental technique. A year of practice in the "woodshed" paid off. In 1960 he was on tour backing Clyde McPhatter, Otis Redding, and Clarence Henry; then he joined the Hawkettes. In 1964, at seventeen, Leo traveled to Detroit to record for Motown. Besides studio work with New Orleans artists, he played on the Supremes' "Where Did Our Love Go?" and made recordings with Martha and the Vandellas, the Temptations, and the Spinners. Drafted into the army, he spent 1964 at Fort Riley, Kansas, with periodic returns to New Orleans and session work for Toussaint. Discharged in 1966, he joined the Neville Sound.

The Neville Sound began with seven members, including Cyril and Aaron Neville as vocalists and Gary Brown on saxophone. In June of 1968 the group consisted of only four men—Art Neville, George Porter, Joe Modeliste, and Leo Nocentelli. By then they had moved to the Ivanhoe Club on Bourbon Street and had developed a dance beat with solid rhythms. "We played as free as we wanted. No one was restricted," George explained. "We didn't say, 'Hey, brother, you got to play this and you got to play that.' Everybody just felt good and comfortable. Really, playin' the gig at the Ivanhoe was the thing that got us tight, 'cause we were playin' six nights a week."

When record offers came, "I looked 'em all over, and decided to go with Allen Toussaint," Art remembers. "I had worked with him, and he seemed to be doing the right thing at the time."[18] Their first Sansu records were released under Art Neville's name—"Bo Diddley," parts one and two, and "I'm Gonna Put Some Hurt on You." Then in late 1968, "after a session for Lee Dorsey," Art recalls, "we decided to put down some things we'd been playin' on the gig." Several instrumental tracks were cut—"straight from the head," just as they were conceived in the morning hours at the Ivanhoe. Toussaint watched and listened.

In New York, Sehorn made a deal with Jubilee Records' president Jerry Blaine, who requested that the group change its name. Art Neville and the Neville Sound was not very commercial. Art was the leader, but everyone felt the name should reflect the group's image. Leo Nocentelli suggested the Mock Four. But in the end, Sehorn and Toussaint named the quartet the Meters. Sehorn and Toussaint also changed the name of the songs. "Art's Thing" became "Sophisticated Cissy," a title borrowed from a popular song in 1967 by Rufus Thomas. "Cissy Strut" and "Here Comes the Meterman" rounded out the first session.

In August of 1969 *Billboard* magazine changed the heading of the rhythm-and-blues charts to *soul* music. As white pop and rock-and-roll had succumbed to the British invasion, contemporary black music was undergoing profound changes. Record companies that had built empires in the 1950s found a dwindling blues market. As political values changed during the civil rights movement, blacks searched for a new music, a new urban voice. As blues receded, gospel exerted greater influence. The frantic shouts and pleading moans of soul shouters, backed with staccato horn lines, solid snare punctuation, and thick treble guitar chords, became known as "soul music." Songs like "Mr. Pitiful" by Otis Redding, "I Got You" by James Brown, and "Knock on Wood" by Eddie Floyd exemplify the period.

Studio technology changed, too. Monophonic recorders gave way to two-track stereophonic, then four-track, and by the mid-sixties, eight-track systems, which became standard in the industry. Thus producers were able to isolate each instrument on one or more tracks, giving each recording greater clarity, better balance, and fuller musical texture. The rhythm section—bass, drums, guitar, piano—moved to the center of the soul sound. In Memphis, the "Stax" sound was led by organist Booker T. Jones. Berry Gordy's Motown and hits from Muscle Shoals, Alabama, also relied heavily on tight, pulsating rhythm sections. All three were directly influenced by the New Orleans sound of the early sixties, borrowing rhythmic concepts from drums and bass.

In the late sixties, *funk* became a new term for black dance music. The origin of the word is unknown. It usually meant bad smelling but more popularly referred to a down-home, loose style of dance. The word began turning up in song lyrics and titles. "Funky Broadway" by Dyke and the Blazers, "Funky Fever" by Clarence Carter, "Do the Funky Chicken" by Rufus Thomas, and Lee Dorsey's "Everything I Do Gonna Be Funky" all contributed to the unfolding pop vocabulary. The Meters' "Sophisticated Cissy" and "Cissy Strut" became New Orleans funk anthems. If, as Mac Rebennack claims, Professor Longhair is the "Father of Funk," then the Meters can be viewed as stepchildren, extending his musical language.

The Meters set a style, a trademark of relaxed rhythmic shadings with loose interplay between instruments. Leo played light jazz chords, influenced by Kenny Burrell and Barney Kessell, his idols, and with a scratch-work technique accenting the rhythm. Modeliste on drums hit polyrhythmic snare lines against George Porter's bulging bass patterns. Art's slicing chords on keyboard occupied the center.

The Meters followed with a string of hits—"Chicken Strut," "Looka-Py-Py," and "Stretch Your Rubber Band." In 1970 the group was named the best rhythm-and-blues instrumental group by both *Billboard* and *Record World* magazines. The Meters toured from coast to coast. George Porter recalls: "Some places we went, people weren't expecting what they got. One place in Roanoke, Virginia, was packed with nothing but faggots. They thought the Meters were faggots 'cause our first records were 'Sophisticated Cissy' and 'Cissy Strut.' But it turned out all right; other people came. We turned the speedometer on the car around several times."[19]

In 1971 Jubilee Records declared bankruptcy, owing the Meters substantial royalties. Sehorn recovered the master tapes, then set about finding a label to properly market their brand of funk. Within the year, Sehorn negotiated a six-figure deal with Warner Brothers Music to administer the Marsaint catalog; the agreement included record contracts for Toussaint and the Meters with Warner's subsidiary, Reprise.

By May of 1972 the Meters released their first Reprise LP, *Cabbage Alley,* named for a tiny New Orleans back street. They pushed the LP on a trip to Trinidad, appearing with the island's star, the Mighty Sparrow. This trip gave inspiration for "Soul Island," a reggae-tinged melody. *Cabbage Alley* sold poorly but led to studio work on Dr. John's celebrated *Right Place, Wrong Time* and a European tour in the summer of 1973 with Professor Longhair and Dr. John.[20]

As the Toussaint/Sehorn partnership grew, both men recognized a large vacuum in the city. No state-of-the-art recording studio existed in New Orleans. Sehorn observed, "If we were going to compete with Nashville and Muscle Shoals, we'd have to have the best facility." It took a lot of talk and salesmanship by Sehorn in light of the city's conservative banking mentality, but by the end of 1973, with $350,000 in financing, the dream studio was built and named SeaSaint. It opened in early 1974. "I think the city is going to blossom," Sehorn said in 1973. "It's going to bloom into a beautiful flower of music. It's going to really happen here. I won't say what it was in the fifties—

it's going to be greater than that . . . Memphis and Muscle Shoals bound into one."[21]

Sehorn's predictions fell short of the mark. While SeaSaint did develop a cadre of local acts, Toussaint concentrated most of his energies on producing out-of-town talent with money provided by major record companies. For his services he received a producer's fee, fees for arranging each song, royalties from sales and airplay, and monies paid for studio rental. Most of these funds arrive before an album is even released. So why take chances on new talent?

Toussaint began working with big name talent when the Band asked him to do horn charts for their song "Life Is a Carnival." He did arrangements for Paul Simon on his *Rhymin' Simon.* When the studio opened, Toussaint began to attract name acts and new talent. The idea of recording in New Orleans was tempting, and Toussaint now had a national reputation. And come they did. British singer Frankie Miller, an all-girl band called Isis, blues singer John Mayall, Taj Mahal, even Paul McCartney, among others. Toussaint in the seventies and eighties produced hit forty-fives, the measuring stick of industry dollars: Labelle's "Lady Marmalade," Joe Cocker's "Funtime," Patti Labelle's "I Don't Go Shopping," and "Girl Callin'" for Chocolate Milk, a New Orleans group.

The Meters, however, were not new talent. Sehorn and Toussaint held the Meters' managerial-production contract, but the band's day-to-day business affairs were a mess. For the European tour, Sehorn hired Rupert Surcouf, a young New Orleanian, as road manager. A graduate student in Germany, Surcouf returned to New Orleans to manage the group full time. Surcouf reflected candidly: "It was my contention that Marshall and Allen had a conflict of interest in that not only were they the managers, but they were also the record producers and the music publisher. The Meters felt, rightly or wrongly, like they were being exploited. I wanted to try and gain for them some control over their destiny."[22]

In New Orleans, the Meters played for mostly black audiences. "I saw them at the Nite Cap," Surcouf said, "and I said, 'Gee whiz, man, this is a white act. They're wasting their time here.' The black people loved them as long as they could dance. But when the Meters wanted to experiment, the blacks didn't relate to that." Surcouf went to work broadening the base, booking them into white clubs.

In 1974 the Meters released *Rejuvenation,* their finest LP. "If ever there was an album made to wear out a stereo needle," wrote one critic, "this is it. The music is honest and natural, unstained by the high-powered commerciality. The Meters just play themselves, part of the great tradition of New Orleans musicians doing their own thing."[23] But the album cover hurt *Rejuvenation* sales—a slinky girl, reclining on a couch, with a bottle of Ripple wine. Sales were poor, but the disc did produce a local hit, "Hey Pocky Way," which helped gain a larger following in New Orleans.

Toussaint continued to use them as session players. Robert Palmer's smash hit "Sneakin' Sally Through the Alley" bore the Meters' touch. Canadian blues singer King Biscuit Boy courted their sound for his 1974 album and took them on the road as back-up band. Joel Selvin wrote in the *San Francisco Chronicle:* "When the opening act backup band steals the entire show, that is rare." The headline read, "The Meters Just Stole It Away."[24] When British rock singer Rod Stewart wanted the Meters for studio work and for touring, Sehorn agreed on the condition that Stewart record at SeaSaint. But when Stewart's representatives flew in and toured the studio, they found it unsuitable for their client. The deal was nixed. "That could have been a really big break," Surcouf reflects sadly.

In the summer of 1975 the Rolling Stones invited the Meters to open the concert on their Tour of the Americas. It was an exciting but grueling trip. Exposed to millions of fans, the Meters found a reception long denied them. But the tour put strains on their inner fabric as men and as artists. Art Neville explains: "You come out of a club, and you're thrown into something like that. This is a test to see how together you really are. Cause your music can be together, and your head *not* be together, and the music won't really mean anything. . . . Some of the attitudes changed. You know, heads went to swelling up."[25]

Egos were not the only problem. Art was more than a decade older than Leo, George, and Zig. The younger Meters had a stronger rock bent. The dichotomy was sharpest between Art and Leo Nocentelli. Art's keyboard and Leo's guitar style had slowly moved in different musical directions. Still, the band was moving, and the Rolling Stones tour gave them a rare charge of energy.

Prior to the Stones' tour, they recorded a new album, *Fire on the Bayou,* with Cyril Neville on vocals and congas. Cyril's dance movements gave the Meters greater visual appeal and his singing complemented that of his brother. With exposure from the Rolling Stones' tour, the LP sold 88,000 copies, still marginal by industry standards. "We were in tremendous debt to Warners," Surcouf explained. "But Warners always had a complex about the Meters. They felt like they owed the Meters something because they thought *Cabbage Alley* and *Rejuvenation* were both gold albums. At the time Warners was not able to do what they had to do with those records because they didn't have a black music department. So they felt like they dropped the ball." By 1975 Warners had a solid rhythm-and-blues promotional staff, charting hits by the Funkadelics, Bootsie's Rubber Band, and the Staple Singers. "But then they realized that the Meters didn't fit into any conventional mold," Surcouf continues. "They didn't know how to pigeonhole it."

For the Meters, it was an extremely frustrating situation. Everyone agreed the music was good, but where were the sales figures? They played to sellout audiences at the Roxy in Los Angeles, the Boarding House in San Francisco, and New York's Bottom Line. Critics were relentless in their praise. "The Meters we heard last week were so astonishingly good," observed a critic for Boston's *Real Paper*, "they could blow virtually any other band in the country right off the stage and out the door. Play with them and you're playing with fire."[26]

In the summer of 1976 the Rolling Stones offered them a second tour, this time in Europe. "Just before the Stones' tour," Art Neville recalls, "we were out in Denver and had decided to split up. But, man, we thought about it, and after all the years we'd been playing together, we realized that regardless of all the b.s., there wasn't anybody else any of us wanted to be playing with."[27] During the tour, Warner Brothers released *Trickbag*—mostly live studio demos, tracks not meant for commercial release. When Warner Brothers had put pressure on Sehorn for a new Meters album, he took the demos, mixed them, and sent them to California. Both the band and Surcouf were angered by the release. The songs were of an experimental nature. "Disco Is the Thing Today" was an obvious attempt to tap a commercial market. (Ironically, Meters' hits of the late sixties indeed influenced the disco fad of the mid-seventies.) The album failed artistically and at the cash register. With losses mounting, Warners still stood by the band, but the company now realized the problem was that the albums were self-produced. Toussaint's name appeared on album jackets as producer, yet he was rarely present at the sessions. The Meters were basically self-produced.

"We made a deal to record in San Francisco with David Rubinson, who was a pretty hot producer," Surcouf continues. "He had the Pointer Sisters, Herbie Hancock; he was doing Carlos Santana. He was acceptable to Warners, and the Meters were happy with him. So we went to San Francisco." Warners increased the studio budget to $80,000 to show good faith. But now tensions were building within the group, bickering led to quarrels, rehearsals caved in before the studio date. To complicate matters, Surcouf, who had worked for four years on a handshake, presented a managerial contract to the group. The Meters reacted angrily to certain clauses. "Really, now that I reflect back on it," Surcouf said, "it was the wrong time to negotiate a contract."

The controversy carried over into the studio, Rubinson was disappointed by their ill-preparedness and poor attitudes. The album went over budget, not a common practice for Rubinson. One bright spot surfaced with an invitation from NBC to perform on "Saturday Night Live." Surcouf comments: "We knew 'Saturday Night Live' had the audience that was going to buy Meters records and go to Meters dates—provided they were exposed to them." The network was planning to broadcast live from the Mardi Gras of 1977. The band flew in from San Francisco to share billing with Randy Newman and the local New Leviathan Oriental Foxtrot Orchestra.

The Meters were scheduled for the first twenty minutes of the show. But when called to dress rehearsal, only half the band was present. An angry producer moved them to the end of the show to play the final number. Fans packed the Theater for the Performing Arts, but as the show progressed, comedy scenes ran overtime. Worse still, a Carnival parade, running late, interrupted the live remote. When credits rolled at midnight, the Meters were still in their dressing room, not a note played.

In a sense, the fiasco marked the end of the Meters. Surcouf quit as manager. After nine years, Neville quit the band, followed by brother Cyril. Porter, Nocentelli, and Modeliste did a make-good engagement on "Saturday Night Live" in New York, but without Art Neville, it simply was not the Meters.

A month after the breakup, Warner Brothers released their final LP, ironically titled *New Directions*. But with no band to push the product, little promotion was done. Some say the album is prophetic—with songs like "I'm Gone" and "Stop That Train, I'm Leavin'." In fact, *New Directions* is a solid piece of music, well-executed, well-produced: an album that could have broken commercial barriers. Instead it ended up in cut-out bins of record stores around the country.

The musicians went their separate ways. George Porter formed a local group called Joyride. Zig Modeliste toured nationally as drummer with the New Barbarians, led by Rolling Stone guitarists Ron Wood and Keith Richards. Leo Nocentelli continued studio work. Art formed the Neville Brothers band.

Financial pressures, artistic conflicts, individual egos cause many bands to split. In that respect, the Meters' dissolution was not exceptional. By the early 1980s, however, the earlier bonds of friendship, rooted in the Thirteenth Ward community life, had brought the four artists back to a common ground of sorts. Although Art's time was largely devoted to the Nevilles, the Meters began performing in periodic "reunion" concerts that continued drawing fans. As late as 1984, *Wavelength* magazine featured the four Meters as a cover story before one such concert. Much of the old fire still rages, but whether the group will ever regroup permanently is doubtful.

As for Toussaint, his musical powers broadened through the 1970s. As a solo artist, he produced four albums. The best of them, *Southern Nights* and *Motion*, feature lyrics that offer hints of Toussaint's self-effacing, often mysterious personality. In the title cut of the former album—a tune Glen Campbell turned into a country hit—Toussaint's vision of an exotic, dreamy Southland has poetic resonances.

Southern nights,
  Have you ever felt a southern night?

Free as a breeze,
  Not to mention the trees,
Whistling tunes
  That you know and love so.

Southern skies,
  Have you ever noticed southern skies?
This precious beauty lies
  Way beyond the eye
Goes rushing through your soul
  Like a story told of old.

As an artist, his skills are perhaps the best of his generation. His melodies are clear and concise, with warm harmonic passages and simple rhythmic punctuations. His compositions have been recorded by scores of artists including Boz Scaggs, Bonnie Raitt, the Oak Ridge Boys, Devo, Little Feat, the Band, and even Lawrence Welk. But Toussaint's character is elusive. He alluded to this in a television interview: "I consider music more spiritual and intangible . . . and I consider business very tangible and non-spiritual."[28]

When asked of business matters, he refers one to Marshall Sehorn. Yet it is impossible to believe that Toussaint does not have intimate knowledge of business transactions under the SeaSaint roof. Indeed, Sehorn's dealings have embittered some musicians. Others, like Lee Dorsey, have built careers under Toussaint's creative hand, backed by Sehorn's business moves. More recently, the studio has produced some younger artists and still remains a primary recording outlet for New Orleans, though other studios have emerged in the 1980s.

A man of great musical expressiveness, Allen Toussaint, however distinguished as an individual artist, holds a potential yet untapped. And there can be no doubt that SeaSaint did fill a crucial gap in the 1970s. Without it, many good recordings would not have been made. Opinions among artists, however, are sharply divided as to how well that gap was filled by SeaSaint.

FOUR

The Caribbean Connection

Chapter Seventeen

IN SEARCH OF
THE MARDI GRAS INDIANS

On Mardi Gras (French for Fat Tuesday), New Orleans teems with parades and music and dancing. The streets fill with radiant maskers, a flood of personas drawn from aging history books and television. But so is Mardi Gras a season, more accurately called Carnival—several weeks of society balls, parades, a rush of musical celebration culminating the night before Ash Wednesday, which signals the beginning of Lent.

The parades are dazzling sights. Long floats, lavishly decorated and drawn by tractors, course through the streets in rhythm with the marching bands. In the night parades black flambeau carriers strut between the bands and the floats, raising poles studded with burning candles. Masked riders throw beads, doubloons, dolls, and trinkets to the thousands jammed on sidewalks, tottering on ladders, yelling "Throw me something, Mister!"

A long and lovely history of costume art is associated with Carnival; so is a growing film and documentary tradition, and a body of lively music,

from jazz and R&B standards to more romantic lyrics played at the fancy balls. Parades and dances move to a distinct Carnival beat. Jukeboxes resonate with Professor Longhair's anthem "Go to the Mardi Gras" and others, like Al Johnson's memorable "Carnival Time." Carnival has spawned many traditions. The upper class enshrined an ornate fictitious royalty: autumn debutantes as winter queens, big businessmen as kings. Black New Orleans has its own society circuit, of which Zulu is the most illustrious ball. But in the early 1970s, a seemingly new tradition burst into popularity, the Mardi Gras Indians.

Before dawn broke on the Mardi Gras of 1979, a video crew set up outside of George Landry's shotgun house on Valence Street. Neighbors gathered, followed by red-eyed revelers from Tipitina's, where the Neville Brothers last set had just ended. Momentarily, Art Neville arrived, joining the small group, waiting in the cold dawn for his uncle, affectionately called Jolley, who was still inside the house. For weeks, neighborhood kids had filed in and out of the room where the old man sewed rhinestones and sequins onto the patches and chest of the suit. Watching the costume emerge had become a ritual in itself, but when the house got too crowded, Jolley made everyone leave. He was Big Chief of the Wild Tchoupitoulas, founded in 1972.

Slowly, the dark sky washed blue. The cameraman waited with his sungun, a strong light encased in a metal sleeve. The first Indian arrived: Norman Bell, portly Second Chief, wearing a pink-feathered suit with billowing ostrich plumes. Next came the Spy Boy, whose suit was vivid yellow. Then the door opened and Big Chief Jolley stepped into the early light wearing a costume red as blood; he crashed the tambourine against his fist and yelled, "Whoaaa, Big Chief! Big Chief Jolleeeyyy!" People parted as he came down the steps, hitting the tambourine. He stopped and raised his tambourine toward the sun in a stunning red profile and cried: "Koochee mighty baum baum, nobody run this mawnin'! Koochee mighty baum baum, make blood chipahoona, make no bow!"

Word had spread that this would be Jolley's last Mardi Gras as Big Chief of the Thirteenth Ward tribe, named for the last uptown street bordering the river. Jolley was passing the mantle to Norman, but no one knew exactly when. Art Neville opened the door of someone's fender-bent convertible and Uncle Jolley stepped in and plopped down on the top of the rear cushion. "I'm gonna ride this one, Norman. You take 'em down."

And it happened just like that. No grand ritual: the convertible chugged off, leaving the cameramen wondering who to follow—Jolley in the car or Norman on foot with the tribe. They stuck with the tribe on the streets. Spy Boy led the procession down Valence Street, his yellow suit aglow in the dawn, while Norman Bell's costume took on a lush rosy hue. People on porches and in yards waved to the black Indians. Their first stop was Dot's Patio Bar, a hole-in-the-wall on

Tchoupitoulas where a hundred and fifty people, about half of them white, stood on the sidewalk and spilled into the street. Besides the Indians, pirates, cowboys, Zorro, and someone dressed as an ear of corn milled around cars, drinking early beers, while inside Dot's the sunguns and camera hit high gear as other Indians danced to the jukebox.

Maybe his majestic arrival was the gesture terminating Jolley's reign as Big Chief. The Indians marched, and Jolley stood in the open car, grinning like a winner at the track, red feathers radiant and his arms outstretched wide, bowing and smiling to cheers on the street. He went into Dot's for a few snorts, and when the tribe emerged, Norman Bell, a hefty former football player, was Big Chief. The weighty pink costume caused Norman's brow to glisten. The tribe formed a gauntlet in front of him; the crowd pressed in tight as Big Chief Norman raised his chin and sang deep from his chest: "Mightyyy Kooti Fiyooooo!" And the tribe, in African call-and-response tradition, handed down from slave ships to field chants into churches and early jazz, came back strong: "Eee Aie, Ayyy."

Norman sang: "Oh I got a Spyyy Boy . . . a Spy Boy . . ."—and up the gauntlet of Wild Tchoupitoulas Indians came the Spy Boy, yellow feathers dripping light, chanting "Koochee mallee, whoa Big Chief!" Big Chief Norman resumed: "The Spy Boy of the nation . . . the whole wide creation . . . oh how I love to hear them call my Indian Red." He introduced other members of the tribe in turn. Jolley sang each response with the chorus, and when the prayer of "Indian Red" was sung, Jolley got into the convertible and Norman led the Wild Tchoupitoulas along the street to the next bar. It was eight o'clock in the morning. Waves of second liners surrounded Big Chief Norman as he led the chant "Hey Pocky Way." No one knew it would be Norman's only Mardi Gras as Big Chief. He was in the hospital the following year and died before spring, so Jolley ended up leading the gang again in 1980.

Who are the Mardi Gras Indians and where did they come from?

We are moving deeper now, beneath the contours of a popular culture, searching for a trail of chiefs embedded in the past. Indians and Africans were beaten people in colonial Louisiana: so much of what we know as history records the lives and deeds of winners. One notion is crucial to our journey. At root, the black tribes are a *spiritual* tradition in which the Indian persona is more than symbolism. The tradition carries a cultural language, of sorts, representing what historian Samuel Charters calls "a procession of spirit figures."[1]

In the 1720s, thousands of slaves were shipped from coastal West Africa to tropical colonies of the New World. Uprooted, these people underwent a massive dislocation under brutal conditions that effectively erased the language and most realities of daily life in Africa. But the disparate tribal peoples shared a primal bond rooted in the mother culture: communication with ancestral spirits.

A basic vision blanketed animist zones of the sub-Saharan map. When a leader died, his memory stayed alive through the enactment of ceremony, with masked dancers representing departed elders. Honoring these ancestors was the core of communal rites, and the attendant instruments—rattles, wooden horns, strings—melded with the singers and drum voices in a percussive stream to which people danced, often in long lines, forming a chain of human movement honoring the dead.

Such expressions varied greatly under the painful arch of New World slavery. North American plantation economies purposely divided slaves from remnants of their tribal family so as to facilitate subjugation. But in other regions tribal groupings were relocated somewhat intact. The Yoruba of what is now Nigeria, retained specific deities and rituals in Cuba and Brazil. However much

was taken from them, the Africans in many enslaved communities—of South America, of the Caribbean islands, of New Orleans—kept alive their primary belief in spirits. Even as the cosmology changed—the faces of African gods turning into visages of Christian saints—the ritual form endured: drums and dances to call the spirits.

"A characteristic of all African music," Francis Bebey writes, "is the fact that it is common property, a language that all members of any one group can understand."[2] In certain African cultures, the tonal vocabulary of drumming embraced real words. Word and tone were one, a drumvoice: "talking drums." Other instruments figured deeply in the African musical family, such as thumb pianos, shakers, gourds, unmetallic horns, string instruments. As the African gods slowly died in the New World, so did the literal language of the drums.

But the spiritual sensibility lived on—more specifically, a *historical memory* in which music rituals gave voice to man's deepest religious yearnings. People summoned spirits, warded away others with rhythmic crossings; people sang and danced to the percussions.

Indians lived in the region near New Orleans long before the first slave ships came. Canadian woodsmen and French soldiers traded peacefully with some of them; Indian women, however, were often taken as concubines by the whites. The earliest slaves came from Senegambia. In 1730 a contingent of about two dozen runaway slaves found harbor with the Chickasaws and returned to slave quarters along the river to foment a rebellion. The plot was exposed, the leaders caught. Four of them were broken on wheels and their heads put on gates of the city. One woman was hanged. The following year an army of French soldiers, using Indian forces and black conscripts, slaughtered rebellious Indians with their own African allies at an upriver post, now named Natchez after the tribe.[3]

Although Indians took slaves in their own tribal wars, those passed on to colonists proved to be poor field workers. More ships arrived bearing slaves from Africa, and slaves continued fleeing plantations. By 1748, writes Carl Brasseaux, "lower river settlements had become a haven for a large, tightly knit and highly efficient band of maroon raiders."[4] In May 1748 the governor of the colony sent troops to suppress them. Until that time, French fear of Indian attacks greatly shadowed concerns over slave uprisings. As the Indians around New Orleans dispersed, scattering seeds of their culture behind them, small groups lived on the fringes of the colony.

In such an environment, rebellion took on different forms. To Africans, religion served as an outlet for these rebellious thoughts. As early as the 1730s, slaves congregated at night to dance the *calinda*. Rural blacks rode their masters' horses to such drum gatherings, and thefts were reported by drunken slaves after *calinda* dances. In 1751 the government took actions to stop the dancing.[5]

A spiritualist sensibility was implicit in those gatherings. Living in quarters set back on the plantation estates, slaves kept alive the memory of animist worship. An earlier generation of scholars, including Harold Courlander, Robert Tallant, and Marshall Stearns, wrote about Haitian influences on New Orleans voodoo. The French imported slaves from various West African tribes to Haiti, but the strongest regional expression came from Dahomey (today the People's Republic of Benin). "It is the vodun of the Fōn-speaking people," Melville Herskovits wrote, "a word that is best translated as 'god.' "[6] Other interpretations are "genius," "protective spirit."[7]

The Fōn monarchy was built on agriculture and used plantation slaves, though the slaves were more of a peasant class than chattel. Dahomean religion centered on a hierarchy of spirits whose literal human pasts lived in rituals of their tribal descendants. These *loa* were not necessarily good or bad deities, rather ones whose responses to the living hinged on the character of a given ceremony. The natural human urge for protection required appeasing worship, otherwise vexed *loa* might react accordingly. Dahomean kings sold two million ethnic peoples to Western slave merchants. In Haiti, the sprouting vodun ritual served both as a link to the mother culture and as a metaphysical impulse. What Western civilization saw as the dark side of voodoo—animal sacrifices, blood as a symbol of life—expressed rebellion via cultural preservation. Voodoo dances melded with the Catholic Mass, kindling the flames of African spiritualism.

But were the sacrifices only an African impulse? In 1730 five hundred Natchez Indians defeated by the French were sent as slaves to the island of Saint Domingue. Moreover, in a study of Haitian voodoo, Maya Deren argues that remnants of the Petro Indians, living in hills of the island in the sixteenth century, fired the African imagination with the rage of New World suffering. Indians and Africans shared compatible beliefs in spirits, in healing herbs and powers, and in a cosmic vision based on ancestral gods. New World Indians were driven by anger over the genocidal warfare of colonial conquerers. Deren writes: "The emphasis on Indian religious practice was aggressive, imperialistic and active, assertively dynamic, which met the New World need of the Negro in a way that his Dahomean religion—almost settled and passive with security—could not match. And finally, the American pattern was strongly colored by the severity of divinities; propitiation had the violent bloody character typical of the Aztecan, Mayan and Incan cultures."[8]

The 1804 liberation of Saint Domingue, which became the Republic of Haiti, triggered an exodus of planters, freedmen, and some slaves. Waves of them settled in New Orleans; the largest number (ten thousand) came after expulsion from Cuba in 1809. Amid the concentration of slaves descended from various African cultures, voodoo cults surfaced in New Orleans. Although voodoo did not exert a direct musical influence on the Mardi Gras Indians, but it was a cornerstone of the cultural tradition out of which they eventually developed—a living link to the African spirit cults of the Caribbean. Whether of Dahomean origin, a re-blending of other animist rituals, or as Deren argues, a fusion of Indian and African beliefs, the voodoo ritual as it became implanted in New Orleans fed a cultural consciousness: opposition to the master class.

Large drum-and-dance convocations by slaves surfaced about 1800 on a grassy field behind the French Quarter, now Louis Armstrong Park. In the late 1700s the area was called the Congo Plains. "No meaner name could be given the spot," George Washington Cable wrote, "the Negro was the most despised of human creatures and the Congo was plebeian among Negroes."[9] Set behind the Vieux Carré, the area was surrounded by swamps and woods. Slave cabins were in the vicinity. Small clusters of Indians lived on the outskirts, too. On Sunday afternoons the Indian villagers played a ballgame called *raquette* with rough-and-tumble whites. Given the extraordinary overlay of ethnic folds in early New Orleans, it is safe to say that blacks, whether slaves or free, played sport with Indians.

The gathering site was called Place Congo—in later years, with English supplanting French as the local language, Congo Square. Drums boomed. Big wooden horns sent out notes. And from the shacks and shanties of the slave quarters came hundreds of men and women to the Sunday gatherings to dance, to make rhythm, to express freedom. However disparate the ethnic strands, however time-removed from the drumvoices and the praises and pleadings to African gods, Congo Square served a critical ceremonial function—a bridge, as it were, over which the inherited historical memory of the ancestral cults advanced in New Orleans.

Music came out of long, hollow drums that lay on the ground, then smaller ones, open at one end and covered by sheepskin at the other. Some were beaten with hands and fists, others were hit like tom-toms. The other instruments varied—triangles, animal jawbones, gourds filled with pebbles, primitive string instruments. No brass is known of, but Cable identifies a "Pan's pipe" made of cane. The kalinda and bamboula dances flourished, as they did in the West Indies.

Drums were the heartbeat of the African instrumental family. The river of percussions tumbling over the watershed of Congo Square and out of Reconstruction split into divergent tributaries; they flowed in years to come beneath the streams of jazz, R&B, and music by the Mardi Gras Indians. But that is to anticipate events. For the moment, it is the dancer who attracts our gaze; the dancer becomes the visible image of historical memory. Whether in secret voodoo gatherings or before thousands of onlookers at Congo Square, the dancer kept alive the cultural reality, the consciousness of spirits. The voodoo dancer is the first in our procession of spirit figures.

Congo Square separates New Orleans from the rest of the South by the more or less unbroken chain, the *form* if not the actual vocabulary of religious ceremony in the motherland. One wonders if Indians danced at Congo Square. The Choctaws made regular visits to the French Market. But it was "more than a market place," Maurice Martinez writes. "It was a social event, a moment when slaves and servants, sent to purchase foodstuffs for the white households, could talk with each other. They bought spices, filé, herbs and other products from the Indians. No doubt, such encounters developed into friendly relationships."[10] By 1890 the word *griffon*, which meant "black Indian" had entered the lexicon of the city's racial code. The Afro-Indian intermarriages formed a startlingly different sociocultural pool than the European-black miscegenation. One bond stemmed from two races thrown together by oppression; the other, infinitely less satisfying, from a guilty sexual imposition of master upon slave.

In many ways, the historical memory of Indians was markedly similar to that of the slaves. The Indian tribes referred to themselves as nations; in Africa, many tribes were called kingdoms. Both had hierarchical community structures, led by chiefs. They worshipped ancestral spirits, albeit different ones, and believed in spirits inhabiting the natural forces around them. Both lived close to the land, with their ceremonies steeped in percussive music.

As a spirit figure, the Indian would never have entered the folk streams of New Orleans music had it not been for Carnival. Congo Square was suppressed about 1835, though some gatherings probably occurred afterward. Voodoo ceremonies endured longer, but they were hardly a mass phenomenon nor particularly attractive to blacks, who by then attended Christian churches. Carnival thus became the stage for a ritual enacting of historical memory.

In Old Italian *carnivale* means "taking away meat," or by other interpretations, "putting away the flesh." Carnival was a celebration common to Greek and Roman societies, a period of feast prior to spring planting. Early Christians changed the time to midwinter, the day before Lent. The French incorporated the tradition into their Catholic calendar. New Orleans had long since begun bidding the flesh farewell when the Krewe of Rex was founded in 1872. The movement of maskers through the streets goes back much farther; the city's early history is fraught with carnivalia. In 1762 the Spanish crown passed an edict permitting only Caucasians to mask. Masquerade balls were legally authorized in 1827. Erroll Laborde writes that in 1841 "as many as four hundred citizens decked themselves out as bedouins (North African desert dwellers) and pranced through town . . . and by 1852, reportedly, they were able to organize a procession of 'thousands' on foot, on horseback, and in wagons."[11] Latin social custom, the French taste for music and fine things, Catholic seasonal feasts, the deep African energy, and the profound urge to dance were currents merging into Mardi Gras. Today, Rex is the king of Mardi Gras, a largely symbolic rule.

Carnival became ever more necessary for black New Orleans. It filled basic needs increasingly denied the people by allowing new identities to take shape. Creoles and the black bourgeois emulated the white aristocracy with society balls, but a network of social aid and pleasure clubs arose around Carnival. The costumes were another matter altogether. To whites, they were largely toy disguises, fancy fleetings reflecting one's humor or élan. To the black consciousness, masking often took on a heightened meaning. The mask became a cover, a new identity, a persona eluding the white policeman or soldier; the mask gave ephemeral freedom; the whole organic presence of the costume could scare people, delight them, it could satirize or do any number of things provided the person inside it fulfilled the role to the core of his imagination. In this way, Carnival became one linear extension of Congo Square. Out of the flickering memory of African spiritualism and percussive ceremony came a procession of spirit figures, an inherited cultural consciousness marching into Carnival.

Over the years, Claiborne Avenue became the meeting place for black Carnival. There were all kinds of costumes, but certain ones reflected primal urges of the mask, the transformation of self into a riveting, new identity. Tribes of skeletons issued out of back neighborhoods, often in the most menacing of marches. There was a rivalry of sorts, between Baby Dolls and Gold Diggers, women decked out in flashy garb, green bills stuffed in their garters and a lot of flirting on the hoof. A satiric tradition arose with the Zulu parade, black men in black face wearing grass skirts. In all of this, the Indian was a hybrid persona, a

Congo Square

Big Chief Jolley (George Landry)

spirit figure anchored in the American sensibility. The traveling wild west shows of the late nineteenth century popularized the Indian as an authentic culture figure, but the common struggle of Indians and Africans in Louisiana predates by many years the influences that such shows (particularly in the dress style of American Plains) probably had in New Orleans. In the final measure, the adaptation by blacks of the Indian persona was an act of ritual rebellion. The liberation inherent in masking required a cultural vocabulary: in chants and body language, in the collective imagery of Indian parades.[12]

But the phenomenon of black Indians sprouted in other carnivals, a wider geographic web of cultural memory. The Indian was a carnival fixture as early as 1847 in Trinidad and has long appeared in Haitian and Brazilian carnivals. These costumes bear some resemblance to those of many downtown Indians, particularly the "Mummy" crown style. Musical idioms arose, too. The calypso descended from the old kalinda dance, which was common to Congo Square and to Trinidad. In the relative isolation of Port-au-Spain, city blacks of Trinidad channeled great creativity into costumes. More than any other aspect of the culture, Carnival masks drew praise as expressions of the inner self. There were Red Indians and Blue Indians and Black Indians of Trinidadian carnival. Yet the colors had symbolic meaning, too. The Reds were believed to have come from Venezuela, while the Blacks were thought of as African.[13]

Edward Kamau Brathwaite, the distinguished Caribbean scholar and poet, has observed that the mother culture, to survive the weight of New World domination, had to go through a submarine or tunneling stage to endure the imposed value system. Through this submersion period of generations, rituals of the mother culture underwent a permutation, surfacing in a visually different form, but with the root sensibility, of dignity, intact. Voodoo conforms to this proposition, as do the spirit cults of Brazil and Cuba, which move to African drumming rhythms.[14]

Beginning in the 1880s, the Mardi Gras Indians started the slow rise out of submersion that the mother culture underwent with the disappearance of Congo Square and voodoo. The Indians' chants were not set to drums, but to hand-percussion instruments such as tambourines. They did not worship spirits per se, but through a slow-evolving body of coded lyrics established a tribal hierarchy that praised the Indian nations and celebrated the bravery of rebellion. The Mardi Gras Indians gave light to the memory of an African past, but in a ritual fashion that embraced the Indian as an adopted spirit figure. It was the highest compliment the African could pay a race of the New World; it stemmed from common struggle, sociocultural intercourse, a shared vision of freedom—but most of all, from a profoundly African ritual retention. The Indian followed the procession of rebellious slaves, voodoo cultists, and Congo Square dancers as a spirit figure in the historical memory.

Not until the 1960s did serious scholarship address the Indians as a historical phenomenon. Subsequently, journalists and academics have advanced key themes, but the article bank is still thin. Where does it all begin? Written sources offer small assistance: no letters culled from dusty trunks. Timeworn memories, lodged in the minds of aging men, guide us down the path.

Our point of entry is the Seventh Ward, where the first black to mask as an Indian, Becate Batiste, founded the Creole Wild West Tribe in the early 1880s. The name suggests he may have borrowed a few ideas from traveling wild west shows of the era. In any event, he was soon joined by his brother, Eugene, a plasterer. The Batistes were of Indian descent, though of how much is unknown. The story of Chief Becate has come down through three generations of a Seventh Ward Creole family. Today, the linear descendant of that tribe is called the Yellow Pocahontas and its chief, Allison "Tuddy" Montana, began leading the tribe after World War II. Trim and sturdy, Tuddy is a folk hero to thousands of blacks in the neighborhood. Born on December 17, 1922, he learned of Chief Becate Batiste—his granduncle—from his grandmother, Jeanne Durrell, who was Becate's sister. Tuddy's father, Alfred Montana, Sr., led the Pocahontas in the 1930s and 1940s.

"Well my grandmother, she always said that we had Indian blood. If you'd seen her, you could tell. She always were bright as you could want. We had the Indian blood mixed in. Just like on my daddy's side. I have some cousins—my daddy's sister's children—man, they look just *like* an Indian. My grandmother died at ninety-eight. In those days they didn't keep birth records like they do now. French and Indian, in them days was all mixed up. Black folks registered as white. Things were all crossed up."[15]

Tuddy Montana states: "The Creole Wild West originated from that house on 1313 St. Anthony Street. That's where the Indians got their start, from my family."

The earliest written reference comes from a slender memoir by Elise Kirsch about her childhood. She was born in 1876; the specific Mardi Gras mentioned in the following passage is apparently 1883. "At about 10:00 A.M. that day there was a band of men (about 60) disguised as Indians who wore the real Indian costumes and their chiefs had turkey feathers running down from around their heads way down in the back. They came along from St. Bernard Avenue on Robertson Street, shouting and screaming war whoops, and carried tomahawks—on their way back would stop and perform war dances, etc., and would run for a block and begin again. Though we were frightened when very young, we always waited for the passing of 'the Indians.'"[16]

Although the citation does not say a *black* "band of men," the street reference suggests they were coming from the Seventh Ward. More

important, the size of the tribe indicates that the idea of masking as an Indian had caught on quickly.

Out of Chief Becate Batiste's tribe, the Creole Wild West, grew a fascinating hierarchy, a tribal structure that spread into different neighborhoods and, by the early twentieth century, formed the organizational patterns of later tribes. The Big Chief leads the tribe; his authority is supreme. He decides where his tribe will rehearse the chants and can admit or eject anyone from the tribe. Although the Indians are a preponderantly male tradition, many women have masked and marched with tribes over the years. They are known as Queens and usually occupy an ancillary slot by virtue of their relationship to the Big Chief.

Other chiefs occupy lower rungs beneath the leader—Councillor Chief, Second Chief, Third Chief, Trail Chief—titles that vary from tribe to tribe. These Indians back up the Big Chief in rehearsal sessions and on marches. "Their roles," one scholar writes, "are more or less to look good, initiate singing and dancing, etc."[17]

One of the most memorable Yellow Pocahontas braves of the early years was the Wild Man. Sometimes called the Medicine Man, the Wild Man is the least restrained Indian: his outrageousness personifies the general liberation impulse. "Wild Man Rock," Tuddy Montana says, "was a cat who lived out by a junk heap, way down Elysian Fields where people dumped their garbage. He fished old cigarettes out the trash and strung them over the roof where he lived, let 'em dry in the sun, and rolled himself cigarettes. And let me tell you: he was *wild*. You never saw him so much until Carnival came. Then he'd come bargin' out with a ring in his nose, carryin' bones and a spear, whoopin' and carryin' on, used to throw that spear and scare all hell out of people."[18]

The most important Indian after the Big Chief is his Spy Boy, who scouts ahead to make sure the road is clear. When another tribe comes in sight, Spy Boy transmits the message back to the Flag Boy (who carries the tribal pennant), in turn passing the word to the Big Chief. Jelly Roll Morton described the workings of the Spy Boy:

They went armed with fictitious spears and tommyhawks and so forth and their main object was to make the enemy bow. They would send their Spy Boys two blocks on ahead. I happened to be a Spy Boy once myself so I know how this went, and when a Spy Boy would meet another Spy Boy from another tribe, he'd point his finger to the ground and say, "Bow-wow!" And if they wouldn't bow, the Spy Boy would use the Indian call, "woo-woo-woo-woo-woo," and that was the calling of the tribes, and many a time in these Indian things, there would be a killing and the next day there would be someone in the morgue.[19]

It is not certain that Morton was ever a Spy Boy. But his comment rings true in other respects. Killings and bloody clashes did occur among Indian tribes of early Carnivals. Although the cellular structure was rooted in African and Indian sensibilities, with dances of African derivation, the larger statement of solidarity and symbolic rebellion must be weighed against social factors. The underlying strength of the Indians was the articulation of a symbolic language, a cultural vocabulary based on pride and the self-image of a tradition.

To mask as an Indian meant that the poorest man could transcend the toil of daily life, however ephemerally, in open defiance of the role society imposed on him. The tribes drew from laborers, dock workers, street hustlers, and common criminals, as well as from descendants of Indians and in later years from occasional musicians. Violence at the hands of whites provoked in some Indians a militant strain, suppressed through normal life, yet freed in Carnival. In the 1850s, Irish Channel whites openly terrorized blacks entering the area.[20] By the 1920s, in the same neighborhood, whites dressed as cavemen fought the Indians with spike-studded cypress clubs. Most of the Indians, especially the uptown tribes, came from impoverished households. Even in the Seventh Ward, with the "self-help" tradition of Creoles, Tuddy Montana recalls "men who'd walk the street here, real dangerous people. I'm talking about men who'd kill you with their fists. Stone killers. Today people run to the Indians. During them days, people would run away from the Indians."[21]

Near the end of the nineteenth century, for unknown reasons, the Creole Wild West moved uptown. A new tribe, the Yellow Pocahontas, formed in the Seventh Ward. Henri Marigny, who had marched with Becate Batiste, became Big Chief. The Creole Wild West was led by Robert Sam Tillman, Jr., known as "Brother Timber." According to Paul Longpre, who marched with Tillman in the 1930s, he was "a desperado. He was a legend in his time. Never worked for nobody. When it came around carnival time, he'd go in hiding. If the police knowed where he was, they would go after him, put him in jail till after Carnival. Because at Carnival, he was clean treacherous."

Longpre, who learned tribal lore from his uncle and stepbrother, claims that Tillman's father controlled the Creole Wild West; however, his interpretation of tribal origins is at variance with Tuddy Montana's. According to Longpre, the elder Tillman "had Louisiana blood in him, and also his wife. I think they was Choctaw." The elder Tillman and a man named Sam Tweed, he contends, founded the Yellow Pocahontas in 1896 in the Garden District, across town from the Seventh Ward. He says they took the name *Pocahontas* from a history book. The *Yellow* was supposedly added "when one guy had on a suit with this yellow fringe from an old-time lamp shade" and a white woman asked "Yellow Pocahontas?" Thus, says Longpre, the name stuck.[22]

Longpre contends that a split between the two men caused Tweed to take the Pocahontas downtown, while the elder Tillman, having seen "the Hagenback Wallace Creole Wild West Show," took the latter name and stayed uptown. This version contradicts Montana's (and that of another source, Arthur "Creole" Williams) by placing the date of tribal origins some thirteen years after the reference in Kirsch's memoir. In fairness to Longpre, it must be said that stories which are passed down through the generations are often cloudy. The available information supports Montana; still, Longpre confirms the Creole Wild West's resurgence as an uptown tribe.

The younger Tillman, also called "Brother Timber," controlled the Creole Wild West in Longpre's youth and devised schemes to evade the law. In 1927 word of his death spread. Police attended his wake, says Longpre, where people wept and mourned. "They put him in the hearse, bringed him to Holt Cemetery. He got out of the casket inside the hearse. When they got to the cemetery, they buried the casket, brought him back. On Carnival morning he had on an Indian suit—returned from the dead!"

The emergence of Indian celebrations in early decades of this century was marked by a dichotomy similar to that between the first jazzmen. A cultural gulf divided the downtown Creole wards and the uptown black neighborhoods. The jazzmen bridged it peacefully. Although the Indians evolved out of family units, too, with Big Chiefs handing down leadership to sons or nephews, the uptown-downtown competition was hardly peaceful. Arthur "Creole" Williams, who was seventy-nine when interviewed, recalls the Mardi Gras of 1921.

Henri Marigny was the chief of the Yellow Pocahontas for years; they didn't have but one gang down here this side of Canal. Uptown, Brother Timber. They used to fight. The Pocahontas hit Louisiana Avenue and St. Charles. The Creole Wild West and two divisions of the Red, White and Blues was coming up Louisiana, about three in the afternoon, foggy. Brother Tillman was leading Creole Wild West. But Henri Marigny wasn't leading the Pocahontas. He was too drunk; they left him around Parish Prison and Britt brought the gang up—him and Little Yam and all the rest of 'em. Most of the gang was with Henri. And then people started *shooting!* They had Wild Mans jumpin' in the cars, a woman got shot in the foot. It was somethin', man. I was there to the last.

Now Eugene Honore used to be Second Chief to Henri . . . big, tall, looked just like an Indian. Eugene is the one that mapped all them songs out—"Indian Red," "Take That Flag Down," he originated those songs.[23]

When the tribes met in neighborhood bars before Carnival, "Indian Red" was traditionally sung at the opening and closing of rehearsal sessions, and again on Mardi Gras morning as the tribe set out. In earlier years, it was called the "Indian Prayer Song." Longpre and Montana say it was often accompanied by recitation of the Our Father and with some tribes, still is. Then the Big Chief slapped the tambourine and sang: "Ma-Day, Cootie-Fiyo." And the braves sang back in slow, rising unison: "Tee-Nah Aaayy." Unraveling the many chants requires a linguist's tools. The Creole dialect, heavily French, had Spanish influences and probably Indian ones, too. Of the Trinidad carnival Indians, Andrew Pearse writes: "One of the most popular song texts begins 'Indurubi,' which may be Spanish for 'Indo Rubi,' meaning 'Indian Red.'"[24] *Matar* in Spanish means "to kill," while *qui tu est fijo* can be translated to "who is immobile to you." Kill who is in your way. This is but one interpretation. More critical to our investigation is Eugene Honore, who "mapped all them songs out."

Vincent Trepagnier, another aging Creole, recalls his experiences with the Yellow Pocahontas in the 1930s. He says Eugene Honore was a Choctaw. "Eugene was seven-foot two-inches tall. He was a real Indian who came with his mama from up the country, somewhere the other side of Baton Rouge. They lived in tents. . . . And when they come in the city, they moved on Burgundy and Toulouse. Eugene was the tallest Indian I ever seen in my life. He had a high cheekbone, beautiful skin, olive complexion, and long black hair. People used to call his mama Miss Cherie, but that wasn't her name. Her name was Miss Choctaw."[25]

New tribes began masking in the 1920s. Brother Timber's shadow loomed over the groups, which had names like the Red, White, and Blues; the Hundred and One's; and in years after World War II, the Wild Magnolias, Black Eagles, and Wild Tchoupitoulas. Brother Timber, a street runner who became fiery during Carnival, was not prone to organization, drifting in and out of tribes, sometimes as Big Chief, other times as Spy Boy. Just before 1920, a new uptown tribe emerged, the Wild Squatoolas, led by Daniel "Dandy" Lambert, otherwise known as "Big Chief Copperwire." "One year," Paul Longpre explains, "when he put his suit together it fell apart, and he hooked it up with this copper wire he got from a guy working on a telephone line. Everybody after that called him Big Chief Copperwire. He had one of the largest gangs of Queens of any Indian on Carnival day."[26]

One attempt at tribal detente occurred when Lambert and Honore ended up in Parish Prison together. "Dandy Lambert was in jail for stealing a truckload of groceries at the French Market." Tuddy Montana continues: "See, Dandy Lambert was from uptown, Eugene was from downtown, and by them bein' friends [in] jail, they got out of jail, the guys downtown allowed them to come from uptown."[27]

When tribes clashed, it was called a "humbug." The most memorable in Vincent Trepagnier's career locked the Yellow Pocahontas and Wild Squatoolas in battle. The Lambert-Honore truce had not held.

We was going uptown to a place they called the Magnolia Bridge. I don't know if you ever heard talk of it. It's torn down now. The two Spy Boys from the Pocahontas and the Wild Squatoolas got into a humbug over the bridge and shooting took place. When that shooting took place, well, that draw the policemen, see?

Now there was nowhere to go, so what we did, we jumped in the New Basin Canal with our clothes on. The policemen came and got some out, and some others they didn't. I stood right underneath the bridge till they left and then come on back home. I couldn't go uptown cause I was all wet.[28]

By the late 1920s, the violent battles began to halt. In Paul Longpre's memory, "1932 was the last actual fight that the Indians had. They increased the number of policemens . . . they wasn't takin' no stuff off the Indians."

Gumbo Ya-Ya contains a report on the Mardi Gras of 1940.

Ten years ago the various tribes actually fought when they met. Sometimes combatants were seriously injured. . . . Once a police officer was badly injured by an Indian's spear. After that occurrence a law was passed forbidding the tribes of maskers to carry weapons.

Today the tribes are all friendly. The following song [probably from the Golden Blades tribe, whose 1940 march is recorded in the book] is a warning against tactics of other days.

Shootin' don't make it, no no no no.
Shootin' don't make it, no no no no.
Shootin' don't make it, no no no no.
If you see your man sittin' in the bush,
Knock him in the head and give him a push,
 Cause shootin' don't make it, no no.
Shootin' don't make it, no no no no.[29]

The law and a heavier police presence were not the only forces behind the ebbing of open warfare among tribes. By the Depression, Indian traditions were about half a century old. There was a purpose behind the battles of old, a resolution of sorts, between the uptown and downtown tribes, long divided by differences of caste. But as neigh-

An Indian rehearsal

The late Percy Lewis, Chief Pete

borhood and class borders became less distinct, so did the tradition itself evolve; higher values and a more positive self-image emerged. The violent clashes had significance: they showed the Indians were unafraid—of white police or of each other. It must be stressed that the Indians, at heart, were not a violent tradition. Violence was but one manifestation of the early years. But the phrase "ritual violence" has lasting resonance. Today Indian rehearsal sessions at local bars constitute a dance-and-music ceremony in which conflicts are symbolically enacted.[30] But challenges from visiting tribes can on occasion cause grudges, and the Big Chief has to be continually on his toes to quell challenges, or he will be shamed.

In the weeks leading up to Mardi Gras, the men crowd into bars. The Big Chief pounds his tambourines; the braves bang percussive instruments of their own—sticks, bottles, shakers—and sing responses to the Big Chief's chants. (Drums, notably congas, and at least one bass drum, are now becoming more popular. Even in parades, drums are becoming common.) One brave challenges another: the confrontation is enacted by dancing. The two men edge close, one drops a scarf or handkerchief on the floor, the competitors veer close to it—the idea is to veer closer and closer but not cross. A mock fight ensues around the symbolic line across the floor. Territory is defended by the strength of the dance. The two men move in the circle to the pounding rhythms of the clapping, chanting, and rising energy of the tribe.[31] And resentments can develop if the challenger crosses the "line."

Although the Indians symbolize violence to some blacks, to many others their chants, marches, and dazzling costumes are a statement of dignity, an articulation of protest, of rebellion, a masculine code of honor that has come down through the years of Carnival in chants and costumed marches as a musical expression. A long tradition of costume art has greatly influenced the evolution of the Mardi Gras Indians by strengthening peaceful bonds among the tribes. One brave said, "We used to fight with knives and guns. Now we compete by the beauty of our costumes."

Much of the Big Chief's prestige comes from the image he presents on Mardi Gras—how beautiful his suit is. The man becomes his art. In early years, these costumes were rough-hewn affairs, drawn from available materials: chicken and turkey feathers, Christmas ornaments, buckskin, ribbons, fringe and long beads stripped from lampshades, molds from egg cartons dipped in glitter and glued on the suit. The early crowns were stiff cardboard pasteups. In the 1920s the "drop crown" came into play, covered with feathers and extending from head to foot. Then came ostrich plumes, which gave the crowns a larger, billowing coloration when winds blew or the sun shone brightly. An old chief called Black Benny said, "I went to Chicago and saw these plumes in the store window. They were dyed red, white, and blue. I bought the whole bunch of them, and that year I was the first to wear plumes in a crown."[32]

After World War II, as more tribes organized and disbanded, the art of costumery took on greater detail. Rhinestones, sequins, and recycled Mardi Gras beads began to fill out headbands, breastplates, and vests. "The costume is just made up out of your head," Tuddy Montana explains.

The Indians traditionally marched on Mardi Gras and again on St. Joseph's Day, the Italian festival in the Catholic calendar. After the final appearance, the braves would take apart the costume and later begin work on next year's suit. It took long hours over many months, designing scenes for the knee pads, vests and breastpads, sewing a thematic design in common with images affixed to the front and backside of the drop crown. As the tradition evolved, suits became more expensive to make. Big Chief Jolley of the Wild Tchoupitoulas remarked that a costume "can cost as less as $300 and as high as $5,000, if you want to spend that kind of money."[33]

An Indian queen

Emile "Bo" Dollis, Chief of the Wild Magnolias, draws a distinction between art patterns of tribes from the two sides of town. "The difference in the uptown style and the downtown style is the pattern. So, the difference in the suits, if you compare the uptown and downtown, is the beadwork and the finishing work. Where they use sequins, we may use rhinestones. Where they may use feathers, we may use ostrich plumes. But they're totally the same thing: they're both beautiful."[34]

Tuddy Montana says, "In the Yellow Pocahontas we don't have no plumes. We all have feathers. They use the beaded designs, which they'll get from a book or somethin'. Maybe an Indian on horseback. A lot of them don't even know how to draw it themselves. They'll bring it to somebody and say, 'Look, man, I want you to draw this for me.' And they'll take it and trace it on canvas, and then they bead it, you see?"

Costumes became a major theme in the songs, set to call-and-response chants. Paul Longpre says the Golden Blades got their name in 1935 at a rehearsal session in an uptown bar near Third and Rocheblave. From 1931 to 1935 they masked as the Creole Wild West with Brother Tillman.[35]

But then we had a split up, because Brother Tillman told us to be in one place and he was in another. We didn't meet him til four o'clock that evening. So, that next year we were going to mask as the Creole Wild West Juniors. We had a guy called Mice, one of the best at singing Indian songs because he could think fast. The idea of singing a Indian song is rhyming something, thinking fast to rhyme it. Mice was singing "My Big Chief Got a Diamond Crown"—

Oh, the diamond crown,
  The diamond crown,
Two-day de-fay-hock,
  Goo-make-who laun-day he,
Big Chief got a diamond crown.

Well one of the ladies happened to walk into practice and Mice was singing "My Big Chief Got a Diamond

Crown," and when he sang that, she say, "Oh, give it to the boys from Third and Rocheblave!" That made him chant and start singing "Third and Rocheblave," then later on he started singing "Give it to the gang from the Golden Blades."

Two-gay-de-hoc
  Ma who-laun-day,
Give it to the boy
  From the Golden Blades,
Oh, the Golden Blades, the Golden Blades,
  We got some low-down ways!

Another 1930s chant by the Wild Squatoolas celebrated the act of costume-making: "Somebody got to sew, sew, sew." More recently, the Wild Magnolias have borrowed the identical rhythm: "Everybody's got soul, soul, soul."

The best-known and most widely sung chant is "Two-way Pocky Way," or as the Meters popularized it, "Hey Pocky Way." It is an old chant, with conflicting translations. In 1950 Alan Lomax translated the words in Creole dialect as *t'ouwais bas q'ouwais*. The refrain *on tendais* probably came from *entendez*, "to understand," or from *attendez*, "wait up," or "listen." But *t'ouwais bas q'ouwais* is more complicated. One possible meaning, which makes sense in the code of Indian concerns, depends on an etymological shift in the dialect enunciation; in standard French *tu n'as pas couilles* means "you don't have balls" (testicles). But if we interpret *t'ouwais* as in derivation from the verb *tuer*, "to kill"—followed by an abbreviation of the Creole phrase *a la bas*, meaning "over there," we get *tuez bas qu'ou est*—or, "kill who is over there."[36]

Other interpretations have been made. Finn Wilhelmsen, a Norwegian scholar who wrote early articles on the Indians, states, "Allegorically, the expression means, 'I don't give a damn.'"[37] Tuddy Montana believes it is in reference to what the singer of a chant has just said before. "Like, 'That's what I say' or 'See what I mean.'" Paul

Longpre opines: "It means, 'You go dis-away'—or 'You go datta-way.' Either one."[38] Unquestionably, the chant has evolved into a series of popular interpretations quite different from its murky origins. But the *on tendais* refrain of old—which has since been dropped—was a tribal refrain, a warning: Stop! Wait! Listen! An educated guess suggests the meaning was close to "kill the one over there."

In the mid-seventies, Indian chants became popular in music recordings as the relative anonymity of the tribes began to peel away. As a cultural phenomenon, the Indians attracted producers, film and television people, oral historians, journalists, and nightclub owners. It was not always a smooth transition: some streets are hostile to white intrusion. But with the current acceleration of Indian tribal rhythms and verse as a new musical force, the tradition begun by Chief Becate Batiste in the early 1880s has come full circle, replicating the birth of jazz: from rooted urges of African consciousness into a spawning musical idiom, reflecting a performance style as African as it is visually native American.

Chapter Eighteen

WILLIE TEE
AND THE WILD MAGNOLIAS

Wilson Turbinton was eleven years old when his family moved to the Calliope Street housing project and Willie discovered the Mardi Gras Indians. By that time, 1954, new tribes had emerged in the massive central city project and in other neighborhoods. Willie was fascinated by their dances, led "by a man called Bo."

It just always intrigued me. There were certain steps and certain moves they'd make that were synonymous with the kind of rhythm they played. They went through a whole ritual where everybody that masked had a significance to the group. They would have about fifteen guys. All through the year they would practice. So, heck, we'd come in the court and just hear this music.

A lot of the stuff they did was the "Hey Pocky Way" kind of thing. That just kind of caught on, but there was things that they were doing that were more intricate rhythmically. . . . And it came so natural to them. They were using tambourines. They had some instruments made out of bottle caps and [they would] nail 'em on sticks, and the sticks would be so long they could actu-

ally beat rhythms on the ground, but also get a thud from the earth. And I made a couple of those and would use 'em. It was the kind of groove that you couldn't resist. The pulse affected you. You find yourself patting your foot, and if you're shy, you just feel it inside yourself.[1]

As a youngster in the Calliope project, Willie played piano with his older brother Earl on saxophone. They had a band called the Seminoles and played talent shows at Lincoln Beach. "The Calliope project was one of the most positive periods in my life. People were intrigued to see a little boy playing piano and singing, so we won a lot of talent shows basically on that."

When Willie was a boy in the project, the language of the Indian tribes was well into its second generation. The old Creole patois chants were undergoing changes. In 1938 Jelly Roll Morton sang "T'ouwais bas q'uowais"—for which the response was "on tendais." In the mid-fifties, Willie heard the chant as "Hey Pocky Way." Other Indians kept a derivation of Morton's version: "Two-way Pocky Way." The tribe Willie heard was the White Eagles; the leader, Bo, was a drummer named Clarence Davis. The White Eagles formed in the late 1940s as an offshoot of the Golden Blades. In 1956 historian Samuel Charters recorded a group of young Indians, including the White Eagles. On the disc, a Seventh Ward brave says: "Any tribe that's brought out the Red, White and Blue, they supposed to hold the Golden Band. It's a symbol, y'unnerstand. An explanation. It's not really a band."[2] The Golden Band is a derivation of the older symbol, the Golden Crown. A tonal current was passing through the generations, how the words were uttered and heard, the sounds they made musically in chants; the dialect of darker uptown blacks began dropping more mellifluous inflections of the downtown Creole patois.

Willie's seventh-grade music teacher, Harold Battiste, started him on saxophone. "The piano was hardly ever used," Turbinton reflects, "but whenever Harold would go to the office, I'd sneak in and play Little Richard. We'd be jamming in class and he'd catch us. Later on, he told me he used to stand outside and listen for awhile, but I wasn't aware of this then. So one day he called my house, telling my momma he needed to talk to her. I thought he was going to say I was putting him through all kinda changes. And he asked her if I could go on a gig with him. And I met Melvin Lastie."[3]

Turbinton's exposure to Lastie, Ellis Marsalis, and other AFO musicians stimulated his prodigious talent. His first single, "Always Accused," was an AFO production. In the mid-sixties, Turbinton organized Willie Tee and the Souls, with brother Earl Turbinton on saxophone, David Lee on drums, and George Davis on bass. In 1965 his recording of "Teasin' You," written by Earl King, was a solid R&B success. Wardell Quezerque, a versatile arranger, produced the disc as well as follow-up tunes for NOLA, a local label, that were released to Atlantic Records.

In one respect, the curve of Willie Tee's career in the late 1960s was an extension of the AFO philosophy: record R&B for money and exposure, play jazz for love and art. The Souls played fraternity circuits in the Deep South, and through Earl Turbinton's involvement with the Jazz Workshop, Willie continued improvisational work, going on to record under Julian Adderly. By the end of the 1960s, when the Jazz Workshop closed, Turbinton's interest in the Indians was largely a memory. About the time the workshop vacated its Decatur Street premises, however, a curious chain of events began sending Willie rummaging back through memories for a musical interpretation of the Indians.

Jules Cahn, who owned the Decatur Street building, was an avocational photographer with an enduring love of New Orleans music and street celebrations. Over the years, he had filmed hundreds of hours of jazz funerals and Indian marches. One night Cahn invited Quint Davis, a young friend, to a Wild Magnolias' practice session in a small central city bar. The Tulane student was dazzled by the chants and rituals. He met Big Chief Emile "Bo" Dollis, a husky and forceful laborer who put great power into the chants. Davis tape-recorded several chants and soon thereafter approached Dollis about cutting a forty-five. The disc, produced in 1970, was "Handa Wanda," parts one and two. "Handa Wanda" is a chant with origins more blurred than "Pocky-Way." Finn Wilhelmsen's research with the Black Eagles led to this conclusion:

"Handa-wandu o mambo": This phrase is sung when the tribe is downtown (according to the uptown tribes) to let everybody know that we are coming. It stands for "I ain't lookin' for trouble, but I ain't gonna run."

Recently, it has been brought to my attention . . . that the expression was invented by another big chief. The other person apparently derived it from an older phrase, "Shallo water o mama." The latter expression has the same meaning as the former.[4]

Here is how Bo Dollis, Big Chief of the Wild Magnolias, leads his uptown braves on the first modern-day Indian tune—with cracking tambourines, whoops, and cries behind the Chief's lead:

Hey annnnhhhh!

Hey-an dan dalu wild mamboula!
Handa wanda o mama!

Said uptown rulers and downtown too!
Handa wanda o mama!

Said Wild Magnolias got Injun blue!
Handa wanda o mama!

My Spy Boy comin' up and down!
Handa wanda o mama!

"Handa Wanda" as recorded is not simply a chant. The syncopated drumming by Zig Modeliste and bulging bass lines by George French deepened the percussive cushion, giving the Indians a foundation of sound more magnified than in the streets; the recording studio allowed their voices to boom and the call-response patterns to work through the instrumental music with tremendous energy. The disc caught on locally. Fans became curious about the Indians.

In the Wild Magnolias, Quint Davis recognized something original, a high expression of black folk culture—and a dazzling performance act. He booked Bo Dollis and the tribe for a night at Tulane University and hired Willie Tee and his band, the Gators, for the opening set. Turbinton had never met Bo Dollis, but that night he saw the musical promise.

They came out and started doing their thing. And we had played before them, okay? So we just kind of started jamming. And it was so hip and natural that, you know, when you strike a groove musically with somebody, it's almost like knowing 'em. You pass up the barriers of getting to know somebody. That's the whole hip thing about musicians. It's a closer look at a person's spirit.

They were singing "Iko Iko" and "Handa Wanda"—basically chants—so we just put a groove with it that fit in the parts. But it just stayed in one key and didn't change, which worked hip for us because by Bo and them just having a raw thing, they didn't know where they were going technically—well, wherever we went, man, Bo could just naturally hear how to sound.[5]

The French producer Philippe Rault had been spending time in New Orleans and began discussions with Quint Davis about producing an album. But to record the Wild Magnolias alone would amount to a folklore documentary. *Music* was crucial to any recording of the Magnolias. Davis broached the idea with Wilson Turbinton, who jumped at the chance to work on the album. Rault secured a contract with Barclay, the Parisian company, then flew to New York and arranged for American distribution under Polydor.

Willie Tee meanwhile began organizing the studio band. Brother Earl would play alto clarinet and soprano sax. Julius Farmer arrived to play bass for the album. Snooks Eaglin was enlisted on guitar, with Larry Panna on drums and Alfred Roberts on congas. The group was called the New Orleans Project. Joining Bo Dollis was Chief Monk Boudreaux of the White Eagles, the Magnolias' rival uptown tribe. The remaining braves—on tambourine, cowbells, whistles, triangle, bongos, and background vocals, respectively—were "Gator June" Johnson, Jr., "Crip" Adams, "Quarter Moon" Tobias, "Gate" Johnson, "Bubba" Scott, and James Smothers.

The Wild Magnolias was recorded at Studio in the Country in Bogalusa, Louisiana. Turbinton had full producing powers and recorded the musical tracks before the Indians arrived. The album has an interesting architecture. Using the old chants as foundation, Turbinton built songs with meanings close to the Indian sensibility, yet very much in the pop vernacular. The first cut, "Handa Wanda," is based on Dollis's first recording, but

Willie Tee

The Wild Magnolias

with Alfred Roberts's popping congas and whip-crack guitar lines by Snooks Eaglin, and Earl Turbinton's warm, arching reeds, the overall sound veers closer to a blend of funk and Afro-Cubano rhythms. "Smoke My Peace Pipe" draws on the stereotypical image of Indians passing the pipe, but the message, rooted in the counterculture, applies to modern tribes as well. Willie Tee sang:

I'm a Big Chief
  I do the best for my tribe
Smoke my peace pipe,
  Smoke it right.

I do what I can
  To keep them satisfied.
Smoke my peace pipe,
  Smoke it right.

Now in my pipe there's some super-bad herb,
  Guaranteed to soothe your nerve.
Smoke my peace pipe,
  Smoke it right.

Just take a few hits,
  Put some peace in your mind.
Smoke my peace pipe,
  Smoke it right.

Another song, "Corey Died on the Battlefield," is the story of a rebellious slave, based on a chant by Bo Dollis. (See the discussion of "Brother John" in the following chapter.) "Two-way Pocky Way" is sung as a long chant, set to an electronic pulse, undergirded by lolling drumbeats, as is "Somebody Got Soul, Soul, Soul." The final tune is Turbinton's arrangement of "The Saints," the traditional marching song, sung by Bo Dollis. In a radio interview with Shepard Samuels, Bo Dollis explained the Indians' role in the recording production. "How we did it in the studio, we put it just like it was on the streets. We went into the studio and put the lyric tracks like in two days, a day and a half. Wasn't nothin' planned or written out. We just went in and did our thing and that

was it."[6] For Turbinton, it was simply a matter of putting the Indians' voices into the musical layer.

The Wild Magnolias was released in 1974. After a press party in New Orleans, Quint Davis, Willie Tee and his band, and the Indians, with costumes carefully packed, took to the road. (Erving Charles, Willie's old friend from Calliope Street, took the place of Snooks Eaglin on guitar for the road dates.) "Smoke My Peace Pipe" became a solid regional hit. "And then," Willie explains, "we were opening for Aretha Franklin, Gladys Knight and the Pips, burning everybody up. So we played five major cities, Virginia and the Carolinas; we played the Capitol Center in Washington. We played Carnegie Hall. To play Carnegie Hall was an ultimate wish for the guys."

The tour moved to the Bottom Line in Greenwich Village for a press party, hosted by Polydor. Turbinton remembers the occasion.

The President of the company [Jerry Schoenbaum] saw me, said, "Willie Tee, I really like the response we're getting. When are you getting dressed? It's almost time for you to go on." I said, "Well, I'm already dressed. You know, I don't wear an Indian costume. We're the band." So the guy says, "What? You mean you're not one of the Indians?" So I say, "No, we're the band." "You mean I don't have the band signed?" So I say, "We're not signed under a contract. You signed the Wild Magnolias."

I didn't understand why that was a problem. So he invited me back to come talk about signing with the label. But the numbers he was talking about weren't right. The experience I had had in the business, by being involved with the Magnolias I got a really decent shake on how I was treated as a producer, financially. So I wasn't really hungry at the time, you know? And then I knew a little something about publishing. I was just coming off of a contract with Capitol Records and I had been through that trip.[7]

Willie Tee held publishing and composer's rights to "Smoke My Peace Pipe" and "Corey Died on the Battlefield," major tunes on the album.

Turbinton claims that Polydor, upon learning this, had a change of heart. After a successful trip to Paris, where Barclay officials were pleased by the reception, the Wild Magnolias concluded the tour, but they did not branch out to the West Coast nor push the album on road dates designed for larger national exposure.

In 1975 a second Wild Magnolias album was recorded, *They Call Us Wild,* under Barclay. By this time, Turbinton had written new material based on the Indian traditions. "New Suit" sings of the costuming art and the old rule that one takes apart the suit to begin work on next year's outfit.

Every year at Carnival time,
We make a new suit.
Red, yellow, green,
Purple and blue.
We make a new suit.

We got rhinestones on our suits,
Shine like diamonds and stars.
We got to be sure we together,
Cause we the soul of Mardi Gras.

We all try to make 'em
As good as we could
Cause when we out at Carnival,
We be lookin' good.

The second Magnolias' disc, a more elaborate and in some ways more sophisticated fusion of funk, Afro-Cubano rhythms, traditional chants, and aural images of Indians, was never released in the United States. Says Turbinton: "The response in Europe was phenomenal. There's a thing that's called the Otis Redding Award for the best R&B record, and the Wild Magnolias won it. I think the second album is definitely a classic." Many critics and record collectors agree. Sadly, no American distribution followed the European release by Barclay.

The Wild Magnolias brought the Indians' music into the mainstream. By 1976, however, Quint Davis had become deeply involved as director of the city's annual Jazz and Heritage Festival, which left no time to continue booking the group or searching for further recording opportunities. Although Willie Tee's days as musical coordinator for the group had drawn to a close, his own career was on the rise. While producing the Magnolias' discs, he was also cutting tracks of his own and carefully putting them aside. When he had accumulated enough for an album, he returned to Studio in the Country, added new material, and finished the master. A week later, Clive Fox, who owned a record company in Los Angeles, called Turbinton looking for new music. Willie Tee signed with Fox, who arranged distribution through United. Turbinton subsequently discovered that Fox was in business with Jerry Schoenbaum, who had been president of Polydor when the first Indians LP was released. Fox reimbursed Turbinton for his expenses incurred while producing the album, but he and Schoenbaum wanted Willie to rework certain tunes.

I still hadn't signed anything in terms of where the publishing was going to go. They were under the assumption that I was going to do a split publishing thing with them. I never signed it. At the finish of the album, I knew some people who were friends of the president at Chappell Music. And Chappell was having a convention in New Orleans, and luckily I got the album packaged, and met Norm Weiser [president of Chappell] and asked him if he'd be interested in the publishing. And he said, yeah, how much did I want? And I came up with a figure off the top of my mind and the cat said, yeah. And my attorney was like right around the corner; I got the guy to come over because I didn't believe he was saying, "yeah."[8]

Wilson Turbinton was paid a $30,000 advance with a guarantee of $10,000 a year to write eighteen songs. The latter clause did not engender long profits, however, as Weiser soon left Chappell Music. United released the album *Anticipation,* which was well-reviewed in the music press. But the company didn't promote the record, which as of 1983 stood as his most sophisticated statement as pianist, composer, and singer.

With the advance, the Turbintons bought a spacious house in a leafy neighborhood near the lakefront, where he lives today with his wife and daughter. In the years since *Anticipation,* Willie Tee has turned down several recording contracts "because the numbers weren't right." He remains, nevertheless, an active figure in New Orleans music, having written scores of new songs and recorded many new tracks, while maintaining his profile on the performing circuit. He sums up his situation thusly: "I'm waitin', man. You got to wait if you want to get the big one. I ain't exactly hurtin', if you know what I mean."

Chapter Nineteen

BIG CHIEF JOLLEY
AND THE NEVILLE BROTHERS

As the years pass, the great virtue of New Orleans music remains its continuity, the strength of one tradition carrying into the next, coloring anew memories of an older vocabulary. As the idioms evolved, one heard distinct echoes in the references to old songs, Carnival rhythms, dialects, street lore, and the rich harmonic resonances of vocal and instrumental lineage. By the mid-seventies, Mardi Gras Indian chants had entered the vernacular of rhythm-and-blues, challenging ideas of rhythm.

Although Willie Tee and the Wild Magnolias charged the popular imagination with certain chants and the exotic stage imagery of Indians, it was the Neville brothers, starting in 1976, who bridged the older tradition with a closer adherence to R&B vocal harmonies, all the while broadening the cultural connotations of Indian rituals with rhythmic accents shaped by Afro-Caribbean percussions. With the resulting repertoire and stage performance, the Neville Brothers toured nationally and in Europe. By 1980 their music had

become the preeminent pop sound in New Orleans. The creative association of four very different brothers, each with his own musical persona, developed gradually over a period of more than twenty years. The family history is a remarkable one, as much for the artistic range as for the struggle, often painful, to succeed professionally as a family act. The Nevilles' story begins with their uncle, George Landry, who as Big Chief Jolley founded the Wild Tchoupitoulas.

George Landry was born on April 4, 1917, in New Orleans. His sister Amelia, two years older, taught George dance routines when he was a young adolescent; the two performed at various theaters in the city, calling themselves Landry and Landry. These early theatrical outings gave George a love for performance and costume; he began sewing his own stage outfits. "I had an old tuxedo, and I cut it around to make a cutaway. I took the pants off and sewed them to make tails. Then I sewed sequins on the lapels."[1]

As a teenager, he started on piano by watching and imitating the licks others played. A man named Nolan "Apeman" Trim gave him his first lesson. Like other pianists, Landry played endless variations of "The Junker" blues. But many years passed before he had daily access to a piano and the time to refine his skills and widen his repertoire. He became a seaman with the merchant marine and spent much of his time away from New Orleans. When he was home, however, he would delight his nephews with tales of the sea, often setting the stories to music. Years later, after his many wanderings, George Landry became a Mardi Gras Indian.

Amelia Landry married Arthur Neville, Sr. The couple had four boys and two girls. Big Arthur, as the patriarch was called, worked as a Pullman porter and later as a merchant marine, sometimes shipping out with brother-in-law George. The two men became close friends, and in World War II they rode supply ships in dangerous waters of the Pacific. The Neville boys came to view these men as explorers. But the long absences were not easy on Amelia Neville, who had to raise the large family when Big Arthur was away. She was a loving, attentive mother and, like the children, treasured those stretches when Big Arthur was home. In later years, he began working in New Orleans. Although neither parent played professionally, they both loved music, brought it into the home, and encouraged the children to play music and to read.

Art's musical efforts influenced Charles, a year younger, born on December 28, 1938. The family origins were multicultural. Charles recalls, "There was African, American Indian, French, maybe Spanish. The island of Martinique I heard mentioned . . . from my grandmother." As a child he showed a cerebral nature, full of curiosity.

I started reading really young, trying to read everything, not just what I had in school. My daddy had a collection of Zane Grey books and I read those Westerns. I identified with that main Zane Grey character, who was strong and silent and able to survive in whatever conditions there were. I saw my father like that; he was the one I was going to live up to. He worked on the railroad as a pullman porter and that to me was one of the big adventures a black man could launch into, to travel the country and meet all kinds of people. I had this idea of going out in the world and making your fortune, being a part of what life was all about.[2]

Charles showed an early preference for the saxophone; at twelve he joined the school band. Rhythm-and-blues songs were played on the radio, influencing Charles's musical education, as they did older brother Art's. After a stint with Art's band, the Hawkettes, Charles, then fifteen, began touring with Gene Franklin and the Houserockers.

This was in 1954 and I traveled and played with the Rabbit's Foot Minstrel Show. We played for Bobby Bland, Junior Parker, Little Walter, and Jimmy Reed. When I first started, money was definitely not what it was all about. It was the feeling we got from playing music. My mother used to joke about it. I would go on the road with the band and be gone three or four months. She'd say, "All you bring back is a suitcase full of dirty clothes." We would make enough to exist on the road, but I was playing with B. B. King, James Brown, and Little Walter. They didn't have to pay me nothing.[3]

In 1956 Charles joined the navy and requested duty on "a ship going anywhere." He ended up in Memphis in aviation mechanics school. "There was a club on the corner of Beale Street and Hernando across from a little square dedicated to W. C. Handy. This was in Mitchell's Hotel. It was like the Dew Drop. I was in the house band, and some of the cats played with B. B. King. He used to come sit in with us. When I was off the navy base, I would stay by his house sometimes."

After two years, marked by AWOL excursions on Charles's part, the navy wisely decided Charles Neville's future did not lie in the realm of national defense, and he received his discharge and returned to New Orleans. He later enrolled in Southern University in New Orleans but in 1962 was arrested on a drug charge. For possession "of two little skinny marijuana cigarettes," he was sentenced to five years at hard labor in the Louisiana State penitentiary in Angola. For a sensitive young man who wanted only to play saxophone, Angola was a cruel fate. Long days of cutting sugar cane in the fields there caused an introspection, shaped by the tumultuous racial conflicts of the mid-sixties.

"I had already read *Diary of an Escaped Slave* and *The Life and Times of Frederick Douglass*. And Angola was just a big old plantation. But there was music. I remember cuttin' in the fields, singing *Ohhh Lawwd have mer-cy . . . Oh, Lawd have mercy on my soul now!* And then we'd get the rhythm of our [cane knives] swinging, and the chops would come on the downbeat."[4]

Charles's time in prison was eased slightly when he was assigned to the music room, but the three-and-a-half years spent at Angola changed his life radically. "Later, I divided my whole life between before Angola and after Angola." Upon release, he moved to New York.

Arthur and Amelia Neville's third son, Aaron, born on January 24, 1941, developed an early love for gospel music. Inspired by the early Sam Cooke and Soul Stirrers' discs, he sang spirituals. Aaron was a child when the family moved from Valence Street to the Calliope Street housing project. "As far as I was concerned," Art recalled, "it was nothin' more than moving to another neighborhood. I remember Charles, Aaron, and me—Cyril wasn't around yet—used to beat on cigar boxes in the windows. 'Hey Pocky Way' was a chant. In the projects that was something you just had to do. Now where it came from, I don't know."[5]

Aaron remembers, "We'd be sitting out on the bench late at night beatin' on hub caps and bottles, anything, we would be harmonizing. Art used to go around to the different theaters and win the talent contests. I used to go to basketball games at Rosenwald gym and sing for the dude, and he'd let us in free. Me and a little podna of mine named Buckwheat."[6]

Singing with Art and in the pick-up groups on the street, Aaron developed a lasting attachment to doo-wop harmonies. Art and Aaron sang tunes of the Spaniels, the Flamingoes, and the Orioles. In gospel, Aaron found the outlet for his remarkable falsetto reach. The tenderness of his vocals cut quite a contrast to his physique: well-honed muscles, deep red-brown skin, and by late adolescence, the overall look of a healthy prizefighter.

Aaron's voice, one of the finest in American popular music, registers a titillating vibrato. It began, he says with understatement, "when I was a little boy. You see, I used to yodel. I was a cowboy, had me a mopstick for a horse. I used to be yodeling and ride off into the sunset. At one time I didn't know how to use it to the full capacity. But through the years when I was going through changes and paying dues, it was a release valve."[7]

In 1958, when he was seventeen, Aaron spent six months in the parish prison for stealing a car. To a restless youth, joyriding had seemed fun. In spite of his aimlessness and hardened exterior—he went out one day and had a dagger tattooed on his cheek, causing Big Arthur to explode—there was a gentle side to Aaron Neville, even behind bars. This softness, which grew in later years as he became religious, translated into a kind of protectiveness in jail. "I always have been big, and I had a partner named Melvin. We would stop the older cats from messing with the youngsters coming in. There was nothing to do but sing and fight. You could pass in front of parish prison and sometimes all the tiers would be singing. They had these iron columns in the middle of the day room and they would make a nice sound when you beat on them. We had a slow beat and a fast beat."[8]

In parish prison, Aaron wrote his first song, a ballad called "Every Day."

Every day along about noon
    I'm dreaming of the day that I'll be home soon
And every day, along about one
    Oh, I remember how we used to have fun.

And every day along about two,
    Oh, how I'm so lonely and, oh, so blue.
And every day along about three,
    Well, I'm dreaming of the day when I'll be free.

Well, every day along about four,
    I cry, oh, I cry til I can cry no more.

And every day along about five,
    I'm writing you a letter with a tear in my eye.
And every day at just about six,
    Oh, how I remember how we used to kiss.

And every day, oh, every day now,
    How it reminds me of you.

Other inmates encouraged him to record the song. Upon release, Aaron sang it for vocalist Larry Williams, a friend of Art Neville. Deejay Larry McKinley then arranged an audition with Allen Toussaint. Aaron recorded "Every Day" and the Toussaint composition "Over You," which made the national R&B charts. Until the recording, Aaron had been singing with the Hawkettes. "Over You" provided impetus for road tours, with Larry Williams sometimes standing in for the burly younger Neville, with no one the wiser. But as Aaron Neville became recognized as a talented vocalist, he began touring the South in his own right.

As the three older Neville brothers moved through their twenties, married, and had children, the pressures of earning a livelihood grew. Art continued as a professional musician, but Aaron took a day job as a stevedore on the Mississippi docks to support his family. He continued recording on the Minit label until Allen Toussaint entered the army. In 1966 he cut "Tell It Like It Is,"

to date his greatest hit. On the success of that song, he renewed his work on the touring circuit, soon fronting a rhythm section led by Art Neville with Leo Nocentelli on guitar, Smokey Johnson on drums, and bassist George French. The band toured the East Coast and Canada. They were in Canada when the news came from home: Big Arthur had died suddenly of a heart attack. His death left the brothers with a stronger commitment to music as a profession. Like Sidney Bechet's father, Big Arthur Neville had been a "musicianer" who wanted music around him and encouraged his sons to play.

Big Arthur and Uncle Jolley influenced the Nevilles greatly, if not always in the traditional sense of role models. The brothers began leaving home at an early age, as their father and uncle had during their younger years. This departure from home put strains on their personal lives yet left each brother stamped with a strong, rugged individuality. Cyril, born on January 10, 1948, was eleven years younger than Art and ten years younger than Charles. He grew close to Aaron, who remembers asking him: "Hey, man, you feel adventurous? Come on, let's go to California. We would leave with a bus ticket, five dollars between us, and a bag of fried chicken. . . . Me and Cyril have had some episodes."[9] Cyril found more than adventure on their excursions. "Me and Aaron used to just up and go, going to seek our fortunes, so to speak. We never found the fortune, but we found a camaraderie between each other that will never be severed."[10]

By 1967, when Art formed the Neville Sound, Cyril had advanced steadily on the conga drums. In a sense, Cyril had come of age in a different musical generation. His three brothers were influenced by rhythm-and-blues and doo-wop, but Cyril was drawn closer to the sound and feel of hand drumming. His other pivotal influence was Uncle Jolley, who by then had resettled in New Orleans and gravitated to the Mardi Gras Indian

The Nevilles in rehearsal. *From right:* Aaron, son Ivan, and brother
Cyril Neville

The Neville Brothers, 1983. *From left:* Charles, Art, Cyril, and
Aaron Neville

tribes. "Most of the natural rhythm that I got involved with came from my Uncle Jolley," Cyril said. "He'd take his tambourine and beat it anywhere, any time. Now, as far as music is concerned, I heard music from my brothers."[11]

Like Jolley, Cyril Neville viewed the street parades and second-line movements as a sound spun from the same loom as the Indians. Cyril took the drum a step further, endowing it with spiritual implications. "The drum comes to me as a symbol of what I, or *we*, used to be. I can't speak on the drums, but I try to convey my feelings. I have never been so fascinated by an instrument like I was the conga drum. I started playing a set of drums with sticks, but I saw the congas as a direct thing that I could play with my hands. I think about Africa when I play. To me right now, my Africa is the drums 'cause when I feel like going back to Africa, I play my drums."[12]

In 1967 Cyril began performing with Art in the Neville Sound. But when the group became the Meters, Cyril and Aaron formed the Soul Machine. In 1972 they left New Orleans to visit Charles in New York, where they formed a trio. For all of the adventure, Harlem was an education in ghetto poverty on a scale neither man had encountered in New Orleans. "You know they call it the Asphalt Jungle," Aaron reflects. "Me and Cyril stepped off the bus and Cyril said, 'I want to go see Harlem, man.' So we went to Harlem and Cyril stood in the middle of the street and said, 'You mean this is what I been reading about and trying to get to all my life—Harlem?' New York is cold-blooded. New Orleans is warm-blooded."[13]

The summer of 1974 found Art in New Orleans leading the Meters, with Aaron, Cyril, and Charles in New York. But a new force was entering their lives: Uncle Jolley's emergence as a Mardi Gras Indian. George Landry had worked at a variety of industrial jobs in his later years, and at one of them was injured while handling asbestos. A settlement with the plant allowed him to retire just before he turned sixty. He had long been fasci-

nated with the Indian rituals, remembering dimly his grandfather who had been part Indian. Landry's first encounter with the Mardi Gras tribes came in 1966. "I was workin' on a truck," he recalled, "and a lady gave me a black-and-white Indian costume. I think her husband belonged to Choctaw. And I wore it that first year. Then I took it apart and made me another one when I ran with the gang in '67, with the Black Eagles. After that, I just got the bug and tried to make me a costume every year."[14] The first few years he marched with different uptown tribes, but in 1972 he founded the Wild Tchoupitoulas, drawing its members from men living in the Thirteenth Ward, an uptown, near-river neighborhood of which Valence Street was a central thoroughfare.

In New York, Cyril and Aaron were working on Indian songs with Charles. Cyril, whom Jolley had influenced the most, explains: "Me and Aaron and Charles did a thing as Wild Tchoupitoulas in New York. We did a thing with the Indian songs—Charles on sax, me on congas, Aaron on piano. I had my drum in a duffel bag. Charles had his horn cases, and we had a shopping bag with the tambourines and cowbells and a washboard sticking out of it. We would catch the subways like that."[15]

In the fall of 1974 Art called Cyril with the offer to join the Meters as a front man, to sing and play congas. Aaron returned with him to New Orleans. Charles remained in New York. By 1975 all the brothers but Charles were living in New Orleans when Amelia Neville, their mother, was struck by an automobile on the way to work and died from the injury. In the absence of both parents, Uncle Jolley became the surrogate patriarch. And, as a musical force, Landry was moving deeper into the Indian currents swirling around his nephews.

For months before Carnival, Chief Jolley's house, a shotgun shared by Aaron and his family in the adjacent apartment, came alive with Indian activity. Rooms filled with pieces of costumes,

Big Chief Jolley at Mardi Gras

feathers, beads, and sequins. Weekly Indian rehearsal sessions were held in small bars near the river. The Nevilles began to see their uncle in a different light. The crusty cast of an aging bluesman bathed his aura as he spent hours playing piano. Moreover, as Big Chief Jolley of the Wild Tchoupitoulas, he had become a neighborhood folk hero. The Indian chants fascinated Aaron and Cyril, who found new themes in them for pop compositions. "We used to go participate at the Indian rehearsal sessions," said Aaron. "We had some of the stuff; Jolley would come by and would put the pattern down, the groove of whatever he was going to do, putting the harmony together."[16]

A large measure of Landry's appeal came from his warm, bluesy voice, powerful enough to articulate the Big Chief's cries for tribal response, yet with sufficient clarity and range for studio recording. He was older than Chief Bo Dollis of the Wild Magnolias. Where Dollis delivered chants with raw power, Jolley's voice had a seasoned quality; he could hold phrases and sang well. As Jolley continued working the chants into harmonies with Cyril and Aaron, Art Neville saw the commercial potential, as did the Meters. A recording contract was drawn up between Landry, the Meters, the Nevilles, and the Toussaint-Sehorn partnership. The call went to New York: come home, Charles. They began cutting tracks in the spring of 1976. The tribal members who sang on the disc were Spy Boy Amos Landry, Flag Boy Carl Christmas, Trail Chief Booker Washington, and Second Chief Norman Bell.

"It was like a family reunion," Cyril recalls. "It was the culmination of everything that I had wanted in my life. To play in a band with all my brothers *and* my uncle, too, was like heaven. I could tell it was fascinating for Jolley to be there with all his nephews. It was like a dream come true for him, too. I had been in the studio lots of times with a lot of different people, but it never felt like that. This was the first joint effort we all made towards one point."[17]

The Wild Tchoupitoulas album, which Marshall Sehorn leased for distribution through Island records, is one of the great musical statements issued from New Orleans, a remarkable fusion of street chants and folk rhythms set to brilliant instrumental and percussive backing. The driving force behind the songs, the throbbing heartbeat of the music, is George Landry. His version of "Indian Red," sung in the uptown vernacular, introduces the braves after the time-honored chant "Mighty kootie-fiyo." But the lyrics broaden the theme of bravery with cultural implications: "We're the Indians of the nation / The wild, wild creation / We won't kneel down . . . not on the ground."

The lyrics of another song, "Brother John," offer an intriguing insight into the oral traditions. As written by Cyril Neville, who adapted the tune from street lore, "Brother John" is a eulogy to John "Scarface" Williams, a vocalist with Huey Smith's Clowns in the 1950s and a Mardi Gras Indian of the 1960s. It was in 1972, according to Jolley, that Williams "got stabbed to death outside a bar at St. Andrew and Rampart. It was right after Carnival when he died. So they made up a song about him, just made up—out in the streets."[18]

Well I remember that mawnin'
    Remember it well
Brother John is gone!

Well, I remember that mawnin'
    My Brother John fell.
Brother John is gone!

Well now, Cora, he died on
    the battlefield . . .

And the rest of his gang
    They wont bow, they wont kneel
Brother John is gone!

On *The Wild Magnolias,* Wilson Turbinton had used a character, Corey, as the seed for lyrical interpretation of a rebellious slave. In citing Cora, Cyril Neville memorialized Brother John as another fallen Indian within the tradition. A much earlier song recorded by Danny Barker, "Corinne Died on the Battlefield," was based on the story Barker had heard of a woman killed in an Indian altercation. According to Paul Longpre, former Chief of the Golden Blades, Cora Anne was a Queen who masked with the Battlefield Hunters. "She got killed in '27 or '28 at the Magnolia bridge. . . . She got caught in a crossfire between the Hunters and the Wild Squatoolas."[19] As the legend evolved by the time of the Wild Tchoupitoulas recording session, Cora had become a man.

The Wild Tchoupitoulas is a more faithful rendering of the old chants than *The Wild Magnolias,* which is not to detract from Wilson Turbinton's intelligent arrangements. In the transfer of a folk tradition into a commercial recording environment, change is sometimes necessary to find a market. How much is changed revolves around musical taste and the producer's judgment. Musically, a wide dichotomy separated the Indians' hand percussions and *a capella* chants from the rush of rhythm-and-blues. But the distance between Afro-Caribbean folk streams and the urban dance idiom was never so great as to erase the common cultural origin.

New Orleans parades and jazz funerals bred intricate crossrhythms—swishes on snare drum accenting the big beat of the bass drum, while the movement of feet on the street and slapping palms of the second liners advanced a subdominant counterrhythm. By contrast, in Jamaica—where volumes of New Orleans R&B carried on radios and as played by itinerant record-spinners in the 1950s—the reggae beat emerged as a stripped-down syncopation on electronic bass, a percussive pulse transferred from the drums.

The Wild Tchoupitoulas song with clearest reggae overtones is "Meet De Boys on De Battlefront" in which the word *de* moves like a bouncing ball over George Porter's protracted cadences on bass line. Jolley sings:

Now de prettiest little thing that I ever did see
Mardi Gras Indians down in New Awleens
Sewed all night and he sewed all day
Mardi Gras morning went all de way

Chorus

Meet de boys on de battlefront
Meet de boys on de battlefront
Meet de boys on de battlefront,
Oh de Wild Tchoupitoulas
  gonna stomp some rump.

But as a distinct body of songs, *The Wild Tchoupitoulas* is hardly a reggae offshoot. The melodies Landry and Cyril Neville arranged from traditional chants balance sophisticated group harmonies, so dear to the Nevilles, with specific spaces for the Indians to voice their chants. What results is a fine tension between the folk sensibility and instrumental prowess: the compositions, with Leo Nocentelli's biting, offbeat guitar lines and Zig Modeliste's sock-cymbal drums pushing the Indians' tambourines, are more rhythmically complex than the Jamaican beat.

The stronger cultural bond between the Indians' music and reggae is a spiritual tradition, expressed lyrically. Bob Marley and other Rastafarians sang a religious vision of liberation, characterizing the West as a decadent Babylon with Haile Selassie, the deceased Ethiopian liberator-turned-dictator, worshiped as a figure of redemptive power. The Indians' songs, much less overtly religious, articulate a lineage of past tribes and great leaders whose collective memory lives in the chants of bravery and spiritual solidarity as passed on through generations of the oral tradition.

The meeting of the Meters and the Wild Tchoupitoulas produced a fused idiom, unique to New Orleans and to America as one clear design in the larger pattern of African-derived urban dance idioms coloring the musical topography of the Caribbean. Trinidad's most illustrious star, the Mighty Sparrow (Slinger Francisco), embellished the calypso beat with pulsing horn charts and a richly layered percussive texture. In a similar vein, the Bahamian-born Exuma, who settled in New Orleans in the late seventies, used the indigenous junkanoo beat as a launch into driving guitar rhythms with streaking whistles and harmonica passages blasted like horns and with his rhythm section racing all the way.

As modern pop music forms, these styles of Trinidad, Jamaica, the Bahamas, and New Orleans vary considerably. But the common denominator —the base from which varied instrumental arrangements grew—is a percussive tradition in which shakers, bells, sticks, and different sizes of drums were first used ceremonially for dancing and parading, particularly during carnivals. In the postwar years, as nightclubs and dance halls filled with dancers, the influence of Western pop styles settled in disparate fashion on musicians of the island cities. In New Orleans, the percussive sensibility, for decades reflected in the parade drumbeats and beautiful body language of the second liners, found the oldest of echoes in the Indian songs. The African percussive tradition, submerged since the denouement of Congo Square and voodoo, surfaced eloquently in Charles Neville's hand percussions and Cyril Neville's conga drumming on *The Wild Tchoupitoulas*. The beauty of the album stems from the fidelity with which the folk tradition is maintained as the center of the musical arrangements, the chants fueled by strongly percussive rhythms hit by Modeliste and the Nocentelli-Porter strings carrying, but never overpowering, the voices. Chief Jolley's "Golden Crown" follows the pattern of praise for the leader's costume beauty.

At the same time, *The Wild Tchoupitoulas*—now a cult classic among European and American collectors—made concessions to the pop market. The Meters' version of "Hey Pocky Way" has little bearing on Indian imagery.

Little bitty boy with a heart of steel,
He can't boogie but his sister sure
  will, yeah
Feel good music, I've been told,
Is good for the body and it's good
  for your soul

Come and get it, now hey, hey, hey, hey
Hey pocky a-way, Hey, hey, hey, hey
Hey pocky-away.

The Tchoupitoulas recording sessions brought the Nevilles and their Uncle Jolley together as a family in a way nothing else had done. The album won plaudits from the rock press, and by 1977, when Art Neville left the Meters to form the Neville Brothers band, many writers started asking when a second Wild Tchoupitoulas LP would be recorded. But George Landry balked, claiming he had not been properly compensated by Toussaint and Sehorn.

Charles resettled in New Orleans as the Nevilles incorporated their band as Neville Productions, Inc. But a tangled legal web still tied the group contractually to Toussaint and Sehorn. The Nevilles hired a lawyer to secure their autonomy. The legal proceedings promised to be long, expensive, and bitter. No one relished the thought of unpleasant publicity. With a massive discovery deposition facing the studio, Toussaint and Sehorn released the Nevilles but retained publishing rights on many songs, including certain of the Tchoupitoulas tunes. By 1977 the Nevilles were on their own.

Their earliest performances that summer at Tipitina's, in the heat of a club with no air conditioning, drew packed houses week after week.

Many old Meters fans transferred allegiances to the Nevilles. For rhythm-and-blues lovers now in their thirties, the chance to finally see Aaron Neville in person brought back memories of "Tell It Like It Is" and their own nostalgic teenage years. From the start, the Nevilles had a large following of fans whose musical tastes had been formed in the fifties and sixties and with the Meters in the seventies.

Nevertheless, to create a musical style that would sell records and move the Nevilles beyond local popularity, far more was needed than local club dates. Rupert Surcouf became the Nevilles' manager and booked them for a month-long engagement at the Bijou in Dallas. The band moved into two apartments. For the first time in twenty-three years, the four Neville brothers were living under the same roof. Bonds were renewed. Art cooked gumbo and red beans and rice. Charles, after nine years in New York, came to know his three siblings better. Aaron had quit his job on the river docks and now devoted himself solely to music. Cyril was writing new material. The Bijou gigs were good ones.

Back in New Orleans, the band received steady booking on the burgeoning club circuit. R&B was in a colorful revival by the late 1970s. Meanwhile, Rupert Surcouf went looking for a record company. In late 1977, on a chance encounter in Los Angeles, he met Jack Nietzsche, a national producer who not only had heard of the Nevilles but was anxious to produce them. The group signed with Nietzsche and with Capitol Records. *The Neville Brothers* album featured a variety of musical styles. Nietzsche, enchanted with Aaron's voice, gave the singer three solos: "Arianne," "Audience for My Pain," and "If It Takes All Night." The LP also featured two songs composed by Cyril Neville. The youngest of the four brothers, in a sense, represents a newer musical generation. To Cyril, musicianship was a role model embodied by his three elder siblings. Cyril's memories of life on the road contrast significantly with Charles's recollections of the 1950s tours through segregated southern states when cops and state troopers harassed blacks. When the Meters toured Europe fronting for the Rolling Stones, Cyril reveled in Spain. "A full moon . . . in a bullring . . . in Barcelona, Spain—something I never thought I'd get a chance to experience, really. And it was received, like, olé, olé, olé."[20]

But *The Neville Brothers* LP did not earn the profits Nietzsche and Capitol had anticipated. The project went overbudget, but worse, a month before the LP's release, the head of Capitol's black music division quit, along with the head of their national rhythm-and-blues promotion. Both men had worked closely with Rupert Surcouf, but with their departure, Capitol did not back the disc with a tour. The band broadened its Gulf South appeal, however, and in 1979 embarked on a well-touted West Coast tour with the Wild Tchoupitoulas and an all-star New Orleans R&B cast. A complicated financial arrangement led to disputes, and the Nevilles had a final quarrel with Surcouf. The following year they found a manager in Bill Johnston, who had guided Gino Vanelli's career. A hard-driving rock promoter and club owner prior to his work with Vanelli, Johnston negotiated a contract with A&M records. *Fiyo on the Bayou* was produced by Joel Dorn, after Bette Midler heard the band (allegedly falling on the floor at Tipitina's in appreciation of Aaron's falsetto) and swayed Dorn's interest. This release features Indian standards "Brother John," sung in a more delicate dual harmony between Aaron and Cyril with a booming drum carrying the beat; "Iko Iko," another Indian standard popularized by Dr. John, the Dixie Cups, and Sugar Boy Crawford; a beautiful "Mona Lisa" by Aaron; and an updated version of Louis Jordan's "Run Joe," salted with calypso accents, with the lyrics changed slightly to tell the story of a cocaine bust. In sum, *Fiyo on the Bayou* was a class act and the Nevilles' best recorded effort since *The Wild Tchoupitoulas* five years earlier.

Why the LP failed commercially is a telling commentary on New Orleans' dilemma as a musical city. The rock press lauded the album; Robert Palmer gave it a long, glowing review in the *New York Times*. A&M sent the band on a tour of the East Coast, Chicago, and California. The Nevilles played several television engagements and fronted for the Rolling Stones again, in Louisville and New Orleans on their 1982 tour. But the problem boiled down to marketing. The Nevilles' eclectic music was difficult for radio stations to peg. Record sales move by the success of single tunes on radio. *Fiyo on the Bayou* was not strictly rhythm-and-blues; nor was it identifiably rock-and-roll. It did not fit the reggae mold either. The album was New Orleans music at its best, a blend of R&B and rock and much more—but the commercial zones of media strategies were elusive. The album, which critics so admired, and the music, which drew large audiences on the group's own promotional tour, simply did not fit a programming slot for the radio.

But the bloodline continues. Ivan Neville, Aaron's son, by his early twenties had become a promising composer and keyboard vocalist. Even more than Cyril, Ivan grew up in the musical glow of his father and uncles, performing often with them as a second keyboard and vocalist. Ivan's tune "Sweet Honey Dripper" became a local hit, and in the mid-eighties he was pursuing a career in Los Angeles, performing with Rufus and Bonnie Raitt, among others. Words cannot adequately describe the sheer physical presence of the Neville band on stage—Cyril's sensual movements on congas and bursting energy on high-tempo songs; Charles, slender and sinuous in the long, flowing streams on alto sax; Aaron, with deep red skin, sunglasses, with falsetto to chill your spine and the presence of a powerful Indian; and Art, pushing fifty, a keyboard sizzler with slick fashions to match, the true leader of the band.

"I think we've felt what the top is all about," Art reflects. "Because being family, there's some-thing that you just can't compare with any amount of money or material value. . . . So I think we are successful at what we been doing, and regardless to what happens, we just gonna keep *doing it*."[21]

The Nevilles represent the newest of the city's neighborhood-endowed idioms. The Thirteenth Ward is synonymous with the family, as is Valence Street, where Art, Charles, and Aaron were living within steps of one another in 1984, with Cyril only a few blocks away. Besides the Nevilles, the immediate vicinity also produced bassist George Porter and drummers Joe Modeliste and Leo Morris, now known as Idris Muhammed and working out of New York. The kids coming up call Valence Street "singer's row." The Nevilles' music, marked by shifting four-part harmonies, is in that sense an outgrowth of R&B; the Afro-Caribbean rhythms woven into so many songs reach back to the hand percussions and *a capella* phrasings of the Indian tribes. As a fusion music, the Nevilles' is both a high reflection of the city's folk culture and a direct link to islands of the south.

The only person missing now is Uncle Jolley. In July of 1980, four and a half months after his final march as Big Chief of the Wild Tchoupitoulas, he died of lung cancer.

His funeral that burning afternoon was one of the most poignant tributes to an artist the city has known. After a Catholic Mass, the casket was ushered out of the church with Big Chief Jolley's headdress draped over it. DeJean's Olympia Brass Band played dirges as the procession began on Constance, a street parallel to Tchoupitoulas and the river. At the rear of the procession, a half dozen Mardi Gras Indians, led by Chief Pete (Percy Lewis) of the Black Eagles and Bo Dollis of the Wild Magnolias, thundered along with tam-bourines crashing and braves chanting, "My big chief got a golden crown." In one dazzling hour, under fierce heat of the tropical skies, one saw the two traditions come together: the old funereal dirges of the brass band, and following the swell of second liners at the rear of the parade behind the hearse, a different kind of music in the Indians' chants and tambourine rhythms.

The procession turned up Valence Street, where George Landry had lived, the crowd by then numbering about five hundred, and when the hearse drew to a halt in front of his house, the Indians divided into double columns, chanting "Hey Pocky Way." Then a young brave in a bright yellow suit danced into the center of the street, knelt, lay flat, and kissed the hot asphalt in Jolley's honor. After the hearse left for the cemetery, several score second liners kept traffic blocked, standing there in a large human circle, a big man in the middle singing and everyone chanting that long refrain: "Brother Jolley's gone . . . Brother Jolley's gone . . . Brother Jolley's gone."[22]

EPILOGUE:
THE CULTURAL AWAKENING

by Jason Berry

There is a rare quality, an almost lyrical sensation, in the life of a city when avenues of creative expression open up and a new dialogue emerges between artists and the general public. Entering the 1980s, New Orleans was still marked by the dichotomy of increased prosperity for whites and deep poverty for blacks. But as the generation of rhythm-and-blues musicians achieved new levels of prominence, a more encouraging phenomenon took root. The revival of R&B, a burgeoning nightclub circuit, the march of Indians into mainstream popularity, and an emergent generation of new jazz and pop artists, many of them white, converged into a thematic current reflected in works by film and video producers, in poster art and theatrical performances. In the long march from a segregated city to one slowly embracing its bicultural heritage, a curious celebration arose. The imprint of a sense of *place* appeared in countless performances, songs, exhibitions, and works of visual art. In a very real sense, the references to New Orleans in seminal R&B tunes widened through the concourses of other creative expressions. The city itself became a prominent theme. Taken as a whole, the work of these men and women, in music and other art forms, constitutes a coming of age, a cultural awakening.[1]

The overlay of ethnic festive traditions has endowed New Orleans, as no other city in America, with an obsessive devotion to drink and dance, to spectacle and outsized manifestations of cultural memory. In all of this, music is the tie that binds. Celebration alone does not constitute a cultural movement. But the theme, and its artistic execution, stems from the social sinews of a community, what human relations are about. In the late 1970s, with the music revival in full swing, several stage musicals appeared, each of them reaching into the southern past to resurrect bygone traditions of black entertainment.

The first, and in many ways most ambitious, of these productions was N. R. Davidson's *The Caricatures,* a review of minstrelsy performed by the Dashiki Theatre. The musical arrangement was done by Coril Joseph. As the cast performed min-strel skits in blackface, Davidson advanced a satir-ical inner play, commenting on racial stereotypes, the burden of minstrelsy. One act ends with a cakewalk, in high-stepping promenade of planta-tion blacks mimicking masters. In Dashiki's cakewalk, the minstrels carried Confederate flags and danced to "Dixie"; with a final bittersweet touch, all flags dropped on the floor.

A more successful venture was *One Mo' Time* by Vernel Bagneris, set in an earthy New Orleans the-ater, circa 1925, on the night thundering blues singer Big Bertha comes to town. The audience once more becomes a crowd within; a jazz ensem-ble plays on stage, while the play shifts from Bessie Smith blues and vaudeville routines to backstage, dressing-room arguments between the male lead, originally played by Bagneris, and the female singers. *One Mo' Time* opened in New York in 1979 and later played Chicago, Los Angeles, London, and Scandinavia. In New Orleans it ran more or less continuously for five years.

The third musical, *Shangri-La*, was conceived by Charles Neville in homage to Dew Drop Inn shows that excited him as a youth. Written by white playwright Dalt Wonk, the story focuses on a 1950s nightclub and the return of a musician from prison to the "subculture within a subculture." Wonk's sensitive script gave body to Neville's dream of an artistic re-creation of the old Dew Drop days. Neville wrote the musical arrange-ments.

Although *One Mo' Time* was the only one to tour nationally, the value of the three productions is important from a larger cultural and musical standpoint. In a town without a theater district, three black musicals were staged in as many years, highlighting black entertainment forms that spanned close to a century—late nineteenth-century minstrelsy, 1920s vaudeville, and 1950s club life. More than this, the plays focused on musicians both as performers and as people, with their personal stories dramatized in light of social barriers of the times. Tensions of life on the road, the loneliness of stage life, racial pressures, and the human price extracted when "the show must go on" figured deeply in the productions—mirror-ing, as it were, the collective struggle of artists whose history this book records.

The popularity of the plays, like the music re-vival happening around them, did not occur by accident. As late as 1968, few clubs hosted racially mixed audiences. If there was a halting level of communication between the races prior to the civil rights movement, by the middle 1970s more black and white artists in New Orleans were get-ting to know one another as peers. The creative exchange Mac Rebennack pursued in the 1950s had become a social reality to a number of whites by the late 1970s. The collaboration between Dalt Wonk and Charles Neville was one of many. Black culture became exploratory terrain for whites working in other art forms. Among the first of these was photographer Michael Smith, who in the early seventies began visiting Spiritual churches and documenting their traditions. Smith's pioneering photojournalism was exhibited nationally, by which time he had begun pho-tographing the Mardi Gras Indians. Another pho-tographer, Syndey Byrd, painstakingly built an impressive inventory of similar subjects in the color medium.

In 1976 Maurice Martinez released *Black Indians of New Orleans,* a film extolling the Carnival ritu-als. Then Les Blank, a California filmmaker who had studied at Tulane, returned to the city; he visited the kitchens of neighborhood seafood eat-eries, followed the Wild Tchoupitoulas, filmed St. Patrick's Day celebrations, and released *Always for Pleasure,* an episodic, melodically impressionistic portrait of the city, perhaps the finest documentary made about New Orleans. These works, and oth-ers like them, struck deep chords of the popular imagination. Indian tribes began performing at the Jazz and Heritage Festival, at Tipitina's and other clubs, at Carnival dances, and once even at the Superdome. A small army of image seekers formed when Indians marched. And as the media romance with the Indians blossomed, other changes began to surface.

Slightly more than a dozen years had passed since an angry Frank Painia went to court to stop police from raiding the Dew Drop. By the early seventies, Painia was dead and the original Dew Drop a fading relic. But now scores of white aficionados, drawn to the myth of the memory, packed into the theater at the Contemporary Arts Center—a massive drugstore warehouse converted in 1977 into the nation's largest alternative art space—where Dew Drop Inn Revisited shows were staged as late-night features of the jazz festival. The festival brought thousands of people out under warm spring skies to celebrate their musical heritage. It brought them together, in harmony with sounds.

So too did the festival spawn a cottage industry in poster sales. The images proliferated swiftly, all kinds of them: old jazzmen, red-feathered Indians, black banjo pickers on plantation porches, eloquent grand marshals, drag queens of Mardi Gras, dreamy saxmen under starry skies. The school of poster art built on the celebrational impulse: images came from the growing ranks of photographers and painters. Scenes from these media began reflecting the bicultural sensibility of the town: crawfish, sizzling food, city vistas, and even visual puns in Dale Milford's parade of corpulent cockroach floats, the city's patron insect. By the end of the 1970s, New Orleans had a serious community of visual artists, many of whom commanded high prices for reputable works.

Various factors contributed to the city's cultural awakening, but the primary one was an unfolding social climate in which certain institutional barriers of race had fallen. New Orleans was hardly an interracial paradise, but a motley assemblage of whites, many who had come through adolescence dancing to rhythm-and-blues, gravitated to the musicians on a personal level. In the spread of these relationships, the *fact* of music, its durability as a language about the city, lent force and substance to the community at large. A new subculture within a subculture took root: on fringes of the musical society there grew a network of friendships, certifying the musical impulse and embracing the artists in the process of celebrating their art. The founding of Tipitina's is a good example. The club was financed by white devotees of Professor Longhair who felt he deserved more recognition than he had received. Tipitina's took the place of the Dew Drop, becoming the spiritual home of New Orleans music.

As veteran musicians regained popularity on the mushrooming nightclub circuit, a pair of irreverent weekly papers, the *Courier* and *Figaro,* competed through the mid-seventies and provided heightened music and cultural coverage. For many years the daily *Times-Picayune/States-Item* has employed no full-time jazz critic or music correspondent, an unfortunate vacuum in view of the paper's heavy coverage of crime. The vacuum was partially filled in 1980 by *Wavelength,* a monthly music magazine. These alternative media played a critical role in fostering the cultural awakening by sending messages of the musical society to many middle-class people who otherwise may not have known about the music. Early documentaries by the Video Access Center, following the films of Martinez and Blank, ushered similar changes in television. WYES, the PBS outlet, produced several music shows in 1980; the commercial stations, which for years had given sporadic music coverage, began airing periodic profile pieces, occasional documentaries, and even a performance series by an independent station.

The most exciting broadcast development of the 1980s was the birth of WWOZ, a community FM radio station devoted to New Orleans music and other indigenous idioms. With a sizable bank of records and tapes, WWOZ built a programming

Left: Lil Queenie (Leigh Harris), 1979. *Below:* A new generation comes of age. *From left:* David Torkanowsky, George Porter, and Leslie Smith

policy around the cultural origins of many musics. The station, founded in 1980 by transplanted Texans Walter and Jerry Brock, featured oral history profiles mixed with songs and the artists' reflections on them—the source of lyrics, circumstances of studio work, and in some cases, candid conversations about difficulties of the past. What emerged was a colorful excursion into music as a life and as a profession. WWOZ became a kaleidoscope of voices, rich in oral imagery—jazzmen, composers, Cajun fiddlers, parade grand marshals, gospel artists and rhythm-and-bluesmen, writers, occasional filmmakers, historians, Mardi Gras Indians, fathers and sons and mothers and daughters of musical families. WWOZ provided intimacy between the musicians and listeners, immeasurably broadening the sense of place.

To understand music as a cultural force one must examine its economic presence. The power of New Orleans music comes from a performance tradition and from dancing. The town, steeped in spectacle and exotica, has long revered showmanship, and showmanship built many of the better reputations to a greater degree than the record sales did. Even now, the club circuit forms the spine of what euphemistically is called a music economy. Several hours after Professor Longhair's funeral, Jerry Wexler sat in a hotel room discussing Byrd's career. Asked why New Orleans has fared so poorly in national recording circles since the R&B boom subsided, Wexler said, "Look, this town is boiling with talent. But where's the new sound? That's what labels look for."[2]

New sounds have consistently come out of New Orleans, but the larger language, the vocabulary of references from neighborhoods, older songs, and lineages like the Mardi Gras Indians are not the stuff of which high-energy pop bands are usually made. National labels have ignored many New Orleans artists because they fit no easily marketable slot. The variety of popular musics played and performed in the city often overlap. In itself, this might have been overcome had New Orleans developed economically in the postwar years, and even in the 1970s, in a way that matched the musical growth. The root problem is the absence of a high-powered, locally financed entertainment industry, with investments to produce records, with professional career managers, national booking strategies, television productions on a scale reflecting the breadth of talent—in short, with a network of businesses to *export* the music. After the flush years of R&B faded into late sixties rock, only a few of the later artists—Dr. John, Allen Toussaint, the Meters, the Nevilles, the Marsalis brothers—broke beyond regional barriers.

The underdeveloped music economy is a cruel irony in light of the heavy role musicians have played in New Orleans's flourishing tourist industry. Millions of people visit the city, hungry for good music. Far less music is sent up the Mississippi, but that cannot be attributed solely to the marketing departments of national record labels. New Orleans's problem goes deeper. Ultimately, it stems from the lingering myopia of an economy that was so recently built on segregation. The society has broadened, to be sure, but certain sectors remain rigid. Most of the artists in our pages are black; the big investment money is white. The psychology of investment in New Orleans is oriented toward restaurants, real estate, boutiques, bars, in sum, things any city without the same musical community might have.

The more deeply one examines this dilemma, the more one finds the impulse, that heartbeat of sounds as old as the city itself and a tradition that just keeps driving. More than a city "boiling with talent," New Orleans is a gold mine waiting to be tapped. Nashville emerged as a recording center, yet its musical heritage has neither the depth nor the longevity that New Orleans possesses. The same is true of Austin. Whether the city's long-slumbering economy will finally build on the musical largess remains an open question. With the proliferation of cable television systems, the potential to reach new markets without expensive tours has only begun to open. Television may well be the medium on which an entertainment industry could build.

In lieu of such an industry, a new trend emerged in the early 1980s with young musicians producing their own works, then seeking independent distribution arrangements. But if their approach to the business is different from that of their predecessors, the influences that guide them are not. The tradition of the musical family continues with artists like Wynton and Branford Marsalis, Ivan Neville, and Charles and Curt Joseph of the Dirty Dozen Brass Band. Wynton and Branford's success opened doors for trumpeter Terrence Blanchard and alto saxophonist Donald Harrison, whose debut disc *New York Second Line* drew the notice of a young jazz movement emerging from the city. This group of artists includes flutist Kent Jordan, whose father, Kidd Jordan, is an educator and, as a composer and saxophonist, is on the cutting edge of the local avant garde.

Like Wynton and Branford, Blanchard, Harrison, and Kent were students of Ellis Marsalis, which prompted jazz critic Gary Giddins of the *Village Voice* to remark that the keyboard master "hasn't unleashed an assemblage of geniuses, but rather a cadre of impeccably schooled musicians."[3]

The Dirty Dozen, a brass band merging bebop flourishes with street songs and blues, contributes a more robust flavor to the new generation. Giddins sees the young New Orleanians as part of a neoclassical trend in the 1980s, a reliance on jazz tradition itself more than experimental work. Yet it remains to be seen in what direction the new generation from New Orleans will extend the improvisational language. There is indeed a neoclassical quality about these young jazzmen, but as artists in a city with a mosaic of rhythms, they seem also to be advancing an impressionist style, creating montages out of varied idioms.

As an environment of sounds, the deep beauty of New Orleans reflects in the range of artists, young and old, actively at work. Lady B. J., who performed in *One Mo' Time,* began her career in church as a gospel singer; her transition to blues and popular vocals was the subject of the feature film *Dreamland.* Walter Washington, a stirring bluesman who provides a stylistic link to Guitar Slim, also grew up in the gospel tradition. A cult figure in the Seventh Ward, he recorded his first album in 1981, *Walter "Wolfman" Washington: Leader of the Pack.*

As a new generation of black artists embraces the tradition passed down to it, more young white artists are pursuing careers in improvisational jazz, blues and R&B, often in association with veteran black artists. Tony Dagradi, David Torkanowsky, A. J. Loria, Jim Singleton, Steve Masakowski, Ramsey McLean, Patrice Fisher, Johnny Vidacovich, Leslie Smith, Angelle Trosclair, the Pfister Sisters, and the group Woodenhead are among those who have promising careers. Similarly, Ed Volker and the Radiators, with a fusion of rock and R&B, have cut two albums and have attracted a large younger following. One of the best acts of the late seventies and early eighties is Leigh Harris, known as Lil Queenie, a dynamic if diminutive redhead who launched an exciting stage act in collaboration with composer-keyboardist John Magnie. Included in her repertoire is one of the finest lyrics about the city, written by Ron Cuccia, a writer and performer of jazz poetry. "My Darlin' New Orleans," as sung by Queenie, appears on Cuccia's second LP, *Music from the Big Tomato.*

My darlin' New Orleans, my brawlin' hometown
Your magnolia melancholy, how it softly sets me down
In corner bars, on streetcars
Hear that foghorn river sound
The big oaks, the old folks
Beads of moss hangin' down.

A city of sounds

My darlin' New Orleans, my praline hometown
Your carnival calliope sets me free to play the clown.
In patios wearing funky clothes
Through the juleps I can hear
Jazz bands and ceiling fans
Play Mardi Gras in my ears.

New Orleans is no easy town to categorize. A city of old traditions does not rush toward world's fairs and forty-story buildings without rubbing harsh against discontents of the poor; they comprise at least one-third of the urban population, and politically very little is done for them. Spend enough time here and the inconsistencies plant the impression that you are not in America at all, but visiting some littoral city-state, carved out of swampy lowlands, American in signature by virtue of its appendage to the continent. White pillars of the Garden District: decaying halls of the Desire Street housing project. A profitless Superdome that looks like it fell from the sky: Mardi Gras Indians. With its balmy warmth, raucous transients, bars that never close, and people who will throw a party at the mention of an excuse, New Orleans resembles Barcelona, Tangier, Marseilles, any number of Caribbean ports. The city has some of the loveliest weather imaginable between October and May: in thick of summer it can be hell on earth.

But for all of the erratic foibles, the debilitating provincialism, the city can still be one sweet place to live; somehow, in its languid pace, New Orleans has entered the late twentieth century with a deep and abiding sense of self, a distinct urban identity resistant to the great leveling of television culture. However flawed, at heart New Orleans bestows a precious measure of civility on those who live within her borders.

A younger generation of artists has already risen from the cradle of jazz, following in the steps of those we have chronicled. In years to come, new generations will doubtless extend the city's musical language, an inheritance of spirit as well as art. Harold Battiste, a pioneer of the heritage jazz that came out of those little clubs near Magnolia project and central city in the 1950s, explains it this way: "New Orleans, the city, has always been the focus. Musicians come and go, and their creations always seem directed at the city. Because after all is said and done, *New Orleans* is the star."[4]

NOTES

Chapter One

MUSICAL FAMILIES: THE FOUNDING TRADITION

1. Lincoln Steffens, *The Autobiography of Lincoln Steffens* (New York, 1931), p. 159.
2. Interview with Danny Barker, by Jason Berry, February 4, 1976, Louis Armstrong Oral History Project (hereafter cited as LAOHP), a grant to Jason Berry from the 1976 New Orleans Bicentennial Commission. Tapes are stored in the William Ransom Hogan Jazz Archive of Tulane University, Howard-Tilton Memorial Library, New Orleans.
3. Interview with James Rivers, by Jason Berry, February 19, 1976, LAOHP.
4. Interview with Alfred Roberts, by Jason Berry and Jonathan Foose, April 30, 1979.
5. Interview with Huey Smith, by Jonathan Foose, February 21, 1978.
6. Interview with Aaron Neville, by Jonathan Foose, August 19, 1978.
7. Henry A. Kmen, *Music in New Orleans: The Formative Years, 1791–1841* (Baton Rouge, 1966), pp. 232–33.
8. John W. Blassingame, *Black New Orleans, 1860–1880* (Chicago, 1973), p. 1.
9. See Marcus Christian, *Negro Ironworkers in Louisiana, 1718–1900* (Gretna, La., 1972); Sally Kittredge Evans, "Creoles of Color," in Samuel Wilson et al., *The Creole Faubourgs*, vol. 4 of *New Orleans Architecture* (Gretna, 1975).
10. Alan Lomax, *Mister Jelly Roll* (Berkeley, 1950), pp. 83–86.
11. Karl Koenig, "The Plantation Belt Brass Bands and Musicians, Part 1: Professor James B. Humphrey," *Second Line* 33 (Fall 1981): 28, 29.
12. Karl Koenig, "Magnolia Plantation: History and Music," *Second Line* 34 (Spring 1982): 35.
13. John Storm Roberts, *The Latin Tinge: The Impact of Latin Music on the United States* (New York, 1979), p. 36.
14. Jason Berry is indebted to Alan Lomax's lecture "The Power of New Orleans Music," given at the Louisiana State Museum in New Orleans on March 10, 1984, for cross-cultural analysis. In an informal discussion after the talk, he answered several questions regarding the urban neighborhood research

methodology employed in this chapter, which proved most helpful.

15. Sidney Bechet, *Treat It Gentle* (New York, 1978), p. 59.

16. H. O. Brunn, *The Story of the Original Dixieland Jazz Band* (Baton Rouge, 1969), p. 5.

17. In the genealogy "Louis Arthidore (1884–1905): Virtuoso with the Onward Brass Band, Clarinet" by Danny Barker, in the William Ransom Hogan Jazz Archive.

18. Interview with Danny Barker, by Jason Berry, May 12, 1981, New Orleans Ethnic Music Research Project (hereafter cited as NOEMRP), a grant to the authors from the National Endowment for the Humanities. Tapes and selected transcripts are stored in the William Ransom Hogan Jazz Archive of Tulane University, Howard-Tilton Memorial Library, New Orleans.

19. Interview with Placide Adams, by Jonathan Foose and Tad Jones, September 19, 1981, NOEMRP.

20. See "Seventh Ward," in *New Orleans Neighborhood Profile Series,* City of New Orleans Office of Policy Planning, in the library of the University of New Orleans.

21. "Claiborne Avenue Design Team 1-10 Multi-Use Study," a report by the Perkins and James Architectural Firm. See chapter 2, "The Historic CADT Area."

22. Ibid.

23. Interview with George French, by Jonathan Foose, June 22, 1981, NOEMRP; interview with Bob French, by Jonathan Foose and Tad Jones, November 27, 1982, NOEMRP.

24. Interview with "Deacon" John Moore, by Jason Berry, January 16, 1982, NOEMRP.

Chapter Two
PROFESSOR LONGHAIR: AT THE ROOTS

1. George W. S. Trow, Jr., "Profile of Ahmet Ertegun," *New Yorker,* June 5, 1978, pp. 50–51.

2. Tad Jones, "Interview with Professor Longhair," *Living Blues* (March–April 1976): 17.

3. Jennifer Quale, "Rocking Along with Professor Longhair," *Dixie* magazine, *New Orleans Times-Picayune,* February 12, 1972, p. 12.

4. Interview with Roy Byrd (Professor Longhair), by Hudson Marquez, New Orleans, July 1969, William Ransom Hogan Jazz Archive, Tulane University.

5. Interview with Isidore "Tuts" Washington, by Tad Jones, July 10, 1977.

6. Interview with Johnny Vincent, by Tad Jones, Jackson, Mississippi, August 8, 1973.

7. Timothy White, "The Professor Longhair Story: Lessons of a Rock and Roll Legend," *Rolling Stone,* March 20, 1980, p. 32.

8. Interview with Dr. John (Mac Rebennack), by Tad Jones, August 29, 1973.

9. Vincent Fumar, "Professor Longhair: A Remembrance," in *Lagniappe* section, *New Orleans States-Item,* February 2, 1980, pp. 6–7.

10. Jeff Hannusch, *I Hear You Knockin': The Sound of New Orleans Rhythm and Blues* (Ville Platte, La., 1985), pp. 26–27.

11. White, "The Professor Longhair Story."

12. Ibid.

13. Ron Cuccia, "Fess Fiesta," *Gris Gris,* December 3, 1979, pp. 42–43.

14. Interview with Alice Byrd, by Jonathan Foose and Tad Jones, September 9, 1981, NOEMRP.

15. The account of Longhair's funeral is based on reporting by Jason Berry, "Tunes and Bitterness at the Funeral of a Jazz Legend," *Washington Post,* February 5, 1980, sec. 2, p. 2.

Chapter Three
ANTOINE DOMINO: THE FAT MAN

1. Interview with David Lastie, by Jonathan Foose, February 12, 1980.

2. Mike Joyce, "Interview with Fats Domino," *Living Blues* (November 1977): 16–20.

3. Interview with David Lastie, by Jonathan Foose, February 12, 1980.

4. Joyce, "Interview with Fats Domino," p. 16.

5. Peter Davis, music instructor at the Colored Waifs Home where Armstrong had been placed, steered many boys from street mishaps into music.

6. Interview with Dave Bartholomew, by Jonathan Foose and Tad Jones, September 23, 1981, NOEMRP.

7. Band members were: Joe Harris, alto; Clarence Hall, Alvin "Red" Tyler, Herbert Hardesty, tenor; Salvador Doucette, piano; Ernest McClean, guitar; Frank Fields, bass; Earl Palmer, drums.

8. Other black artists recorded by Chudd for Imperial included Poison Gardner, Charlie Davis, Lloyd Glenn, and King Porter.

9. John Broven, "Interview with Earl Palmer," *Blues Unlimited* (September–October 1975): 5.

10. Arnold Shaw, *Honkers and Shouters: The Golden Years of Rhythm and Blues* (New York, 1978), p. 261.

11. Interview with Lew Chudd, by Tad Jones, September 3, 1973.

12. David Hershkovits, "Cosimo Matassa," *New Orleans Courier,* July 29–August 4, 1976, p. 7.

13. John Broven, *Rhythm and Blues in New Orleans* (Gretna, La., 1978), p. 14.

14. Ibid.

15. Interview with Dave Bartholomew.

16. "Domino Keeps 'Em Happy," *Louisiana Weekly,* January 19, 1957, p. 14.

17. Vincent Fumar, "Dave Bartholomew," in *Lagniappe* section, *New Orleans States-Item,* August 5, 1978, p. 8.

18. *New York Times,* September 12, 1955, p. 38.

19. Dick Clark and Richard Robinson, *Rock, Roll, Remember* (New York, 1976), p. 130.

20. Interview with Dave Bartholomew.

21. *Newsweek,* September 20, 1970, p. 12.

22. Hans J. Massaquoi, "Fats Domino: The Man Who Gambled Away $2 Million Without Going Broke," *Ebony* 39 (May 1974): 155.

23. *Newsweek,* September 20, 1970, p. 11.

Chapter Four
THE LASTIES: A NINTH WARD FAMILY

1. Interview with Frank Lastie, by Jason Berry, February 25, 1976, LAOHP.

2. Interview with Frank Lastie and Lewis Rock, by Jason Berry and Jonathan Foose, March 11, 1982, NOEMRP.

3. Interview with Frank Lastie.

4. Interview with Frank Lastie and Lewis Rock.

5. James A. Perry, "The Deacon Finds His Calling," *New Orleans Times-Picayune/States-Item,* September 18, 1980, sec. 4, p. 1.

6. Interview with Frank Lastie.

7. Jason Berry and Jonathan Foose, producers, *Up from the Cradle of Jazz* (video documentary), 1980.

8. Lyle Saxon, Robert Tallant, and Edward Dreyer, *Gumbo Ya-Ya* (New York, 1945), pp. 209–10.

9. Berry and Foose, *Up from the Cradle of Jazz* (video documentary).

10. The spiritual religious movement apparently came to New Orleans in 1919 when Leith Anderson, a woman of mixed Indian and African ancestry, began proselytizing in the Irish Channel and established churches. WPA interview digests with her disciples may be found in the Robert Tallant collection in the New Orleans Public Library. See also Michael Smith's "Exploring Underground Black Religion," *New Orleans Magazine* (December 19, 1975): 30, and Andrew Kaslow's learned account "Prophecy, Healing, and Power: The Afro-American Spiritual Churches of New Orleans," monograph, Department of Anthropology and Geography, University of New Orleans, 1981.

11. Interview with Frank Lastie, by Jason Berry and Jonathan Foose, March 11, 1982, NOEMRP.

12. Videotaped interview with Frank Lastie, by Jason Berry and Jonathan Foose, March 1979.

13. Videotaped interview with Alice Lastie by Jason Berry and Jonathan Foose, March 1979.

14. Ibid.

15. Berry and Foose, *Up from the Cradle of Jazz.*

16. Interview with Ornette Coleman, by Jonathan Foose, November 6, 1981, New York City.

17. Interview with David Lastie, by Jonathan Foose, February 12, 1980.

18. Berry and Foose, *Up from the Cradle of Jazz.*

19. Interview with Walter Lastie, by Jonathan Foose, February 6, 1980.

20. Berry and Foose, *Up from the Cradle of Jazz.*

21. Interview with Harold Battiste, by Jonathan Foose and Tad Jones, April 27, 1980.

22. Berry and Foose, *Up from the Cradle of Jazz.*

23. Interview with Betty Ann Lastie, by Jonathan Foose, February 2, 1981.

24. Berry and Foose, *Up from the Cradle of Jazz.*

Chapter Five
CLUB LIFE

1. Edward F. Haas, *DeLesseps S. Morrison and the Image of Reform: New Orleans Politics, 1946–1961* (Baton Rouge, 1974), p. 29.
2. Information concerning nightclubs is taken from various issues of the *New Orleans States-Item,* 1954–1957.
3. Videotaped interview with Charles Neville, by Jason Berry and Jonathan Foose, January 20, 1979.
4. *New Orleans Times-Picayune,* March 18, 1938, sec. 1, p. 1.
5. *Louisiana Weekly,* October 3, 1942, p. 6.
6. Interview with Johnny Donnels, by Jonathan Foose, February 3, 1981.
7. Videotaped interview with Charles Neville.
8. Interview with Gerri Hall, by Jonathan Foose, January 16, 1981.
9. Videotaped interview with Charles Neville.
10. Interview with Placide Adams, by Jonathan Foose and Tad Jones, March 20, 1981, NOEMRP.
11. Videotaped interview with Charles Neville.
12. Interview with Patsy Valdalia, by Jonathan Foose, March 11, 1981, NOEMRP.
13. Videotaped interview with Charles Neville.
14. Interview with Earl King, by Tad Jones, March 18, 1981, NOEMRP.
15. Interview with James Rivers, by Jason Berry, May 12, 1981.
16. Interview with Placide Adams.
17. Interview with Earl King.
18. *New Orleans Times-Picayune,* November 18, 1952, p. 16.
19. Interview with Earl King.
20. Interview with Huey Smith, by Jonathan Foose, January 12, 1981, NOEMRP.
21. Gloria Bolden, in conversation with Jonathan Foose, December 12, 1980.
22. Interview with Bobby Marchan, by Jonathan Foose, January 16, 1981, NOEMRP.
23. Gloria Bolden, in conversation with Jonathan Foose.
24. Interview with Bobby Marchan.

Chapter Six
MIDNIGHT ROCKERS AND SWEETHEARTS OF THE BLUES

1. Interview with Vernon Winslow, by Jason Berry and Jonathan Foose, March 12, 1981.
2. Interview with Vernon Winslow, by Jason Berry, July 3, 1981.
3. Ibid.
4. John Broven, "Roy Brown: Good Rockin' Tonight, Part I," *Blues Unlimited* (January–February 1977): 4.
5. Bill Bentley, "Roy Brown: Still Rockin' Tonight," *Los Angeles Weekly,* July 23–31, 1981, p. 56.
6. Jonas Bernholm, "The Roy Brown Story," *Crazy Music* (March–June 1977): 41.
7. John Broven, "Roy Brown: Good Rockin' Tonight, Part II," *Blues Unlimited* (March–April 1977): 15.
8. Ibid.
9. Bentley, "Roy Brown: Still Rockin' Tonight," p. 56.
10. Jeff "Almost Slim" Hannusch, "Roy Brown: Hard Luck Blues," *Wavelength* 1 (August 1981): 9–12.
11. Interview with Teddy Riley, by Jonathan Foose, June 29, 1981, NOEMRP.
12. Interview with Vernon Winslow, July 3, 1981.
13. Interview with Isidore "Tuts" Washington, by Tad Jones, July 10, 1977.
14. Interview with Isidore "Tuts" Washington, by Tad Jones, August 13, 1981, NOEMRP.
15. Hannusch, *I Hear You Knockin',* p. 245.
16. Interview with Thomas Jefferson, by Tad Jones, August 15, 1981, NOEMRP.
17. Interview with Vernon Winslow, July 3, 1981.
18. According to Isidore "Tuts" Washington, the music for "Tee Nah Nah," as recorded by Smiley Lewis in 1950, evolved from a set of standard blues changes that was frequently played in New Orleans during the 1930s and 1940s. The lyrics Lewis sang were a variation of the old standard "Junkers Blues," but the title can be traced back to 1910. In that year, Grunewald's, a New Orleans firm, published an instrumental "Indian" rag, "Te Na Nah," written by Harry Weston. The title would resurface in 1912, this time spelled "Te Na Na," as a dance/vocal melody published by the I. Seidel Music Publishing Company of Indianapolis, Indiana. Smiley Lewis's version was soon covered by Harry Van Wells's Or-

chestra with Spider Sam (Brownie McGee) on vocals for the Atlantic label.

19. Interview with Thomas Jefferson.
20. *Louisiana Weekly,* March 19, 1966, sec. 2, p. 10.
21. Interview with Vernon Winslow, July 3, 1981.
22. Interview with Shirley Goodman, by Tad Jones, April 4, 1981.
23. Interview with Leonard Lee, by Tad Jones, September 15, 1974.
24. Interview with Vernon Winslow, July 3, 1981.
25. Interview with James "Sugarboy" Crawford, by Tad Jones and Terry Patterson, April 29, 1975.
26. Ibid.
27. Jason Berry, "Gospel Music Is Voices Singing of Good News," *Figaro,* February 23, 1981, p. 24.

Chapter Seven
HUEY "PIANO" SMITH AND GUITAR SLIM

1. LeRoi Jones, *Blues People: Negro Music in White America* (New York, 1963), 82.
2. Jon Newlin, "Earl King: Voodoo Dolls to 'Trick Bags,'" *Figaro,* October 7, 1972, p. 5.
3. Interview with Huey Smith, by Jonathan Foose, September 12, 1978.
4. Interview with Virginia Dumas, by Jonathan Foose, August 9, 1980, Greenville, Mississippi.
5. Letter from Martin Gross to Jim O'Neal, December 1, 1977, courtesy of Jim O'Neal.
6. Hammond Scott, "New Orleans' Cousin Joe," *Living Blues* (January–February 1975): 22.
7. Interview with Huey Smith, by Jonathan Foose, August 14, 1978.
8. Interview with Gerri Hall, by Jonathan Foose, January 16, 1981.
9. *Louisiana Weekly,* August 26, 1950, p. 9.
10. Interview with Percy Stovall, by Tad Jones, December 27, 1977.
11. Interview with Earl King, by Tad Jones, June 10, 1977.
12. Jeff "Almost Slim" Hannusch, "Making a Hit: The Rise and Fall of New Orleans Music Parallels the History of Ace Records," *Figaro,* December 1, 1980, sec. 1, p. 33.
13. Broven, *Rhythm and Blues in New Orleans,* 114.
14. Hannusch, "Making a Hit," p. 33.
15. Broven, *Rhythm and Blues in New Orleans,* p. 52.
16. Interview with Johnny Vincent, by Tad Jones, August 8, 1973, Jackson, Mississippi.
17. Huey Smith, in conversation with Jonathan Foose, February 12, 1979.
18. Interview with Bobby Marchan, by Jonathan Foose, January 16, 1981.
19. Interview with Huey Smith, August 14, 1978.
20. Broven, *Rhythm and Blues in New Orleans,* 122.
21. Interview with Gerri Hall.
22. Interview with Bobby Marchan.
23. Interview with Huey Smith, August 14, 1978.
24. Interview with Bobby Marchan.
25. Interview with Lloyd Lambert, by Tad Jones, March 22, 1978.
26. Interview with Clarence Ford, by Tad Jones and Richard B. Allen, December 10, 1975, in the William Ransom Hogan Jazz Archive of Tulane University.
27. Interview with Harry Nance, by Tad Jones, January 21, 1981.

Chapter Eight
HAIL, HAIL, ROCK-AND-ROLL

1. Willie Morris, *North Toward Home* (Boston, 1967), p. 180.
2. Langdon Winner, "The Sound of New Orleans," *The Rolling Stone Illustrated History of Rock and Roll,* edited by Jim Miller (New York, 1980), p. 35.
3. Jonathan Kamin, "The White 'R&B' Audience and the Music Industry, 1952–1956," *Popular Music and Society* 4 (1976): 183.
4. Interview with Duke Dugas, by Tad Jones, September 30, 1981.
5. Jeff "Almost Slim" Hannusch, "Bobby Mitchell Remembers New Orleans Music," *Wavelength* 1 (November 1980): 7.
6. Interview with Chuck Carbo, by Tad Jones, December 1, 1973.
7. From "Little Richard Is Big on Jesus," a taped sermon given by Richard Penniman at the First Assembly Church of God, New Orleans, Louisiana, May 10 and 11, 1981.

8. Langdon Winner, "Little Richard," in *The Rolling Stone Illustrated History of Rock and Roll,* p. 48.

9. Penniman, "Little Richard Is Big on Jesus."

10. Charles White, *The Life and Times of Little Richard: The Quasar of Rock* (New York, 1984), p. 30.

11. Shaw, *Honkers and Shouters,* p. 74.

12. Penniman, "Little Richard Is Big on Jesus."

13. Interview with Bobby Marchan, by Jonathan Foose, January 16, 1981, NOEMRP.

14. White, *The Life and Times of Little Richard,* p. 37.

15. Broven, "Interview with Earl Palmer." *Blues Unlimited* (September–October 1975): 5.

16. Interview with Dave Bartholomew, by Jonathan Foose and Tad Jones, November 16, 1981, NOEMRP.

17. Interview with Frank Fields, by Jonathan Foose, August 27, 1981, NOEMRP.

18. Interview with Alvin "Red" Tyler, by Tad Jones, August 20, 1973.

19. Interview with Dave Bartholomew.

20. Interview with Frankie Ford, by Tad Jones, June 4, 1973.

21. La Bostrie says she wrote "Tutti Frutti" herself after a girlfriend ordered tutti-fruitti ice cream at a local drugstore. See Hannusch, *I Hear You Knockin',* p. 222. Her version of the song's origin is at variance with Blackwell's and Richard's. In White's biography of Richard, he lists Penniman/La Bostrie/Lubin as writers; however, Lubin is not identified in the text.

22. Interview with Lee Diamond, by Jonathan Foose and Tad Jones, August 29, 1981, NOEMRP.

23. Ibid.

Chapter Nine
DEEJAYS AND TEEN IDOLS

1. Shaw, *Honkers and Shouters,* p. 509.

2. Albert Murray, *Stomping the Blues* (New York, 1976), p. 189.

3. Interview with Jim Russell, by Jason Berry, November 10, 1981.

4. Interview with Larry Regan, by Jason Berry, October 15, 1981.

5. Ibid.

6. Vincent Fumar, "Poppa Stoppa," *Vieux Carre Courier,* November 23, 1972, pp. 6–7.

7. Interview with Larry Regan, by Jason Berry, October 15, 1981.

8. Interview with Keith Rush, by Jason Berry and Tad Jones, September 15, 1981.

9. William Hammel, in conversation with Jason Berry, November 1981.

10. Interview with Duke Dugas, by Tad Jones, September 30, 1981.

11. Interview with Ken Elliott, Jr., by Tad Jones, October 21, 1981.

12. Interview with Bobby Charles, by Tad Jones, September 11, 1973.

13. Interview with Jimmy Clanton, by Tad Jones, September 9, 1973.

14. Ibid.

15. Interview with Frankie Ford, by Jonathan Foose, October 12, 1981.

16. Huey Smith, in conversation with Jonathan Foose, January 12, 1981.

17. Interview with Frankie Ford, by Jonathan Foose, October 12, 1981.

Chapter Ten
ALLEN TOUSSAINT AND THE MINIT SOUND

1. City of New Orleans Office of Policy Planning, "Gert Town/Zion City," *New Orleans Neighborhood Profile Series,* vol. 14, p. 12D.

2. Interview with Allen Toussaint, by Richard B. Allen, April 20, 1978, in "Jambalaya" series, New Orleans Public Library.

3. Timothy White, "When Toussaint Goes Marching In," *Crawdaddy* (May 1975): 43.

4. Stevenson Palfi, producer, *Piano Players Seldom Play Together,* a video documentary, 1981.

5. Interview with Allen Toussaint, by Tad Jones, May 12, 1973.

6. Shaw, *Honkers and Shouters,* pp. 455–56.

7. Broven, *Rhythm and Blues in New Orleans,* p. 150.

8. Ibid., pp. 150–51.

9. Interview with Larry McKinley, by Jonathan Foose, October 27, 1981.

10. Interview with Joe Banashak, by Tad Jones, November 30, 1981.
11. Interview with Allen Toussaint, by Tad Jones, May 12, 1973.
12. Ibid.
13. Jeff "Almost Slim" Hannusch, "The In-Kredible Ernie K-Doe," *Wavelength* 1 (March 1981): 6.
14. Musicians who played for Minit recording sessions included: Red Tyler (baritone sax); Nat Perrilat (tenor sax); Roy Montrel, Snooks Eaglin, George Davis (guitar); Chuck Badie, Frank Fields, Richard Payne (bass); John Boudreaux (drums).
15. Interview with Benny Spellman, by Tad Jones, July 6, 1973.
16. Hannusch, "The In-Kredible K-Doe," p. 7.
17. Interview with Irma Thomas, by Jonathan Foose, October 21, 1981.
18. Interview with Irma Thomas, by Jonathan Foose, November 30, 1981.
19. It is Banashak's contention that on the night of the Minit auditions, he offered Irma Thomas a contract that she verbally accepted. The following day, without notifying Banashak, she signed with Ron Records.
20. Interview with Irma Thomas, by Jonathan Foose, November 30, 1981.
21. Ibid.
22. Interview with Larry McKinley, by Jonathan Foose, October 27, 1981.
23. Interview with Chris Kenner, by Tad Jones, September 3, 1973.
24. Interview with Ike Favorite, by Jonathan Foose, October 29, 1981.
25. Ibid.
26. Interview with Joe Banashak, by Tad Jones, November 30, 1981.
27. Interview with Larry McKinley, by Jonathan Foose, October 27, 1981.
28. Interview with Joe Banashak, by Tad Jones, May 12, 1973.

Chapter Eleven
DECLINE AND EXODUS

1. Broven, *Rhythm and Blues in New Orleans*, p. 191.
2. Interview with Mac "Dr. John" Rebennack, by Tad Jones, August 29, 1973.

3. Interview with Cosimo Matassa, by Jonathan Foose, December 16, 1981.
4. Tad Jones, "Interview with Earl King," *Living Blues* (July–August 1978): 42.
5. Earl King quotations in this chapter are taken from a two-part article by Tad Jones, "Interview with Earl King," *Living Blues* (May–June 1978): 7–19 and (July–August 1978):17–22, 39–43.
6. Broven, *Rhythm and Blues in New Orleans*, p. 78.
7. Interview with Oliver Morgan, by Jonathan Foose, June 26, 1981.
8. Interview with Cosimo Matassa, by Jonathan Foose, October 26, 1981.
9. Ibid.
10. Ibid.
11. Interview with Lee Diamond, by Jonathan Foose and Tad Jones, August 29, 1981, NOEMRP.
12. Interview with Cosimo Matassa, December 16, 1981.

Chapter Twelve
THE NEW JAZZ AND AFO

1. Interview with Al Belletto, by Jason Berry, October 28, 1981, NOEMRP.
2. James Lincoln Collier, *The Making of Jazz* (Boston, 1978), p. 352.
3. Paul Lentz, "Keeping Up with Al Belletto," *Downbeat* 39 (June 22, 1972): 16.
4. Interview with Al Belletto.
5. Rhodes Spedale, in conversation with Jason Berry, February 1982.
6. Collier, *The Making of Jazz*, p. 418.
7. Interview with James Drew, by Jason Berry, January 4, 1982.
8. Some of the biographical information on AFO artists comes from the twenty-eight-page booklet Harold Battiste wrote to accompany the four-LP set *New Orleans Heritage Jazz, 1956–1966* (1979) that he produced.
9. Interview with Harold Battiste, by Jonathan Foose and Tad Jones, April 27, 1980.

10. Pierce Lewis, *New Orleans: The Making of an Urban Landscape* (Cambridge, Mass., 1976), p. 42.

11. Andrew Kaslow, "Central City: The Ethnohistory of a New Orleans Neighborhood," in *Perspectives on Ethnicity in New Orleans* (University of New Orleans, 1980), p. 36.

12. A. B. Spellman, *Black Music: Four Lives* (New York, 1966), p. 103. In Spellman's chapter on Ornette Coleman, the musician identified as Melvin Lassiter is Melvin Lastie.

13. Ibid, pp. 114–15.

14. Valerie Wilmer, "The Drummer: Street Parade Fan," *Melody Maker,* March 9, 1968, p. 10.

15. Interview with Edward Frank, by Jonathan Foose, January 9, 1982, NOEMRP.

16. Interview with Ellis Marsalis, by Jason Berry, October 20, 1981, NOEMRP.

17. Interview with James Black, by Jason Berry, January 22, 1982, NOEMRP.

18. Interview with Edward Frank.

19. Interview with James Black.

20. Interview with Ellis Marsalis.

21. Interview with Ornette Coleman, by Jonathan Foose, November 6, 1981, New York.

22. Interview with Harold Battiste, by Jonathan Foose and Tad Jones.

23. Interview with Tami Lynn, by Jonathan Foose, October 20, 1981, NOEMRP.

24. Broven, *Rhythm and Blues in New Orleans,* p. 163.

25. Ibid.

26. Interview with Harold Battiste.

Chapter Thirteen
JAZZ AND BLUES KEPT COMING

1. Interview with Earl Turbinton, by Jason Berry, October 15, 1981, NOEMRP.

2. Interview with Earl Turbinton, by Jason Berry, February 15, 1982.

3. Interview with Earl Turbinton, October 15, 1981.

4. Ibid.

5. Ibid.

6. Interview with James Rivers, by Jason Berry, February 19, 1976, LAOHP.

7. Interview with James Rivers, by Jason Berry, May 28, 1981.

8. Interview with James Drew, by Jason Berry, January 4, 1982.

9. Interview with Luther Kent and Charlie Brent, by Jason Berry, February 18, 1983, NOEMRP.

10. Ibid.

11. A. James Liska, "Interview with Wynton and Branford Marsalis, A Common Understanding," *Downbeat,* December 1982, p. 15.

12. Ellis Marsalis, telephone interview with Jason Berry, January 29, 1982.

13. Kalamu Ya Salaam, "Talking to Wynton Marsalis: Double Tonguing, Triple Tonguing, Slurring and Phrasing," *Wavelength* 3 (February 1984): 40.

14. Ibid.

15. Stanley Crouch, liner notes to *Wynton Marsalis* (Columbia, 1982).

16. Gary Giddins, *Rhythm-A-Ning: Jazz Tradition and Innovation in the Eighties* (New York, 1985), p. 160.

Chapter Fourteen
PIANO PLAYERS

1. Interview with Dave Williams, by Jonathan Foose, December 9, 1981, NOEMRP.

2. Al Rose, *Storyville, New Orleans* (University, Ala., 1974), p. 115.

3. Lomax, *Mister Jelly Roll,* p. 43.

4. Interview with Dave Williams.

5. Interview with Oliver Morgan, by Jonathan Foose, October 28, 1981, NOEMRP.

6. Interview with Dave Williams.

7. Al Rose and Edmond Souchon, *New Orleans Jazz: A Family Album* (Baton Rouge, 1967), pp. 12, 46, 82.

8. Interview with Dave Williams.

9. Interview with Edwin Bocage, by Jonathan Foose, December 19, 1981, NOEMRP.

10. *Gumbo* LP liner notes, ATCO Records, 1972.

11. Interview with Edwin Bocage.

12. Ibid.

13. Interview with Tommy Ridgley, by Jonathan Foose, January 20, 1982, NOEMRP.

14. Broven, *Rhythm and Blues in New Orleans,* p. 104.

15. Interview with Edward Frank, by Jonathan Foose, January 9, 1982, NOEMRP.
16. Interview with James Booker, by Jonathan Foose, December 17, 1981.
17. Interview with Betsy Lizana, by Jonathan Foose, January 5, 1982, Bay St. Louis, Mississippi.
18. Interview with Edward Frank.
19. Interview with James Booker, by Jason Berry, June 23, 1976.

Chapter Fifteen
DR. JOHN'S GUMBO ROCK

1. Interview with Dorothy M. Rebennack, by Tad Jones, November 4, 1981, Orange, California.
2. Interview with Mac "Dr. John" Rebennack, by Tad Jones, August 29, 1973.
3. Interview with Dorothy M. Rebennack.
4. Shirley Goodman, in conversation with Tad Jones, 1981.
5. Interview with Mac Rebennack, by Tad Jones, February 25, 1977.
6. Richard Williams, "The Dr. John Story," *Melody Maker* (May 20, 1972): 12.
7. Interview with Henry Geuraneaux, by Tad Jones, June 11, 1977.
8. Interview with Al Farrell, by Tad Jones, March 29, 1981.
9. Interview with Mac Rebennack, August 29, 1973.
10. Interview with James Herring, by Tad Jones, June 4, 1977.
11. Interview with Mac Rebennack, August 29, 1973.
12. "Up to His Ears in Tunes," in *Dixie* magazine, *New Orleans Times-Picayune*, June 21, 1959, p. 14.
13. Interview with Eddie Hynes, by Tad Jones, May 31, 1977.
14. Interview with Tommy Ridgley, by Tad Jones, June 6, 1973.
15. Williams, "The Dr. John Story," p. 12.
16. Interview with Harold Battiste, by Tad Jones, July 5, 1976.
17. Williams, "The Dr. John Story," p. 12.
18. Interview with Ronnie Barron, by Tad Jones, November 6, 1981, Reseda, California.
19. John Swenson, "Dr. John, Finally in the Right Place," *Crawdaddy* (June 1974): 40.
20. Interview with Harold Battiste.
21. Albert Goldman, "Pale Voodoo Hands Across the Sea," *Life*, March 14, 1969, p. 14.
22. Interview with Dorothy M. Rebennack.
23. Vance du Rivage, "NOLA's Own Voodoo Pop Star," *Vieux Carre Courier*, July 7–13, 1972, p. 5.

Chapter Sixteen
ALLEN TOUSSAINT AND THE METERS

1. Interview with Marshall Sehorn, by Tad Jones, July 19, 1973.
2. Interview with Lee Dorsey, by Tad Jones, July 1, 1973.
3. Ibid.
4. Interview with Allen Toussaint, by Tad Jones, May 12, 1973.
5. Joe McEwen, "Performance," review of the Meters concert at Paul's Mall, Boston, on September 6, 1976, in *Rolling Stone*, November 4, 1976, p. 94.
6. Interview with Art Neville, by Jonathan Foose, May 16, 1978, Dallas, Texas.
7. Ibid.
8. Interview with Art Neville, by Tad Jones, May 31, 1974.
9. Art Neville, in conversation with Jonathan Foose, November 1980.
10. Interview with George Porter, by Tad Jones, April 23, 1974.
11. Ibid.
12. Cyril Neville, in conversation with Jonathan Foose, November 1980.
13. Bunny Matthews, "Let's Get Fired Up," *Figaro*, September 1, 1980, sec. 1, p. 17.
14. Interview with Joe Modeliste, by Jason Berry, May 15, 1981.
15. Interview with Joe Modeliste, by Tad Jones, November 22, 1974.
16. Kathleen Austen, "Guitar Players," *Wavelength* 2 (March 1982): 13.
17. Interview with Leo Nocentelli, by Tad Jones, November 22, 1974. See also Jason Berry, "The Ballad of Jack Nocentelli: Poet Laureate of Elysian

Fields," *Southern Exposure* 5 (Summer–Fall 1977): 156.

18. Interview with Art Neville, May 31, 1974.

19. Interview with George Porter, April 23, 1974.

20. The song "Cabbage Alley" by the Meters is a melodic rendition of Professor Longhair's "Hey Now, Baby." The publisher, Rhinelander Music, owned by Marshall Sehorn and Allen Toussaint, did not view this as a copyright infringement. Royalties were not paid to Byrd or his heirs.

21. Interview with Marshall Sehorn.

22. Interview with Rupert Surcouf, Jr., by Tad Jones, February 10, 1982.

23. *Stereo Review* 33, no. 6 (December 1974): 124.

24. Joel Selvin, "The Meters Just Stole It Away," *San Francisco Chronicle*, July 12, 1974.

25. Interview with Art Neville, May 16, 1978.

26. "Meet the Meters: This Shit Be Fire," *Boston Real Paper*, September 18, 1976, p. 36.

27. Interview with Art Neville, May 16, 1978.

28. Marcia Kavanaugh and Ross Yockey, producers, *Crescent City, Soul of Rock 'n Roll*, WDSU-TV, New Orleans, 1979.

Chapter Seventeen
IN SEARCH OF THE MARDI GRAS INDIANS

1. Samuel Charters, *The Roots of Blues: An African Search* (London, 1981), pp. 68–69. On a research trip to the Gambia, Charters encountered a group of masked villagers, parading to music. "Where had I seen it before? It was in New Orleans, on a Mardi Gras morning in the 1950s. It was the first time I'd seen the 'Indians.' . . . What I saw in New Orleans was this same procession of a spirit figure, only in New Orleans the spirit had become an 'Indian,' through all the confusions of the new culture and new religion."

2. Francis Bebey, *African Music: A People's Art* (Westport, Conn., 1980), p. 116.

3. See *Negro Insurrections*, vol. 2 of *Louisiana*, edited by Alcee Fortier (Madison, Wisc.. 1914), p. 213; Henry E. Chambers, *A History of Louisiana*, vol. 1 (Chicago and New York: American Historical Society, 1925), pp. 209–11.

4. Carl Brasseaux, "The Administration of Slave Regulations in French Louisiana, 1724–1766," *Louisiana History* (1980): 155.

5. Ibid., p. 146.

6. Melville J. Herskovits, *Life in a Haitian Valley* (Garden City, N.Y., 1971), p. 23.

7. Janheinz Jahn, *Muntu: An Outline of the New African Culture* (New York, 1961), pp. 32–33.

8. Maya Deren, *Divine Horsemen: The Voodoo Gods of Haiti* (New York, 1970), pp. 58–66.

9. George Washington Cable, "The Dance at Place Congo," in *Creoles and Cajuns* (New York, 1959), p. 3.

10. Maurice M. Martinez, "Delight in Repetition: The Black Indians," *Wavelength* 16 (February 1982): 21.

11. "The Carnival," *The WPA Guide to New Orleans* (New York, 1983), p. 175. Mitchell Osborne and Errol L. Laborde, *Mardi Gras! A Celebration* (New Orleans, 1981), pp. 42–44.

12. Martinez, "Delight in Repetition," p. 21.

13. See Andrew Pearse, "Carnival in the Nineteenth Century," *Caribbean Quarterly* 4, nos. 3–4 (1956):175–93.

14. See Edward Brathwaite's "Caribbean Culture—Two Paradigms," in *Missile and Capsule*, edited by Jurgen Martini (Bremen, Germany, 1983), pp. 28–54. Brathwaite's thematic observations in previous works are applied to New Orleans in an excellent article by Tom Dent, "A Critical Look at Mardi Gras," *Jackson* (Mississippi) *Advocate*, February 18, 1982, sec. B, p. 1.

15. Interview with Allison "Tuddy" Montana, by Jason Berry, March 13, 1982, NOEMRP.

16. Elise Kirsch, *Downtown New Orleans in the Early Eighties: Customs and Characters of Old Robertson Street and Its Neighborhoods* (New Orleans, 1951), p. 9.

17. Finn Wilhelmsen, "Creativity in the Songs of the Mardi Gras Indians of New Orleans, Louisiana." The appendix to Wilhelmsen's manuscript, which he gratuitously sent after an initial correspondence, was published, in part, in *Louisiana Folklore Miscellany* 3 (1973): 56–74.

18. Interview with Allison Montana.

19. Lomax, *Mister Jelly Roll*, p. 15.

20. Robert Tallant, *Mardi Gras* (New York, 1948), pp. 107–8.
21. Interview with Allison Montana.
22. Interview with Paul Longpre, by Jason Berry and Jonathan Foose, February 13, 1982, NOEMRP.
23. Interview with Arthur "Creole" Williams and Allison Montana, by Jason Berry, March 13, 1982, NOEMRP.
24. Pearse, "Carnival in the Nineteenth Century," p. 180.
25. Andrew Kaslow, "Folklore: Talking to Some Glorious Mardi Gras Indians," *Figaro*, February 1, 1976, sec. 1, p. 19.
26. Interview with Paul Longpre.
27. Interview with Arthur Williams and Allison Montana.
28. Kaslow, "Folklore."
29. Saxon, Dreyer, and Tallant, *Gumbo Ya-Ya*, pp. 20–21.
30. Alan Lomax, "The Power of New Orleans Music," a lecture at the Louisiana State Museum, New Orleans, March 10, 1984, sponsored by the Louisiana Committee for the Humanities. An enlightening study for comparative purposes is John Stewart's "Stickfighting: Ritual Violence in Trinidad," Smithsonian Institution, Research Institute on Immigration and Ethnic Studies, 1980.
31. See also Finn Wilhelmsen, "Verbal, Body and Territoriality Communications Concepts Among the Mardi Gras Indians of New Orleans, Louisiana," p. 33. A seminar report to Professor H. Jause, Department of Anthropology, Tulane University, March 1972.
32. Martinez, "Delight in Repetition," p. 24.
33. Berry and Foose, producers, *Up from the Cradle of Jazz*.
34. Interview with Emile "Bo" Dollis, by Sheperd Samuel, February 20, 1978, WTUL Radio, New Orleans.
35. Interview with Paul Longpre.
36. Lomax, *Mister Jelly Roll*, pp. 14, 280. Jason Berry is indebted to George Reinecke, Department of English, University of New Orleans, for interpretation of "q'ouwais" as possibly meaning "couilles."
37. Wilhelmsen, "Creativity."
38. Paul Longpre, in conversation with Jason Berry, March 10, 1982.

Chapter Eighteen
WILLIE TEE AND THE WILD MAGNOLIAS

1. Interview with Wilson Turbinton, by Jason Berry, March 3, 1982.
2. From the recording *The Music of New Orleans, the Music of the Streets, the Music of Mardi Gras*. Folkways FA 2461.
3. Interview with Wilson Turbinton.
4. Wilhelmsen, "Verbal, Body and Territoriality Communication Concepts Among the Mardi Gras Indians," p. 32.
5. Interview with Wilson Turbinton.
6. Interview with Emile "Bo" Dollis, by Shepard Samuels, February 20, 1978, WTUL Radio, New Orleans.
7. Interview with Wilson Turbinton.
8. Ibid.

Chapter Nineteen
BIG CHIEF JOLLEY AND THE NEVILLE BROTHERS

1. Videotaped interview with George Landry, by Jason Berry and Jonathan Foose, January 25, 1979.
2. Videotaped interview with Charles Neville, by Jason Berry and Jonathan Foose, January 20, 1979.
3. Ibid.
4. Berry and Foose, producers, *Up from the Cradle of Jazz* (video documentary).
5. Ibid.
6. Interview with Aaron Neville, by Jonathan Foose, May 16, 1977, Dallas, Texas.
7. Ibid.
8. Jason Berry and Jonathan Foose, "The Nevilles: At the Roots," *Figaro*, August 2, 1978. sec. 2, p. 7.
9. Videotaped interview with Aaron Neville, by Jason Berry and Jonathan Foose, March 3, 1979.
10. Videotaped interview with Cyril Neville, by Jason Berry and Jonathan Foose, April 20, 1979.

11. Berry and Foose, *Up from the Cradle of Jazz* (video documentary).
12. Videotaped interview with Cyril Neville.
13. Videotaped interview with Aaron Neville.
14. Berry and Foose, *Up from the Cradle of Jazz.*
15. Interview with Cyril Neville, by Jonathan Foose, March 2, 1982.
16. Interview with Aaron Neville, by Jonathan Foose, February 15, 1982.
17. Interview with Cyril Neville.
18. Berry and Foose, *Up from the Cradle of Jazz.*
19. Paul Longpre, telephone interview with Jason Berry, March 15, 1982.
20. Berry and Foose, *Up from the Cradle of Jazz.*
21. Ibid.
22. Jason Berry, "Jazz Funerals," *New Orleans Magazine* 18 (November 1981): 90.

EPILOGUE: THE CULTURAL AWAKENING

1. Jason Berry, "The City's Cultural Awakening," *Figaro*, April 16, 1979, sec. 2, p. 1.
2. Interview with Jerry Wexler, by Jason Berry, February 2, 1980.
3. Giddins, *Rhythm-A-Ning*, p. 267.
4. Interview with Harold Battiste, by Jonathan Foose and Tad Jones, April 27, 1980.

BIBLIOGRAPHY

BOOKS AND PAMPHLETS

Apel, Willi. *Harvard Dictionary of Music.* Cambridge, Mass., 1974.

Armstrong, Louis. *Satchmo: My Life in New Orleans.* New York, 1954.

Balliet, Whitney. *Dinosaurs in the Morning.* Philadelphia, 1962.

Bebey, Francis. *African Music: A People's Art.* Westport, Conn., 1980.

Bechet, Sidney. *Treat It Gentle.* New York, 1978.

Belz, Carl. *The Story of Rock.* New York, 1969.

Benjaminson, Peter. *The Story of Motown.* New York, 1979.

Blassingame, John W. *Black New Orleans, 1860–1880.* Chicago, 1973.

Blesh, Rudi. *Shining Trumpets: A History of Jazz.* New York, 1978.

Blesh, Rudi, and Harriet Janis. *They All Played Ragtime.* New York, 1971.

Broven, John. *Rhythm and Blues in New Orleans.* Gretna, La., 1978.

Brunn, H. O. *The Story of the Original Dixieland Jazz Band.* Baton Rouge, 1969.

Buerkle, Jack V., and Danny Barker. *Bourbon Street Black: The New Orleans Black Jazzman.* New York, 1973.

Cable, George Washington. *Creoles and Cajuns.* New York, 1959.

Case, Brian, and Stan Britt. *The Illustrated Encyclopedia of Jazz.* New York, 1978.

Chambers, Henry E. *A History of Louisiana.* Vol. 1. Chicago and New York, 1925.

Charles, Ray, and David Ritz. *Brother Ray: Ray Charles' Own Story.* New York, 1978.

Charters, Samuel B. *The Legacy of the Blues.* New York, 1977.

_____. *New Orleans Jazz, 1885–1963.* New York, 1963.

_____. *The Roots of the Blues: An African Search.* London, 1981.

Chernoff, John Miller. *African Rhythm and African Sensibility: Aesthetics and Social Action in African Musical Idioms.* Chicago, 1979.

Christian, Marcus. *Negro Ironworkers in Louisiana, 1718–1900.* Gretna, La., 1972.

Christovich, Mary Louise, ed. *The Cemeteries.* Gretna, La., 1974. Vol. 3 of *New Orleans Architecture.*

Christovich, Mary Louise, and Roulhac Toledano, eds. *Faubourg Treme and the Bayou Road.* Gretna, La., 1980. Vol. 6 of *New Orleans Architecture.*

Clark, Dick, and Richard Robinson. *Rock, Roll, Remember.* New York, 1976.

Collier, James Lincoln, *Louis Armstrong: An American Genius.* New York, 1983.

———. *The Making of Jazz.* Boston, 1978.

Davis, Stephen, and Peter Simon. *Reggae Bloodlines: In Search of the Music and Culture of Jamaica.* New York, 1977.

Deren, Maya. *Divine Horsemen: The Voodoo Gods of Haiti.* New York, 1970.

The Federal Writers' Project of the Works Project Administration for the City of New Orleans, *The WPA Guide to New Orleans.* New York, 1983.

Ferris, William. *Blues from the Delta.* New York, 1978.

Gara, Larry. *The Baby Dodds Story.* Los Angeles, 1959.

Genovese, Eugene. *Roll, Jordan, Roll: The World the Slaves Made.* New York, 1974.

Gert zur Heide, Karl. *Deep South Piano.* London, 1970.

Giddins, Gary. *Rhythm-A-Ning: Jazz Tradition and Innovation in the Eighties.* New York, 1985.

———. *Riding on a Blue Note.* New York, 1981.

Gillett, Charlie. *Making Tracks: The Story of Atlantic Records.* New York, 1974.

———. *The Sound of the City.* New York, 1970.

Gutman, Herbert. *The Black Family in Slavery and Freedom, 1750–1925.* New York, 1977.

Haas, Edward F. *DeLesseps S. Morrison and the Image of Reform: New Orleans Politics, 1946–1961.* Baton Rouge, 1974.

Haley, Alex. *Roots: The Saga of an American Family.* New York, 1976.

Hannusch, Jeff. *I Hear You Knockin': The Sound of New Orleans Rhythm and Blues.* Ville Platte, La., 1985.

Haralambos, Michael. *Right On: From Blues to Soul in Black America.* New York, 1975.

Hentoff, Nat. *The Jazz Life.* New York, 1961.

Hentoff, Nat, and Nat Shapiro, eds. *Hear Me Talkin' to Ya.* New York, 1955.

Herskovits, Melville J. *Life in a Haitian Valley.* Garden City, N.Y., 1971.

———. *The Myth of the Negro Past.* Boston, 1958.

Hirshey, Gerri. *Nowhere to Run: The Story of Soul Music.* New York, 1984.

Jahn, Janheinz. *Muntu: An Outline of the New African Culture.* New York, 1961.

Jepsen, Jorgen Grunnet. *Jazz Records, 1942–1965.* Holte, Denmark, 1966.

Jones, LeRoi. *Blues People: Negro Music in White America.* New York, 1963.

Jones, Max, and John Chilton. *Louis: The Louis Armstrong Story, 1900–1971.* Boston, 1971.

Keil, Charles. *Urban Blues.* Chicago, 1966.

Kirsch, Elise. *Downtown New Orleans in the Early Eighties: Customs and Characters of Old Robertson Street and Its Neighborhoods.* New Orleans, 1951. A pamphlet in the New Orleans Public Library, apparently self-published.

Leadbitter, Mike, and Neil Slaven. *Blues Records, 1943–1966.* New York, 1968.

Levine, Lawrence E. *Black Culture and Black Consciousness: Afro-American Folk Thought from Slavery to Freedom.* New York, 1977.

Lewis, Pierce. *New Orleans: The Making of an Urban Landscape.* Cambridge, Mass., 1976.

Lomax, Alan. *Mister Jelly Roll.* Berkeley, 1950.

Malone, Bill C. *Country Music U.S.A.: A Fifty-Year History.* Austin, Tex., 1968.

———. *Southern Music, American Music.* Lexington, Ky., 1979.

Manning, Patrick. *Slavery, Colonialism and Economic Growth in Dahomey, 1640–1960.* Cambridge, England, 1982.

Marcus, Greil. *Mystery Train: Images of America in Rock and Roll.* New York, 1975.

Marquis, Don. *In Search of Buddy Bolden: First Man of Jazz.* Baton Rouge, 1978.

Métraux, Alfred. *Voodoo in Haiti.* New York, 1972.

Miller, Jim, ed. *The Rolling Stone Illustrated History of Rock and Roll.* New York, 1980.

Morris, Willie. *North Toward Home.* Boston, 1967.

Murray, Albert. *Stomping the Blues.* New York, 1976.

"Negro Insurrections." In vol. 2 of *Louisiana,* edited by Alcee Fortier. 3 vols. Madison, Wisc., 1914.

Osborne Mitchell, and Erroll L. Laborde. *Mardi Gras! A Celebration.* New Orleans, 1981.

Palmer, Robert. *Deep Blues.* New York, 1981.

———. *Jerry Lee Lewis Rocks!* New York, 1981.

Peters, Gordon. *The Drummer Man.* Wilmette, Ill., 1975.

Randel, Don Michael. *Harvard Concise Dictionary of Music.* Cambridge, Mass., 1978.

Roberts, John Storm. *Black Music of Two Worlds.* New York, 1972.

_____. *The Latin Tinge: The Impact of Latin Music on the United States.* New York, 1979.

Rose, Al. *Eubie Blake.* New York, 1979.

_____. *Storyville, New Orleans.* University, Ala., 1974.

Rose, Al, and Edmond Souchon. *New Orleans Jazz: A Family Album.* Baton Rouge, 1967.

Russell, Ross. *Bird Lives! The High Life and Hard Times of Charlie (Yardbird) Parker.* New York, 1973.

Sargeant, Winthrop. *Jazz Hot and Hybrid.* New York, 1975.

Saxon, Lyle, Robert Tallant, and Edward Dreyer. *Gumbo Ya-Ya.* New York, 1945.

Schafer, William J., and Johannes Riedel, with assistance from Michael Polad and Richard Thompson. *The Art of Ragtime: Form and Meaning of an Original Black American Art.* Baton Rouge, 1973.

Shaw, Arnold. *Honkers and Shouters: The Golden Years of Rhythm and Blues.* New York, 1978.

Spellman, A. B. *Black Music: Four Lives.* New York, 1966.

Stagg, Tom, and Charlie Crump. *New Orleans: The Revival.* Dublin, Ireland, 1973.

Stearns, Marshall. *The Story of Jazz.* New York, 1956.

Steffens, Lincoln. *The Autobiography of Lincoln Steffens.* New York, 1931.

Tallant, Robert. *Mardi Gras.* New York, 1948.

_____. *Voodoo in New Orleans.* New York, 1974.

Tirro, Frank. *Jazz: A History.* New York, 1977.

Titon, Jeff Todd. *Early Downhome Blues: A Musical and Cultural Analysis.* Urbana, Ill., 1979.

Warner, Keith. *Kaiso! The Trinidadian Calypso.* Washington, D.C., 1982.

Whitburn, Joel C. *Top Rhythm and Blues Records: 1949–1970.* Menomonee Falls, Wisc. 1973.

White, Charles. *The Life and Times of Little Richard: The Quasar of Rock.* New York, 1984.

Wilson, Samuel, et al. *The Creole Faubourgs.* Gretna, La., 1975. In vol. 4 of *New Orleans Architecture.*

ARTICLES AND MONOGRAPHS

Austen, Kathleen. "Guitar Players." *Wavelength* 2 (March 1982): 13.

Bentley, Bill. "Roy Brown: Still Rockin' Tonight." *Los Angeles Weekly,* July 23–31, 1981, p. 56.

Bernholm, Jonas. "The Roy Brown Story." *Crazy Music* (March–June 1977): 41–47.

Berry, Jason. "A.C., D.C.—New Orleans Mardi Gras Indians Bring a Little Electricity to Static Washington, D.C." *Figaro,* November 10, 1980, sec. 1, p. 12.

_____. "The Ballad of Jack Nocentelli: Poet Laureate of Elysian Fields." *Southern Exposure* 5 (Summer–Fall 1977): 156.

_____. "The Caribbean Connection." *New Orleans Magazine* 19 (May 1985): 68.

_____. "The City's Cultural Awakening." *Figaro,* April 16, 1979, sec. 2, p. 1.

_____. "Claiborne Carnival Comeback." *Gambit,* November 14, 1981, p. 20.

_____. "Controversy Swirls Around Mardi Gras Indians." *New Orleans Times-Picayune,* February 18, 1980, sec. 1, p. 18.

_____. "Drumvoices: The Roots of New Orleans Rhythm." *Wavelength* 1 (July 1981): 19.

_____. "Goodbye, Chief Pete." *Gambit,* November 14, 1981, p. 20.

_____. "Gospel Music Is Voices Singing of Good News." *Figaro,* February 23, 1981, p. 24.

_____. "Jazz Funerals." *New Orleans Magazine* 18 (November 1984): 90.

_____. "Pomp and Circumstance of the Mardi Gras Indians." *Dynamic Years* 16 (March 1981): 42.

_____. "Tunes and Bitterness at the Funeral of a Jazz Legend." *Washington Post,* February 5, 1980, sec. 2, p. 2.

_____. "Young Man with a Horn." *Gambit,* February 6, 1982, p. 17.

Berry, Jason, and Jonathan Foose. "Neighborhood Roots." *Figaro,* April 15, 1978, sec. 1, p. 18.

_____. "The Nevilles: At the Roots." *Figaro,* August 2, 1978, sec. 2, p. 7.

Borde, Percival. "The Sounds of Trinidad: The Development of the Steel Drum Bands." *Black Perspective in Music* 1 (July 1981): 45.

Boyd, Richard, and John Pope. "Heart Attack Kills New Orleans' Musical Mentor, Professor Longhair." *New Orleans States-Item*, January 31, 1980, sec. 1, p. 1.

Brasseaux, Carl. "The Administration of Slave Regulations in French Louisiana, 1724–1766." *Louisiana History* 21 (1980): 139–58.

Broven, John. "Interview with Earl Palmer." *Blues Unlimited* (September–October, 1975): 5.

————. "Roy Brown: Good Rockin' Tonight, Part I." *Blues Unlimited* (January–February 1977): 4.

————. "Roy Brown: Good Rockin' Tonight, Part II." *Blues Unlimited* (March–April 1977): 15.

————. "We Had Some Good Times: Interview with Marshall Sehorn." *Blues Unlimited* (February–March 1974): 15–16.

City of New Orleans Office of Policy Planning, "Gert Town/Zion City." *New Orleans Neighborhood Profile Series*, vol. 14, p. 12D.

————. "Seventh Ward Neighborhood Profile." In *Neighborhood Characteristics Summary*. Office of City Planning, Analysis Unit, City of New Orleans, Ernest M. Morial, mayor. December 1979.

Cost, Deborah. "Allen Toussaint: Funk's Patron Saint." *Gris Gris*, July 10–16, 1978, p. 5.

Crowley, Donald J. "The Traditional Masques of Carnival." *Caribbean Quarterly* 4 (1956): 194–223.

Cuccia, Ron. "Fess Fiesta." *Gris Gris*, December 3, 1979, pp. 42–43.

————. "With His Eye on a Star: An Interview with James Booker." *Gris Gris*, July 17–23, 1978, pp. 9–11.

Davis, Jack. "Why Aren't the Meters a Bigger Deal in New Orleans?" *Figaro*, May 13, 1972, sec. 1, pp. 1, 5.

DeCaro, Francis. "Folk Festival Film." *Journal of American Folklore* 91 (January–March 1978): 625.

Dees, Diane. "Irma Thomas Cries On." *Figaro*, April 23, 1979, sec. 2, pp. 5–6.

Dent, Tom. "A Critical Look at Mardi Gras." *Jackson* (Mississippi) *Advocate*, February 18, 1982, sec. B, p. 1.

"Domino Keeps 'Em Happy." *Louisiana Weekly*, January 19, 1957, p. 14.

du Rivage, Vance. "NOLA's Own Voodoo Pop Star." *Vieux Carre Courier*, July 7–13, 1972, p. 5.

"Fats Ain't Blue." *Newsweek*, October 19, 1970, p. 24.

"Fats Domino's Rock 'n Roll Too Much for GIs." *Louisiana Weekly*, September 29, 1956, p. 15.

"Fats on Fire." *Time*, June 10, 1957, p. 71.

Fein, Art. "The Meters: The Beat Is Their Meat." *Circular* 6 (July 29, 1974): 1, 6.

Foose, Jonathan. "Frank Fields: Rhythm and Blues." *Wavelength* 1 (October 1981): 31.

"Frank Painia Seeks Relief in U.S. Courts from Raids." *Louisiana Weekly*, February 15, 1964, p. 1.

Fumar, Vincent. "Dave Bartholomew." In *Lagniappe* section, *New Orleans States-Item*, August 5, 1978, p. 8.

————. "Poppa Stoppa." *Vieux Carre Courier*, November 23, 1972, pp. 6–7.

————. "Professor Longhair: A Remembrance." In *Lagniappe* section, *New Orleans States-Item*, February 2, 1980, pp. 6–7.

Goldman, Albert. "Pale Voodoo Hands Across the Sea." *Life*, March 14, 1969, p. 14.

Grevatt, Ren. "On the Beat." *Billboard*, September 9, 1957, p. 64.

Hannusch, Jeff "Almost Slim." "Bobby Mitchell Remembers New Orleans Music." *Wavelength* 1 (November 1980): pp. 6–8.

————. "The In-Kredible Ernie K-Doe." *Wavelength* 1 (March 1981): 6–7.

————. "Making a Hit: The Rise and Fall of New Orleans Music Parallels the History of Ace Records." *Figaro*, December 1, 1980, sec. 1, pp. 31–37.

————. "Roy Brown: Hard Luck Blues." *Wavelength* 1 (August 1981): 9–12.

Hershkovits, David. "Cosimo Matassa." *New Orleans Courier*, July 29–August 4, 1976, p. 7.

Jones, Tad. "Interview with Earl King." *Living Blues* (July–August 1978): 42.

————. "Interview with Professor Longhair." *Living Blues* (March–April 1976): 17.

————. "The Radiators." *Wavelength* 1 (September 1981): 12–14.

Joyce, Mike. "Interview with Fats Domino." *Living Blues* (November 1977): 16–20.

Kamin, Jonathan. "The White 'R&B' Audience and the Music Industry, 1952–1956." *Popular Music and Society* 4 (1976): 170–88.

Kaslow, Allison. "The Mardi Gras Indians." *Louisiana Folklore Miscellany* 3 (1972): 48–49.

Kaslow, Andrew. "Central City: The Ethnohistory of a New Orleans Neighborhood." In *Perspectives on Eth-*

nicity in New Orleans, University of New Orleans, 1980.

————. "Folklore: Talking to Some Glorious Mardi Gras Indians." *Figaro,* February 1, 1976, sec. 1, p. 19.

————. "Prophecy, Healing, and Power: The Afro-American Spiritual Churches of New Orleans." Monograph, Department of Anthropology and Geography, University of New Orleans, 1981.

"King of Rock 'n Roll: Fats Domino Hailed as New Idol of Teen-agers." *Ebony* (February 1957): 26–31.

Koenig, Karl. "Magnolia Plantation: History and Music." *Second Line* 34 (Spring 1982): 28–38.

————. "The Plantation Belt Brass Bands and Musicians." *Second Line* 33 (Fall 1981): 24–40.

Lentz, Paul. "Keeping Up with Al Belletto." *Downbeat* 39 (June 22, 1972): 16.

Lombard, Rudy, et al. "Claiborne I-10 Multi-Use Study." Louisiana Department of Highways, November 1976.

McEwen, Joe. "Performance." Review of the Meters concert at Paul's Mall, Boston, on September 6, 1976. In *Rolling Stone,* November 4, 1976, p. 94.

Martinez, Maurice M. "Delight in Repetition: The Black Indians." *Wavelength* 16 (February 1982): 21.

Massaquoi, Hans J. "Fats Domino: The Man Who Gambled Away $2 Million Without Going Broke." *Ebony* 39 (May 1974): 155.

Matthews, Bunny. "Can the Nevilles Survive Now?" *Figaro,* October 22, 1979, sec. 2, pp. 1–4.

————. "Let's Get Fired Up." *Figaro,* September 1, 1980, sec. 1, p. 17.

————. "Why the Meters Broke Up." *Figaro,* March 30, 1977, sec. 2, pp. 10, 14.

"Meet the Meters: This Shit Be Fire." *Boston Real Paper,* September 18, 1976, p. 36.

Morthland, John. "The Nevilles Tighten Up, Get Loose." *Village Voice,* June 23, 1980, pp. 61–62.

Newlin, Jon. "The Allen Toussaint Story: He Wrote All Those Songs." *Figaro,* July 22, 1972, sec. 1, pp. 5, 7.

————. "Earl King of New Orleans: A Seventh Ward Son Makes Good Music." *Figaro,* October 7, 1973, pp. 1, 5.

————. "Earl King: Voodoo Dolls to 'Trick Bags.' " *Figaro,* October 7, 1972, pp. 4–5.

————. "Ernie K-Doe: At 35, Rock's Grand Old Man." *Figaro,* July 8, 1972, pp. 4–5.

————. "Fats Domino Comes Home." *Figaro,* November 11, 1972, pp. 1–2, 4.

————. "Irma Thomas: New Orleans' Best Female Rocker Returns." *Figaro,* January 13, 1973, pp. 7–8.

————. "Man of a Thousand Dances: Chris Kenner." *Figaro,* June 17, 1972, pp. 1, 4.

Palmer, Robert. "The Heart and Soul of New Orleans Rock." *New York Times,* July 10, 1977, pp. 18–19.

————. "New Orleans Inspires the Neville Brothers." *New York Times,* June 28, 1981, p. 28.

————. "A Tale of Two Cities: Memphis Rock and New Orleans Roll." Department of Music, School of Performing Arts, Brooklyn College of the City University of New York, *Institute for Studies in American Music,* no. 12.

Partridge, Robert. "Everything I Do Gonna Be Funky." *Melody Maker* 48 (July 31, 1973): 38–39.

Patoski, Joe Nick. "Allen Toussaint Listens to New Orleans." *Rolling Stone,* July 28, 1977, pp. 30–31.

Pearse, Andrew. "Carnival in the Nineteenth Century." *Caribbean Quarterly* 4, nos. 3–4 (1956): 175–93.

Perry, James, A. "The Deacon Finds His Calling." *New Orleans Times-Picayune/States-Item,* September 18, 1980, sec. 4, p. 1.

Peterson, Betsy. "The Record Industry That Failed." *Vieux Carre Courier,* October 1–7, 1971, p. 1.

Pope, John. "Cosimo Matassa: New Orleans' Rock 'n Roll Record King." *Dixie* magazine, *New Orleans Times-Picayune/States-Item,* July 19, 1978, pp. 14–15.

Quale, Jennifer. "Rocking Along with Professor Longhair." *Dixie* magazine. *New Orleans Times-Picayune/States-Item,* February 12, 1972, pp. 12–13.

Salaam, Kalamu Ya. "Talking to Wynton Marsalis: Double Tonguing, Triple Tonguing, Slurring and Phrasing." *Wavelength* 3 (February 1984): 40.

Schroder, Anita. "Indians Parade in Regalia Ritual." *New Orleans Times-Picayune,* February 8, 1974, sec. 3, p. 8.

Scott, Hammond. "New Orleans' Cousin Joe." *Living Blues* (January–February 1975): 20–22.

Shaw, Greg. "The Dr. John Story." *Phonograph Record* 3 (July 1973): 18–22.

Smith, Michael. "Exploring Underground Black Religion." *New Orleans Magazine* (December 19, 1975): 30.

Stewart, John. "Stickfighting: Ritual Violence in Trinidad." Smithsonian Institution, Research Institute on Immigration and Ethnic Studies, 1980.

Swenson, John. "Dr. John, Finally in the Right Place." *Crawdaddy* (June 1974): 40–44.

Trow, George W. S., Jr. "Profile of Ahmet Ertegun." *New Yorker,* June 5, 1978, pp. 50–51.

"Up to His Ears in Tunes." *Dixie* magazine, *New Orleans Times-Picayune,* June 21, 1959, p. 14.

White, Timothy. "The Professor Longhair Story: Lessons of a Rock and Roll Legend." *Rolling Stone,* March 20, 1980, p. 32.

_____. "When Toussaint Goes Marching In." *Crawdaddy* (May 1975): 42–46.

Wilhelmsen, Finn. "Creativity in the Songs of the Mardi Gras Indians of New Orleans, Louisiana." Part of appendix appears in *Louisiana Folklore Miscellany* 3 (1973): 56–74.

_____. "Verbal, Body and Territoriality Communications Concepts Among the Mardi Gras Indians of New Orleans, Louisiana." Department of Anthropology, Tulane University, March 1972.

Williams, Richard. "The Dr. John Story." *Melody Maker* (June 9, 1968): 10.

Wilmer, Valerie. "The Drummer: Street Parade Fan." *Melody Maker* (March 9, 1968): 10.

FILMS

Berry, Jason, and Jonathan Foose, producers. *Up from the Cradle of Jazz,* 1980.

Blank, Les, producer. *Always for Pleasure,* 1977.

Kavanaugh, Marcia, and Ross Yockey, producers. *Crescent City, Soul of Rock 'n Roll,* WDSU-TV, New Orleans, 1979.

Martinez, Maurice, producer. *Black Indians of New Orleans,* 1976.

Palfi, Stevenson, producer. *Piano Players Seldom Play Together.*

DISCOGRAPHIES AND TRADE PERIODICALS

Ace Records Discography, 1955–1963.

Billboard Magazine, 1954–1958. Issues on file at the Country Music Library, Country Music Foundation, Nashville, Tennessee.

Cashbox Charts, 1948–1968.

Imperial Records Discography, 1960–1963.

Minit Records Discography, 1960–1963. In *Soul Bag* magazine, no. 38, 1975.

Ruppli, Michel. *Atlantic Records: A Discography (1957–1966).* Westport, Conn., 1979.

Specialty Label Singles Listing, 1946–1964.

Topping, Ray. *New Orleans Rhythm and Blues Record Label Listing.* Bexhill-on-Sea, East Sussex, England, 1978.

OTHER REFERENCES

The Blue Jay, 1954–1958. Jesuit High School, New Orleans.

Louisiana Weekly, 1947–1961.

Polk New Orleans City Directory, 1938–1965.

Soard's New Orleans City Directory, 1880–1937.

DISCOGRAPHY

Adams, Johnny. *From the Heart.* Rounder 2044.

———. *Heart and Soul.* SSS International SSS 5.

———. *The Tan Nightingale.* Charly Records CRB 1058 (England).

AFO, *New Orleans Heritage Jazz.* 1956–1966. Opus 43.

Archibald. *The Complete New Orleans Sessions.* Krazy Kat 7408 (England).

Barron, Ronnie. *Blues Delicacies.* Sunshine SPD1023.

Bartholomew, Dave. *Jump Children.* Pathe Marconi/EMI 1546601 (France).

———. *The Monkey.* Pathe Marconi/EMI 1561352 (France).

Batiste, Alvin. *Clarinet Summit, Vol. II, In Concert at the Public Theatre.* India Navigation Company IN-1067.

———. *Musique D'Afrique Nouvelle Orleans.* IN-1046.

Belletto, Al. *The Big Sound.* King 716.

———. *Coach's Choice.* ARTCO LPJ986 LD.

———. *Half and Half.* Capitol T751.

———. *An Introduction to Al Belletto.* Capitol EAP 1-6508.

———. *Somebody Loves Me.* Bethlehem BCP76.

———. *Sounds and Songs.* Capitol T6514.

———. *Whisper Not.* Capitol T901.

Blanchard, Terence, and Donald Harrison. *New York Second Line.* Concord GW-3002.

Bo, Eddie. *The Other Side of Eddie Bo.* Bo-Sound EB55379.

———. *Watch for the Coming.* Bo-Sound ED55379.

Booker, James. *Blues and Ragtime from New Orleans.* Aves Int. 146.530 (Germany).

———. *Classified.* Rounder 2036.

———. *Junko Partner.* Island Help 26-A.

———. *King of New Orleans Keyboard.* Vol. 1. JPS Records 1083.

———. *King of New Orleans Keyboard.* Vol. 2. JPS Records 1086 (England).

———. *Mr. Mystery.* Sundown CG 709-09 (Dutch).

———. *New Orleans Piano Wizard: Live!* Rounder 2027.

———. *The Piano Prince from New Orleans.* Aves Int. 146.509 (Germany).

Brown, Roy. *Boogie at Midnight.* Charly Records CRB 1093 (England).

———. *Good Rockin' Tonight.* 1947–1954. Route 66 KIX6 (Sweden).

———. *Hard Luck Blues.* Gusto GD5036X(2).

_____. *I Feel That Young Man's Rhythm.* Route 66 KIX-26 (Sweden).

_____. *Laughing But Crying.* 1947–1959. Route 66 KIX2 (Sweden).

Charles, Bobby. *Bobby Charles.* Bearsville/Island IRSP26.

_____. *Hark Back to the 60's.* Jewel/P-Vine Special PLP714 (Japan).

Crawford, James "Sugarboy." Chess/Vogue VG 306 427017 (French).

_____. *New Orleans Classics.* Pathe Marconi 1561351 (France).

Cuccia, Ron. *The Jazz Poetry Group.* Takoma TAK7072.

_____. *Music from the Big Tomato.* Oblique PB002.

Dagradi, Tony. *Lunar Eclipse.* Gramavision 8103.

_____. *Oasis.* Gramavision 8001.

Darnell, Larry. *I'll Get Along Somehow.* Route 66 KIX19 (Sweden).

Dirty Dozen Brass Band. *My Feet Can't Fail Me Now.* The George Wein Collection/Concord GW-3005.

Dixie Cups. *Teen Anguish. Vol. 1,* Charly CRM2004 (England).

Domino, Fats. *The Fats Domino Story.* Vols. 1–6, United Artists (England).

_____. *Greatest Hits.* United Artists UAS9958.

_____. *Rock! Rock! Rock 'n Roll!* Mercury/Phonogram 6463043 (Germany).

Dorsey, Lee. *All Ways Funky.* Charly CRB 1036 (England).

_____. *The Best of Lee Dorsey—Holy Cow.* Arista ALB6-8387.

_____. *Gonna Be Funky.* Charly CRB 1001 (England).

Drew, James. *Barrio Frances.* MX 101.

Dr. John. *The Brightest Smile in Town.* Clean Cuts 707.

_____. *City Lights.* A&M/Horizon SP-732.

_____. *Desitively Bonnaroo.* ATCO SD 7043.

_____. *Dr. John Plays Mac Rebennack.* Clean Cut CC 705.

_____. *Gris-Gris.* ATCO SD 33-234.

_____. *Gumbo.* Atlantic P8356A (Japan).

_____. *In the Right Place.* ATCO SD 7018.

_____. *Remedies.* ATCO SD 33-316.

_____. *Such a Night.* Live in London. Spindrift Records SPIN 107.

_____. *The Sun, the Moon and Herbs.* ATCO SD 33-362.

_____. *Triumvirate.* Columbia KC 32172.

Excelsior Brass Band. *Jolly Reeds and Steamin' Horns.* Great Ones 1011.

Fisher, Patrice. *Jasmine-Tropical Breeze.* Inner City IC1155.

Ford, Frankie. *Let's Take a Sea Cruise.* Ace/Vivid Sound VS 10009 (Japan).

_____. New Orleans Dynamo. Ace Records CH 116 (England).

Gayten, Paul. Annie Laurie: *Creole Gal.* Route 66 KIX8 (Sweden).

_____. *The Crescent City Roll, 1957.* Paul Gayten, Alonzo Stewart, Roland Cook, and Charles Williams. Chess PLP 6028-9 (Japan).

Guitar Slim. *The Things I Used to Do.* Specialty 2120.

Henry, Clarence. *You Always Hurt the One You Love.* Chess/Viking AUSLP 1009 (Australia).

Hill, Jessie. *Can't Get Enough of That Ooh Poo Pah Doo.* Bandy 70016.

Kenner, Chris. *Land of 1000 Dances.* Atlantic P-6172A (Japan).

_____. *The Name of the Place.* Bandy 70015.

Kent, Luther. *World Class.* RCS-A-1002.

Kent, Luther, and Trickbag. *It's in the Bag.* Renegade 1001.

K-Doe, Ernie. *Ernie K-Doe.* Gandy 7004.

King, Earl. *Street Parade.* Charly CRM-2021 (England).

_____. *That Good New Orleans Rock 'n Roll.* Sonet SNTF 719 (England).

_____. *Those Lonely, Lonely Nights.* Ace/Vivid Sound VS-1012 (Japan).

_____. *Trick Bag.* Pathe Marconi (EMI) 2C06883299.

Lewis, Smiley. *The Bells Are Ringing.* United Artists UAS 30186 (England).

_____. *Hook, Line and Sinker.* KC.102 (England).

_____. *I Hear You Knocking.* United Artists UAS 30167 (England).

_____. *Ooh La La.* Pathe Marconi/EMI 1561391 (France).

Little Richard. *Grooviest 17 Original Hits.* Specialty SPS 2113.

McLean, Ramsey, and Tony Dagradi. *The Long View.* Prescription Records, P.O. Box 3081, New Orleans 70117.

Marsalis, Branford. *Scenes in the City.* Columbia FC 38951.

Marsalis, Ellis. *Ellis Marsalis and Eddie Harris.* Spindletop Records STP 105.

——. *Fathers and Sons.* Columbia FC 37972.

——. *Solo Piano Reflexions.* Elm Records 001-A (reissue).

——. *Syndrome.* Elm Records.

Marsalis, Wynton. *Black Codes (From the Underground).* Columbia FC 40009.

——. *Fathers and Sons.* Columbia FC 37972.

——. *Hot House Flowers.* Columbia FC 39530.

——. *Think of One.* Columbia FC 38951.

——. *Trumpet Concertos.* With the National Philharmonic Orchestra. Haydn, Hummar, and Mozart: CBS Masterworks IM 37846.

——. *Wynton Marsalis.* Columbia FC 37574.

Masakowski, Steve. *Mars.* Prescription Records (New Orleans) PR-04.

Meters. *Cabbage Alley.* Reprise MS 2076.

——. *Fire on the Bayou.* Reprise MS 2228.

——. *New Directions.* Warner Brothers BS 3042.

——. *Rejuvenation.* Reprise MS 2200.

——. *Second Line Strut.* Charly CRM 1009 (England).

——. *Trickbag.* Reprise MS 2252.

Mitchell, Bobby, and the Toppers. *I'm Gonna Be a Wheel Someday.* MRR&B R&B 101 (Sweden).

Neville, Art and Aaron. *The Best of Art and Aaron.* Bandy 70013.

Neville Brothers. *Fiyo on the Bayou.* A&M SP 4866.

——. *The Neville Brothers.* Capital ST 11865.

——. *Neville-ization.* Black Top Records BT 1031.

Price, Lloyd. *Collectables.* MCA 1503.

——. *Greatest Hits.* Specialty/Vivid Sound VS 2011 (Japan).

Professor Longhair. *Crawfish Fiesta.* Alligator 4718.

——. *The Last Mardi Gras.* Atlantic/Deluxe SD2-4001.

——. *Mardi Gras in New Orleans.* Krazy Kat 7408 (England).

——. *Mardi Gras in New Orleans.* 1949–1956. Nighthawk 106.

——. *New Orleans Piano.* 1949 and 1953. Atlantic SD 7225.

——. *Rock 'n Roll Gumbo.* Dancing Cat Records DC 3006.

Radiators. *Heat Generation.* Croaker CR-1442.

——. *Work Done on Premises.* Croaker CR-114.

Re-Birth Jazz Band. *New Orleans Here to Stay.* Arhoolie 1092.

Ridgley, Tommy. *The New King of Stroll.* Flyright LP 519 (England).

Rivers, James. *The James Rivers Quartet: The Dallas Sessions.* Spindletop Records STP 101.

——. *Ole.* JB's, JB 103.

——. *Thrill Me.* JB's, JB 101.

Shirley and Lee. *Let the Good Times Roll.* Imperial LAX 302(M) (Japan).

Smith, Huey. *For Dancing.* Ace/Vivid Sound US 1007 (Japan).

——. *Havin' a Good Time.* Ace/Vivid Sound US 1006 (Japan).

——. *The Imperial Sides.* 1960–1961, Pathe Marconi/EMI PM 231 (France).

——. *Rockin' Pneumonia and the Boogie Woogie Flu.* Chiswich (England).

Spellman, Benny. Bandy 70018.

Spiders. *I Didn't Want to Do It.* Imperial LAX 303(M) (Japan).

The Stokes with Allen Toussaint. Bandy 70014.

Tee, Willie. *Anticipation.* United Artists US-LA 655 G-0698.

Thomas, Irma. *Down at Muscle Shoals.* Chess P-Vine 6014 (Japan).

——. *In Between the Tears.* Charly CRB 1020 (England).

——. *Irma Thomas Sings.* Bandy 70003.

——. *The New Rules.* Rounder 2046.

——. *Wish Someone Would Care.* Imperial LP 9266 (Japan).

Toussaint, Allen. *From a Whisper to a Scream.* Kent Records KENT 306 (England).

——. *Life, Love and Faith.* Reprise 2062.

——. *Motion.* Warner Bros. BSK 3142.

——. *Southern Nights.* Reprise 2186.

Tyler, Alvin "Red." *Heritage.* Rounder 2044.

Washington, Tuts. *New Orleans Piano Professor.* Rounder 2041.

Wild Magnolias. *The Wild Magnolias.* Polydor PD 6026.

Wild Tchoupitoulas. *The Wild Tchoupitoulas.* Island AN 7052.

Williams, Dave. *I Ate Up the Apple Tree.* New Orleans NOR 7204.

ALBUM COLLECTIONS AND ANTHOLOGIES

Ace of New Orleans Sound. Ace/Vivid Sound VS 1013 (Japan).

Ace Story: Volume One. Chiswich CH11 (England).

Ace Story: Volume Two. Chiswich CH12 (England).

All These Things. Bandy 70007.

Going Back to New Orleans. Earl King, Jerry Byrne, Art Neville, Ernie K-Doe, Lloyd Price, and Guitar Slim. Specialty SNTF 5021 (England).

It's Raining. Bandy 70012.

Love You New Orleans. Bandy 70008.

Mardi Gras in New Orleans. Earl King, Professor Longhair, Al Johnson, Wild Magnolias, Bo Dollis, and the Hawkettes. Mardi Gras MG 1001.

The Music of New Orleans, the Music of the Streets, the Music of Mardi Gras. Folkway FA 2461.

New Orleans Blues. Vol. 1, *Black Music in the 1950's.* Dave Bartholomew and Joe August. P-Vine Special PLP-9034 (Japan).

New Orleans Blues. Vol. 2, *New Orleans Radio Live, 1951.* Paul Gayten, Larry Darnell, and Cubby Newsome. P-Vine Special PLP-9059 (Japan).

New Orleans Gospel Quartets, 1947–1956. Heritage HT 306 (England).

New Orleans Heritage Jazz, 1956–1966. AFO Orchestra, OPUS 43.

New Orleans: Home of the Blues. Bandy 7006.

New Orleans Soul Variety. Vol. 1, Earl King and Allen Toussaint JVC-VIP 4085 (Sansu-4006) (Japan).

The Official New Orleans Rhythm and Blues Anniversary Album. Vol. 1, Johnny Adams, Frankie Ford, Lee Dorsey, Ernie K-Doe, Earl King, and Robert Parker. Dese Days Records 101.

Plenty More, Keep Score. Bandy 70011.

Sehorn's Soul Farm. Various artists. Charly CRB 1032 (England).

We Sing the Blues. Bandy 70010.

CREDITS

LYRICS

ILLUSTRATIONS

Pages 6–7: Street rhythms, photograph by Michael Smith.

Page 15: Danny Barker, photograph by Syndey Byrd. Deacon John Moore, photograph by Michael Smith. David and Melvin Lastie, family photograph.

Page 23: Street life, photograph from the Ralston Crawford Collection, William Ransom Hogan Jazz Archive, Howard-Tilton Memorial Library, Tulane University, New Orleans.

Page 25: Professor Longhair, both photographs by Michael Smith.

Page 27: Second line, photograph from the Ralston Crawford Collection, Jazz Archive, Tulane University.

Page 32: Dave Bartholomew and Fats Domino, both photographs by Michael Smith. Harrison Verrett, photograph from the Ralston Crawford Collection, Jazz Archive, Tulane University.

Page 37: Cosimo Matassa, photograph by Michael Smith. Fats Domino, publicity still.

Pages 44–45: Spirits visit the faithful, photograph by

Michael Smith. Mother Catherine, photographer unknown, courtesy of Deacon Frank Lastie.

Page 47: Deacon Frank Lastie, photograph by Ellis Lucia, courtesy of the *New Orleans Times-Picayune/States-Item.* Walter Lastie, photograph by Syndey Byrd. The Lasties, publicity still.

Page 55: Jamming at Club Tiajuana and Female impersonator at the Dew Drop, both photographs from the Ralston Crawford Collection, Jazz Archive, Tulane University.

Page 59: Only in New Orleans . . . , photograph from the Ralston Crawford Collection, Jazz Archive, Tulane University.

Page 61: Exotic dancer, Justin Adams, Saturday night function, and Dancing at the San Jacinto Club, all photographs from the Ralston Crawford Collection, Jazz Archive, Tulane University.

Page 63: A subculture within a subculture and Female impersonators at the Dew Drop, both photographs from the Ralston Crawford Collection, Jazz Archive, Tulane University. Ernie K-Doe, photograph by Michael Smith.

Page 71: Smiley Lewis, publicity still. Dr. Daddy-O, publicity still. Roy Brown, photograph by Syndey Byrd.

Page 75: Shirley and Lee, courtesy of Shirley Goodman. Sugar Boy and the Sugar Lumps, publicity still.

Page 83: Huey Smith, junior high school graduation, family photograph. Huey "Piano" Smith, 1979, photograph by Michael Smith. Guitar Slim, photographer unknown.

Page 87: Bobby Marchan, publicity still.

Page 89: Gerri Hall, photograph by Syndey Byrd. Earl King and Johnny Vincent, photograph by Kevin M. Shea.

Page 99: Alvin "Red" Tyler and Lee Allen, photograph by Michael Smith. Richard "Little Richard" Penniman, publicity still.

Page 109: Deejay Poppa Stoppa with Dr. John, photograph by Michael Smith.

Page 113: Frankie Ford, publicity still. Lloyd Price, publicity still.

Page 119: Allen Toussaint, photograph by Michael Smith.

Page 123: Joe Banashak, photograph by Michael Smith. Irma Thomas and Ernie K-Doe, both photographs by Syndey Byrd.

Page 135: Clarence "Frogman" Henry, publicity still.

Aaron Neville, publicity still. Earl King, photograph by Michael Smith.

Page 145: Ellis Marsalis, photograph by Michael Smith. Al Belletto, publicity still.

Page 149: AFO executives, photographer unknown. James Black, photograph by Syndey Byrd.

Page 157: Earl Turbinton, photograph by Michael Smith.

Page 163: Wynton Marsalis, photograph by Marc Karzen, courtesy of Columbia Records. Luther Kent, photograph by Syndey Byrd. James Rivers and Bernard Dixon, photograph by Michael Smith.

Page 170–71: Papa Jellie Bellie, photograph from the Ralston Crawford Collection, Jazz Archive, Tulane University.

Page 173: Tommy Ridgley and Eddie Bo, both photographs by Michael Smith.

Page 175: James Booker, Piano Prince, photograph by Michael Smith. James Booker as a child, family photograph.

Page 183: Mac Rebennack starting out, courtesy of Dorothy Rebennack. Mac Rebennack at the Children's Mardi Gras Ball, photograph from the Historic New Orleans Collection.

Page 185: Dr. John at Tipitina's, photograph by Michael Smith.

Page 193: Allen Toussaint and Marshall Sehorn, photographer unknown. Lee Dorsey, publicity still. The Meters, publicity still.

Page 209: Congo Square, courtesy of Faruk von Turk. Big Chief Jolley, photograph by Michael Smith.

Page 215: An Indian rehearsal and Percy Lewis, both photographs by Michael Smith.

Page 217: An Indian queen, photograph by Michael Smith.

Page 223: Willie Tee and the Wild Magnolias, both photographs by Michael Smith.

Page 231: The Nevilles in rehearsal, photograph by Michael Smith. The Neville Brothers, photograph by Syndey Byrd.

Page 233: Big Chief Jolley at Mardi Gras, photograph by Syndey Byrd.

Page 243: Lil Queenie, photograph by Tomio L. H. Thomann. A new generation comes of age, photograph by Michael Smith.

Pages 246–47: A city of sounds, photograph by Michael Smith.

INDEX